Marxism Against Postmodernism in Educational Theory

Edited by

Dave Hill, Peter McLaren, Mike Cole, and Glenn Rikowski

LEXINGTON BOOKS
Lanham • Boulder • New York • Oxford

LEXINGTON BOOKS

Published in the United States of America
by Lexington Books
A Member of the Rowman & Littlefield Publishing Group
4720 Boston Way, Lanham, Maryland 20706

PO Box 317
Oxford
OX2 9RU, UK

Cover artwork by Roger Hill

British Library Cataloguing in Publication Information Available

Library of Congress Cataloging-in-Publication Data

Marxism against postmodernism in educational theory / edited by Dave Hill . . . [et al.].
    p. cm.
    Rev. ed. of: Postmodernism in educational theory. 1999.
    Includes bibliographical references and index.
    ISBN 0-7391-0345-8 (cloth : alk. paper)—ISBN 0-7391-0346-6 (pbk. : alk. paper)
    1. Communism and education. 2. Socialism and education. 3. Postmodernism and education. I. Hill, Dave, 1945– II. Postmodernism in educational theory.

HX526 .M35 2002
370'.1—dc21

                              2001050669

Printed in the United States of America

♾™ The paper used in this publication meets the minimum requirements of American National Standard for Information Sciences—Permanence of Paper for Printed Library Materials, ANSI/NISO Z39.48–1992.

Marxism Against Postmodernism
in Educational Theory

WITHDRAWN

Praise for

Marxism Against Postmodernism in Educational Theory

"The importance of a work that grounds critical educational theory in its Marxist foundations and that constitutes an uncompromising socialist project dedicated to educating toward a just society, cannot be understated. This book will provocatively engage all scholars who consider the multiple roles of schooling in society."
—**Jill Pinkey Pastrana**, California State University, Long Beach

"For those of us who still dare to envision a world liberated from the imperatives of capital and the brutalities of market-discipline, the individual and collective efforts of Glenn Rikowski, Mike Cole, Dave Hill, and Peter McLaren help us all sustain our cautious optimism for the future."
—**David Gabbard**, East Carolina University

"I applaud the book's timeliness and its authors' courage."
—**Zeus Leonardo**, California State University, Long Beach

"There is undoubtedly a need for a contemporary rigorous Marxist-inspired critique of postmodernism and poststructuralism in educational settings and this book is certainly that."
—*British Journal of Educational Studies*

"The essential message is that Marxism still matters, and this collection highlights the importance of this perspective in educational theory."
—*Educational Research*

"The scholarship is impressive. . . . It is a book which will certainly be of interest to any educators who want to build a society where socialism can flourish."
—*Journal of In-Service Education*

"Quite simply, this is a brilliant book."
—**Paula Allman**, University of Nottingham

"This book is an aid to thought, not just interpretation. Its central theme (that education is of necessity a political activity) is one that needs debate outside the walls of academia."
—*Times Educational Supplement*

Contents

Preface

This book is an expanded and partially updated version of our earlier *Postmodernism in Educational Theory:Education and the Politics of Human Resistance.*[1] For this Lexington Books edition there are two completely new chapters—chapter 2, Glenn Rikowski's "Prelude: Marxist Educational Theory after Postmodernism," and chapter 3, Peter McLaren and Ramin Farahmandpur's "Breaking Signifying Chains: A Marxist Position on Postmodernism." A number of other chapters have been substantially revised. These are Glenn Rikowski and Peter McLaren's chapter 1, "Introduction: Postmodernism in Educational Theory," Mike Cole and Dave Hill's chapter 5, "'Resistance Postmodernism'—Progressive Politics or Rhetorical Left Posturing?" and chapter 8, "Marxism, Class Analysis and Postmodernism" by Dave Hill, Mike Sanders and Ted Hankin.

We want to thank, in particular, Jason Hallman at Lexington Books for his interest, encouragement and advice regarding the realization of this new and expanded edition, which allows us to gain wider access to a United States and international readership. Jason has been unfailingly courteous, encouraging and enthusiastic throughout the revision and production process.

We also thank Robert Albury and Janet Holland at Tufnell Press for encouraging us, in 1998, to write the original first edition. They provided tremendous support, technical expertise and understanding in our original enterprise.

And for both editions, we thank Christie Fox of Running Heads Editorials for her insightful, expert and humorous editorial advice and work.

Things have moved very quickly since that Tufnell Press edition of *Postmodernism in Educational Theory* appeared in late 1999, both in terms of political events and in terms of the intellectual analysis and portrayal of those events, as well as the deepening capitalization and commodification of humanity. The pace of privatization and marketization in education has quickened, spurred on by drive of the World Trade Organization (WTO) to open the doors of all sectors of education to profit-making and the law of money (see chapter 2, and Glenn Rikowski's book *The Battle in Seattle: Its Significance for Education*).[2] However, the events in Seattle in late 1999 have given the Left in general and the educational Left new heart and confidence, with subsequent anticapitalist protests in Washington, Davos, Prague and elsewhere maintaining the 'spirit of Seattle.' Since Seattle, radical educators have turned the spotlight on the WTO's education agenda.[3] The cover is being blown on the relationship between the agenda of the WTO and other international capitalist organizations for education and the increasing takeovers of schools, colleges and universities by corporate capital. It is an issue we took up in our booklet, *Red Chalk: On Schooling, Capitalism and Politics*[4] (itself, a substantially expanded version of our interview in the *International Journal of Education Reform*). We look forward to further work from the educational Left along these lines.

We hope this book helps to fuel debate within the educational Left internationally regarding the need for useful theoretical work for the movement. We also offer our readers some propositions on this score. First, we hold that Marxist educational theory has a key role in generating ideas that challenge educational orthodoxies and 'justifications' for educational inequalities. Second, it can help us set a course for socialist transformation of education. Third, postmodernism in education (and in general) cannot generate a vital politics of human resistance to neoliberal policies in education. Postmodernism provides an inadequate set of theoretical resources for the liberatory education that is required for the new century.

Notes

1. Dave Hill, Peter McLaren, Mike Cole and Glenn Rikowski, eds., *Postmodernism in Educational Theory: Education and the Politics of Human Resistance* (London: Tufnell Press, 1999), <http://www.tufnellpress.com> (May 1, 2001).

2. Glenn Rikowski, *The Battle in Seattle: Its Significance for Education* (London: Tufnell Press, 2001).

3. See for example, Nico Hirtt, "The 'Millennium Round' and the Liberalisation of the Education Market," *Education and Social Justice* 2, no. 2 (2000): 12–18; Bhumika Muchhala, *Student Voices: One Year After Seattle* (Washington, D.C.: Institute of Policy Studies, 2000), and <http://www.ips-dc.org> (April 9, 2001); Rikowski, *Battle in Seattle*; Jonathan Rutherford, "Scholars squeezed by market muscle," in *Times Higher Education Supplement*, January 26, 2001.

4. Mike Cole, Dave Hill, Peter McLaren and Glenn Rikowski, *Red Chalk: On Schooling, Capitalism and Politics* (Brighton, U.K.: Institute of Education Policy Studies, 2001), <http://www.ieps.org.uk> (May 1, 2001); Peter McLaren, Mike Cole, Dave Hill and Glenn Rikowski, "An Interview with Three British Marxist Educators," *International Journal of Education Reform* (2001). See also Dave Hill and Mike Cole, eds., *Schooling and Equality: Fact, Concept and Policy* (London: Kogan Page, 2001).

Part I

Introduction

Chapter 1

Postmodernism in Educational Theory

Glenn Rikowski and Peter McLaren

Introduction

In many parts of the capitalist world, postmodernist politics still attests to contemporary relevance. Indeed, it claims to be the only politics available. The authors of this book collectively discern a need to clear the decks of such junk theory and debilitating 'political' posturing because of the urgent tasks ahead for socialists. We also, in various ways, stress the significance of education and training as resources for constructing a future based on the struggle against capital, the social forms and institutions it engenders, and the social inequalities that arise from its market mechanisms.

Some 'Left' postmodernisms, or 'postmodernisms of resistance,' appear to hold out prospects for a fruitful consummation of postmodernist and Marxist outlooks. We aim to dispel that illusion. Education has a crucial role to play in the struggle for a future where the domination of capital and its value-form of labor do not close off social, economic and political options.

Postmodernism is an obstacle to the formation of open and radical perspectives that challenge inequalities and the deepening of the rule of capital in all areas of social life. As Helen Raduntz notes, postmodernism "constitutes a sterile theoretical cul-de-sac with no political program for transformative change."[1] In recent years, postmodernism has assumed an educational form, as educational theory—postmodernized modes of 'reflective' teacher practice, postmodern educational research methods, and so on. Hence, it poses a particular challenge to those viewing education as a resource for social equality and democracy.

The incursion of postmodernism into U.K. educational circles has been a relatively recent phenomenon. It appears to have followed what has been described as the 'cultural turn' in social theory: a focus on symbolic meaning after decades of research dominated by structural, functionalist and empirical approaches within the human sciences. Ian Stronach and Maggie MacLure note that the *British Education Index* had no postmodern entries between 1986 and 1991. There was one for 1992, two for 1993 and fifteen for 1994.[2] Thus, 1994 seems to be a significant milestone for British educational postmodernism, and the publication of Robin Usher and Richard Edwards' *Postmodernism and Education* in that year heralded the 'arrival' of postmodernism within the British educational milieu. In 1997, Stronach and MacLure's *Educational Research Undone* and Stuart Parker's *Reflective Teaching in the Postmodern World* consolidated the position of postmodernism within educational research and pedagogy, respectively, within the British context.[3] In the United States, postmodernism appeared in educational theory and research much earlier and much more extensively. The late 1980s and early 1990s saw an explosion of education books and articles written from postmodernist perspectives, the first being Peter McLaren's critique of postmodernism, *Postmodernity and the Death of Politics: A Brazilian Reprieve* in 1986, followed by Stanley Aronowitz and Henry Giroux's *Postmodern Education* in 1990, and in 1991 by Patti Lather's *Getting Smart: Feminist Research and Pedagogy With/in the Postmodern* (as leading examples).[4] During this period, some American education journals became clearing houses for educational postmodernism.

Attempts to 'define' postmodernism and 'educational postmodernism' are fraught with difficulty. Daring to spell out differences between postmodernism and postmodernity[5] easily brings down accusations of oversimplification and crassness from postmodernists.[6] Even taking Usher and Edwards' rendering of postmodernism—as a certain "attitude" toward "life" or a certain "state of mind," as ironical, self-referential posture and style, a different "way of seeing"[7]—still begs the question of why this *particular* 'attitude' is superior, more relevant, or politically 'cool' than any other. For us, a commitment to social justice that seeks to end social inequalities is a better 'attitude' to adopt.

At the popular level, postmodernism reflects a certain celebration of aimless anarchism, captured by Martin Jay as "a world in which Beavis and Butthead have replaced Horkheimer and Adorno as the reigning champions of negation."[8] As a social-theoretical project, postmodernism is excessive: within the realm of 'discourse' (which functions as a parallel universe) it knows no bounds. Yet in the social universe, in the real world (which, for us, incorporates 'discourse'), we face structural constraints, collectively and individually, on our form of life; constraints set by capital and its social relations.[9] For postmodernists, all concepts are decentered (fragmented, splattered) and all dualisms (such as the Marxist notion of two major social classes) are deconstructed. The search for 'meaning' within texts as within discourse is infinitized, comprising endless academic work for postmodernists. As Mike Cole, Dave Hill and Glenn Rikowski show, through a critique of the work of Nigel Blake, postmodernism "as excessive social-theoretical practice" attempts to negate the Enlightenment project, and with it reason and rationality, along with any attempts to secure 'knowledge.' Meta-narratives, ethics and value, and any appeals to 'truth' are also scuppered.[10] The effects of postmodernism are predictable: relativism; nihilism; solipsism; fragmentation, pathos, hopelessness. Worse, it acts as obfuscation and veil for the projects of the Radical Right[11] and continues to obscure them under the guise of the 'Third Way.'[12]

Of course, postmodernists might argue that their object and purpose is just 'playfulness.' In 1996 and 1997, Nigel Blake claimed that he was merely appraising and assessing postmodernism's value for educational philosophy; Geoff Waite, on the other hand, holds that such indulgences can more accurately be viewed as acts invoking *self-destruction*.[13] Facing the harsh rule of capital, we need to build ourselves up, find similarities between us (as opposed to emphasizing differences and fractured, hybrid identities) and to enhance our strengths based on *labor in and against capital*.[14] We need to become a social and political force of substance, not virtual forces in the ethereal realm of 'discourse.' And while it is true that in some respect there is a materiality to discourse as a form of practice, postmodernists fail to make the necessary connections between discursive materiality and social relations of production.

It is the political uselessness and debilitating effects of postmodernist discourse that jar most. These can be best illustrated through an example. At the 1997 British Association's Annual Festival of Science, Alan Smithers indicated that some education research efforts were "a desperate waste of time."[15] To illustrate the general point, Smithers picked on Nigel Blake's 1996 article, "Between Postmodernism and Anti-Modernism."[16] Educational research in general and postmodernist educational perspectives in particular, continued to take a battering, the critics spurred on by Chris Woodhead from the U.K. Government's Office for Standards in Education (OFSTED).

In an article in the *Times Education Supplement*, Blake struck back in 1997, arguing that "discussions about [educational] policy and practice can be informed by *rational argument* and critique" (our emphasis). However, Blake's appeal to rational discourse as arbiter of the value of education research flies in the face of the postmodernist tendency (including his own, in his 1996 article) to be skeptical about, or to undermine, 'Western' or 'Eurocentric' notions of 'reason' and rationality. After attempting to rescue himself with the enemy's poison, Blake then confusedly argues postmodernist perspectives on educational research can be of value.[17] This indicates that not only is postmodernism useless as a basis for self-defense, *even for postmodernists*, but as a resource for defending the poor, informing class struggle and arguing against the reality of social inequality it is likely to be even more unhelpful.

Identity Politics and Contemporary Crises

Postmodernist 'politics,' such as it is, largely rests upon the concepts of identity and difference. As Jenny Bourne shows in chapter 9, the "politics of identity and difference [are] being clearly used to justify the break with class politics." The problem with basing a 'Left' politics on notions of identity and difference is that these concepts, when driven through the mill of postmodernism, become an *anti-politics*, a kind of "game of despair."[18] This is because, in pointing toward the fragmentation of 'selves' and a corresponding lack of a *core* to personhood, to the hybridity of 'identities' (we are legion), and the infinite play of 'differance' based on social context, perspective, infinite interpretation and variegated relations to the Other—we are left with *little or nothing in common* upon which to build a politics of resistance to capital. This applies to a prospective politics of gender, 'race,' disability and sexuality as much as it does for a politics based upon class struggle. Postmodernists reflect what Peter Sloterdijk calls "cynical reason," which is an "enlightened false consciousness" or a "hard-boiled, shadowy cleverness that has split courage off from itself, holds anything positive to be a fraud, and is intent only on somehow getting through life."[19]

The hyper-tech cousins of the postmodernists, the post-human and transhuman theorists who emphasize our march toward the cyborg (fused human-machine entity), add another layer of thought which throws a politics of *commonality* off-balance (although some hold out prospects for a new *cyberpolitics* based on our shared evolutionary destiny).[20] However, what postmodernists and post/trans-human theorists[21]—protagonists for a cyborg future—blatantly ignore or deny is that our lives and 'selves' are, after all, very much centered: by *capital*, as social force and social relation. As capital is a social force that exists as a range of contradictory social drives and flows through capitalist social relations, and insofar as we become capital, then *our everyday lives are lived through and express these contradictions*. Our lives *are* fragmented, shattered and unbalanced—and postmodernism reflects this, though only at the level of 'discourse' and the 'text'—but this strikes a chord only because the 'human' has historically become capital, human-capital. Thus, as well as causing havoc *externally* to individuals, capital is also the 'horror within' personhood; we live our lives through its forms (money, value, state, commodity and so on) and its contradictions. As Glenn Rikowski indicates in chapter 6, the struggle against the horror within cannot be undertaken internally—through some form of Marxist psychotherapy. Rather, the need is for a politics aimed at the abolition of the value-form of labor—the dissolution of capital itself— and this involves our *uniting* as labor against capital.

Beyond our fragmented selves, international capital is going through a severe crisis. As Peter McLaren and Ramin Farahmandpur note in chapter 11,[22] the outcomes of the current crisis of capital accumulation include the redistribution of income from poor to rich; the erosion of welfare benefits; the socialization of risks to capital; the suppression of labor incomes; the re-enforcement of surplus-value extraction (longer working hours); a raft of anti-labor laws in many Western countries; increased casualization, job insecurity and flexibilization of labor (temporary contracts, part-time and low-paid McJobs in the service sector); and increasing social division within the working class, accompanied by profound weaknesses within labor movements in many countries. Furthermore, many governments have reacted to the crisis by looking to education and training to give businesses within their national capitals a competitive edge in the global marketplace, by reforming education and training systems (for example, in the context of the ideologies of globalization and modernization, as Mike Cole shows).[23] In the United Kingdom in particular, human capital theory (largely implicitly, but increasingly explicitly) is at the foundation of education and training policy development. Reform mania has resulted, powered by a generalized drive to rise the quality of human capital (labor-power) throughout British capital. This is certainly the case with respect to current U.S. school reform efforts, discussed in chapter 9. The special emphasis on labor-power quality results from the (erroneous) perception by governments that they can at least control *this* commodity, if no other.

There is a need for a socialist response to these developments. One of the aims of this book is to provide a range of such responses. But we are not just reacting against the poverty of postmodern theory and current economic and educational crises. Our project aims to go further and much deeper. The various contributions in the book highlight the contradictory roles of education and training in capitalism. On the one hand, education and training are implicated in the social production of labor-power and in social inequalities and divisions, but on the other can become critical forces for change. With respect to the latter, Peter McLaren[24] emphasizes the critical, revolutionary and contraband role that pedagogies can play. Michael Neary in chapter 7, and Dave Hill, Mike Sanders and Ted Hankin in chapter 8, make clear that education and training have significant roles to play in strategies of human resistance to the rule of capital in everyday life, and in struggles for social justice and social equality.

Outline

This book incorporates three major themes: the appraisal and critique of postmodernism within educational theory; the explication of Marxist and socialist-feminist alternatives to postmodernism; and human resistance to capital and its associated forms of inequality. With respect to education and training, the focus is fourfold: first, there is an emphasis on the degeneration of educational theory through the 'postmodern turn' (and the effects for educational politics, policy and perspectives); second, attention is given to the ways capitalist education and training are implicated in the social production of labor-power, the living commodity on which the whole capitalist system rests; third, a range of educational inequalities are analyzed and theorized, and various implications for the struggle for equality within education are drawn out; finally, and most importantly, the subversive, critical and emancipatory aspects of education are explored, with an emphasis on *critical, revolutionary and contraband pedagogies*—pedagogies that run against the grain of capitalist educational and social life.

With these themes and foci in view, the book is organized into four parts. This chapter and the next, the "Prelude," constitute Part I, the "Introduction." The second part, "Postmodern Excess," comprises chapters 3, 4 and 5, which are focused on the general critique of postmodernism and specific criticisms of postmodernism in educational theory. In Part III, "Human Resistance against Postmodernism," chapters 6–10 bring to the fore education as a form of human resistance to capital and social inequalities and divisions (for example, Glenn Rikowski on 'the human', Michael Neary on youth, Jane Kelly on feminism, Jenny Bourne on 'race' and Dave Hill, Mike Sanders and Ted Hankin on social class). Finally, chapters 11 and 12 constitute Part IV, "Pedagogy, Reprise and Conclusion." This explores the importance of radical (contraband) pedagogy as a form of human resistance to capitalist education, brings the key arguments of the book together and says "Adieu" to postmodernism in conclusion. The specifics of the individual chapters are as follows.

In chapter 2, Glenn Rikowski presents a brief survey of prospects for Marxist educational theory. He argues for the need for such theory in today's neoliberal times, when capital runs rampant throughout the globe, and uncovers evidence for cautious optimism, charting the volume of Marxist and Left writings on education since 1994. Secondly, he critiques the important work of Elizabeth Atkinson,[25] which appeared after *Postmodernism in Educational Theory*[26] was published in 1999. In her articles and also her paper presented at the British Educational Research Association Conference of 2000, Atkinson provides an explicit and wide-ranging critique of Marxist educational theory from within what she calls "postmodern thought." Atkinson asserts that she is seeking to critique unwelcome trends and developments within education policy and practice as a "responsible anarchist," yet her critique of contemporary education is shown to be not that radical at all; rather, it is a form of *repressed* dissent (as further explicated by Cole and Hill in chapter 5, as well as by the article "Between Postmodernism and Nowhere").[27] Thirdly, Glenn Rikowski outlines in chapter 2 some of the key tasks ahead for Marxist educational theory.

Peter McLaren and Ramin Farahmandpur take up the issue of the prospects for Marxist analysis in the face of 'post-Marxism' in chapter 3. They argue that Marx and Marxist analysis are required now more than ever before in the history of capitalism. Globalization (capital is everywhere) and neoliberalism (representatives and procapitalist organizations are seeking to *deepen* capital's hold on all aspects of everyday life—including education, health and social services) call forth the need for radical critique on a scale hitherto unimagined. Avoidance of the relevance of Marx and Marxism in today's situation, argue McLaren and Farahmandpur, cannot be politically or intellectually justified. They indicate how 'new times' and post-Marxist theories are inadequate to the task of grasping the depth of horror generated by capitalist globalization and neoliberalism, and are also poor foundations for effective resistance movements. McLaren and Farahmandpur also expose postmodernism and educational postmodernism as brakes on the radicalization of theory and for understanding developments in educational and social life in order to transform them (a theme they expand further in chapter 11). They proceed to note the 'tragedy' of fragmentation, in which social movements have disempowered themselves by largely turning their backs on Marxist theorizations, and they indicate how postmodern thought has played its part in bringing this unfortunate situation about.

In chapter 4, Michael W. Apple and Geoff Whitty argue that the pendulum has swung too far away from the social and educational theories and traditions informing change in curriculum and pedagogy. Postmodernist and poststructuralist alternatives, although superficially 'cool,' have sometimes merely thrown up old forms of social and educational outlooks where social control becomes the dominant leitmotif. Apple and Whitty advocate a shift from a postmodernist obsession with *meaning* in educational discourse toward a concern with *critical action*. They call for a re-emphasis on the *political economy of education*, though not to the neglect of cultural aspects of contemporary social and educational life. The chapter provides analyses of educational 'reforms' of the last ten years (mainly in a British context, but also with examples from the United States and New Zealand) and asks the question: Can these be characterized as instances of *postmodern* educational reforms? Apple and Whitty argue that analysis of changes in capitalist accumulation processes is a more useful starting point for exploring these 'reforms.' Although they point toward some positive effects of postmodern theory, they are critical of its excessive moments and flights of fancy.

The main targets of chapter 5, by Mike Cole and Dave Hill, are 'postmodernisms of resistance.' They contrast these false pretenders with straightforwardly reactionary forms of postmodernism. Fashionable postmodernisms of resistance seek to provide alternatives to Marxist educational perspectives. The authors provide trenchant criticisms of postmodernist thought in general, and postmodernisms of resistance in particular, before showing how *all* forms of postmodernist discourse disempower those aiming to uncover and struggle against a range of social and educational inequalities. Finally, they provide arguments indicating that postmodernist educational research and writing gloss over the major division within capitalist society: the social class divide.

In chapter 6, Glenn Rikowski indicates that a politics of human resistance to the rule of capital faces a particular problem: *we are capital*. Most of the chapter is taken up with demonstrating how we become capital, and the ways that 'human' life is capitalized. Criticisms of fashionable trans/post-human theories are provided en route. Special emphasis is given to the social production of labor-power in capitalism, and to the parts that education and training play in the formation of human-capital: humanity *as* capital. Finally, the chapter points toward the role that critical pedagogy can play in understanding and resisting our predicament as human-capital.

Michael Neary, in chapter 7, problematizes the concept of youth and, inter alia, the sociology of youth and youth cultural studies. By delving deeply into Marxist theory, Neary provides an innovative critique of conventional theories of human resistance. Through focusing upon some of Marx's basic structuring concepts—*value, labor, labor-time* and so on—Neary expresses how capital is an impersonal form of social domination created by labor itself, and takes the form of abstract labor. In this analysis, Neary exposes some weak points within capitalist domination. He then proceeds to explore these vulnerabilities through an historical account of the "production of a specific form of human sociability: youth, through a particular form of regulation: training." Neary does this by examining the U.K. Employment and Training Act 1948, showing how the re-sultant training 'culture' *was set against human resistance* (to capital's domina-tion). Neary's exploration of the Act, in relation to the post-war and contempo-rary youth condition, shows how we can theorize resistance beyond orthodox accounts of working-class struggle and perceive that human resistance to capital "cannot be contained."

In chapter 8, Dave Hill, Mike Sanders and Ted Hankin provide compelling arguments for a "return to class analysis" as the basis for a rejuvenated educa-tional theory and politics. These authors show how we still live in a class-divided society and unearth some of the key facts regarding social class differ-ences. They go on to show the deleterious effects of postmodernist discourse on contemporary educational debate and politics. The main part of the chapter is taken up with working through problems and issues in class analysis, prior to showing the relevance of social class to a range of contemporary policy devel-opments. They end with an argument for reinvigorating the secondary curricu-lum through a pedagogy that enlightens young people about the (capitalist) na-ture of the society in which they live and that provides resources for critical analyses of contemporary society.

Jenny Bourne, in chapter 9, critiques postmodernist and poststructuralist positions on 'race.' She shows how these perspectives have de-radicalized the study and politics of 'race,' while simultaneously undermining social class analysis. Bourne provides an account of the rise of postmodernist theory from its beginnings in 'cultural studies' to its eventual flowering in the hokum of 'new times' and theories of identity and identity 'politics.' She shows how we can reclaim radical 'race' perspectives, pinpointing criticisms within culturalism and positions that make positive claims for a 'politics of identity/difference,' and showing how 'Left' postmodernists have betrayed the oppressed. Bourne concludes with a critique of the work of Phil Cohen on youth and education. This critique illuminates the poverty of postmodern perspectives. Postmodern-ism, argues Bourne, is useless as a basis for understanding and resisting racism.

In chapter 10, Jane Kelly critically surveys postmodernist and poststruc-turalist feminisms. She charts the development of these theories within femi-nism and then exposes their incoherence. For Kelly, "postmodernized femi-nism" is on a road to nowhere: bereft of political direction, imbued with theoretical drift. Through an historical and empirical analysis of the position of women in Britain, Kelly finds that there is still much about which to be angry. The position of women on a range of issues—from pay, to working conditions and beyond—requires clear theoretical analysis that can function as guide to effective political action for changing women's lives for the better. The preoccupations of postmodernism are elsewhere. Postmodernism is not only excessive in its effects but also a form of self-indulgence, argues Kelly.

Peter McLaren and Ramin Farahmandpur begin chapter 11 with a wide-ranging critique of neoliberal ideology, pinpointing some of the contemporary attacks on workers and oppressed groups committed in its name. While McLaren and Farahmandpur acknowledge some positive aspects of postmodern theory, they note its failure to become a force for effective opposition to neoliberal policy drives. They develop critical positions on globalization and the marketization of social life, and then go on to demonstrate the 'naughtiness' of postmodernism in its collusion and synergy with neoliberalism. Following a return to class analysis and an extensive review of the relevance of social class to understanding key aspects of capitalist inequalities, McLaren and Farahmandpur set about "re-enchanting the project of critical educational theory" through developing a contraband pedagogy.

In the final chapter, McLaren, Hill, Rikowski and Cole focus on the notion of human resistance, and show how the various chapters in this volume inform and theorize this issue. They explore concrete ways through which we can resist the degenerative tendencies of contemporary capital, and examine where education fits into strategies for human resistance. At this juncture, the authors make a case for forms of critical and revolutionary pedagogy, and explicate the roles they can play within anticapitalist politics of human resistance.

Notes

1. Helen Raduntz, "Researching a Hegelian-Marxian dialectic for a theory of Australian Catholic schooling" (modified version of a paper presented at the Conference of the Australian Association for Education Research (RSD 98259: 1998), 14.

2. Ian Stronach and Maggie MacLure, *Educational Research Undone: The Postmodern Embrace* (Buckingham, U.K.: Open University Press, 1997), 32.

3. Robin Usher and Richard Edwards, *Postmodernism and Education: Different Voices, Different Worlds* (London: Routledge, 1994); Stronach and MacLure, *Educational Research;* Stuart Parker, *Reflective Teaching in the Postmodern World: A Manifesto for Education in Postmodernity* (Buckingham, U.K.: Open University Press, 1997).

4. Peter McLaren, "Postmodernity and the Death of Politics: A Brazilian Reprieve," *Educational Theory* 36, no. 4 (fall 1986): 389–401; Stanley Aronowitz and Henry Giroux, *Postmodern Education: Politics, Culture and Social Criticism* (Minneapolis: University of Minnesota Press, 1990); Patti Lather, *Getting Smart: Feminist Research and Pedagogy With/in the Postmodern* (London: Routledge, 1991).

5. As in Mike Cole, Dave Hill and Glenn Rikowski, "Between Postmodernism and Nowhere: The Predicament of the Postmodernist," *British Journal of Educational Studies* 45, no. 2 (1997): 187–200; Shaun Fielding and Glenn Rikowski, "Resistance to Restructuring? Post-Fordism in British Primary Schools" (unpublished paper, School of Education, University of Birmingham, U.K.), 1996.

6. Cf. Nigel Blake, "A Postmodernism Worth Bothering About: A Rejoinder to Cole, Hill and Rikowski," *British Journal of Educational Studies* 45, no. 3 (1997): 293–305.

7. Usher and Edwards, *Postmodernism and Education*, 1–2.

8. Martin Jay, *Cultural Semantics: Keywords of Our Time* (Amherst: University of Massachusetts Press, 1998), 108.

9. Moishe Postone, *Time, Labour and Social Domination: A Reinterpretation of Marx's Critical Theory* (Cambridge: Cambridge University Press, 1996).

10. See Cole, Hill and Rikowski, "Between Postmodernism and Nowhere," for a critique of N. Blake, "Between Postmodernism and Anti-Modernism: The Predicament of Educational Studies," *British Journal of Educational Studies* 44, no. 1 (1996): 371–393.

11. Dave Hill and Mike Cole, "Marxist State Theory and State Autonomy Theory: The Case of 'Race' Education in Initial Teacher Education," *Journal of Education Policy* 10, no. 2 (1995): 221–232; Cole and Hill, "Resistance Postmodernism: Emancipatory Politics for a New Era or Academic Chic for a Defeatist Intelligentsia?" in *Information Society: New Media, Ethics and Postmodernism*, ed. K. Gill (London: Springer-Verlag, 1996).

12. Dave Hill, *New Labour and Education: Policy, Ideology and the Third Way* (London: Tufnell Press, 1999) and *Education, Education, Education: Capitalism, Socialism and 'The Third Way,'* ed. D. Hill (Brighton, U.K.: Institute for Education Policy Studies, 2002).

13. Blake, "Postmodernism and Antimodernism" and "Postmodernism Worth Bothering About;" Geoff Waite, *Nietzsche's Corps/e: Aesthetics, Politics, Prophecy, or the Spectacular Technoculture of Everyday Life* (Durham, N.C.: Duke University Press, 1996).

14. Michael Neary, *Youth, Training and the Training State: The Real History of Youth Training in the Twentieth Century* (Basingstoke, U.K.: Macmillan, 1997).

15. Nick Barnard, "Most research is 'waste of time,'" *Times Educational Supplement*, September 12, 1997, 6; David Halpin, "Getting By through Failing to Deliver Simple Truths," *British Journal of Educational Studies* 46, no. 1 (1998): 1.

16. Nigel Blake, "Postmodernism and Antimodernism."

17. Nigel Blake and Richard Smith, "Beware a Totalising Society," *Times Educational Supplement*, October 10, 1997, 23.

18. Mike Cole and Dave Hill, "Games of Despair and Rhetorics of Resistance: Postmodernism, Education and Reaction," *British Journal of Sociology of Education* 16, no. 2 (1995): 165–182.

19. Peter Sloterdijk, *Critique of Cynical Reason* (London: Verso, 1988), 546.

20. Robert Pepperell, *The Post-Human Condition* (Exeter, U.K.: Intellect Books, 1997); Donna Haraway, "Situated Knowledges: The Science Question in Feminism and the Privilege of Partial Perspectives," *Feminist Studies* 14, no. 3 (1988): 575–599, and *Simians, Cyborgs, and Women: The Reinvention of Nature* (New York: Routledge, 1991).

21. Postmodernism and post/trans-human theory are outlined and discussed by Glenn Rikowski in chapter 6.

22. See also Peter McLaren, "Revolutionary Pedagogy in Post-Revolutionary Times: Rethinking the Political Economy of Critical Education," *Educational Theory* (fall 1998).

23. See Mike Cole, "Globalisation, Modernisation and Competitiveness: A Critique of the New Labour Project in Education," *International Studies in Sociology of Education* 8, no. 3 (1998): 315–332.

24. Peter McLaren, "Critical Pedagogy and Globalization: Thirty Years After Che" (keynote address at the Annual Convention for the National Association for Multicultural Education, Albuquerque, New Mexico, October 31,1997).

25. Elizabeth Atkinson, "The Promise of Uncertainty: Education, Postmodernism and the Politics of Possibility," *International Studies in Sociology of Education* 10, no. 1 (2000): 81–99, also "The Responsible Anarchist: Postmodernism and Social Change" (paper presented to the Symposium "If We Aren't Pursuing Improvement, What Are We Doing?" at the British Educational Research Association Conference, Cardiff University, Wales, September 7–9, 2000) and "Critical Dissonance and Critical Schizophrenia: The Struggle between Policy Delivery and Policy Critique," *Research Intelligence*, no. 30 (November 2000): 14–17.

26. Dave Hill, Peter McLaren, Mike Cole and Glenn Rikowski, eds., *Postmodernism in Educational Theory: Education and the Politics of Human Resistance* (London: Tufnell Press, 1999).

27. See also Cole, Hill and Rikowski, "Between Postmodernism and Nowhere."

Chapter 2

Prelude: Marxist Educational Theory after Postmodernism

Glenn Rikowski

Radical Dinosaurs

This book is powered by three drives: first, the critique of postmodernism (with special reference to educational theory); second, the rethinking and renewing of Marxist educational theory after postmodernism; and third, the generation of a politics of human resistance to capitalist social life and its educational forms. However, the primary drive of these three is the critique of postmodernism. Our original text, *Postmodernism in Educational Theory: Education and the Politics of Human Resistance* by Dave Hill, Peter McLaren, Mike Cole and Glenn Rikowski, was published in 1999, and an assessment of some recent developments is now essential. Furthermore, as Peter McLaren and Ramin Farahmandpur indicate in chapter 3, the extension of our initial text yields more to a consideration of Marxist educational theory than did the original. The purpose of this chapter is to examine the prospects for Marxist educational theory 'after postmodernism.'

Why I choose Marx rather than anyone else as starting point for generating a critique of capitalist education and training, and why I stand on his shoulders rather than stand on the tainted ground of capitalism all by myself requires brief explanation. Certainly, my own biographical and intellectual history, as illustrated in *Red Chalk: On Schooling, Capitalism and Politics*[1] indicates leading facts about my personal and political development that inclined me toward Marxism. In particular, my experience as an educator and as an education researcher has catapulted Marxism to the forefront of the interpretation of the experiences constituting my 'everyday life.' But personal trajectories cannot, by themselves, sustain commitment to a theory as oppositional as Marxism. The penalties involved are all too clear, in terms of career devaluation and various forms of discrimination, persecution and surveillance. That commitment is nurtured by the explanatory possibilities and the hopefulness, love and potential for overcoming oppression incorporated within the theory itself. For me, Marxist theory affords potentialities for articulating a multitude of forms of oppression in relation to people of color, women, gays and lesbians, and other social groups de-valued by capitalist society. Furthermore, Marxism expresses, theoretic-politically and empirically, the dynamics of social class as the form of oppression within capitalist society that is constituted by its own development. Marxist theory also allows me to perspectivize gender, 'race' and other forms of oppression through the lens of social class.[2] Finally, it articulates the fragility of capitalist oppression.[3] It expresses the scream of refusal, but also gives form to the shrieks of power of the oppressed as they resist and confront capital's insurgence into all spheres of social life.

Reverting to the personal outlook: while living life as a Marxist educator, theorist and activist has its risks, I would argue that the enriched experience of life it affords, of life's intensity and significance, is mightily magnified. I am no self-sacrificing ego-less altruist. However, what I would say is that as capital is a social force that colonizes the whole of social existence, including 'the human' itself (see chapter 6) on an exponential scale, then the contradictions of capital are incorporated within human life (within my life). In these circumstances, humans will seek to solve these contradictions within their 'everyday lives.' Yet real and lasting solutions depend upon the abolition of the social force that generates these contradictions within the 'human': capital. Our lives are an expression of this contradiction in an extreme form. I am an extremist insofar as I give vent to the operations of the force that generates contradictions within my social existence: capital. However, I am no different from anyone else in this respect; all are oppressed by capital as social force. We live in the social universe of capital. Although capital drives us all to be extremists as its social drives are infinite,[4] yet its survival depends on us avoiding and hiding this fact of life, and therefore living as schizophrenics in denial or manic acceptors of 'Capital's Fate for Us.' It is the clash of personal biography and general determinants within this social universe that socially produced me as a dissident seeking to erase the social conditions underpinning my own rage and the impoverished and alienated lives of billions. This is illustrated in the *Red Chalk*[5] book, where relations between aspects of my individual trajectory and some general determinants of capitalist social life (particularly social class) are explored in more depth. Thus, for me, Marxism provides a materialist explanation of my own personal responses to capitalist social life. This deep pedagogy and subterranean thought as expressed through my own life also provides a window for viewing, explaining and formulating strategies of resistance to processes of the capitalization of humanity. Marxist theory, for me, illuminates the contradictory nature of my own 'personhood' as an effect of capital as social force invading the human. It also informs regarding the contradictions of social life thrown up by antagonistic social relations. In addition, Marxism provides understanding of inequalities and forms of oppression. However, most significantly, it also indicates fragile spots within the rule of capital and why an oppositional force of millions is necessary to break open these weak links within the radical chains that bind us all.

Some postmodernists might insist that my perspective on Marx is erroneous, on the basis that Marx "saw ignorance as inevitable in anything less than a fully qualified communist state."[6] However, on the preceding account of Marxism, I disagree. Marxist theory enables understanding of our own personal and social predicaments. It seeks to banish ignorance on these matters to the effect and extent that the understanding and explanation gained can be dangerous to the social domination of capital. I can know dangerous stuff. It is this that stops me from being a 'Marxist dinosaur.' Michael Hardt and Antonio Negri in *Labor of Dionysus* take on the postmodernist charge that Marxists are dinosaurs in a way that is, for me, very instructive. The opening section of their first chapter is called "Dinosaurs," and Hardt and Negri note that some readers may be surprised that the book speaks "not only of labor, exploitation, and capitalism, but also of class conflict, proletarian struggles, and even communist forces. Do dinosaurs walk the earth?" They note that:

> We cast our discussions in these terms not from obstinacy or any obscure orthodoxy, but simply because we believe that, when submitted to a continual process of reconsideration so as to be in line with our desires and our interpretation of the contemporary world, these are the most useful categories for political and social analysis.[7]

If these and other Marxist concepts—such as value, abstract labor, alienation and so on—were inadequate to the task of functioning as tools for an understanding of capitalist life, and hence for a form of politics with the potential to implode it, then I would be a dinosaur indeed. However, the working class fired by the flame of Marxist theory is a "terrible beast" that induces fear in representatives of capital. Despite wishful and superficial postmodern thought, "this monster was never extinct and continues to express its power throughout our modern and postmodern history."[8]

I advance the argument that in order to survive we must mutate into radical dinosaurs. Marxist theory as the critique of capitalist social life must expand and adapt until its usefulness dissolves as the force of millions implodes capitalist social relations. At that point, Marxist theorists truly become dinosaurs, with extinction imminent! The point at which Marxism as a negative social theory—that is, a theory against capitalist society and not just a theory of it—loses its social existence is when it plays its final part in the unraveling of capitalist society. Then it melds into communist science: the science of the constitution of communist society. This form of science already exists but is suppressed within capitalism (as is communism itself). Marxist theory, tailored to ending capital's reign, can be viewed as a particular expression of communist science that is moving toward its own extinction consonant with the abolition of capitalism. Thus, let us all become dinosaurs, radical dinosaurs, and struggle simultaneously for our own extinction as capitalist life forms and our evolution as humanity with an open future—a future free of the chains of capitalist social relations.

Marxist Educational Theory:
Is There Life after Postmodernism?

The publication of *Schooling in Capitalist America* in 1976 and *Learning to Labour* in 1977[9] heralded Marxist educational theory's high point: the late 1970s to early 1980s. The period following this, from the economic recession of the early 1980s right up to the mid-1990s, was both tragic and bumpy. The tragedy lay in the fact that writers within the field of Marxist educational theory avoided pushing it into new and exciting directions. Some writers in the field were attempting to shore up the defects[10] contained within these seminal texts.[11] Many were merely content to criticize these master texts to death. There were exceptions. A few were explicitly attempting to forge new tracks for Marxist educational theory. John Freeman-Moir and Rachel Sharp[12] were most clearly seeking to break free from the problems of the 'old' Marxist educational theory.[13] In 1988, Mike Cole's edited collection *Bowles and Gintis Revisited*[14] sought a serious re-appraisal of Marxist educational theory after *Schooling in Capitalist America*. The work of Richard Brosio and Kevin Harris[15] also inspired those few still working within the small pond of Marxist educational theory in those hard times.

The bumpy road for the 'old' Marxist educational theory was constructed from a number of corrosive materials.[16] These materials comprised the determinism flowing from crude applications of the base/superstructure model, the obverse problems associated with theorizing agency through Willisite resistance theory, and the weaknesses of Althusserian relative autonomy theory for theoretically situating schools in capitalist social space. Furthermore, the 'old' Marxist educational theory was also beset by threats external to its development: the 'death of Marxism' syndrome after the fall of the Soviet Union and Eastern Bloc countries into the empire of capital, and the rise of postmodernism as a seemingly 'radical' alternative. These two developments were mutually reinforcing; the 'death of Marxism' seemed to justify, or validate, a movement toward postmodernism, which at least seemed to have a future.

While confidence in a future for Marxism in general suffered briefly in the early 1990s, only to bounce back quite quickly, the future for Marxist *educational* theory seemed bleak indeed during the early 1990s, nearly twenty years since it had gathered any energy or vibrancy. Some education journals in the United States seemed to be clearing-houses for educational postmodernism in the early 1990s. In the United Kingdom, the publication of Robin Usher and

Richard Edwards' *Postmodernism and Education*[17] in 1994, seemed to be the first nail in the coffin of Marxist educational theory.[18] Postmodernism in education seemed to be sweeping all before it. Extinction was the prospect facing Marxist educational theory in the run-up to the millennium's end. Yet just at that instant of oblivion, survival was ensured. In the same year that Usher and Edwards' blockbuster was published, three significant developments occurred that gave Marxist educational theory a new lease of life. First, Richard Brosio published his 1994 epic, *A Radical Democratic Critique of Capitalist Education*.[19] This book demonstrated the inherent contradiction between democracy and capitalism with a mine of historical and contemporary examples and evidence, while also addressing the theoretical problems within the writings of many Marxist educational theorists as a backdrop to the main argument. Second, Kevin Harris' *Teachers: Constructing the Future*[20] also came out in 1994, giving heart to Marxists seeking a materialist understanding of teachers' work and their strategic significance both for the reproduction of capitalist society and for being leading players in its social transformation into socialism. Third, Andy Green's spirited and oft-referenced critique of postmodernism in state education also came out in 1994,[21] thus making it seem the critical year.

The years since 1994 have witnessed an explosion of Marxist work on education. This work proves beyond doubt that there is 'life after postmodernism' for Marxist educational theory, of which there are many examples.[22] In 1996, Charlie Bertsch's "The Pedagogy of the Depressed" appeared on the Internet.[23] Ross Longhurst's "Education as a Commodity," a Marxist analysis of English further education (FE) after the 'incorporation' of colleges in 1993, is still the best analysis of the FE sector we have today.[24] It moves on a deeper and more sophisticated level of analysis than anything else written on FE, asks penetrating questions (unheard of within almost all writing on English FE), and provides interesting and provocative answers. Overall, the works of the radical pedagogy movement and new interpretations of Antonio Gramsci and Paulo Freire are considerably larger than can be indicated here, and the renewed interest in education by Left organizations is hardly represented at all (although the latter development dates a few years prior to 1994).[25] The contributions of Mike Cole, Dave Hill, Peter McLaren and myself, the editors of this volume, add to the pertinent body of work.[26] Marxist educational theory is here to stay; its existence secured by the degenerative forms of education and training assumed in contemporary capitalism.

There is life for Marxist educational theory. Ironically, the neoliberal frame of much education policy during the 1980s and 1990s that generated the urgency to explain and resist key trends—such as marketization, privatization, opening school and college doors to capital—simultaneously highlights the continued need for an integrated theory and practice of resistance. The heavy managerialism, bureaucratization and regulation of education flowing from its manifestation as an aspect of the state-form of capital, and the drive to reduce education and training to labor power production 'on the cheap,' have also underpinned the relevance of Marxist analysis for educational struggles. In the last few years, the deepening of attacks on pedagogic conditions, the corralling of education research into national programs for capital-friendly education, and the narrowing of curricula on the basis of perceived 'needs' of capital accumulation, all call for a radical perspective on education as offered by Marxism. Intensified efforts of national capitals to reduce education to labor power production and enhancement at the expense of other goals and purposes of education have uncovered the basic instinct within the monster that is capitalist education. It devours all other forms of educational life. These developments have pushed some postmodernists toward attempting to give their educational theorizing a cutting edge, to take on and critique the increasingly impoverished forms of education and educational research on offer. However, these exercises in 'radicalism' by postmodern thinkers are severely circumscribed by the theorists' own presuppositions. As I now want to indicate, postmodern dissent in the face of the capitalization of education and of all social life exists in a repressed form. Postmodern thinkers on education disallow, curtail and denigrate a form of social analysis that can yield dangerous consequences for the very things that they seem to object to within education and training policy: Marxism.

The Spectacle of the Repressed:
The Limits of Postmodern Dissent

For me, the work of Elizabeth Atkinson[27] is most instructive regarding the limits of postmodern dissent. Mike Cole and Dave Hill critique Atkinson's work in detail in chapter 5. Here, my focus is on how this work represses radicalism.

Obviously, I share the unease and distaste expressed by Atkinson regarding many contemporary developments in education policy and education research. But Atkinson responds with a *repressed* critique of these developments. The resources provided by postmodernism cannot explain them (not that postmodernists seem particularly interested in explanation) nor generate pertinent political projects and forms of resistance to them. Furthermore, postmodern thinking seems irrelevant to the search for analysis of, and resistance to, the education policies Atkinson seems to object too. There is a rift between some depressing facts of contemporary educational and social life presented by Atkinson and the postmodern thought she fast-forwards as the basis of critique of those uncomfortable happenings. Hence, repressed critique. Atkinson uncovers the phenomenon in an extreme form, in the body of work I am addressing.

In a paper presented at the British Educational Research Association Conference in 2000,[28] Atkinson introduces herself[29] as a "responsible anarchist" rather than an "irresponsible nihilist." Her portrayal of postmodernism rests on the

- resistance of certainty and resolution.
- rejection of fixed notions of reality, knowledge, or method.
- acceptance of complexity, of lack of clarity and of multiplicity.

- acknowledgment of subjectivity, contradiction and irony.
- irreverence for traditions of philosophy or morality.
- deliberate intent to unsettle assumptions and presuppositions.
- refusal to accept boundaries or hierarchies in ways of thinking.
- disruption of binaries which define things as either/or.[30]

These points can all be challenged, and Cole and Hill take up the specifics of, and problems with, Atkinson's overall theorization in chapter 5.[31] For Atkinson, postmodern thinking "challenges the automatic acceptance of the beliefs" upon which multiple projects "might be founded," and "opens up the way" to "a critical questioning of the concepts on which notions of morality and justice are based," so that:

> Through this critical challenge, postmodernism presents itself as an inevitable agent for change: it challenges the educator, the researcher, the social activist or the politician not only to deconstruct the certainties around what they might see as standing in need of change, but also to deconstruct their own certainties as to why they hold this view.[32]

Atkinson avoids several problems, such as how postmodernists explain the changes they (inevitably) bring as they 'think the postmodern' and how it is possible that 'certainties' can be deconstructed, thus rendering their prior official status as certainties most problematic. But these issues do not concern me here. Since a comprehensive critique of postmodernism emerges from the subsequent chapters of the book, I aim simply to show how Atkinson's separation of 'facts' from postmodern thinking makes the latter redundant. Likewise, I do not wish to unravel her ludicrous claim that Marxists believe in the "forward march of progress,"[33] when so many Marxist analysts have pointed to retrogression in aspects of education policy, labor practices and welfare standards in leading capitalist nations. Rather, I focus on Atkinson's definition of deconstruction. Relying on a summary from Judith Butler,[34] Atkinson notes that to deconstruct "is not to negate or to dismiss, but to call into question and, perhaps most importantly, to open up a term," to a "re-usage or redeployment that previously has not been authorized."[35] It seems to me that calling concepts into question, opening up terms for re-use (recycling them) constitutes mainstream academic practice. Atkinson's appeal to 'authority' merely pinpoints postmodernist hang-ups that Marxists worth their salt would not have; the challenge to 'authority' (especially in its guise as representatives of the state or capital) goes without saying for Marxists! From Atkinson's outlook on postmodernism, I now approach the question of how she utilizes her postmodern thinking in the critique of aspects of existing capitalist social reality.

Atkinson begins an article for *Research Intelligence*, on the critique of education policy, with a string of facts and observations that have resonance with, and hold significance for, Marxist educational theorists and Left activists. On the experience of education policy initiatives in England and Wales during the last ten to twelve years, Atkinson makes a number of observations and signals degenerative elements within the educational landscape that capture some pertinent features of certain depressive aspects therein. These include the fact that Initial Teacher Training (ITT) in England and Wales has "suffered steady erosion of professional and academic autonomy" due to "an unprecedented increase in central control over the content and delivery both of teacher training itself and of the curricula trainees are taught to deliver in schools."[36] Atkinson points toward the debilitating and corrosive effects on teacher professionalism and autonomy of the National Curriculum for school students, of the National Curriculum for ITT and the inquisitorial and punitive inspection system for teachers carried out through the Office for Standards in Education (OFSTED). She also notes the mealymouthed, euphemistic and misleading terms in which these policies are described in official reports and legislation: "quality," "accountability," "excellence" and the like. Atkinson also conjures up some friendly spirits following the "accidental deaths" of both educational philosophy and educational autonomy at the hands of central government murderers, reminding us of times when thinking was central to what education was about.[37]

Now, for me, it is a useful first step for critical educational theorists to list some of the most objectionable education and teacher training policies of the last ten to twelve years. But to leave the list unattended to is superficiality squared. Such negligence is hopeless for teachers, teacher trainers and student teachers struggling to resist these policies and trends; we are only telling them things they already know and experience in their everyday lives. Critical educational analysts need to dive deeper and to explore the generation of these diabolical policies and initiatives. However, this depth is not best provided by the strategy of infinite deconstruction. Diving deep involves exploring the strange creatures at the bottom of the lagoon: social class, value, surplus value, abstract labor, labor-time and other monsters. With these abominable concepts, explanations of phenomena on the surface of society, such as education policies and practices, can demonstrate how they are generated.

As a postmodern thinker, Atkinson is attempting to "unsettle the certainties on which government policies are founded," an aspect of her portrayal of deconstruction noted earlier. This is at best standard academic practice, at worst a paper tiger. Furthermore, I just don't believe Atkinson when she says that she is aiming to "unsettle the certainties on which government policies are founded." Many times, we have argued—Mike Cole, Dave Hill, Peter McLaren and I—that labor power (human capital) development and enhancement drives education policy.[38] Many non-Marxist radical/critical educators acknowledge this point too. Thus, if Atkinson was really serious about "unsettling the certainties" underpinning contemporary education policy, she ought to check out the assumption that increasing the quality of labor power raises productivity for the nation and for individual enterprises, and then examine its effects for education policy and practice. However, her critique is repressed at this point, as she needs to consider the role that labor power (human capital) plays in society, the generation of value and profit, the social production of labor power and the role that education plays in this productive form, among other things. In toto, this would involve Atkinson in an exploration of the constitution of capitalist society. Of course, she may be one of those postmodernists who are skeptical about the existence of the 'social' and would be loath to acknowledge the pertinence of Marxist concepts in uncovering the phenomenon in question (i.e., labor power)—in which case the project is aborted. But if she isn't one of these hyper-deconstructors, then deconstruction alone—as characterized by her Conference paper[39]—is inadequate. This is because to substantially unsettle the assumptions surrounding the magical qualities of 'human capital' for national well-being, we have to explore and explain how the drive to enhance human capital results in the despicable education policies we witness today. More fundamentally, this substantive 'unsettling' rests upon the need to give an account of why raising the quality of human capital exists as an *infinite social drive* at all. For this, mere analysis of 'concepts' or deconstructing them holds little purchase. What is required is a materialist account of the generation of these ideas and the policies they spawn. This account presupposes a prior analysis of the constitution of society—capitalist society, or the *social universe of capital.*[40]

In Atkinson's postmodern thought, there is a vertiginous rift between the distasteful facts and trends she outlines and her deconstructive moments. The potential for the deconstructive moments to seriously disrupt, to really 'unsettle,' to be truly dangerous is repressed by the refusal to partake in analyses based on a critique of the constitution of capitalist society. The consequences are predictably depressing: "critical schizophrenia." As she notes:

> For those who are engaged in a critique of government policy, this situation leads to a condition of 'critical schizophrenia,' brought about by delivering government policies with one hand, while critiquing them with the other. Ironically, this condition is worsened by trying to do both jobs well: as a professional teacher-trainer, with responsibility for the academic welfare and ultimate success of hundreds of students each year, I find myself promoting exactly the sort of single-track, single-focus learning and teaching against which I protest in my academic writing.[41]

For Atkinson, the task of critique in education research and writing involves the analyst seeking to "deconstruct the concepts and terminology on which National Curricula and National Strategies are based."[42] Marxist critique, however, involves explaining the social existence of ideas, policies and national strategies with reference to the deep phenomena structuring their appearance on the surface of society: value, exchange-value, use-value, abstract labor, labor-time and so on. Thus, Atkinson's conception of critique and my own are radically different. For me, Atkinson misses the first and most important critical moment: explaining the social existence of phenomena by exploring the social forms they attain in capitalist society and their relations within a developing totality. In the case of capitalism, this totality is nothing less than the social universe of capital whose substance is value.[43] The fact that education and training play a role in the creation of value, through the laborer's labor power, fixes these as processes constitutive of this social universe. It is this fact about capitalist society that lays at the roots of the form and nature of any possible education and training policies. This is the starting point for substantive critiques of capitalist schooling and training, as opposed to superficial conceptual deconstruction that represses fundamental critique.

In a much longer article, Atkinson provides more examples of education policies to which Left educators and researchers would object. But in terms of the form of her argument and its consequences, nothing really changes. This is despite providing a long list of what postmodern thinking can do for education, by enabling us to:

1. Question the power structures underlying the contexts in which research and teaching are conducted, and the relationship between knowledge and power which exists in educational and social settings.
2. Question the relationship of researcher to researched, and its implications for both the process and the products of research activity.
3. Question the traditional oppositions between 'theory' and 'practice,' 'researcher' and 'researched' and 'practitioner,' 'insider' and 'outsider,' 'knowledge' and 'intuition' which frame much current research and teaching.
4. Question views of the growth of knowledge (in both research and teaching) which see it as linear, structured, predictable, stable and controllable.
5. Question the possibility of discovering objective 'truths' through empirical inquiry, and of representing such 'truths' with language.
6. Question notions of a fixed, stable identity for 'teacher,' 'pupil,' 'parent,' 'researcher' in the context of teaching and research.
7. Recognize the possibility of multiple meanings and interpretations (for all participants and all 'users') in educational research and practice.
8. Distrust language as a fixed signifier and question the search for universal or transcendental meanings as a basis for understanding education.
9. Question 'the ethnographic belief that "reality" is somehow out there waiting to be captured by language.'[44]

What is interesting about this list is why we need something called 'postmodern thinking' to do all this questioning, recognition and distrusting (of language). Radical sociology of the late 1960s would, for me, be a more useful starting point for tackling them. Even some not-so-radical sociology might have the edge on postmodern thinking for some of the above (traditional role theory might be more useful for point number 6, it could be argued). Second, it is far from obvious that these questions, by themselves, will cause much disruption and unsettling of educational certainties—just an infinite task of deconstructing concepts (as education policies come and go). Third, it is unsubstantiated that these questions would be the best starting points for critique even if one was serious about unsettling capitalist schooling with this approach. Fourth, it is not clear that Atkinson's notion of 'doing something for education,' and the role that postmodern thinking can play in this, are really fundamentally different from any modernist notion of 'improvement.' Finally, the previous point underscores the realization that Atkinson's project for educational critique is *abstract*: it is divorced from consideration of the constitution of capitalist society. Postmodern thinking, therefore, yields no dangerous consequences for informing actions and struggles that threaten to practically disrupt the constitution of capitalist society, as this is left unexplored; capitalism remains an enigma safe from any amount of postmodern question-posing and deconstruction. Postmodern idealism is the result—the position previously thought to be impossible as postmodernists are often viewed as Nietzschean destroyers of 'ideals.'

At the end of this longer article, Atkinson is no better off. The lack of interest in the deep structure of capitalist society represses and suppresses any really radical conclusions, much less action. The repressed anarchist, however, is a pretty poor specimen of an anarchist. The blocks such people place on their own capacity to generate radical ideas is a gift to a future where the social universe of capital continues to expand.

Education after Seattle and the Tasks Ahead

The World Trade Organization (WTO) is currently engaged in pursuing the capitalization of education, of opening up education to corporate capital on a scale unthinkable only a few years ago.[45] Through the General Agreement on Trade in Services (GATS), the WTO is actively seeking to encourage national governments to open up all education institutions—including compulsory schooling—to private capital, to the maximum. Analysis of the penetration of higher education by business interests has proceeded apace in the last ten years,[46] but the 'businessification' of compulsory schooling in leading capitalist countries is gathering pace. There is an obvious need to chart these trends and devise strategies of resistance. However, Marxist educational theory's key task is to indicate the significance of education for the anticapitalist struggles of the future and for socialist transformation.[47]

A politics of human resistance to the capitalization of social life, including education, calls forth a number of key theoretical tasks for Marxist educational theory. Very generally, for me, these are to:

- Show the role of education and training in the generation of value via their links to labor power.

- Explore the links between social class, education and training and value creation in contemporary capitalism.

- Examine the ways in which 'difference' (gender, 'race,' age, sexuality etc.) is conditioned by social class and value production, with special reference to the struggle for economic and social justice.

- Indicate the significance of education, especially radical pedagogy, for breaking capital's weakest link: its reliance on our labor power to generate the labor that creates the substance of the social universe of capital—*value*.

These are massive and urgent tasks, and by no means the only ones for Marxist educational theory. Collectively, in our writings, the four of us have made contributions on all four fronts. Much work is nevertheless required, again on all four fronts.

What is clear is that post-Seattle, with the growing anticapitalist offensive, theories of education based on the works of Karl Marx will finally come into their own. What is also clear is that postmodernism in general, and educational postmodernism in particular, may be useful up to a point (that point at which they become repressed forms of thought and dissent, or are positively dangerous as Radical Right camouflage). Although I welcome attempts such as Atkinson's[48] to radicalize postmodernism and educational postmodernism, I nevertheless hold that such attempts must inevitably fall well short of generating any dangerous perspectives that substantially challenge the domination of capital in society today.

Notes

1. Mike Cole, Dave Hill, Peter McLaren and Glenn Rikowski, eds., *Red Chalk: On Schooling, Capitalism and Politics* (Brighton, U.K.: Institute for Educational Studies, 2001); Dave Hill, Peter McLaren, Mike Cole and Glenn Rikowski, eds., *Postmodernism in Educational Theory: Education and the Politics of Human Resistance* (London: Tufnell Press, 1999).

2. Peter McLaren, *Che Guevara, Paulo Freire, and the Pedagogy of Revolution* (Lanham, Md.: Rowman & Littlefield, 2000); Peter McLaren and Ramin Farahmandpur, "Educational Policy and the Socialist Imagination: Revolutionary Citizenship as a Pedagogy of Resistance," *Educational Policy* 15, no. 3 (July 2001): 343–378.

3. Glenn Rikowski, "Third Fantasy from the Right," *Education and Social Justice* 1, no. 3 (1999): 26.

4. Glenn Rikowski, "Education and Social Justice within the Social Universe of Capital," paper presented to the British Educational Research Association seminar on "Approaching Social Justice in Education: Theoretical Frameworks for Practical Purposes," Faculty of Education, Nottingham Trent University, U.K., April 10, 2000.

5. Cole et al., *Red Chalk*.

6. Nigel Blake, Paul Smeyers, Richard Smith, and Paul Standish, *Education in an Age of Nihilism* (London: Routledge/Falmer, 2000), 216.

7. Michael Hardt and Antonio Negri, "Labor of Dionysus," *Theory Out of Bounds* (Minneapolis: University of Minnesota Press, 1994), 2.

8. Hardt and Negri, "Labor of Dionysus," 4.

9. Sam Bowles and Herb Gintis, *Schooling in Capitalist America: Educational Reform and the Contradictions of Economic Life* (London: Routledge and Kegan Paul, 1976); Paul Willis, *Learning to Labour: How Working Class Kids Get Working Class Jobs* (Farnborough, U.K.: Saxon House, 1977).

10. Madan Sarup's classic *Marxism and Education* (London: Routledge and Kegan Paul, 1978) provided a trenchant critique of Bowles and Gintis' *Schooling in Capitalist America*. Daniel Liston's wide-ranging methodological critiques of Bowles and Gintis completed the job, see *Capitalist Schools: Explanation and Ethics in Radical Theories of Schooling* (London: Routledge and Kegan Paul, 1988), and "Faith and Evidence: Examining Marxist Explanations of Schools," *American Journal of Education* 96, no. 3

(1988): 323–350. For critiques of Willis, *Learning to Labour*, see Glynis Cousin, "Failure through Resistance: Critique of Learning to Labour," *Youth and Policy* 10 (autumn 1984): 37–40; also Hugh Lauder, John Freeman-Moir and Alan Scott "What Is to Be Done with Radical Academic Practice?" *Capital and Class* 29 (1986): 83–110.

11. See Michael W. Apple, *Education and Power* (London,: Ark Paperbacks, 1985); David Livingstone, "Searching for the Missing Links: Neo-Marxist Theories of Education," *British Journal of Sociology of Education* 16, no. 1 (March 1995): 53–73.

12. John Freeman-Moir, "Reflections on the Methods of Marxism," *Educational Philosophy and Theory* 24, no. 2 (1992): 98–128; Freeman-Moir, Scott and Lauder, "Reformism or Revolution: Liberalism and the Metaphysics of Democracy," in *Bowles and Gintis Revisited: Correspondence and Contradiction in Educational Theory*, ed. Mike Cole (London: Falmer Press, 1988); John Freeman-Moir and Alan Scott, "Looking Back at Education: The Abandonment of Hope," *New Zealand Journal of Educational Studies* 26, no. 2 (1991): 109–124; Rachel Sharp, "Introduction" in *Capitalist Crisis and Schooling: Comparative Studies in the Politics of Education*, ed. Rachel Sharp (South Melbourne: Macmillan Company of Australia PTY, 1986).

13. Analyzed in Glenn Rikowski, "Scorched Earth: Prelude to Rebuilding Marxist Educational Theory," *British Journal of Sociology of Education* 18, no. 4 (1997): 551–574.

14. Mike Cole, ed., *Bowles and Gintis Revisited: Correspondence and Contradiction in Educational Theory* (London: Falmer Press, 1988).

15. Richard Brosio, "One Marx, and the Centrality of the Historical Actor(s)," *Educational Theory* 35, no. 1 (winter 1985): 73–83, and "Capitalism's Emerging World Order: The Continuing Need for Theory and Brave Action by Citizen-Educators," *Educational Theory* 43, no. 4 (fall 1993): 467–482; Kevin Harris, "Two Contrasting Theories," *Education with Production* 3, no. 1 (July 1984): 13–33, "Teachers, Curriculum and Social Reconstruction," *Forum of Education* 47, no. 2 (1988): 3–21, and "Schooling, Democracy and Teachers as Intellectual Vanguard," *New Zealand Journal of Educational Studies* 27, no. 1 (1992): 21–33.

16. I define these in Rikowski, "Scorched Earth."

17. Robin Usher and Richard Edwards, *Postmodernism in Education: Different Voices, Different Worlds* (London: Routledge, 1994).

18. In chapter 1, Peter McLaren and Glenn Rikowski provide the story of the rise of educational postmodernism in more detail.

19. Richard Brosio, *A Radical Democratic Critique of Capitalist Education* (New York: Peter Lang Publishing, 1994).

20. Kevin Harris, *Teachers: Constructing the Future* (London: Falmer Press, 1994).

21. Andy Green, "Postmodernism and State Education," *Journal of Education Policy* 9, no. 1 (January–February 1994): 67–83. The critique of postmodernism in general and educational postmodernism in particular is developed further in his *Education, Globalization and the Nation State* (Basingstoke, U.K.: Macmillan, 1997).

22. See Nick Adnett, "Recent Education Reforms: Some Neglected Macroeconomics and Misapplied Microeconomics," *Review of Policy Issues* 3, no. 3 (summer 1997): 59–77; Paula Allman, *Revolutionary Social Transformation: Democratic Hopes, Political Possibilities and Critical Education* (Westport, Conn.: Bergin and Garvey, 1999), also *Critical Education against Global Capital: Karl Marx and Revolutionary Critical Education* (Westport, Conn.: Bergin and Garvey, 2001), and "Foreword: Education on Fire!" in Cole et al., *Red Chalk*, 10–14; Paula Allman and John Wallis, "Gramsci's Challenge to the Politics of the Left in 'Our Times,'" *International Journal of Life-*

long Learning 14, no 2 (March–April 1995): 120–143; Michael W. Apple, "Remembering Capital: On the Connections between French Fries and Education," *Journal of Curriculum Theorizing* 11, no. 1 (spring 1995): 113–128, and "Can Critical Pedagogies Interrupt Rightist Policies?" *Educational Theory* 50, no. 2 (spring 2000): 229–254; Grant Banfield, "Schooling and the Spirit of Enterprise: Producing the Power to Labour," *Education and Social Justice* 2, no. 3 (summer 2000): 23–28; Richard Brosio, "Late Capitalism and Postmodernism: Educational Problems and Possibilities," *Studies in Philosophy and Education* 15, no. 1 (January–April 1996): 5–12, and *Philosophical Scaffolding for the Construction of Critical Democratic Education* (New York: Peter Lang Publishing, 2000); Barry Burke, "Karl Marx and Informal Education: What Significance Does Marx Have for Educators Today?" <http://www.infed.org/thinkers/et-marx.htm> (November 6, 2000); Helen Colley, "Exploring Myths of Mentor: A Rough Guide to the History of Mentoring from a Marxist Feminist Perspective" (paper presented at the British Educational Research Association Annual Conference, Cardiff University, September 7–10, 2000); Moacir Gadotti, *Pedagogy of Praxis: A Dialectical Philosophy of Education* (Albany: State University of New York Press, 1996); Paul Gee, "On Mobots and Classrooms: The Converging Languages of the New Capitalism and Schooling," *Organization* 3, no. 3 (1996): 385–407; Henry Giroux, "Radical Pedagogy and Prophetic Thought: Remembering Paulo Freire," *Rethinking Marxism* 9, no. 4 (winter 1997): 76–87; David Harvie, "Alienation, Class and Enclosure in U.K. Universities," *Capital and Class*, no. 71 (2000): 103–132; Dennis Hayes, "Confidence and the Academy" (paper presented at the British Educational Research Association Conference 2000, Cardiff University, September 7–10, 2000); Tom Hickey, "Class and Class Analysis for the Twenty-first Century," in *Education, Equality and Human Rights*, ed. Mike Cole (London: Routledge–Falmer, 2000), 162–181; International Communist Union, "Public Education under Attack," *Class Struggle*, no. 30 (January–February 2000): 14–19; Jane Kelly, "Gender and Equality: One Hand Tied Behind Us," in *Education, Equality*, ed. Cole; Deb Kelsh, "Desire and Class: The Knowledge Industry in the Wake of Poststructuralism" (Parts 1 and 2), *Cultural Logic* 1, no. 2 (spring 1998), <http://eserver.org/clogic/1-2/kelsh.html> (May 2001); Mark Kleinberg Neumark, "If It's So Important, Why Won't They Pay for It? Public Higher Education at the Turn of the Century," *Monthly Review* 51, no. 1 (1999): 20–31; Les Levidow, "Marketizing Higher Education: Neoliberal Strategies and Counter-Strategies," *Education and Social Justice* (summer 2001); David Livingstone, "Searching for the Missing Links," 53–73; Simon Marginson, *Markets in Education* (St. Leonards, NSW: Allen and Unwin, 1997); Frank Margonis, "Theories of Conviction: The Return of Marxist Theorizing," *Educational Theory* 48, no. 1 (winter 1998): 87–101; Phil Mizen, *The State, Young People and Youth Training: In and against the Training State* (London: Mansell, 1995); Michael Neary, *Youth, Training and the Training State: The Real History of Youth Training in the Twentieth Century* (Basingstoke, U.K.: Macmillan, 1997); Yair Neuman and Zvi Bekerman, "Organic versus Symbolic Pedagogy: Against the Commercialization of Knowledge," *Education and Society*, 17, no. 1 (1999): 53–61; Helen Raduntz, "Researching a Hegelian-Marxist Dialectic for a Theory of Australian Catholic Schooling" (paper first presented at the Conference of the Australian Association for Education Research 1998, RAD 98259, revised version, January 1999), also "A Marxian Critique of Teachers' Work in an Era of Capitalist Globalization" (paper presented at the AARE-NZARE Conference, RAD 99520, Melbourne, Victoria, November 19–December 2, 1999); Chanie Rosenberg and Kevin Ovenden, "Education: Why Our Children Deserve Better than New Labour" (London: Socialist Workers Party, 1999); Murray Saunders and Helen Sambili, "Can Vocational Programmes Change Use and Exchange Value Attributions of School Leavers?" *Educa-*

tional Review 47, no. 3 (November 1995): 319–331; Colin Sparks, "The Tories, Labour and the Education Crisis," *International Socialism*, no. 74 (spring 1997): 3–40; Gary Taylor, "Socialism and Education: Marx and Engels," *General Educator*, no. 32 (January–February 1995): 22–23, also "Socialism and education: 'The German Ideology'" *General Educator*, no. 33 (March–April 1995): 21–23, and "Marx on Education, Industry and the Fall of Capitalism," *General Educator*, no. 35 (July–August 1995): 19–22; Geraldine Thorpe and Patrick Brady, "The Labour Process in Higher Education" (paper presented at "Restructuring the Left" Conference of Socialist Economists, University of Northumbria at Newcastle, July 12–14, 1996); Colin Waugh, "Marx and Engels' Concept of Education" (unpublished paper, 1996), also "Marx and Engels' Concept of Education," *General Educator*, no. 43 (December 1996): 21–23; Paul Willis, "Labour Power, Culture, and the Cultural Commodity," in *Critical Education in the New Information Age*, ed. Manuel Castells, Ramon Flecha, Paulo Freire, Henry Giroux, Donald Macedo and Paul Willis (Lanham, Md.: Rowman & Littlefield, 1999); Oswaldo Yamamoto and Antonio Neto, "Sociology of Education and Marxism in Brazil," *Sociological Research Online* 4, no. 1 (1999), <http://www.socresonline.org.U.K.> (April 2001); Michael Yates, "An Essay on Radical Labor Education," *Cultural Logic* 2, no. 1 (fall 1998), <http://eserver.org/clogic/2-1/yates.html>(May 19, 2001). This range of examples by no means constitutes the total sum of the renaissance in Marxist educational theory since 1994.

23. Charlie Bertsch, "Pedagogy of the Depressed," *Bad Subjects*, no. 27 (September 1996), <http://eserver.org/bs/01/Bertsch.html> (April 2001). Further interesting articles on education appear on the *Bad Subjects* web site <http://eserver.org/bs/>.

24. Ross Longhurst, "Education as a Commodity: The Political Economy of the New Further Education," *Journal of Further and Higher Education* 20, no. 2 (summer 1996): 49–66. On April 1, 1993, FE colleges in England became 'incorporated' as individual corporations operating in a FE quasi-market with a complex funding system based on student recruitment, retention and qualification outputs. They lost their previous links to local democratic control. Following incorporation, the Further Education Funding Council funded colleges. Since April 1, 2001, FE colleges have been funded and directly controlled by new Learning and Skills Councils, which have strong employer representation. Thus, it is for the period April 1993–April 2001 that Longhurst's 1996 analysis holds: the development of new Learning and Skills Councils accompanies significant changes that require updated analysis.

25. I indicate this in "Left Alone: End Time for Marxist Educational Theory?" *British Journal of Sociology of Education* 17, no. 4 (December 1996): 415–451.

26. For example: Mike Cole, "Globalisation, Modernisation and Competitiveness: A Critique of the Labour Project in Education," *International Studies in Sociology of Education* 8, no. 3 (1998): 315–332, also *Business, Business, Business: New Labour's Education Policy*, ed. Martin Allen, Caroline Benn, Clyde Chitty, Mike Cole, Richard Hatcher, Nico Hirtt and Glenn Rikowski (London: Tufnell Press, 1999); Mike Cole and Dave Hill, "Games of Despair and Rhetorics of Resistance: Postmodernism, Education and Reaction," *British Journal of Sociology of Education* 16, no. 2 (1995): 165–182, also "Postmodernism, Education and Contemporary Capitalism: A Materialist Critique," in *Teacher Education and Values Education*, ed. Odete Valente, Amália Bárrios, Alberto Gaspas and V. D. Teodoro (Lisbon: Faculty of Science, Department of Education, University of Lisbon, 1995), and "Ex-Left Academics and the Curse of the Postmodern," *Education and Social Justice* 1, no. 3 (1999): 28–30; Cole, *Red Chalk*; Dave Hill, *New Labour and Education: Policy, Ideology and the Third Way* (London: Tufnell Press, 1999), also "Social Class," in *An Introduction to the Study of Education*, ed. D. Matheson

and I. Grosvenor (London: David Fulton, 1999), "Reclaiming Our Education from the Neo-Liberals: Markets in Education, James Tooley, and the Struggle for Economic and Social Justice" (paper prepared for the Campaign for Free Education Conference on "Reclaiming Our Education," University of East London, August 11–12, 2000), "The Third Way in Britain: Capitalism, Neo-Liberalism and Education Policy" (paper presented at the European Educational Research Association Annual Conference, University of Edinburgh, Scotland, September 20–23, 2000), "New Labour's Neo-Liberal Education Policy," *Forum for Promoting Comprehensive Education* 42, no. 1 (2000): 8–11, "Radical Left Principles for Social and Economic Justice in Education Policy" (paper presented to "Approaching Social Justice in Education: Theoretical Frameworks for Practical Purposes," Faculty of Education, Nottingham Trent University, Clifton Hall, April 10, 2000); "State Theory and the Neo-Liberal Reconstruction of Schooling and Teacher Education: A Structuralist Neo-Marxist Critique of Postmodernist, Quasi-postmodernist, and Culturalist Neo-Marxist Theory," *British Journal of Sociology of Education* 22, no. 1 (2001): 137–156, *Education, Education, Education: Capitalism, Socialism and the Third Way* (Brighton, U.K.: Institute for Education Policy Studies, 2002), "The National Curriculum, the Hidden Curriculum and Inequality in Schooling" and "Equality, Ideology and Education Policy" in *Schooling and Equality: Fact, Concept and Policy*, ed. Dave Hill and Mike Cole (London: Kogan Page, 2001); Dave Hill and Mike Cole, eds., "Marxist State Theory and State Autonomy Theory: The Case of 'Race' Education in Initial Teacher Education," *Journal of Education Policy* 10, no. 2 (1995): 221–232; Peter McLaren, *Revolutionary Multiculturalism: Pedagogies of Dissent for the New Millennium* (Boulder, Colo.: Westview Press, 1997), also "Revolutionary Pedagogy in Post-Revolutionary Times," *Educational Theory* 48, no. 4 (1998): 431–462, "The Educational Researcher as Critical Social Agent: Some Personal Reflections on Marxist Criticism in Post-Modern Times of Fashionable Apostasy," in *Multicultural Research: A Reflective Engagement with Race, Class, Gender and Sexual Orientation*, ed. C. Grant (London: Falmer Press, 1999), "Traumatizing Capital: Oppositional Pedagogies in the Age of Consent" in *Critical Education in the New Information Age*, ed. Castells et al., also *Che Guevara*; Peter McLaren and Ramin Farahmandpur, "Critical Multiculturalism and the Globalization of Capital: Some Implications for a Politics of Resistance," *Journal of Curriculum Theorizing* 15, no. 4 (1999): 27–46, also "Reconsidering Marx in Post-Marxist Times: A Requiem for Postmodernism?" *Educational Researcher* 29, no. 3 (2000): 25–33, and "Socialist Dreaming"; Glenn Rikowski, "Education Markets and Missing Products" (paper presented at the Conference of Socialist Economists, University of Northumbria at Newcastle, July 7–9, 1995), also "Apprenticeship and the Use-Value Aspect of Labour Power" and "Revealed Recruitment Criteria through the Use-Value Aspect of Labour Power" (papers for the ESRC seminars on "Apprenticeship," Nene College, Northampton, May 31, 1996), "Nietzsche's School? The Roots of Educational Postmodernism" (paper presented at the Education Research Seminar "A Marxist Critique of Postmodernism," School of Education, Inter-Area Group, University of Brighton, November 19, 1997), "Scorched Earth," and "Only Charybdis: The Learning Society through Idealism" in *Inside the Learning Society*, ed. Stewart Ranson (London: Cassell, 1998); "Three Types of Apprenticeship, Three Forms of Mastery: Nietzsche, Marx, Self and Capital" (Departmental paper, University of Birmingham, School of Education, 1998), "Nietzsche, Marx and Mastery: The Learning unto Death," in *Apprenticeship: Towards a New Paradigm of Learning*, ed. Patrick Ainley and Helen Rainbird (London: Kogan Page 1999), "Lifelong Learning and the Political Economy of Containment" (paper, Faculty of Education, University of Central England in Birmingham, Novmber 1999); "Third Fantasy," 25–27; "Why Employers Can't Ever Get What They

Want. In Fact, They Can't Even Get What They Need" (paper presented to the School of Post-Compulsory Education and Training, Staff/Student Seminar, University of Greenwich, March 27, 2000), "Education and Social Justice," "New Labour's Knowledge Economy versus Critical Pedagogy: The Battle in Seattle and Its Significance for Education" (paper presented at the Conference of Socialist Economists "Global Capital and Global Struggles: Strategies, Alliances, Alternatives," University of London Union, July 1–2, 2000), "Marxist Educational Theory Transformed," *Education and Social Justice* 2, no. 3 (2000): 60–64, "Messing with the Explosive Commodity: School Improvement, Educational Research and Labour-Power in the Era of Global Capitalism" and "That Other Great Class of Commodities: Repositioning Marxist Educational Theory" (papers presented at British Educational Research Association Conference, Cardiff University, September 7–9, 2000), "The Rise of the Student-Worker," in *A Compact for Higher Education*, ed. Moti Gokulsing and Cornel DaCosta (Aldershot, U.K.: Ashgate, 2000), *The Battle in Seattle: Its Significance for Education* (London: Tufnell Press, 2001); "Education for Industry: A Complex Technicism," *Journal of Education and Work* 13, no. 1 (2001): 27–47, "Marxist Educational Theory Unplugged," *Historical Materialism: Research in Critical Marxist Theory* (forthcoming, 2002), and "The Repressed Anarchist: Postmodernism as Theoretic Anxiety Attack, and the Consequences for Educational Theory, Practice and Politics," *Education-line,* <http://www.leeds.ac.U.K./educol/> (forthcoming, 2002).

27. Elizabeth Atkinson, "The Promise of Uncertainty: Education, Postmodernism and the Politics of Possibility," *International Studies in Sociology of Education* 10, no. 1 (2000): 81–99; "The Responsible Anarchist: Postmodernism and Social Change" (paper presented to the Symposium on "If We Aren't Pursuing Improvement, What Are We Doing?" at British Educational Research Association Conference, Cardiff University, Wales, September 7–9, 2000); "Critical Dissonance and Critical Schizophrenia: The Struggle between Policy Delivery and Policy Critique," *Research Intelligence* 30 (November 2000):14–17.

28. Atkinson, "Responsible Anarchist."

29. This description follows Ian Stronach and Maggie MacLure, *Educational Research Undone: The Postmodern Embrace* (Buckingham, U.K.: Open University Press, 1997).

30. Atkinson, "Responsible Anarchist," 1–3.

31. See also Cole, "Educational Postmodernism;" Rikowski, "Repressed Anarchist."

32. Atkinson, "Responsible Anarchist," 5.

33. Atkinson, "Responsible Anarchist," 6.

34. Judith Butler, "Contingent Foundations: Feminism and the Question of 'Postmodernism'" in *Feminists Theorize the Political*, ed. Judith Butler and Joan Scott (New York: Routledge, 1992).

35. Atkinson, "Responsible Anarchist," 8.

36. Atkinson, "Critical Dissonance," 14.

37. Atkinson, "Critical Dissonance," 14–15.

38. The argument I refer to can be followed in Cole, "Globalisation, Competitiveness," "Globalisation, Modernisation" and *Red Chalk*; also Hill, *New Labour* and "State Theory;" McLaren, "Revolutionary Pedagogy," *Che Guevara*, and "Gang of Five," in *Red Chalk*; McLaren and Farahmandpur, "Reconsidering Marx;" Rikowski, "Nietzsche," "Lifelong Learning," "Why Employers," *Battle in Seattle* and "Education for Industry."

39. Atkinson, "Responsible Anarchist."

40. Rikowski, "Education and Social Justice" and "New Labour's Knowledge."

41. Atkinson, "Critical Dissonance," 15.

42. Atkinson, "Critical Dissonance," 16.

43. Rikowski, "Messing with the Explosive" and "That Other Great Class."

44. Atkinson, "The Promise of Uncertainty," 87.

45. Rikowski, *Battle in Seattle.*

46. For examples, see Marxist Collective at Syracuse University (MCSU), "Capitalism and Your University Education," *The Alternative Orange* 3, no. 2 (1993), <http://www.geocities.co./CapitolHill/ Lobby/2072/ AOVol2—2CapUniv.html> (April 19, 2001); Harvie,"Alienation"; Levidow, "Marketizing."

47. Allman, "Revolutionary Social Transformation."

48. Atkinson, "The Promise of Uncertainty," also "The Responsible Anarchist" and "Critical Dissonance."

Part II

Postmodern Excess

Chapter 3

Breaking Signifying Chains: A Marxist Position on Postmodernism

Peter McLaren and Ramin Farahmandpur

Capital is dead labor which, vampire-like, lives only by sucking
living labor, and lives the more, the more labor it sucks.
—Karl Marx

The proletarians have nothing to lose but their chains. They have
a world to win. WORKERS OF ALL COUNTRIES, UNITE!
—Karl Marx and Frederick Engels

Introduction

This chapter attempts to address some fundamental problems with postmodern
theory, as it currently informs the field of educational research.[1] Our position is
that postmodern theory has overwhelmingly debauched the field of Leftist
criticism. However, we have not undertaken an analysis of specific postmodern
educationalists (this being achieved by many of the other chapters in this book).
Rather, we set forth counterpositions to claims put forth in the literature by
postmodern theorists. We give a positive appraisal of postmodern theory in
certain instances where we feel it has contributed to the field of Leftist critique.
In the main, however, our position remains unwaveringly critical. This is largely
a result of our contention that postmodern theorists advocate an expansion of
existing bourgeois forms of democratic social life into wider arenas of society,
by means of a reformist politics in the tradition of Western liberalism. Such a
politics views culture as partially independent of the state. Such a move only
makes sense, however, within a larger politics of anticapitalist struggle. Yet
postmodernists fail to challenge existing social relations of production and the
larger social totality of capitalist social relations. As a result, their work has very

little to contribute to the uprooting of the contradictions between capital and labor.

The Fin-de-Siécle Millennium and the Vertigo of Global Capitalism

Regardless of where we position ourselves at the crossroads of history, our location is always precarious and risky. Though we are tempted always to look beyond the agony of the present moment into the sublime abyss of the unknown, we cannot avoid encountering the violent clash between labor and capital. We are at a peculiar juncture in human history that tantalizes us with the promise of redemption and liberation while delivering on its threat of corruption and despair. We are suspended precariously between the revolution and counter revolution, which Rosa Luxemburg so forcefully referred to as a choice between socialism and barbarism.

We face the future much like the observers of *The Ambassadors*, a masterpiece painted by Hans Holbein the Younger in 1533 that now hangs in London's British Museum. Below the figures of two ambassadors is a large skull that appears drastically out of proportion when viewed head-on. The distortion corrects itself, however, when viewed at a sharp angle from below the bottom right hand side of the painting. The painting was meant to be viewed from below, possibly as one walked up the stairs to one's bedroom to pray before sleeping. Presumably, the observer would be reminded of one's mortality. The lesson for us voyagers in the new millennium is that we need to position ourselves from below, from the perspective of the suffering masses, in order to see what is happening in the capitalist world system, and how mortality is something the masses confront on a daily basis, and not because they can afford to commission a painting, much less own a house in which to hang it.

Marx's description of capitalism as the sorcerer's dark power that has become uncontrollable is even more apt today than it was in Marx's time, despite the fact that Marxism has been relegated by the postmodernists to the Icarian status of failed aspiration. No other individual has been able to analyze the Frankensteinian dimensions of capital accumulation with the same intensity and foresight as Marx, who wrote, "If money . . . 'comes into the world with a congenital blood-stain on one cheek,' capital comes dripping from head to foot, from every pore, with blood and dirt."[2] Never before has a Marxian analysis of capitalism been so desperately needed than at this particular juncture in history, especially in view of the global push toward finance and speculative capital. It is becoming increasingly clearer that the quality of life in capitalist nations such as the United States is implicated in the absence of freedom in less developed countries. Global carpetbaggers and 'bankerist Overworlders' profiteering from human suffering, and bargain basement capitalists with a vision of transforming the environment into Planet Mall, are bent upon reaping short-term profits at the expense of ecological health and human dignity and drawing ever more of existence within their expanding domain, cannibalizing life as a whole. On the soil of our former Cold War opponent, a clique of wealthy Russian oligarchs now follow the Western path to redemption, pillaging existing state property—the refineries, steel mills, smelters, pipelines, mineral deposits and factories.[3] The state picks up the bill, while the former proletariats surf the black market for rent money. The World Bank calls it "tough love."

James Gibb Stuart notes, "Greed has become the seed corn of free-market capitalism," in a period marked by the intensification of class polarization and the upward redistribution of wealth.[4] Capitalism, according to Terry Eagleton, has a "built-in dynamic to universalize itself," and "is bound to ensnare itself in its own strength, since the more it proliferates, the more fronts it breeds on which it can become vulnerable."[5] Marx's prophetic warning against capitalism is no less true for those of us who work in schools of education, where the logic of privatization abounds and where postmodernism has more than encroached on Leftist educational discourse; it has taken up permanent residence.

Neoliberalism—'capitalism with the gloves off' or 'socialism for the rich'—refers to a corporate domination of society that supports state enforcement of the unregulated market, engages in the oppression of nonmarket forces and antimarket policies, guts free public services, eliminates social subsidies, offers limitless concessions to transnational corporations, enthrones a neomercantilist public policy agenda, establishes the market as the patron of educational reform, and permits private interests to control most of social life in the pursuit of profits for the few (i.e., through lowering taxes on the wealthy, scrapping environmental regulations, and dismantling public education and social welfare programs). It is undeniably one of the most dangerous politics that we face today. As described by Robert W. McChesney, neoliberalism is "the immediate and foremost enemy of genuine participatory democracy, not just in the United States but across the planet, and will be for the foreseeable future."[6] John McMurtry avers, noting that the restructuring of the United States economy constitutes the "revenge of the rich against those who advocate a more democratic and egalitarian social order."[7] So much has been made of the wonders of the U.S. economic model, yet its so-called success can be measured in its complete rejection of social and environmental capital for the short-term gains of investors and consumers. As John McMurtry remarks:

> Cheaper goods and costs come by the loss of tens of millions of secure domestic jobs. Real lower taxes for upper income brackets are achieved by stripping social assistance programs for the poor and unemployed. Equity values are increased by non-productive mergers, laundered drug billions, internet stocks with no earnings, and leveraged debt and asset-flip money. Low unemployment figures are achieved by massive increases in part-time and starvation-wage jobs and a staggering 2,000,000 citizens in prison off the employment rolls (over 12 times the number of US citizens caged as in 1968,

and about six times the Western European rate). The new regime rules the globe behind bars of money and iron.[8]

If Marxism appears to have lost its epochal footing and does not yet enjoy a new, refunctional status as the official opponent of neoliberalism and the downsizing of democracy, this does not mean that educators should remain inactive until history is suddenly served by a wake-up call that will make Marxism relevant again. History has already done so, for those who have the eyes to recognize the current crises of capitalism and its implications for the future of education. The globalization of capital has occasioned what István Mészáros describes as the "downward equalization of the differential rate of exploitation" where workers all over the world—including those in advanced capitalist countries such as the United States—are facing a steady deterioration of working conditions, due to the structural crisis of the capitalist system, a crisis of fast-track, push cart capitalism of the "grab-the-profits-and-run" variety.[9]

Yet at the same time, capitalism has never been so blindly infatuated with its own myth of success. Corporate leaders in the United States and dominant media have inured us into accepting the capitalist marketplace as the only possible social reality. Walter Mosley puts it thus: "The juggernaut of capitalism, having broken the bonds of its imprisonment—national borders—exacts its toll in an equal opportunity manner. It is the nature of capitalism to apply its value system to everything."[10] David McNally writes: "Having vanquished all challengers, having apparently tamed labor, anti-imperialist, and radical social movements," capitalism "can now calmly go about the business of making us all rich."[11] McNally traces the current capitalist triumphalism to the antihistorical character of bourgeois ideology. He also notes that contemporary procapitalist ideology "betrays a remarkable amnesia about capitalism itself: it forgets its bloody past, its recurrent crises; it denies everything that hints at the historically specific limits of the capitalist mode of production."[12] To wit, it naturalizes the exploitation of the world's poor and powerless, reducing workers to the market price of their sweat and blood.

Floodlit by post-Communist, end-of-history ideologies and decorated with crudely binaristic, David and Goliath mythologies of good prevailing over evil, today's discourses of advanced capitalism have been severely compressed, their semiotic potency made sacred by the corporate logo, the iconographic representation of a new period of idol-worshipping for a generation of youth who have been savagely seduced into the salivating jaws of consumption. As the Golden Calves of 'hype'-reality, corporate logos like Nike's promote a capitalist ethics of individualism and greed; they constitute the religious signifiers of a new wave of technocrazed global robber barons whose capitalist plunder proceeds remorselessly apace. Read Mercer Schuchardt captures this ethos thus:

> If sport is the religion of the modern age, then Nike has successfully become the official church. It is a church whose icon is a window between this world and the other, between your existing self (your overweight slob) and your

Nike self (your god of fitness), where salvation lies in achieving the athletic Nietzschean ideal: no fear, no mercy, no second place. Like the Christian fish, the Swoosh is a true religious icon in that it both symbolizes the believer's reality and actually participates in it. After all, you do have to wear something to attain this special salvation, so why not something emblazoned with the Swoosh?[13]

Due to the fast-paced and frenetic changes taking place around us in the wired realms of global technologies and free trade initiatives, we are hard pressed to chart out the vast reach of our daily struggles against oppression and exploitation. As we attempt to flee a psychopathological culture of endless acquisition, we find ourselves at the mercy of an even more terrifying corporate culture shaping our subjectivities. We worship at the altar of the Lords of Finance Capital and Transnational Commerce who have been ordained as the world's new global caretakers. Corporate leaders have become the doyens of advanced citizenship, transformed into public icons who rival the status held by athletes and film stars. Bill Gates now masquerades as Dickens' spiritually redeemed Ebenezer Scrooge, offering a gift of one billion dollars worth of scholarship funds to economically disfranchised students of color in the role of Tiny Tim. Education has become reduced to a subsector of the economy.

The 1980s and 1990s has witnessed the growing economic and political power and influence of corporations. Corporate discourse has increasingly converged with the family values and ideology of the Christian Right (represented by organizations such as Jerry Falwell's 'Moral Majority' and Pat Robertson's 'Christian Coalition'). The Christian Right has openly declared war on the working class by supporting anti-abortion legislature, school prayer, favorable tax cuts for the rich, instituting partial privatization of Social Security, pushing forth welfare reform, and reducing government intervention in the unregulated free market. It has provided the necessary framework for the alignment of moral and ethical issues with neoliberal social and economic policies, and has succeeded in decapitating the struggle for economic equality from its moral and ethical foundation.[14]

Entrenched social, political, and economic disparities and antagonisms compel us as educators and cultural workers to create alternatives to the logic of capitalist accumulation. We are struggling and suffering (some of us more than others) through a time when there exists an inordinate and frightening corporate control over job growth and job loss, in a capitalist system whose inequalities are becoming more glaringly evident that ever before. The real problem posed by the global economy is that it has increased the influence of large corporations over the daily lives of most Americans. This influence is revealed in corporate control over job growth and job loss, media control of information, and the role of big money in the world of national politics. At the same time that this growing influence is revealed on a daily basis, it has become increasingly clear that the major corporations have abandoned any sense of allegiance to, or special responsibilities toward, American workers and their communities.[15]

On the one hand, the manufacturing sector of the economy has been relocated in Third World and developing countries, where labor is cheaper and unions are considerably weaker than in industrialized nations. On the other hand, the service sector of the United States' economy has expanded dramatically, in effect creating a large pool for temporary part-time employment. The flexibilization of labor markets has allowed unregulated capital to move freely around the globe in search of the cheapest labor markets, without government intervention. Christa Wichterich remarks ruefully, "The labor market has become a kind of shopping center for itinerant executives, who help themselves to local labor, infrastructure and investment incentives according to where the greatest profits lie."[16] Flexible methods of production typify a "cowboy-style poaching" of cheap labor in the international markets, where Third World economies are forced to follow the logic of the market by moving from economic self-reliance and self-sufficiency to economic dependency on Western products. The "McDonaldization of food" is leading to economic concentration and forced industrialization in the hands of transnational corporations to cite only one example.[17]

The Crisis of Global Capitalism

In the wake of its triumphant victory over socialism, global capitalism has successfully integrated all types of differences within its borders. The term *liberal democracy* is, for the most part, an oxymoron. Although liberalism lived up to its name by expanding the welfare state after the Second World War, it nevertheless has become more intimately associated with capitalism than with democracy's rule of the majority. Especially over the last several decades, liberal democracy has failed to adequately address the democratic citizenship of marginalized groups, since it has consistently failed to recognize that social inequality is embedded within capitalist property relations.[18]

Neoliberal free market economics—the purpose of which is to avoid stasis and keep everyone in healthy flux—has become the desideratum of the new corporate barons and continues to advance across the current stage of history, proudly unfurling its laundry list of achievements as the Magna Carta of the new world order: deregulation, unrestricted access to consumer markets, downsizing, outsourcing, flexible arrangements of labor, intensification of competition among transnational corporations, an increasing centralization of economic and political power, and finally, widening class polarization. The twenty-first century represents at once the incalculably expanded scope of the culture of consumption and the implosion of social relations into a universal signifier—namely capital—which Marx metaphorically referred to as the "universal pimp." Marx likened money to a "visible god," which in the generalized commodity-form,

> spreads this illusory perception throughout society, dissolving all previous identities and distinctions, and remolding human consciousness in its own image. In the fully developed form of capital, money achieves an active, self-regulating power through which it shapes the lives of concrete individuals.[19]

Many prominent social theorists maintain that physical labor has become less significant in what they claim to be the postindustrial information economy.[20] However, we believe this to be misleading. Computer technology has not reduced the need for physical labor (someone had to build the polished steel information cathedrals of Silicon Valley that house the new dot.com billionaires). Rather, computer technology has led to an automation of labor, making it more productive and efficient while at the same time cheapening it.

For those who believe that the economy is self-regulated by Hayekian archangels who mysteriously ensure that the feedback mechanisms of the unfettered 'free' market are 'fair,' that only democracy will spring forth from its famously spontaneous order, and that the common good will magically advance from its networked complexity, there is reason to be wildly optimistic about the future. But for those, like us, who refuse to fetishize the social system under capitalism as a self-organizing totality, the future appears perilous indeed. We refuse to treat the economy as a thing and endow it with democratic agency. After Marx, we view the economy as a social relation and not a natural entity. Capitalism is not a natural, self-regulating system but rather one overburdened by exploitation, the quest of endless accumulation, and class conflict. Peter Hudis raises an important question that merits attention: Can capital be controlled?[21] In response, he argues that capital does not come with a human face. It cannot be tamed or restrained. Consequently, it must be completely abolished. Capital is a social relation of abstract value. It is also a value-relation because the substance of value is abstract labor. Because it is a repository of surplus value, capital is driven toward an endless accumulation of value by transforming concrete labor into abstract, undifferentiated labor. The prime objective of capital is to have command over objectified labor.

The supporters of the free market claim that the free market is equipped with self-regulating mechanisms. They believe that producers and consumers enter into economic transactions at their own free will and that supply and demand automatically reach a state of equilibrium. However, capitalist exchanges are not equal exchanges because they depend on the private ownership of the means of production, which allows capitalists to have control over the production and distribution process.[22] Capital is a social relation which relies on the unequal property relations existing between individuals and social groups. Capitalist relations propagate the illusion that the necessary conditions for economic growth, stability, and prosperity are hinged upon the existence of capital. Yet, capital is a destructive force that has caused immense disparities for the overwhelming majority of human beings who lack capital. As Allan Engler suggests:

Capital is a social relation. It is the right to profit from the labor of others—the right to a kind of private taxation. It is the right to claim ownership of social assets and the right to exclude others from means of livelihood. So long as capitalist property relations prevail, wealthowners will decide who prospers and who does not, but the wealth they control was not created by capital.[23]

The Charge of the Lite Brigade

Radical theorists such as Paulo Freire and Antonio Gramsci have been disinterred from the Marxist soil where they first drew breath, and their graves now sprout the saplings of postmodern theory. It is all part of the postmodernization of the Left and its accompanying retreat from class struggle and latent support of laissez-faire evangelism. Radical pluralists who champion the cause of the new social movements have ripped Gramsci's concept of civil society out of its intended framework and have massaged it away from the context in which Gramsci intended it to be understood—namely, within a socialist political strategy that included the seizure of state power by the working class and the creation of a socialist society.[24] The same type of domestication has occurred with the work of Paulo Freire.[25]

Postmodern theory has made a significant contribution in helping educators grasp the politics that underwrite popular cultural formations, mass media apparatuses, the technological revolution's involvement in the global restructuring of capitalism, the ideological machinations of the new capitalism, from Schumpeter to Keynes, and the reconceptualization of schooling practices in the interest of making them more related to (racial, gender, sexual, and national) identity formation, within postcolonial, geopolitical and cultural spaces. However, its ability to advance (let alone sustain) a critique of global capitalism, corporate anorexia (downsizing and outsourcing) and the contemporary reign of money, has been severely compromised. Too eager to take a wide detour around political economy, postmodern educators have been hampered by a number of factors: (a) by their tacit—and often overt—acceptance of a market economy; (b) their joining in the chorus of post-Marxists celebrating the death of universalism and grand narratives; (c) their impatience to strike a novel posture in the theater of educational transgression; (d) their predilection for allowing their politics to be distracted by their postcolonial cultural performances of dissent; and (e) by their failure to recognize that, in the words of Robin D. G. Kelley, "We are hardly in a 'postcolonial' moment. The official apparatus might have been removed, but the political, economic, and cultural links established by colonial domination still remain with some alterations."[26] Teresa Ebert goes so far as to argue that within postmodern theory, the "assumption of the deimperialism of the center is an act of concealed imperialism."[27] Although postmodern 'masters of suspicion' have managed to deftly map the semiotic fault lines of the contemporary *fracture social*, have uncovered the necessity hidden under the appearance of contingency, have challenged stable genres of discourse, have ruptured the Eleatic cohesiveness of master narratives, have transgressed hidebound and sacred binarisms and rent them apart, and have brazenly and with percipience challenged the right-wing philippics of William Bennett-style cultural brokers, they have failed in the main to challenge in any deep or sustained way the engineered misery of neoliberal fiscal regimes and—more importantly—capitalist relations of exploitation. Consequently, the postmodern Left remains hostage to its own strategic ambivalence about capital. Not only have postmodern theorists been woefully remiss in explaining how cultural representations and formations are indentured to capitalism, they have often confused socialism with, at worse, the history of Stalinism, and, at best, the welfare state reformism often associated with Scandinavian countries such as Denmark and Sweden. As James O'Connor notes:

> The theory of capital accumulation and crisis, pioneered by Marx and fine-tuned by three or four generations of Marxist economists, is the baby thrown out with the dirty bathwater of totalitarian socialism. Just at the moment that capital triumphs globally, the greatest theorist of capital is relegated to the status of a wrongheaded 19th-century ideologue. . . . This irony, or anomaly, is so pervasive today that we are forced to turn one of Hegel's most famous lines on its head. The great dialectician wrote that "the owl of Minerva spreads its wings only at dusk," meaning that only after a particular historical event or change is it possible for reason to apprehend what has happened and why.[28]

Mocked as a 'modernist' form of outmoded phallomilitary and 'totalizing' demagoguery, Marxism is now relegated to history's cabinet of lost revolutionary dreams where it is abandoned to those romantic images of guerrillas of the Sierra Maestra. While elegiac hymns to Che Guevara still abound in the courtyards of the diminishing Left, this should not detract from the fact that, when read sharply against Guevarian challenges to imperialism and Marxist challenges to social relations of production and global regimes of capitalist exploitation, postmodernist theory frequently collapses into a form of toothless liberalism and airbrushed insurgency.

While to its considerable credit, postmodern theory—especially through the insights of its pantheon of progenitors such as Nietzsche, Toynbee, Heidegger, C. Wright Mills, Horkheimer, and Adorno—has troubled the primary status of the colonizer, peeled back the horizon of culture to reveal the trace marks of the antipodal, broken the semiotic gridlock of reigning binarisms, prevented the authoritative closure that serves to reenlist alterity into the ranks of Western imperialism, and revealed how temporal structures of dislocation constitute rather than describe our geographies of identity, it has often reconfirmed as much as contested capitalist relations of exploitation. Although it is important to follow postmodernists in introducing subaltern readers of texts, such texts need to be acknowledged as speaking through the ventriloquism of Western epistemologies linked to imperialist and capitalist social relations. Progressive educators need to ask: *how does the semiotic warfare of the postmodern or postcolonial critic reinscribe, repropose, and recohere capitalist social relations of production through decentering and rerouting cultural representations?* This is a central question that postmodernists routinely sidestep and to do so at this current historical conjuncture of titanic capitalist forces is, to say the least, perilous. As the dust finally settles we are troubled by the fact that much of what is called postmodern education is freighted with insoluble contradictions that unwittingly push radical critique toward the center. As Dave Hill writes,

> postmodernism's tunnel vision and myopic limitations have particular consequences when it comes to, *first,* the theoretical de-constructive analysis and assessment of developments within state policy, and, *second,* an inability to agree on and define a re-constructive socially and economically transformatory vision of the future. A *third* consequence is its inability to draw up and develop a politically and effective project and detailed program to work toward and actualize that social and economic vision, and a *fourth,* to define, or secure a politically effective agreement on a political strategy—to suggest how to get there. A *fifth* consequence is an inability to define what *effective* and solidaristic role radical educators might play in that political strategy. As far as I am aware, no postmodernist theorist, of any theoretical bent, has gone beyond *de*construction into constructing a coherent program for *re*construction. This is precluded by a postmodern theoretical orientation.[29]

Capitalism and democracy share a forced intimacy: their marriage has been arranged so that the families of the global ruling class can consolidate their power and set limits on how and what questions concerning equality and emancipation can be raised and in what contexts. The preservation of capital remains entombed within postmodernism's own ineffable logic and "conceals the true contradictions of advanced capitalist societies."[30] This remains the case even though some postmodernists like to imbibe the miasmically iconoclastic aura of Marx without, we might add, necessarily engaging in radical (let alone revolutionary) politics. As postmodernists look amusingly at what Charlie Bertsch and Joe Lockard call "the widely successful repackaging of *The Communist Manifesto* as a pricey fetish object for the upwardly mobile," they can play out their cathartic fantasies of the *guerrillero/a* while continuing to trash the politics that underlies revolutionary praxis.[31]

In many instances, postmodernists have dismissed Marxism as a form of ideological Neanderthalism, or a crusted-over antediluvian memory, and have tried to disabuse progressive educators and other cultural workers of the notion that there are practical and workable alternatives to capitalism worth considering. In their less generous moments, they recycle Marxist theory as contemporary farce. We don't want to deny the crimes against humanity committed by regimes claiming to be Marxist, to ignore the problems associated with Eastern and European Communist parties in their unregenerate Stalinist aspects, or to defend Marxism's recidivistic retreat into bureaucratic authoritarianism, dogmatism, and economic determinism. Nor do we wish to defend what Eagleton calls "the long tragedy of class-society," corporate governance, the ill-gotten gains of financial profiteers and speculators, and the history of imperialism and international terrorism committed by Western "democracies." [32] On the other hand, we don't believe that Marxism should be dismissed because it appears to have reached its apex in the decades before the collapse of the Soviet Union and Russia's new gangster capitalism, red bourgeoisie, and forms of primitive accumulation. We admit that Marxist theory may be out of fashion (in the United States at least) but it still has a full tank of conceptual fuel for the kind of analysis urgently needed at this point in the history of capitalism. In fact, in the light of current debates about the globalization of capital, there is a renewed interest in and reappraisal of Marx's work among social scientists. As Peter Hudis puts it:

> Some may find such talk of Marx a bit odd, given the abject failure of the communist regimes that claimed to rule in his name. Yet as Marx scholars have long pointed out, the communist regimes had little in common with Marx's actual ideas. Marx opposed centralized state control of the economy (he called those who advocated it "crude and unthinking communists"); he passionately defended freedom of the press (he made his debut as a radical journalist espousing it); and he ridiculed the notion that a small "vanguard" of revolutionaries could successfully restructure society without the democratic consent of its citizens. If anything, the collapse of communism seems to have spurred new interest in Marx, since it makes his predictions concerning the global reach of capitalism seem even more timely. [33]

The Postmodern Promise

Postmodernism has made impressive advances in helping educators map the hidden trajectories of power within the processes of representation (especially the political optics of mass media), enabling teachers as cultural workers to strip back the epistemological scaffolding that props up essentialist claims to authenticity, and to peel away layers of ideological mystification that shroud the assertion of truth and validity made by positivists within the empirical sciences. Postmodern theory's articulations of the epistemic subject have been, for the most part, invigorating and innovatory. In this regard, postmodernism has offered up a veritable cornucopia of research tools for the analysis of identity and has helped uncover ways in which universal narratives are based on masculinist and heteronormative practices of exclusion.

Despite its successes, postmodern dissent is symptomatic of the structural contradictions and problematic assumptions within postmodern theory itself. By too often displacing critique to a field of serial negation without fully grasping its prefigurative or emancipatory potential, postmodern criticism frequently traps intelligibility and meaning internally, that is, *inside* the texts of culture. In revealing the inconsistencies, aporias, and contradictions within the text of culture, postmodernism often fails to connect the significance of these contradictions, inconsistencies, and equivocations by comprehending their necessity. Consequently, it often blunts an understanding of contemporary society and unwittingly agitates for a re-enactment of the fate of society that constitutes the object of its critique. This line of fracture is emblematic of the problem that has plagued the postmodern Left over the last several decades. At this moment, we are compelled to ask: Is the practice of ignoring these contradictions and inconsistencies of culture structurally advantageous to capitalist relations of exploitation? Do such contradictions left conspicuously unaddressed merely—or mainly—provide ballast to reigning hegemons and the international division of labor, as argued by Cole and Hill in this volume? Postmodernists appear loathe to raise such questions yet continue unrepentantly to dismiss an analysis of the so-called economic 'base' in favor of the cultural 'superstructure.' While postmodernists encourage an examination of the cultural discourses of capitalism as open-ended sites of desire, Marxists, by contrast, treat discourses not as sanctuaries of difference barricaded against the forces of history but as always an interpretation naturalized by the libidinal circuits of desire wired into the culture of commerce and historically and socially produced within the crucible of class antagonisms. Marxist criticism uncoils the political economy of texts by remapping and rethinking systems of signification in relation to the material and historical practices that produce them, thus valorizing the "structural endurance of histories" over the "contingent moment."[34] In doing so it examines not the present's lack of coincidence with itself, or its lack of self-identity, but rather its ability to surpass its own limitations.

The shift toward a postmodernism layered with a thin veneer of cultural Marxism, scaffolded by identity politics and postsocialist ideology, sprayed by aerosol terms such as 'difference' and 'indeterminacy, and dipped in the gurgling foam of jacuzzi socialism and window-dressing democracy, has witnessed the categories of cultural domination and oppression replace those of class exploitation and imperialism as capitalism's reigning antagonisms.[35] At the same time, a politics of representation has deftly outflanked the issue of socioeconomic redistribution.[36] The postmodernist and postsocialist assumption that culture has suddenly found ways of winning independence from economic forces, and that somehow the new globalized capitalism has decapitated culture from the body of class exploitation by constructing new desires and remaking old ones, in ways that are currently unmappable and unfactorable within the theoretical optics of political economy, has not only contributed to the crisis of Western Marxism, but has effectively secured a long-term monopoly for capitalist market ideology. Gospelized and accorded a sacerdotal status in the temple of the new postsocialist Left, postmodern theory has failed to provide an effective counterstrategy to the spread of neoliberal ideology that currently holds educational policy and practice in its thrall. In fact, it has provided neoliberalism with the political stability it needs to reproduce its most troublesome determinations.

Our purpose here has not been to establish, evidentially, instance by instance, or *in toto*, the dilemmas, pitfalls, and shortcomings of postmodern theory, but rather to sound a rather basic caution with respect to its potential for mounting an effective counter-hegemonic project against global capitalism and its discontents. In doing so we raise the following questions, echoed by the epigones of the modernist project: Does returning to Marx reveal the ultimate sources of the patriarchal and colonizing venture of the West's master narratives? Will re-embracing Marxism somehow summon a new coherent identity for the patriarchal West? Is Marxism a quixotically romantic quest for liberation that can only serve as a stimulant for the passion of the Western master narrative? Can Marxist writings today be anything more than a dirge on the death of the communist dream?

The position we take on the issues raised by these questions is unambiguous. We believe that Marxist analysis should serve as an axiomatic tool for contesting current social relations linked to the globalization of capital and the neoliberal education policies that follow in its wake. Educational researchers ignore Marxist analyses of globalization and the quotidian poetics of the everyday at their peril. This is because Marxism enables the development of a dialectical grasp of the opposition between capital and labor, and the social relations of labor, that are concealed in the product and process of exchange. In doing so, it provides the political backdrop for a challenge to the rule of capital itself. At the same time, we admit that Marxist theory constitutes a social system of analysis that inscribes subjects and is seeped in the dross of everyday life. As such, it must continually be examined for its underlying assumptions. We believe that a critical reflexive Marxist theory—undergirded by the categorical imperative of striving to overthrow all social conditions in which human beings are exploited and oppressed—can prove foundational in the development of current educational research traditions, as well as pedagogies of liberation.

Postmodern Politics

Following tectonic shifts in the geopolitical landscapes of the 1980s and 1990s, postmodern social and political theory—with its preening emphasis on language, culture, and identity—has become the *de rigeur* conceptual attire among social scientists attempting to make sense of contemporary social life within late capitalism. Mining the terrain of identity politics, consumer fetishism and privatopia has become a central academic activity and is now considered *theoretical chic*. In contrast, Marxism has been mummified along with Lenin's corpse, and its scholarly exercise has been likened to tampering with historical relics.

The joint ambition of uncovering the hidden ideologies secreted within Western representations of the 'other' and refashioning the antifoundational self, has disposed postmodern theorists to dampen their euphoria surrounding social transformation at the level of relations of production and to heighten their regard for reforming and decentering dominant discourses and institutional practices at the level of cultural transactions. According to Sam J. Noumoff, postmodern politics attempts (a) to separate culture from ideology, (b) to employ culture as a construct that diminishes the centrality of class, (c) to insert a neoliberal political system of intelligibility and policy agenda, (d) to perpetuate the belief in the ultimate futility of the socialist project, and (e) to promote an assortment of 'post' concepts—such as post-structuralism, post-modernism, post-history, post-ideology—as a way of limiting the theoretical direction of inquiry and preempting socialist challenges to new objective realities brought about by the globalization of capital.[37]

Hilary Wainwright rightly asserts that much of what passes as postmodern politics not only lacks a coherent social and political vision with which to actively challenge the Radical Right, it also endorses a number of the Right's main tenets in progressive and radical discourses. She writes that postmodernism does not "provide adequate tools to answer the radical right . . . the tools of postmodernism produce only a more volatile version of the radical right. . . . Postmodernism cuts the connection between human intention and social outcome."[38]

Postmodern theory's stress on micropolitics and local struggles transforms what are essentially social struggles into discursive struggles, at the level of the superstructure, that overvalue economies of desire at the expense of political economy and a philosophy of praxis. In the main, postmodernists refute the idea that any particular social group or class is capable of transforming the existing social relations of production under capitalism. At the same time, however, they fail to lay the conceptual foundations for building necessary political alliances among oppressed and marginalized social groups. Ehrenberg underscores this vividly:

> It will not do to claim that knowledge is local, "identity" and "difference" are the key categories in modern social life, human relations are constituted by language and "discourse," "culture" is the site of struggle, and no single agent of human liberation can even be theorized. The inexorable concentration and centralization of capital stand in eloquent opposition to the claim that fragmentation and discontinuity have eliminated all possibilities for collective action toward a common end which can cut across the multiple, shifting and self-defined "identities" that make up the social world.[39]

While postmodern politics tends to focus on particular forms of oppression, the irrefragable power of Marxist theory resides in its ability to reveal how all forms of social oppression under capitalism are mutually interconnected.[40] While both Marxism and postmodernism address the "interlocking triumvirate" of race, class, and gender, Marxist theory attempts to reveal how all of these forms of oppression are linked to private ownership of the means of production and the extraction of surplus labor.

It is a cardinal position in postmodernism to place under suspicion master narratives, universalism and objectivity, on the grounds that they are particular epistemological and moral discourses camouflaged under the guise of universal discourses. Enlightenment ideals come under fire as well, since they putatively aim at creating homogenous discourses which are based on scientific progress associated with European economic, social, and political dominance.[41] Postmodernists additionally dismiss the Enlightenment's claim and appeal to universalism by associating it with European imperialism and colonialism which, in their view, aided the Spanish, Portuguese, and British conquest of the 'New World.' However, history demonstrates that prior empires did not rely on specific universal discourses similar to the Enlightenment ideas to justify their atrocities, genocide, and territorial conquest. On the contrary, Enlightenment thinkers frequently stressed the significance of other cultures' moral and ethical commitments by comparing and contrasting them to their own European origins. According to Willie Thompson:

> The Spanish conquistadors did not require the Enlightenment to commit genocide upon the populations of the Caribbean, Mexico and Peru and subject the remnant to slavery, nor Genghis Khan to do similar things in Central Asia during the earlier period. These acts were committed by cultures with no pretensions to universalism (unless Christianity is to be regarded as such, in which case the root of all evil has to be sought a lot further back).[42]

Post-Marxists such as Laclau and Mouffe tend to look at social contradictions as semantic problems, whereas Marxists are strongly inclined to see social contradictions as anchored in the objective nature of everyday life; they are part of the structural determinations of the social.[43] In rejecting dialectical thought, and in abandoning the notion that capitalist exploitation is linked to the law of value and the extraction of surplus value, Laclau and Mouffe reduce exploitation to a linguistic process in a purely semantic universe. Yet the oppressed know differently. For them, exploitation takes place in a concrete fashion, in the bowels of everyday contradictions that expel relations of equality. Workers might not be able to theorize this, or link it up to a working definition of resistance, but they live such contradictions in their bones. Unlike Laclau and Mouffe, we do not believe that resistance has to be conscious on the part of workers in order to stipulate that exploitation has occurred. Relations of subordination are antagonistic in relation to an ideology (a logic of capital) that rationalizes—hence naturalizes—this relationship.

The problem with post-Marxists such as Laclau and Mouffe is that the notion of materiality is often subsumed under or replaced by the signifier, or abstracted out of existence as a form of radical contingency or pure heterogeneity. The material is reduced to an integument that encapsulates a core of pre-existing codes. This collapses the material into a type of mediating exteriority that gives birth to the abstract production of ideas. Collapsed in the process is capitalism's mode of production; obliterated is the fundamental tension between labor and capital as the motor force of history. Callinicos has noted that postmodern theory has become so institutionalized in university departments throughout the Western academy that it has become an unchallengeable orthodoxy; in fact, he argues that "postmodernism has become the Parsonian sociology of our fin-de-siécle."[44] Atilio Boron has also linked the work of Laclau and Mouffe to Parsons, but for a different reason. For Boron, the work of Laclau and Mouffe, far from superseding Marxism, is, in effect, reproductive of some of the fundamental conservative expressions of United States sociology of the 1950s, as found in the work of Talcott Parsons.[45]

Postmodern theory's decentering of the 'official' discourses of the dominant culture, while not limited in referential range, is certainly limited in its scope of possible political outcomes in the here-and-now of the ongoing historical process, and does little to challenge the unbrokerable collective agency of ruling class interests and the superintendence of the state. Such efforts at decentering reigning discourses cannot effectively contest the laws of motion of surplus value extraction, and the systematically exploitative and antagonistic economic order. Class-for-itself action is the only secure and effective means of securing the legal and political apparatuses necessary for controlling the state and its economic hegemony. Of course, the composite consciousness of the working class is not a reflex of large-scale indoctrination of the masses within the social anatomy of the bourgeoisie, but rather is a consequence of rival interpretations of the world. The development of revolutionary consciousness attempts to elaborate the understanding that the working class has of its own interests and capacities. This requires extensive ideological and organizational preparation in sites such as schools. It is within such sites that a critical pedagogy must been born that refuses to compromise with the interests of the capitalist class.

The New Social Movements? A Hit-and-Miss Proposition

The new social movements in the 1980s and 1990s signaled the decline of class politics and the rise of social struggles existing outside of the economic sphere and based on "extra-economic identities" of individuals and groups.[46] As a result, social struggles became diversified around the particular interests of social groups such as environmentalists, feminists, gays and lesbians, and peace activists. While there is much to praise in the work of these new social movements, our celebration of their practices is not unqualified or unreserved. Only a minority of these social movements has been class-based. Many lack a common interest and are primarily organized around the interests of the middle class.[47] We would also like to point out that capitalism is not necessarily endangered by the ethnic, racial, gender, or sexual identities of the social groups that it seeks to exploit. Capitalism can survive antiracist and antisexist practices because it is a social system based on economic exploitation and the ownership of private property.[48] Of course, antiracist and feminist struggles *can* help bring capitalism down, but they are necessary and not sufficient struggles. We believe that in its failure to recognize capitalism as a fundamental determinant of social oppression, and in its focus on racism, sexism, and homophobia delinked from their attachment to White patriarchal epistemologies, the law of value, and the international division of labor, identity politics falls prey to a facile form of culturalism. In our opinion, certain contexts arise in which identity politics tends to hamper and weaken working-class struggles. In some instances, for example, by blaming only Whites for the oppression of Blacks, men for the oppression of women, and heterosexuality for the oppression of gays and lesbians, identity politics fails to situate White racializing and racist practices, as well as patriarchal and heteronormative practices, as *conjunctional practices* within the wider context of capitalist relations of exploitation.

The accusation of some postmodernists that classical Marxism leaves virtually untroubled the issue of gender ignores the contributions of Marxist feminists and multiculturalists, not to mention Marxist revolutionaries.[49] We refer to the programmatic documents on the oppression of women produced by the Fourth International. Trotsky, for example, argued for the liberation of women from unpaid domestic labor as part of the advance toward socialism. And in his criticism of the effects of the Stalinist counter-revolution on the family, he wrote:

> How man enslaved women, how the exploiter subjected them both, how the toilers have attempted at the price of blood to free themselves from slavery and have only exchanged one chain for another—history tells us much about this. In essence, it tells us nothing else. But how in reality to free the child, the woman, and the human being? For that we have as yet no reliable models. All past historical experience, wholly negative, demands of the toilers at least of all an implacable distrust of all privileged and uncontrollable guardians.[50]

Some postmodern feminists have argued that classical Marxism is shrouded in claims to universal truth and has overlooked the specificity of women's labor. They assert that historical materialism is reductive because it reduces all types of oppression into class exploitation, ignoring racism, sexism, and homophobia. Carol Stabile responds by describing this attack on Marxism as underwritten by what she calls "theoretical essentialism." Stabile argues that the end to sexual domination does require ending class exploitation. She notes:

> Without considering class position and its centrality for capitalism, socialist-feminism ceases to exist. Only economic analyses can force academic and similarly privileged feminists to confront the unevenness of

gender oppression and undermine its methodological centrality. Only along the frictionless plane—a location where social relations and class antagonisms hold little or no critical purchase—can the category of class be so easily dismissed.[51]

Jane Kenway astutely recognizes that in the work of negotiating among competing discourses in pedagogical processes and practices, materialist feminists are more attentive to extra-discursive (that is, economic) factors than are postmodern feminists. She writes:

> University and schools can be seen to consist of fragile settlements between and within discursive fields and such settlements can be recognized as always uncertain; always open to challenge and change through the struggle over meaning, or what is sometimes called the politics of discourse; that is, interdiscursive work directed toward the making and remaking of meaning. Materialist feminists participate in this struggle over meaning but recognize more fully than do postmodernist feminists that this struggle is overdetermined by the distribution of other resources. It is neither naïve nor voluntaristic.[52]

Consider the following comment by Lynne Segal: "despite the existence of the largest, most influential and vociferous feminist movement in the world, it is US women who have seen least *overall* change in the relative disadvantages of their sex, compared to other Western democracies."[53] Taking into account the existing social, economic and political conditions, Segal notes that

> at a time when the advances made by some women are so clearly overshadowed by the increasing poverty experienced so acutely by others (alongside the unemployment of men of their class and group) it seems perverse to pose women's specific interest *against* rather than *alongside* more traditional socialist goals.[54]

Finally, Segal argues that identity politics by itself "can offer little more than enjoyment of an endless game of self-expression played out on the great board of Identity."[55] By focusing on identity politics, postmodernists tend to lose sight of the determinate character of global capitalist relations. The challenge posed by theorists like Judith Butler—to see identity as performance and as a corporeal exhortation to mobilize against oppression—is undeniably important, but must be accompanied by a critique of the cultural formations in which performance as a material practice is produced within existing social relations of production.[56] Otherwise postmodern performance as a 'practice of the self' always remains at the level of the cultural disruption of existing discourses instead of the transformation of relations of production—that is, the transformation of the exploited labor-power of the proletariat and private ownership of the means of production.

Over recent years, the division between the supporters of class politics and of identity politics has become intensified. Supporters of the latter—postmodernists, feminists, and cultural studies theorists—have accused the former of engaging in 'class reductionism' and 'orthodox economism.' In the case of racism, for instance, Alex Callinicos argues that racial differences are invented within specific political economies associated with the mode of production.[57] Racism occurs when the characteristics which justify discrimination are held to be inherent in the oppressed group. This form of oppression is peculiar to capitalist societies; it arises in the circumstances surrounding industrial capitalism and the attempt to acquire a large labor force. Racism is thus no mere epiphenomenon of a determinant social process, but a fundamental component of that process. Callinicos points outs three main conditions for the existence of racism as outlined by Marx: economic competition between workers; the appeal of racist ideology to white workers; and efforts of the capitalist class to establish and maintain racial divisions among workers.

In a historically specific sense, racial hostility in the United States did not antecede the founding of the plantocracy in seventeenth-century Virginia. Steve Martinot notes that systematic racism involved the traversing of the sociohistorical gap between economic structure (plantation slavery) and social racialization (white hegemony).[58] More specifically, the invention of race, racism, and whiteness in the United States was hastened by the interaction between the slave market and the legislation of sexuality within the corporate structure of the colony. Chattel bond-labor became the juridical standard for the plantation system as Africans became its primary labor source. Children of mixed marriages between Africans and indentured English bond-laborers or impoverished tenant farmers working for debt relief were given the servitude status of the mother—a move that was clearly in the economic interest of the plantocracy and one that produced a social distinction between English women and African women, the latter reduced to mere 'breeding stock.' White women were subject to careful surveillance because any mixed children they might bear would be free. The 'purity condition' of English women was a necessary ideological condition for establishing the social reality of the white race. Martinot also points out that all women were reduced to productive resources, as the corporate structure of the colony was reproduced in all personal affairs and interactions. When African slaves participated in common cause with English bond-laborers, bearing arms together during Bacon's Rebellion, it strongly suggested that the antipathy felt by the English toward the Africans was essentially class-based (Bacon's Rebellion refers to the actions initiated by Nathaniel Bacon, a large landholder, who had organized bond-laborers and tenant farmers to wage war against the Algonquin in order to seize more land and create more wealth for the colony). The plantocracy responded by devising ways of turning the Africans and the English bond-laborers against each other through 'policing' privileges granted to the English. In addition, the plantocracy launched campaigns to demonize and bestialize Africans and passed laws against miscegenation. White laborers were conscripted to the task of enforcing the slave codes; poor whites were given the role or function of guardians of white privilege by policing the 'unruly' 'transgressive' or 'insurrectionary' behavior of Africans. The result was the diffusion of conflict from economic competition between small and large farms and the prevention of an agrarian class revolution.

The corporate state that emerged out of the plantocracy was able to survive and flourish by granting membership to the white bond-laborer who had the responsibility of preventing rebellion against the dominant center. Poor white laborers were offered membership in the control stratum for the subalterned nonwhite labor force. Whites were thus given a double role: as workers and as white people. The structure of white solidarity defined the white laborers' existence as the latter group was given membership at the center of the corporate plantation structure while still serving as a marginalized labor force, outside the main class relation. Thus, by using whiteness as a means of guaranteeing allegiance, the plantocracy secured its hegemony through white solidarity and the integration of labor relations (wage labor, prison labor, etc.) into the white confraternal society, or what Martinot calls the "overarching white social machine."[59] He writes:

> Whiteness and white supremacy did not evolve out of race relations, but were themselves the sociopolitical relations that brought race into existence. Indeed, if whiteness can engender itself as such only by racializing others, it can only be understood as a social relation, a social hierarchy of racialized identities. White racialized identity is constituted through identification with that social structure; whites become a self-constituting group only within the relations of racialization. In that relation, the other is interior and essential to white identity, yet separate and inimical as other. The substance and essence of white identity are external to it in the racialized other; its meaning as white exists through that other. With dominance comes dependency; with denigration comes indispensability. . . . Racism and white supremacy were not invented to "divide and rule" the working class, within an existing class structure, but to serve as the primary mode of organizing the structure of labor itself. Racism is the very name of the process whereby a class structure itself was produced. [60]

Clearly, whiteness or white solidarity became an "administrative apparatus" of the slave/class economy that served as a "matrix of social cohesion" and located whites "in a structural relation to each other."[61] Whiteness became such a powerful social/corporate social position that class struggle often fell short of actually challenging the basis of the corporate structure because such a structure was synonymous with profitability and allegiance. The white working class—in order to become a class in itself and for itself—had, tragically, to exist in collaboration with white capital. Martinot skillfully argues that the racialization of the working class in the United States has produced a double economy, comprised of two qualitatively different systems of political economy, overlaid upon each other. The plantocracy created the relation between the white socioeconomy and those nonwhite peoples who existed on its periphery or margins. Here, white corporate society functioned as the ruling class with respect to the nonwhite people that it exploited. The second system was the white economy itself, whose principle of cohesion and allegiance was racialization. Martinot notes that "the first economy conditions the integrity of the white economy as a corporate society and culture."[62] Martinot further points out that because white workers in the United States have a different relation to black workers (since the former belong to the corporate state), and because the primary relation between white workers and capital is not mainly across the means of production but through a social administrative hierarchy, whose purpose is to administer those 'Others' who exist outside the corporate state, the idea of working-class struggle aimed at the overthrow of class society "has never made sense to the white working class in the United States" whose resistance to class exploitation rarely attempted to undermine profitability or contested its legitimacy.[63] Martinot concludes that "Marxism has never extended itself beyond trade union consciousness because it was never able to fathom the structure of white solidarity by which the white working class was constructed."[64] African-Americans today are sometimes granted the status of recognition of black worker, but only as "adjuncts to white hegemony" or as "white-by-association."[65] Thus, "the very condition for working-class unity in the United States is the condition for its disunity."[66] This no doubt goes a long way in explaining why, for instance, the United States labor movement does not call for solidarity with Mexican workers against NAFTA, but remains in solidarity with the U.S. business/corporate order even as it protests unfair labor practices.

We think it is important to connect racism, sexism, and other forms of oppression to the mode of production and the historically specific political economies of capitalist exploitation, since the fundamental axis of systematic oppression is linked to the appropriation of labor power of the many by the few and its conversion into private property. Consequently, we don't want to claim that racism, sexism or homophobia are not serious forms of oppression—they can be devastating and life-threatening forms of violence. As Chomsky notes, "For people's lives, racism and sexism may be much worse than class oppression. When a kid was lynched in the South, that was worse than being paid low wages.[67] However, Chomsky agrees that the abolition of racism and sexism doesn't necessarily mean class oppression will cease. He writes:

> the United States could become a color-free society. It's possible. I don't think it's going to happen, but it's perfectly possible that it would happen, and it would hardly change the political economy at all. Just as women could pass through the "glass ceiling" and that wouldn't change the political economy at all. That's one of the reasons why you commonly find the business sector

reasonably willing to support efforts to overcome racism and sexism. It doesn't matter much for them. You lose a little white-male privilege in the executive suite, but that's not all that important as long as the basic institutions of power and domination survive intact.[68]

We are attempting, here, to establish a central linkage between race and class. And we are criticizing the way that identity politics often articulates race, gender and sexuality as existing in gated communities of cultural production, barricaded against the messy terrain in which value is extracted from human labor. In other words, it refuses to see, for instance, that racism and class oppression are dialectically linked. The goal of Marxism is to abolish class society so that every individual—regardless of age, gender, sexuality, race, ethnicity—enjoys the material resources necessary to develop his or her differences and enhance the creative capacities denied to them by capitalism. Many proponents of identity politics fail to situate racism and sexism within the arena of class struggle. Following from this line of argument, we are interested in how racism, sexism and homophobia are implicated in the contradictory and dialectical movement between the forces and relations of production. More specifically, we are interested in how the exploitative social relations of production under capitalism impact the ideological production of racist, sexist, and homophobic cultural identities. In other words, class oppression is linked (in historically specific ways) to other modalities of oppression and together they constitute a dialectically mediated constellation of totality. Identity politics may therefore be said to be conditioned by class struggle but not determined by it. At the same time, we believe that it needs to be located *within* class struggle.

Take the example of class and gender: in contemporary capitalism, women are objectively 'worth less' than men on the basis of exchange-value, on the *average*. Capitalism systematically discriminates against women, no matter what their (or men's) 'subjective' perceptions or feelings or interpretations, justifications, evasions, or the exceptions (growing in number over the last thirty years) that we can point toward. On this basis, capitalism is an abomination for visions of gender equality. Yet it is important not to confuse race or gender with social class. Social class is not the same as gender or race, on the grounds that it is a necessary feature of capitalist society. One could imagine a posthuman future where we are both sexes (or none), where we choose our 'color' (as a fashion statement)—indeed the trans/posthumanists actively seek to bring about such a future (see Glenn Rikowski in chapter 6). However, this would not invalidate capitalism as such. If, on the other hand, we arranged things such that people did not have to sell their labor powers then that, in a stroke, would make value an impossibility: as value is based on abstract labor, which in turn is based on the labor-time performed at the level of socially average labor power. Hence: no labor power expenditure at all, then the end of value, surplus value and capital. Class, therefore, is different if you maintain this broad definition, that is, the 'working class' is the vast majority pressed into selling their labor powers. Of course, a whole set of inequalities arises from whether they can *actually* sell their labor powers at any point in time. Further inequalities arise from the conditions upon and prices for which they sell their labor powers to capitalist enterprises (as observed by Glenn Rikowski, in a personal communication).

While in an important sense identity politics personalizes in different ways, in different contexts, for different groups, and for different generations of people, the often grinding and impersonal nature of class exploitation, it cannot objectively put an end to class oppression any more than the elimination of class hierarchies can automatically put an end to oppressive discrimination based on race, ethnicity, sexual orientation, etc. Although we argue that class oppression often grounds or anchors other forms of oppression linked to identity politics, we want to underscore the point that, to a large extent, all forms of oppression are important and dialectically interactive with each other. Modes of alienation and anomie resulting from living in a racist, sexist and homophobic society are deeply underlayed by the primary contradiction of class society: the tension between labor and capital. Regrettably, the political emphasis of many of the new social movements within the U.S. Left has taken away the primary emphasis on collective class struggle, a struggle linked to the objective requirements of capitalism to accumulate more and more surplus value. Antiracist struggle or antisexist struggle can never be self-validating but must be situated in the labor/capital divide. Of course, every struggle is always and necessarily incomplete since there exists an excess that cannot be accounted for. This is because dialectics itself cannot escape the marketplace.

In his criticism of cultural politics, Terry Eagleton argues that the shift from politicizing culture to culturalizing politics demonstrates the bankruptcy of the Left and progressives who have altogether abandoned the Enlightenment project.[69] Cultural theorists fail to make the distinction between culture and politics. Not all political problems stem from cultural antagonisms, nor can all cultural differences be classified as political. Eagleton argues that people from different social hierarchies (of race, class, gender) can share the same culture, if by culture we mean particular social practices that are associated with identity. However, under capitalist social relations of production, individuals from different class backgrounds cannot share the same class interests. Terry Eagleton maintains that we should emphasize the politics of culture rather than cultural politics since "politics are the conditions of which culture is the product."[70] Politics cannot be described or identified as cultural. For example, the struggle between the Palestinians and Israeli settlers manifests itself in religious and cultural struggles. However, a closer examination would reveal that they are political and economic struggles over land, self-determination, and nationhood. Cultural practices become political under certain historical conditions and as a result of antagonisms between social forces. Eagleton remarks compellingly that cultural practices

> are not innately and eternally political; they become so only under specific
> historical conditions. . . . They become political only when they are caught up

in a process of domination and resistance—when these otherwise innocuous matters are turned for one reason or another into terrains of struggle.[71]

The fashionable strain of Nietzschean irrationalism, cynicism, and nihilism being advanced in today's theatre of postmodern cultural criticism reeks of a regressive mutation of modernism. Samir Amin distinguishes between the "negative utopia" of postmodernism and the "positive utopia" of Marxism that seeks to transform the existing social and economic relations of production. Amin emphasizes that postmodernism "expresses capitulation to the demands of capitalist political economy in its current phase, in the hope—the utopian hope—of 'humanely' managing the system."[72] Postmodernism—with its often puerile and declamatory call for diversity and its refusal of allegiance to the positive value of Marxist labor theory—lives in bourgeois time and on occasion skirts the suggestive obscurities of New Age philosophy.

Like graffiti sprayed across the tropes and conceits of modernist narratives, postmodern theory remains a soft form of revolt. It constitutes a transgression of the 'already said' in the name of the poetics of the 'unsaid.' Slouching under the Promethean hubris of avant-garde cosmopolitanism, postmodern theorists privilege the poetics of the sublime over the drab flux of quotidian existence; evanescent immateriality over the concrete materiality of lived experience; the imponderability of representations over the historically palpable concreteness of oppression; the autonomy of cultural and political practices over the political and economic determinations of capitalism's law of value; fashionable apostasy over the collective ideals of revolutionary struggle from below (*bas materialisme*); the salubriousness of aesthetic subversion over political insurrection; the bewitchment and exorcism of signs over the class struggle that shapes their epistemological character; transgressive pedagogy over the pedagogy of revolution.

Lulled into political complacency by their centrist adaptations to the reformist practices of their liberal colleagues, the postmodern Left is sharing a bed with mainstream progressive educators whose work remains untroubled by a critique of capitalist social relations and is exhibiting a generic tendency to evade an analysis of schooling from the perspective of political economy. As one of us has written elsewhere:

> While not all postmodern theory is to be rejected, there is a species of it that remains loyal to capital's promotional culture where parody can be paraded as dissent and cultural parasitism masqueraded as subversion and where one can avoid putting political commitment to the test. The academy is a place where Marxism is dismissed as innocent of complexity and where Marxist educators are increasingly outflanked by fashionable, motley minded apostates . . . for whom the metropole has become a riotous mixture of postmodern mestize narratives and where hubris shadows of those who remain even remotely loyal to causal thinking. For these voguish hellions of the seminar room, postmodernism is the toxic intensity of bohemian nights, where the

proscribed, the immiserated and the wretched of the earth simply get in the way of their fun.[73]

Mas'ud Zavarzadeh argues that "post-ality" (the term he uses to refer to discursive modalities within postmodernism) represents "post-ideologies," "post-production," and "post-labor" theories.[74] He offers a powerful critique of post-ality by revealing the mechanisms by which these discourses conceal the logic behind capitalist social relations of production, through their stress on language, representation, identity, and structures of feeling. He suggests that what are frequently and seriously overlooked by post-al discourses are issues related to economic exploitation, labor, and class inequality. The seduction of post-al theories within academic discourses suggests the existence of a deep-seated pessimism among scholars surrounding the possibility of the working class becoming the revolutionary agent of social transformation.

Postmodern social theorists maintain that in postindustrial society, consumption is equally as significant as the production of commodities. Yet they overlook how commodities are produced and the relationship each individual has to the means of production, preferring to occupy themselves with how commodities are consumed. Mas'ud Zavarzadeh suggests that "post-ality attempts to solve—in the theoretical imaginary—the historical and material contradictions of capitalism caused by the social division of labor."[75] He adds that "knowledge, beyond elementary practical everyday problem solving, becomes possible only through the concealed labor of the other—that is, when the social division of labor frees some workers to engage in theoretical analysis."[76] Postproduction theorists fail to provide a persuasive critique of property relations and the social relations of production which are at the core of capitalist exploitation. The shift from production practices toward consumption practices removes labor and class as the central categories of social organization, and instead replaces them with discourses stressing the politics of desire and consumption. Postmodern theory has both shifted and replaced discourses on economic production, and the objective interests of the working class, with the subjective interests of the bourgeoisie. We follow Mas'ud Zavarzadeh in claiming that: "Class is the repressed concept in all theories of post-ality."[77] Finally, Mas'ud Zavarzadeh suggests that postmodernists and postindustrialist theorists confuse employment patterns with class structures. In other words, the expansion of service industry sectors and the managerial class does not alter the class composition and class conflict between the two main social classes: those who are wage earners and those who live off the surplus value of workers. The existence of a middle class does not alter the overall relations of exploitation between workers and the ruling class. Following Mészáros, Zavarzadeh suggests that capitalism must produce new theories to legitimize and justify the existing social and economic order and to conceal its internal contradictions.[78]

We are not convinced that we have entered into a postindustrial economy where production can be moved easily from advanced capitalist countries in the North to developing countries in the South. As Kim Moody has noted, most production still occurs in the North and foreign direct investment is still controlled by the North. In fact, 80 percent of this investment is invested in the North itself.[79] While it is true that northern industries are being transplanted to the south to take advantage of the cheaper labor markets, the North merely modernizes its economic base while making it more technologically sophisticated. We don't believe that the state has withered away under the onslaught of an information economy or information-based capital. In fact, we have not seen a qualitative rupture in capitalist relations of production. We still live within monopoly capitalism or late capitalism, and internationally the struggle between capital and labor as part of the practice of imperialism has not seen a qualitative change or shift in direction. For this reason, we still regard the working class as the privileged agent for fundamental social change with the state still serving as the central target of the revolutionary struggle of the masses. This is because the state is still the main agent of globalization, in that it continues to maintain the conditions of accumulation, undertakes a rigid disciplining of the labor force, flexibly enhances the mobility of capital while ruthlessly suppressing the mobility of labor, and serves as a vehicle for viciously repressing social movements through the state apparatuses of the police, the military, the judicial system, etc. That the state is still the major target of working-class struggle should be clear from the recent mass political strikes in France, South Korea, Italy, Belgium, Canada, Panama, South Africa, Brazil, Argentina, Paraguay, Bolivia, Greece, Spain, Venezuela, Haiti, Columbia, Ecuador, Britain, Germany, Taiwan, Indonesia, Nigeria, and elsewhere.

We remain skeptical of the new social movements dedicated to democratizing civil society but leaving the state apparatuses largely untouched. We are not interested in ways to democratize civil society if that means (and it usually does) that capitalism will be strengthened in the process. The new social movements mistakenly believing that industrial production has declined in relevance, engage in a self-limiting radicalization of the public sphere, largely struggle on behalf of bourgeois rights for the petty-bourgeoisie, fail to consider the state as a unitary agent of intervention and action in promoting structural reform, and eschew the goal of revolutionary Marxists of taking over the state and the economy. In fact, John Holst notes that at a time when segments of the Left have embraced a politics of discursive struggle and fragmentation, capitalism as a world economic system has become more universal and unified.[80]

Home-Spun Domination and the Global Reach of Power

The presence of capitalism floats in the air like the avuncular aroma of pipe tobacco wafting through your bedroom window from a neighbor's veranda. It tickles the nostrils with a mixture of familiarity and security. It instills a capitalist nostalgia, a deep yearning for a time when success appeared inevitable, when progress was ensured, when hunger and disease would be wiped out by the steady advance of industrial wealth and technological prowess. Mesmerized by the scent of money, we willfully ignore the ramifications of capitalism's current capital flight; its elimination of multiple layers of management, administration and production; and processes such as deindustrialization, the ascendancy of financial and speculative capital, the expansion of transnational circuits of migrant workers, and the casualization of the labor force. We ignore the monopolies, the oligopolies, the cartels, the new corporate carpetbaggers, the prophets of privatization, the Wal-Martization of the global lifeworld, and the transfer of capital investments to cheaper markets offering higher rates of exploitation. We pretend we don't see the reduced social expenditures in health, education, and social services, the business counterattack against labor, the state's growing indebtedness to corporate bondholders, the privatization of municipal services, the assault on trade unionism and the draconian attacks on the social safety net. We want to believe all of this will soon pass, leaving us once again curled up beside the glowing hearth of the American Dream.

Marx's utopian vision of a democratic society has much to offer today's educators, as it does the world's exploited classes. Its task has been "less to imagine a new social order than to unlock the contradictions which forestall its historical emergence."[81] We believe that capital has a unique reifying force and peculiar durability. We agree with Robert Albritton that "capital is the most important single determinant of modern history."[82] In our view, Marxist social theory's conception of the dynamic and organic nature of social relations of production under capitalism is more convincing than the triumphalistic, self-congratulatory and self-centered effusions associated with the neoliberal ideologues claiming the 'end of Marxism.' Ian McKay informs us that "Marx's transcendental yet this-worldly vision is at once ethical, realist and historical."[83] We remain confident that Marxist theory will continue to play a critical role as both theoretical and practical tools in the struggle for social justice. McKay explains it thus:

> Unless Marx was completely wrong, and conditions of social and political inequality vanish under capitalism, the kinds of analysis he undertook of class power will always be of direct interest to people who want to explain and change the world around them. Marxist hypotheses are probably going to be a continuing interest to radical movements of all kinds because Marx was likely right in thinking that there are intractable conflicting forces and tendencies in

capitalism, and new liberals and Keynesians wrong in thinking that such forces could be permanently overcome by the general welfare state.[84]

The unforeseeable future of Leftist educational practice is, in part, linked to the outcome of the following questions: can a renewed, retooled, or conceptually redrawn Marxism—absent of its most vulgar and dogmatically rigid trappings—provide the epistemological machinery for explaining and transforming the complex determinations and indeterminacies of culture, as well as theorizing the gap between empirical contingencies and eternal structures, better than a depoliticized and depleted postmodernism can? Can educational theorists escape the vulgarities that compromise the emancipatory potential of Marxism? Can Marxists sufficiently salvage a form of 'totalizing' thought within the Marxian optic in such a way that does not forfeit empirical complexity by means of a reductive synthesis? Can educators excise from the grid of causal determination a Marxism that escapes a generalized formalism and monolithic idealism? We believe that these questions can be answered resoundingly in the affirmative. We believe that critical educators can surmount the crisis of credibility of the socialist project. Establishing the conditions of possibility for the restoration of historical materialism will not be easy but the hermeneutic expansion of Marxism that is already taking place in some precincts of the academy is promising.[85] We share a guarded optimism about the extent to which educators can become tactically prepared and ideologically predisposed to carry out a 'war of position' on sequestered fronts, waged in the interest of building oppositional cultures of revolutionary workers. Recent anti-WTO protests provide us with confidence that future struggles will further point the way to alternatives to the rule of capital.

If anyone doubts the power of collective struggle in the developed Western countries like the United States, they should be reminded of what happened in Seattle on November 30, 1999. On that fateful day, young and old political activists from labor, educational, environment, legal, agricultural, industrial, and trade union groups lay siege to the city—despite a curfew declared by city officials and fierce resistance in the form of 200 National Guard troops, 300 state troopers and state police in riot gear armed with batons, rubber bullets, concussion grenades, and canisters and rubber pellets filled with pepper spray—and prevented the World Trade Organization summit from holding a successful first day in what has become known as the 'battle in Seattle.' In the same city that hosted the bloody general strike of 1919, the titans of business, the chieftains of corporate finance, neoliberal global planners, political leaders, and global robber barons were put on notice by tens of thousands of extraordinary ordinary people taking back the streets in the largest export city in the United States that boasts the headquarters of Microsoft, Starbucks, and Boeing.

The all-embracing social revolution of which Babeuf, Marx, Lenin, Luxemburg, Trotsky and others so eloquently spoke is exceedingly relevant today, despite the interminably changing social conditions facing us. History undoubtedly will point us further in the direction of a socialist future but whether we will have the will and the courage to bring it about is quite another story. Capitalism doesn't come equipped with air bags. On its collision course with history, vast numbers of human fatalities are a certainty. No one escapes injury, especially the exploited classes. The answer is not to acquire customized protection for the masses against the ravages of capital but to create a different historical trajectory altogether by cutting capitalism off at the knees. The alternative is to wait for capitalism to bring us down to ours. If we reduce the past to the postmodern texts that are currently used to write about it or cling to the belief that the future is limited to the post-Marxist discourses currently employed to predict it, we condemn ourselves to the brain-stunting banality and mind-numbing apologetics that are carried by contemporary winds of desperation and, in the long run, we engender a fatal disconnection between hope and possibility.

Notes

1. An earlier version of this chapter has appeared as a paper in *Educational Researcher* and *The Working Papers Series in Cultural Studies, Ethnicity, and Race Relations*. It will also appear in *Enclitic* (forthcoming).
2. Karl Marx, *Capital: A Critique of Political Economy, Volume 1* (Moscow: Foreign Languages Publishing House, 1959), 760.
3. See William Krehm, "The Co-Failure of Communism and Capitalism in Russia," *Comer* 12, no. 7 (2000): 9, 19.
4. James G. Stuart "A Place for Faith," *Comer* 12, no. 7 (2000): 7.
5. Terry Eagleton, "Utopia and Its Oppositions," in *Socialist Register 2000*, ed. Leo Panitch and Colin Leys (Suffolk, U.K.: The Merlin Press, 1999), 37.
6. Robert W. McChesney, "Introduction," in *Profit over People: Neoliberalism and Global Order*, ed. Noam Chomsky (New York: Seven Stories Press, 1999), 11.
7. John McMurtry, "A Failed Global Experiment: The Truth about the US Economic Model," *Comer* 12, no. 7 (2000): 10.
8. McMurtry, "Failed Global," 10.
9. See István Mészáros, "Marxism, the Capital System, and Social Revolution: An Interview with István Mészáros," *Science and Society* 63, no. 3 (1999): 338–361.
10. Walter Mosley, *Workin' on the Chain Gang: Shaking off the Dead Hand of History* (New York: Ballantine Publishing Group, 2000), 11.
11. David McNally, "The Present as History: Thoughts on Capitalism at the Millennium," *Monthly Review* 51, no. 3 (1999): 134.
12. McNally, "Present as History," 135.
13. See Reader Mercer Schuchardt, "Swoosh! The Perfect Icon for an Imperfect Postliterate World," *UTNE Reader*, no. 89 (1998): 77.
14. See Michael Zweig, *The Working Class Majority: America's Best Kept Secret* (London: ILR Press, 2000).
15. Robert Perrucci and Earl Wysong, *The New Class Society* (Boulder, Colo.: Rowman & Littlefield, 1999), 100.
16. See Christa Wichterich, *The Globalized Woman: Reports from a Future of Inequality*, trans. Patrick Camiller (London: Zed Books, 2000), 3.

17. Wichterich, *Globalized Woman.*

18. See Duncan Kelly, "Multicultural Citizenship: The Limitations of Liberal Democracy," *The Political Quarterly* 71, no. 1 (2000): 31–41.

19. David Hawkes, *Ideology* (London: Routledge, 1996), 101–102.

20. See Jeremy Rifkin, *The Age of Access: The New Culture of Hypercapitalism Where All of Life Is a Paid-for Experience* (New York: Tarcher-Putman Books, 2000).

21. See Peter Hudis, "Can Capital Be Controlled?" *News and Letters* (2000), <http://www.newsandletters.org/4.00_essay.html> (March 1, 2001).

22. See Allen Engler, *Apostles of Greed: Capitalism and the Myth of the Individual in the Market* (Boulder, Colo.: Pluto Press, 1995).

23. Engler, *Apostles of Greed*, 161.

24. For example Peter Mayo, *Gramsci, Freire and Adult Education: Possibilities for Transformative Action* (London: Zed Books, 1999); Paula Allman, *Revolutionary Social Transformation: Democratic Hopes, Political Possibilities and Critical Education* (Westport, Conn.: Bergin & Garvey, 1999); John Holst, *Social Movements, Civil Society, and Radical Adult Education* (Westport, Conn.: Bergin & Garvey, 2001).

25. Peter McLaren, *Che Guevara, Paulo Freire, and the Pedagogy of Revolution* (Lanham, Md.: Rowman & Littlefield, 2000).

26. Robin D. G. Kelley, "A Poetics of Anticolonialism," *Monthly Review* 51, no. 6 (1999): 18.

27. Teresa L. Ebert, *Ludic Feminism and After: Postmodernism, Desire, and Labor in Late Capitalism* (Ann Arbor: University of Michigan Press, 1996), 285.

28. James O'Connor, *Natural Causes: Essays in Ecological Marxism* (New York: Guilford Press, 1998), 281.

29. Dave Hill, "State Theory and the Neoliberal Reconstruction of Schooling and Teacher Education: A Structuralist Neo-Marxist Critique of Postmodernist, Quasi-postmodernist, and Culturalist neo-Marxist Theory," *British Journal of Sociology of Education* 22, no. 1 (March 2001): 140.

30. Jorge Larrain, "Identity, the Other, and Postmodernism," in *Post-ality: Marxism and Postmodernism*, ed. Mas'ud Zavarzadeh, Teresa Ebert and Donald Morton (Washington, D.C.: Maisonneuve, 1995), 288.

31. Charlie Bertsch and Joe Lockard, "Marx without Monsters," *Bad Subjects*, no. 45 (1999) <http://english-www.hss.cmu.edu/bs/45/editors.html> (November 30, 1999).

32. Eagleton, "Utopia," 35.

33. See Peter Hudis, "Marx in the Mirror of Globalization," *Britannica.com* 2000 <http://www.britannica.com/bcom/original/article/print/0.5749.11673.00.html> (January 1, 2001).

34. Aijaz Ahmad, "The Politics of Literary Postcoloniality, " *Race and Class* 36, no. 3 (1995): 15.

35. We acknowledge that there are many 'postmodernisms' just as there are many 'Marxisms.' Our criticism is directed against postmodern theories that do not sufficiently contest capitalist relations of production. Our approach to Marxism could be described as classical in that we argue that the root of exploitation is directly connected to private property and the extraction of surplus labor from workers by the capitalist class.

36. See Nancy Fraser, *Justice Interruptus: Critical Reflections on the 'Postsocialist' Condition* (New York: Routledge, 1997).

37. See Sam J. Noumoff, *Globalization and Culture* (Pullman: Washington State University Press, 1999).

38. Hilary Wainwright, *Arguments for a New Left: Answering the Free Market Right* (London: Blackwell, 1994), 100.

39. John Ehrenberg, "Civil Society and Marxist Politics," *Socialism and Democracy* 12, nos. 1–2 (1998): 43.

40. See, for example, Ebert, *Ludic Feminism*; Fredric Jameson, *Postmodernism or the Cultural Logic of Late Capitalism* (Durham, N.C.: Duke University Press, 1991); Rosemary Hennessy, *Materialist Feminism and the Politics of Discourse* (New York: Routledge, 1993); Ellen Meiksins Wood, *Democracy against Capitalism: Renewing Historical Materialism* (Cambridge: Cambridge University Press, 1996); Peter McLaren and Ramin Farahmandpur, "Critical Pedagogy, Postmodernism, and the Retreat from Class: Towards a Contraband Pedagogy," *Theoria*, no. 93 (June 1999): 83–115.

41. See Willie Thompson, *The Left in History: Revolution and Reform in Twentieth-century Politics* (London: Pluto Press, 1997).

42. Thompson, *The Left in History*, 219.

43. See Ernesto Laclau and Chantal Mouffe, *Hegemony and Socialist Strategy: Towards a Radical Democratic Politics* (London: Verso, 1985).

44. Alex Callinicos, *Social Theory: A Historical Introduction* (New York: New York University Press, 1999), 297.

45. See Robert Albritton, *Dialectics and Deconstruction in Political Economy* (New York: St. Martin's Press, 1999).

46. See Laclau and Mouffe, *Hegemony*.

47. See David Croteau, *Politics and the Class Divide: Working People and the Middle-Class Left* (Philadelphia: Temple University Press, 1995); Meiksins Wood, *Democracy against Capitalism*.

48. Our position as Marxist theorists is not to privilege class over race, gender, or sexual orientation but to see class relations as dealing with the process of producing, appropriating, and distributing surplus value. As such, it is the strongest totalizing force that lies at the very roots of racism and sexism.

49. See, for example, Ebert, *Ludic Feminism*; Rosemary Hennessy, *Materialist Feminism and the Politics of Discourse* (New York: Routledge, 1993).

50. Leon Trotsky, cited in Jane Kelly, Mike Cole, and Dave Hill, "Resisting Postmodernism and the Ordeal of the Undecidable: A Marxist Critique" (paper presented at the meeting of the British Educational Research Association, September 1999).

51. Carole A. Stabile, *Feminism and the Technological Fix* (Manchester, U.K.: Manchester University Press, 1994), 157.

52. Jane Kenway, "Having a Postmodern Turn or Postmodernist Angst: A Disorder Experienced by an Author Who Is Not Yet Dead or Even Close to It," in *Education: Culture, Economy, Society*, ed. A. H. Halsey, Hugh Lauder, Philip Brown and Amy Stuart Wells (Oxford: Oxford University Press, 1997), 141.

53. Lynne Segal, "Whose Left? Socialism, Feminism and the Future," *New Left Review*, no. 185 (1991): 88.

54. Segal, "Whose Left?" 90.

55. Segal, "Whose Left?" 91.

56. See Judith Butler, *Bodies That Matter: On the Discursive Limits of Sex* (London: Routledge, 1993) and *Excitable Speech: A Politics of the Performative* (London: Routledge, 1997).

57. See Alex Callinicos, *Race and Class* (London: Bookmarks, 1993).

58. See Steve Martinot, "The Racialized Construction of Class in the United States," *Social Justice* 27, no. 1 (2000): 43–60.

59. Martinot, "Racialized Construction," 50.

60. Martinot, "Racialized Construction," 52.

61. Martinot, "Racialized Construction," 52.
62. Martinot, "Racialized Construction," 56.
63. Martinot, "Racialized Construction," 56.
64. Martinot, "Racialized Construction" 56.
65. Martinot, "Racialized Construction," 56.
66. Martinot, "Racialized Construction," 57.
67. Noam Chomsky, *The Prosperous Few and the Restless Many* (Tuscon, Ariz.: Odonian Press, 1994), 71–72.
68. Chomsky, *Prosperous Few*, 70–71.
69. Terry Eagleton, *The Idea of Culture* (Oxford, UK: Blackwell, 1999).
70. Eagleton, *Idea of Culture*, 122.
71. Eagleton, *Idea of Culture*, 122–123.
72. See Samir Amin, *Specters of Capitalism: A Critique of Current Intellectual Fashions* (New York: Monthly Review Press, 1998), 101.
73. McLaren, *Che Guevara*, xxiv–xxv.
74. See Mas'ud Zavarzadeh, "Post-ality: The (Dis)simulations of Cybercapitalism," in *Post-ality*.
75. Zavarzadeh, "Post-ality," 1.
76. Zavarzadeh, "Post-ality," 11–12.
77. Zavarzadeh, "Post-ality," 42.
78. See István Mészáros, *The Power of Ideology* (New York: New York University Press, 1991).
79. Kim Moody, *Workers in a Lean World: Unions in the International Economy* (London: Verso, 1997).
80. Holst, *Social Movements*.
81. Eagleton, "Utopia," 35.
82. Albritton, *Dialectics*, 2.
83. Ian McKay, "The Many Deaths of Mr. Marx: Or, What Left Historians Might Contribute to Debates about the 'Crises of Marxism,'" *Left History*, nos. 3.2, 4.1 (1995–1996): 42.
84. McKay, "The Many Deaths," 79.
85. See Mike Cole, Dave Hill, and Glenn Rikowski, "Between Postmodernism and Nowhere: The Predicament of the Postmodernist," *British Journal of Educational Studies* 45, no. 2 (1997): 187–200; Mike Cole, Dave Hill, Peter McLaren, and Glenn Rikowski, *Red Chalk: On Schooling, Capitalism and Politics* (Brighton, U.K.: Institute for Education Policy Studies, 2001); Ebert, *Ludic Feminism*; Jameson, *Postmodernism*; Hennessy, *Materialist Feminism*.

Chapter 4

Structuring the Postmodern in Education Policy

Michael W. Apple and Geoff Whitty

Education Policy and the Conservative Restoration

There has been a breakdown in the accord that guided a good deal of educational policy since World War II. Powerful groups within government and the economy, and within 'authoritarian populist' social movements, have been able to redefine—often in very retrogressive ways—the terms of debate in education, social welfare, and other areas of the common good. No longer is education even seen as part of that fragile social alliance which combined many 'minority' groups, of women, teachers, community activists, progressive legislators and government officials, and others who acted together to propose (limited) social democratic policies for schools (e.g., expanding educational opportunities, limited attempts at equalizing outcomes, developing special programs in bilingual and multicultural education, and so on).

A new alliance has been formed, one that has increasing power in social and educational policy. This power bloc combines multiple fractions of capital, neo-conservative intellectuals, authoritarian populist religious fundamentalists—which in the United States are increasingly powerful—and a particular fraction of the management oriented new middle class. Its interests are less in increasing the life chances of women, people of color, or labor. (These groups are obviously not mutually exclusive.) Rather, in general, it aims at providing the educational conditions believed necessary both for increasing international competitiveness, profit, and discipline and for returning us to a romanticized past of the 'ideal' home, family, and school.[1]

In essence, the new alliance in favor of the conservative restoration has integrated education into a wider set of ideological commitments. The objectives in education are the same as those that serve as a guide to its economic and social welfare goals. They include the expansion of that eloquent fiction—the 'free market'—the drastic reduction of government responsibility for social needs, the reinforcement of intensely competitive structures of mobility, the lowering of people's expectations for economic security, and the popularization of what is clearly a form of Social Darwinist thinking, as, for example, the recent popularity of Herrnstein and Murray's *The Bell* Curve,[2] published in 1994 in the United States, so clearly and distressingly indicates.

The political right in the United States and Britain has been very successful in mobilizing support against the educational system and its employees, often exporting the crisis in the economy onto the schools. Thus, one of its major achievements has been to shift the blame for unemployment and underemployment, for the loss of economic competitiveness, and for the supposed breakdown of 'traditional' values and standards in the family, education, and paid and unpaid workplaces from the economic, cultural, and social policies and effects of dominant groups to the school and other public agencies. 'Public' is now the center of all evil; 'private' is the center of all that is good.[3]

Unfortunately, major elements of this restructuring are rendered virtually invisible in discussions among some of the groups within the critical and 'progressive' communities within education itself, especially by some (not all) of those people who have turned uncritically to postmodernism and poststructuralism. What we shall say here is still rather tentative, but it responds to some of our intuitions that a good deal of the academic debate over the politics of one form of textual analysis over another or even whether we should see the world as a 'text,' as discursively constructed, for example, is at least partly beside the point and that 'we' may be losing some of the most important insights generated by, say, other critical traditions in education and elsewhere.

In what we say here, we hope that we do not sound like unreconstructed reductionists. We simply want us to remember the utterly essential—not essentialist—understandings of the relationships (admittedly very complex) between education and relations of power that we need to consider, but seem to have forgotten a bit too readily.

Between Neo and Post

The growth of the multiple positions associated with postmodernism and poststructuralism is powerful and important. It is indicative of the transformation of our discourse and understandings of the relationship between culture and power. The rejection of the comforting illusion that there can (and must) be one grand narrative under which all relations of domination can be subsumed, the focus on the 'pragmatic' and on the 'micro-level' as a site of the political, the illumination of the utter complexity of the power-knowledge nexus, the extension of our political concerns beyond the 'holy trinity' of class, gender, and race, the stress on multiplicity and heterogeneity, the idea of the 'decentered' subject where identity is both non-fixed and a site of political struggle, the focus on the politics and practices of consumption, not only production—all of this has been important, though not totally unproblematic to say the least.[4]

With the growth of postmodern and poststructural literature in critical educational and cultural studies, however, we have tended to move too quickly away from traditions that continue to be filled with vitality and provide essential insights into the nature of the curriculum and pedagogy that dominate schools at all levels. Thus, for example, the mere fact that class does not explain all can be used as an excuse to deny its power. This would be a serious error. Class is of course an analytic construct as well as a set of relations that have an existence outside of our minds. Thus, what we mean by it and how it is mobilized as a category need to be continually deconstructed and rethought. Thus, we must be very careful when and how it is used, with due recognition of the multiple ways in which people are formed. Even given this, however, it would be wrong to assume that, since many people do not identify with or act on what we might expect from theories that link, say, identity and ideology with one's class position, this means that class has gone away.[5]

As we indicated earlier, we are certainly cognizant of the fact that there are multiple relations of power—not only that 'holy trinity' of race, class, and gender. We also recognize that conflicts not only among these relations but within them as well are crucial and that power can be productive as well. While we don't totally agree with Philip Wexler that in schools and the larger society class difference is always the overriding organizing code of social life,[6] we are deeply worried that issues of class have been marginalized in critical work in education. It took so long for questions about class and political economy to come to the fore in our understanding of educational policy and practice—especially in the United States, where class discourses have been much more muted than in Europe[7]—that it would be a tragic circumstance if, just when a fuller understanding of these dynamics is needed the most, they were marginalized. The neoliberal and neoconservative economic and ideological offensive that is being felt throughout the world demonstrates how very important it is that we take these dynamics seriously.

The same must be said about the economy. Capitalism may be being transformed (and perhaps not totally in the ways suggested by 'post' theorists), but it still exists as a massive structuring force. Many people may not think and act in ways predicted by class-essentializing theories, but this does not mean that the structures of the racial, sexual, and class divisions of paid and unpaid labor have disappeared; nor does it mean that relations of production (both economic and cultural, since how we think about these two may be different) can be ignored if we do it in non-essentializing ways.[8]

We say all this because of the very real dangers that now exist in critical educational studies. While there has been great and necessary vitality at the 'level' of theory, a considerable portion of critical research has often been faddish, moving from theory to theory rapidly. The rapidity of its movement through recent French cultural theory and its partial capture by an upwardly mobile fraction of the new middle class within the academy—so intent on mobilizing its cultural resources within the status hierarchies of the university that it has lost any but the most rhetorical connections with the multiple struggles against domination and subordination at universities, schools, and elsewhere—has as one of its effects the denial of gains that have been made in other traditions. Sometimes, it merely re-states them in new garb, without acknowledgment of the intellectual work that has gone before. At worst, it may actually move backwards, as in the re-appropriation of, say, Foucault into just another (but somewhat more elegant) theorist of social control, a discredited and a-historical concept that denies the power of social movements and historical agents.[9] Unfortunately, in the rush to poststructuralism and postmodernism and in the supposed rejection of 'the' Enlightenment project, many of us may have forgotten how very powerful the structural dynamics are in which we participate. In the process, cynical detachment often replaces our capacity to be angry.

We want to stress again that, though sometimes overstated, there are significant parts of what are sometimes called 'postie' approaches that are insightful and need to be paid close attention to, especially the focus on identity politics, on multiple and contradictory relations of power, on non-reductive analysis, and on the local as an important site of struggle. These positions have taught us and continue to teach us a good deal. However, the way they have been introduced into education has sometimes involved stylistic arrogance and a blatant stereotyping of other approaches. There is too, amongst 'posties' in education, sometimes a concomitant certainty that they've got 'the' answer to issues we've all been struggling with for years, a cynical lack of attachment to any action in real schools, and a trendy rhetoric that when unpacked often says some rather commonsensical things that reflective educators have known and done for as long as we can remember. Let us hasten to add that this is true for only a portion of these approaches; but all of this gives cause for concern.

Thus, there is a fine line between necessary conceptual and political transformations and trendiness. Unfortunately, the latter sometimes appears in the relatively uncritical appropriation of postmodernism by some educational theorists. For example, as one of us has argued at greater length elsewhere and as we shall go into more detail in the second half of this chapter, there certainly are (too many) plans to turn schools over to market forces, to diversify types of schools and give 'consumers' more choice. Various commentators, such as Stephen Ball, have claimed to see in these new forms of schooling a shift from the 'Fordist' school of the era of mass production to the 'post-Fordist school.'[10] The emergence of new and specialized sorts of school may be the educational equivalent of the rise of flexible specialization driven by the imperatives of differentiated consumption, and taking the place of the old assembly-line world of mass production. This certainly has a postmodern ring to it, although it also contains elements of a correspondence theory oddly similar to that which underpinned earlier arguments about the relationship between education and the economy and which were highly questionable even then.[11]

Yet, in many of the new reforms being proposed, there is less that is 'postmodern' than meets the eye. Even in those that are self consciously marketed as "new schools for new times," there is usually "an underlying faith in technical rationality as the basis for solving social, economic, and educational problems." Specialization is just as powerful as—perhaps even more powerful than—any concern for diversity.[12] Rather than an espousal of 'heterogeneity, pluralism, and the local'—although these may be the rhetorical forms in which some of these reforms are couched—what we also may be witnessing is the revivification of more traditional class and racial hierarchies. An unquestioning commitment to the notion that 'we' are now fully involved in a postmodern world may make it easier to see surface transformations (some of which are undoubtedly occurring) and yet at the same time may make it that much more difficult to recognize that these may be new ways of reorganizing and reproducing older hierarchies.[13] The fact that postmodernism as a theory and postmodernity as a set of experiences may not be applicable to an extremely large part of the population of the world should make us a bit more cautious as well.[14]

Thus, it is important not to evacuate a critical (and self-critical) structural understanding of education. While being cautious of economic reductionism, this does require that we recognize that we live under capitalist relations. Milton Friedman and the entire gamut of privatizers and marketizers who have so much influence in the media and in the corridors of power in corporate boardrooms, foundations, and our governments at nearly all levels, spend considerable amounts of time praising these relations. If they can talk about them, why can't we? These relations don't determine everything. They are constituted out of and reconstituted by race, class, gender and multiple other relations, but it seems a bit odd to ignore them. There is a world of difference between taking economic logics and dynamics and the state seriously and reducing everything down to a pale reflection of them. While some postmodern and poststructural analyses in education do in fact place emphasis on the state as well, too often it is treated as if it floats in thin air.[15]

We are fully cognizant that there are many dangers with such a structural approach, no matter how flexible it is. It has as part of its history attempts to create a 'grand narrative,' a theory that explains everything based on a unitary cause. It can also tend to forget that not only are there multiple and contradictory relations of power at both 'macro' and 'micro' levels in nearly every situation, but that the researcher herself or himself is a participant in such relations.[16] Finally, structural approaches at times can neglect the ways our discourses are constructed out of, and themselves help construct, what we do and the very power relations under scrutiny. These indeed are issues that need to be taken as seriously as they deserve. Poststructural and postmodern criticisms of structural analyses in education have been fruitful in this regard, especially when they have come from within the various feminist and postcolonial communities,[17] although it must be said that some of these criticisms have created wildly inaccurate caricatures of the neo-Marxist traditions.

Yet, even though the 'linguistic turn,' as it has been called in sociology, education, and cultural studies, has been immensely productive, it is important to remember that the world of education and elsewhere is not only a text. There are gritty realities out there, realities whose power is often grounded in structural relations that are not simply social constructions created by the meanings given by an observer. Part of our task, it seems to us, is not to lose sight of these gritty realities in the economy, in the state, and cultural practices, at the same time as we recognize the dangers of reductive and essentializing analyses. Our point is not to deny that many elements of 'postmodernity' exist, nor is it to deny the insights of aspects of postmodern theory. Rather, it is to avoid over-statement, to avoid substituting one grand narrative for another (a grand narrative that barely ever existed in the United States for example, since as we mentioned class, state, and political economy only recently surfaced in critical educational scholarship there, and were only rarely seen in the form found in Europe where most postmodern and poststructural criticisms of these explanatory tools were developed. It would help if it was remembered that the intellectual and political histories of the United States and many other nations were very different than that castigated by some postmodern critics). Reductive analysis comes cheap and there is no guarantee that postmodern positions, as currently employed by some in education, are any more immune to this danger than any other position.

To put it in a polemical way, one of the main problems on which a critical analysis of education should focus is not only "meaning and its [supposedly] non-existent foundations, as poststructuralists would, by inversion, have it, but action and its consequences, in particular the structuration of opportunities to act, including to signify and make meanings." Structural conditions "cannot simply be thought 'away,' they must be thought 'through' in order to be 'acted away,' and our 'thinking' will never be fully up to the task."[18] We need, then, to continue to 'think through' the complicated structural and cultural conditions surrounding schools, to uncover the cracks in these conditions, and in doing so to find spaces for critical action.

Between Structure and Agency

A focus on critical action is of immense importance here. In any analysis that retains a core of critically reflective structural concerns, ordinary people aren't 'crushed' by structural forces. They are actors, individually and collectively, historically and currently. Of course, our very language and perspectives may cause us to miss this, especially the language of efficiency, cost-benefit analysis, and human capital on the right, and the language of people as puppets of structural forces or as being totally formed out of 'discourses' and hence having no real agency within some parts of the more 'progressive' academic communities.

Of course, it is the former language—of bureaucracy, of the colonization of all of our lives by the metaphors of markets, profit, and the accountant's bottom line, and so on—that circulates more widely. It leads to what can only be called a loss of memory, an assumption that such approaches were and are neutral technical instrumentalities that if left alone will ultimately solve all of our problems in schools and the larger society (on the terms of dominant groups, of course).

Take the case of our current fascination with management systems and cost cutting, within the conservative restoration, to make us all 'more efficient and productive.' These things are not neutral techniques. Efficiency, bureaucratic management, employing economic models to understand everything—all of these are ethical constructs. Adopting them involves moral and political choices. Their institutionalization needs to be understood as an instance of cultural power relations. "Where the origin of social arrangements in political, cultural, and moral choices has disappeared or has come to appear as a neutral technical matter . . . one faces a situation of cultural and political hegemony." Yet, in order for these forms of understanding and organization to become dominant, those in dominance have had to engage in the hard work (and it is and has to be hard work) of eliminating or marginalizing any serious alternatives.[19]

Bruce Curtis reminds us that,

> No bureaucracy can function unless those subject to it adopt specific attitudes, habits, beliefs, and orientations; attitudes toward authority, habits of punctuality, regularity, and consistency, beliefs about the abstract nature and legitimacy of authority and expertise: orientations to rules and procedures. These attitudes, habits, beliefs, and orientations do not spring into existence out of technical necessity; they are the products of complex and protracted conflicts.[20]

Relations of dominance, and of struggles against them, are not theoretical abstractions, then, somewhere out there in an ethereal sphere unconnected to daily life. Rather, they are based on and built out of an entire network of daily social and cultural relations and practices.[21] In understanding this, it is dangerous to assume that they are not also partly produced out of the structural positions that people occupy. Dominance depends on both leadership and legitimation. That it is not simply an imposition is a key part of any Gramscian analysis. Dominance also partly relies on "an element of moral obligation between rulers and ruled, through which both make sense of and come to terms with relations of domination." Such an obligation "does not imply simple acceptance, but rather offers a set of justifications for political relations and defines the limits of legitimate dominance." Because of this, for political, economic, and cultural leadership to be successful, those who speak for the most powerful groups in society must engage in serious "intellectual work." Such intellectual work involves attempting both to anchor dominant understandings in a particular reading of history and to point toward a "better future" if the way forward generated out of this way of understanding is followed.[22]

Take as an example today's powerful movements toward educational 're-form' such as national testing and marketization. The forms of understanding underlying these efforts are based on economic discourse as the primary (only?) way to act on the world. The path toward a better future, we are constantly told, involves making closer connections between all of our social and cultural institutions and an economy in crisis so that 'we' are more competitive nationally and internationally. A contradictory and paradoxical combination of policies such as those on education for employment, tight control over official or legitimate knowledge, and 'choice' are what we need to 'go forward into the twenty-first century.' Yet, who is the 'we' who will be helped by this combination of neoliberal and neoconservative policies? This is one of the most important questions to ask, since as is shown elsewhere, such policies are immensely destructive both nationally and internationally. But the task of changing our commonsense (a fully Gramscian concept), so that freedom equals the market, so that failure is only the result of individual character flaws, and so that democracy is simply guaranteeing the unattached individual a choice among consumer products, has been more than a little successful.[23]

All of this clearly is occurring within an economic context, but not in any simple 'correspondence' way. And we believe that anything that diminishes our understanding of the economic and ideological context within which such policies are situated also needs to be very carefully thought through. However, when we say this we want to be cautious of not overstating the case. We need to stress again that these conditions are not caused by this context in any linear, unidimensional way. But to ignore this context, as a very powerful set of forces in moving societies in particular directions, is to live in a world divorced from reality. We live in a society in which we are expected, in the words of John Major, "to condemn a little more and understand a little less."[24] Unleashing the 'free market' will be the solution. If the poor still are poor after this society is radically transformed around 'the private' then we'll know that they got poor the old-fashioned way; they earned it. If it weren't so damaging a set of policies, the assertions would be laughable.

Talking about the extension of market principles into education, Stephen Ball puts it this way:

> The market offers a powerful response to a whole set of technical, managerial, and ideological problems. It appears to give power to all parents, while systematically advantaging some and disadvantaging others, and effectively reproducing the classic lines of the social and technical division of labour. It plays its part in the reformulation generalized. . . . And it serves to generalize the commodity form, a basic building brick of capitalist culture and subjectivity.[25]

This emphasis on individual choice, seen by some rightist commentators as the very essence of democracy, facilitates a denial of the importance of structural disadvantage. It invites us to focus our attention on examples of individuals who, for example, have 'escaped' or been 'rescued' from failing schools as a result of choice policies, without paying attention to the continuing relative disadvantages of working class and black communities as a whole.

In the process of doing this, an understanding of society as a collection of possessive individuals is revivified and any serious sense of the common good is marginalized. The ideological effects of this have been damaging. Our very idea of democracy has been altered so that democracy is no longer seen as a political concept, but an economic one. Democracy is reduced to stimulating the conditions of "free consumer choice" in an unfettered market.[26] The world becomes a vast supermarket. The metaphor of the market is an apposite one, for, just as in the real world of the supermarket, some people have the resources to go inside and purchase anything they desire while many, many people must stand outside, looking through the windows and consuming with their eyes only. It is these people who engage in 'postmodern consumption'; they can only consume the image. In a world in which we are moving increasingly toward a double-peaked economy, where the gap between the affluent and the poor grows larger and larger, where worsening conditions within our inner cities and rural areas should be the cause for national embarrassment,[27] we instead reinstall a belief that the possessive individual—the 'consumer'—is the solution. The common good will somehow take care of itself.

From this, it should be clear that there is a cultural project as well as an economic project at work here. One of the goals of the rightist coalition is to separate national identity from origin and ethnicity, to divide history from politics, and to pry loose social consciousness from social experience. Using the language of pluralism and a full range of "consumer choices" in a market, it actually paradoxically aims at what might be called "depluralization," for it articulates a vision of a classless, homogeneous society of consumers within a common, transcendent culture.[28]

This last point about the Right's cultural project is important. We do not want to stress the economy at the expense of cultural and political dynamics and processes, especially in education—a field that is deeply implicated in cultural and political relations of power—and both of us have been at pains to stress the power of these dynamics and processes for many years. In a time when capitalist relations seem even more powerful, it is easy to be reductive. Hence, it is even more important to remember not to try to squeeze everything into being simply a mere reflection of economic relations for conceptual and political reasons.

Education does indeed have a significant degree of 'relative autonomy.' One of the dangers we face has been a tendency to ignore the space education does have to maneuver "within the institutional complexes of the state, [economy], and cultural forms."[29] This is especially true in those overly structural theories that ignore the role of the local, the contingent, and of individual propensities in accounting for what education does. And this is where some postmodern and poststructural theories that emphasize the local and the contingent are helpful. The influence of such contingent circumstances can be seen in the kinds of people who tended to be recruited into school administration when centralization and bureaucratization first arose as a project in the last century in North America, for example. Let us give an example from the life of an early school administrator who was deeply involved in rationalizing education and bringing it 'under control.'

Some of those who were deeply committed to 'improving' schools through the use of tightened control and accountability (the state as the panopticon, in Foucault's terms), were apt to employ the criterion of efficiency even to their own lives. Thus, Dexter D'Everado, a strong supporter of centralized school authority in Canada, who was appointed as inspector of education for the Niagara region in 1846, was a very model of efficiency. When sitting down to eat a meal, he "consistently placed his watch in front of him so he could monitor the time he spent chewing each mouthful of food."[30] (Whether this increased his culinary delight is not known.)

Yes, D'Everado ate his meals in a particular time and within a particular economic context. But his need to apply the norms of efficiency to even the most mundane elements of his daily life—to say nothing of schools—cannot be fully understood (if such a thing is possible) by totally reducing D'Everado back into mirror reflections of the structural realities of that context. There is a tension—if we may be permitted to use some old-fashioned words from social theory—between structure and agency here. It speaks to the necessity of trying to understand both the larger social content and the contingent, local circumstances of daily life inside and outside of schools. This is the balancing act that must be attempted.

We shall attempt such a 'balancing act' by instantiating a number of our arguments within an analysis of the recent history of educational reform in England and, to some extent, elsewhere. This will require that we extend the largely conceptual and political arguments we have made into the 'real world' of education. Thus, it is now time to examine empirically many of the issues we have raised. How might we understand recent transformations in education policy? When taken together, do they constitute a compelling case that supports major aspects of postmodern theory? We shall suggest that by unquestioningly assuming that this is the case there is a danger of establishing a new grand narrative. In a chapter of this length, we cannot deal with all aspects of postmodern theories. In what follows, we shall focus on certain key elements: the issues of the supposed break with modernity's grand narratives of progress, diversity, difference, fragmentation, multiplicity, heterogeneity, and choice.

Is Recent Education Reform a Postmodern Phenomenon?

Writing about English education policy and inner cities in the mid-1980s, one of us suggested that, during the preceding decade, 'corporatist' and 'market' alternatives to traditional social democratic policies had been vying for position.[31] In the late 1980s, the Conservative government of Margaret Thatcher, increasingly dominated by the 'New Right,' displayed a clear preference for the market alternative. While state intervention rather than the vicissitudes of a capitalist market economy came to be blamed for the industrial decline and social dislocation that characterized the urban landscapes of England and Wales, the interventionist policies of Left-wing local education authorities (LEAs) were blamed for the poor educational performance of inner city schools. Just as privatization was now seen as the key to reviving the economy, so the solution to the educational problems of urban areas was seen to lie in creating a 'market' (or quasi-market) in education.[32]

Many of the provisions of the 1986 Education Acts and the 1988 Education Reform Act were thus intended to enhance clients' rights of 'voice,' 'choice' and 'exit.' These were seen by many people on the New Right as important rights and liberties per se. But, in addition to the philosophical case for choice, it was also claimed that giving parents greater control over their children's schools and introducing more diversity into the system would make schools more responsive and thereby more effective. Referring to schooling in the capital, Kenneth Baker, the government minister responsible for the Act of 1988, argued that "choice and diversity are the key elements to improve the quality of education for all London's children."[33]

In retrospect, even the earlier 1980 Education Act can now be seen to prefigure some of the later elements of education policy under the Thatcher government— namely, the use of public money to support the provision of education by private providers and the attempt to make the public sector behave more like the private sector by encouraging competition and choice. These policies of the Thatcher years posed a particular challenge to what is arguably the centerpiece of social democratic social engineering of the postwar years, the system of common comprehensive secondary schools under LEA control. In reducing the powers of LEAs to engage in the detailed planning of provision, they can also be seen as opening the way for a restructuring of the system as a whole and eventually perhaps the abolition of LEAs themselves. Alongside the apparent devolution of power to individual schools, there has also been a strengthening of the powers of central government, most noticeably in the establishment of a National Curriculum, which was a product of the thinking of neoconservative members of the New Right rather than the market-oriented neoliberals.[34]

Political Fashion or Postmodernity?

We want to consider whether some of the changes that have been happening in education over the past ten years or so can be regarded as the abominations of Thatcherism (and similar political tendencies in other countries), or whether they are perhaps an indication of something deeper. Although parts of the British government's Education Reform Act of 1988 could be seen as a typical New Right crusade to stimulate market forces at the expense of 'producer interests' in general, and the Left educational establishment in particular, that is only one way of looking at it. In some ways, the espousal of choice and diversity in education can be seen to resonate with notions of an open, democratic society as well as with a market ideology.

Put in those terms, current policies have a potential appeal far beyond the coteries of the New Right. Part of their appeal is a declared intention to encourage the growth of different types of school, responsive to needs of particular communities and interest groups. Furthermore, we are told that diversity in types of schooling does not necessarily mean hierarchy. Thus, one former government minister has characterized the drift away from comprehensive education toward more specialized and differentiated types of school not as a return to elitist approaches to educational provision, but as happening "without any one [type of school] being regarded as inferior to the others."[35]

More sociologically, this apparent encouragement of a diversity of modes of provision might be seen as reflecting some of the characteristics of postmodernity. In organizational terms, current developments might then be not merely the product of the short-term ascendancy of a free-market ideology within the Conservative Party, but part of a wider retreat from modern, bureaucratized state education systems—the so-called 'one best system' in the United States for example[36] —that are perceived as having failed to fulfil their promise and now seem inappropriate to societies of the late twentieth century. Viewed alongside changes in the way the state regulates other areas of social activity, they might be seen as new ways of resolving the core problems facing the state.

Such policies might also be seen as a response to changes in the mode of accumulation. As we mentioned earlier, the emergence of new sorts of school is sometimes characterized as the educational equivalent of what Stuart Hall describes as the rise of "flexible specialization in place of the old assembly-line world of mass production."[37] The physical appearance of some of the new shopping mall-style City Technology Colleges, and moves toward 'niche marketing' of schools, might seem to support such a 'correspondence thesis.' A broader view might see these moves toward different types of schools as a response to the complex patterns of political, economic and cultural differentiation in contemporary English society, which have replaced the traditional class divisions upon which comprehensive education was predicated. Support for schools run on a variety of principles, including those of religious minorities, might also be seen as recognizing a widespread collapse of a commitment to modernity. Or, put another way, a rejection of the totalizing narratives of the Enlightenment Project, whether in liberal or Marxist versions, and their replacement by "a set of cultural projects united [only] by a self-proclaimed commitment to heterogeneity, fragmentation and difference."[38]

Support is certainly being given to the diversification of provision and of site-based control of schools from a variety of political perspectives, as well as in countries with different political regimes. Thus, although school choice policies in the United States received particular encouragement from Republican presidents Reagan and Bush, the growth in site-based management policies, magnet schools, and other schools of choice has received much broader support. A market approach to education has now entered mainstream social thinking in the United States and is by no means narrowly associated with the New Right.[39] Furthermore, similar policies have been pursued by Labour governments in Australia and New Zealand while, in parts of Eastern Europe, the centrally planned education systems of the Communist regimes are also being replaced with experiments in educational markets. Even Japan, where the standardization of educational provision is often seen as having contributed to the nation's modernization and its extraordinary economic success, has recently been considering policies to enhance choice and diversification, "so as to secure such education as will be compatible with the social changes and cultural developments of our country."[40]

Many feminists have seen attractions in the shift toward the pluralist models of society associated with postmodernism and postmodernity, and there are also some parallels in the educational policies currently being pursued by ethnic minorities. In the United States, the recent reforms of the school system in Chicago are indicative of some of the dilemmas faced by such groups in relation to New Right policies. Those reforms sought to dismantle the vast bureaucracy under which the Chicago Schools District was perceived by many commentators to be failing the majority of its students, even when controlled by black politicians. The devolution and choice policies were enacted as a result of a curious alliance between New Right advocates of school choice, black groups seeking to establish community control of their local schools, together with disillusioned white liberals and some former student radicals of the 1960s. In New Zealand, too, advocates of community empowerment have united with exponents of consumer choice against the old bureaucratic order.[41] Such alliances appear paradoxical at first sight, but less so in the context of postmodernity, which is seen by Lyotard, one of its leading philosophers, as a pluralist, pragmatic and restless set of partially differentiated social orders. Social development is not then seen as "the fulfillment of some grand historical narrative" but as "a pragmatic matter of inventing new rules whose validity will reside in their effectivity rather than in their compatibility with some legitimating discourse."[42] In that context, the notion of 'unprincipled alliances,' which at one time might have prevented such a political configuration as emerged in Chicago, is less appropriate. If major attempts at social engineering have been perceived as failing, less ambitious aspirations may now be in order.

In Britain, recent softening of Labour Party policies toward choice and diversity in education might be seen as reflecting a similar shift away from grand master narratives associated with class-based politics. The emergence of comprehensive education in England was itself linked to a politics that assumed that social class was the most significant dimension of social differentiation. The party's traditional social democratic policies have certainly been perceived as unduly bureaucratic and alienating by many black parents, who it is sometimes claimed welcome the new opportunities offered by the Reform Act to be closer to their children's schools.[43] While not necessarily endorsing the Thatcherite dream in its entirety, some aspects of it may resonate with their aspirations. Policies that seem to emphasize heterogeneity, fragmentation and difference may thus represent more than a passing fashion amongst neoliberal politicians. They may reflect the multiplicity of lines of social fissure that are emerging and a deeper change in modes of social solidarity.

However, some of the groups that may benefit from the devolved and pluralistic patterns of educational provision which such thinking encourages themselves espouse philosophies that are rather more totalizing in their aspirations than the broadly social democratic ones which have dominated educational politics in the recent past. This is one argument that has been used against state funding of new religious schools in Britain, particularly Moslem schools with their assumed stance on the role of women.[44] This criticism, though, can itself be seen as a product of arrogant Enlightenment thinking, reflecting a prevailing stereotype of eastern culture which maintains the West's sense of its own cultural superiority.[45]

The issues are far from straightforward and the political implications of postmodernist tendencies and theories of postmodernity are notoriously difficult to 'read.'[46] Far from reflecting a real change in the nature of society, analyses that celebrate fragmentation and the atomization of decision-making at the expense of social planning and government intervention may merely be replacing one oppressive master narrative with another, that of the market. Furthermore, the espousal of heterogeneity, pluralism and local narratives as the basis of a new social order is still seen by many sociologists as mistaking phenomenal forms for structural relations. David Harvey asks whether postmodernist cultural forms and more flexible modes of capital accumulation should be seen "more as shifts in surface appearance rather than as signs of the emergence of some entirely new post-capitalist or even post-industrial society."[47] While we cannot answer this question with finality, it is clear that we do damage to reality if we see what is happening in education policy as fully postmodern.

The Rhetoric and Reality of 'Choice' and 'Diversity'

So, if the rhetoric of choice and diversity can be read in various ways, what can we make of the reality of the policies which are currently in place in Britain? Are they encouraging choice and diversity anyway? It is, of course, too early to draw any hard and fast conclusions. However, there is some evidence that enables us to give a sense of what Jennifer Ozga has termed "the bigger picture." It will be important to do this, since Ozga suggests that current studies of policy smuggle in a pluralist orthodoxy and detract from theoretical attempts to understand the coherence (or even incoherence) of education policy as a whole.[48]

Looked at overall, the early analyses of the effects of the various market-oriented policies of the Thatcher government would seem to suggest that, as we hinted earlier in this chapter, far from producing a genuine pluralism and interrupting traditional modes of social reproduction, they may be providing a legitimating gloss for the perpetuation of long-standing forms of structural inequality. There is little evidence of a postmodernist 'break.' The Education Reform Act certainly seems as likely to produce greater differentiation between schools on a linear scale of quality and esteem as the positive diversity that some of its supporters hoped for. If so, the recent reforms represent a continuity with a long history in English education chronicled by O. Banks in *Parity and Prestige in English Secondary Education.*[49]

G. Walford and H. Miller claim that while comprehensive schools attempted to overcome the historic links between diversity of provision and inequalities of class and gender, "City Technology Colleges have played a major part in re-legitimizing inequality of provision for different pupils." Indeed, they argue that the "inevitable result" of the concept of City Technology Colleges, especially when coupled with Grant Maintained Schools and Locally Maintained Schools, is "a hierarchy of schools with the private sector at the head, the CTCs and GMSs next, and the various locally managed LEA schools following."[50] A senior Labour Party spokesperson on education has recently asserted that the creation of a hierarchy from elite private schools, through to CTCs and Grant Maintained Schools to a residual provision of Council schools was deliberate Conservative Party policy, a charge which is in some danger of creating a self-fulfilling prophecy.

But, whether deliberate or not, there is little evidence yet that the Education Reform Act is providing a structure that will encompass diversity and ensure equality of opportunity for all students. Rather, there is some evidence that the reforms further disadvantage those unable to compete in the market and that they do actually create a hierarchy of schools. This will have particular consequences for the predominantly working class and black populations who inhabit the inner cities. While they never gained an equitable share of educational resources under social democratic policies, the abandonment of planning in favor of the market seems unlikely to provide a solution. Indeed, there is a real possibility that an educational underclass will emerge in Britain's inner cities, much like that which is so prevalent in the United States.

On this argument, whatever the intentions of their sponsors, present policies are as likely to increase structural inequalities as challenge them, while fostering the belief that their championing of choice does provide genuinely equal opportunities for all those individuals who wish to benefit from them. For those members of disadvantaged groups who are not sponsored out of schools at the bottom of the status hierarchy, either on grounds of exceptional academic ability or alternative definitions or merit, the new arrangements are effectively just another way of reproducing deeply entrenched class and race divisions. Visions of our moving toward a postmodern education system in a postmodern society may thus be premature or reflections of surface appearances—perhaps merely a mirage. At the very most, current reforms would seem to relate to a version of postmodernity that emphasizes 'distinction' and 'hierarchy within a fragmented social order,' rather than one that positively celebrates (or even tolerates) 'difference' and 'heterogeneity.' [51]

National Curricula

This linearity is also evident when one looks at the National Curriculum in England, the one element of recent reforms that seemed to contradict the Thatcher government's espousal of market forces.[52] The National Curriculum established by the 1988 Education Reform Act specifies programs of study and attainment targets for the three 'core' subjects, English, Mathematics and Science, and seven other 'foundation' subjects. While some of the extreme neoliberals of the New Right would have liked to see the curriculum itself left to the market, the government seems to have been more persuaded on this score by the argument of neoconservative pressure groups such as the Hillgate Group. This group argues that, even if market forces should ultimately be seen as the most

desirable way of determining a school's curriculum, central government imposition of a National Curriculum on all state schools is a necessary interim strategy to undermine the vested interests of a 'liberal educational establishment'
that threatens educational standards and traditional values. While there are complex alliances and motivations involved, this is the case as well in the attempt in
the United States to move toward national curricula, national standards, and
national testing.[53]

In England, the Hillgate Group is particularly concerned to counter the
pressure for a multicultural curriculum that "has been felt throughout the Western world, and most notably in France, Germany, and the United States, as well
as in Britain." It joins those "who defend the traditional values of Western societies, and in particular who recognize that the very universalism and openness of European culture is our best justification for imparting it, even to those
who come to it from other roots." While happy to see the emergence of new and
autonomous schools, including Islamic schools and such other schools as parents desire, its commitment to market forces is in the context of an insistence
that all children "be provided with the knowledge and understanding that are
necessary for the full enjoyment and enhancement of British society." At the
same time, "Our" culture, being part of the universalistic culture of Europe,
"must not be sacrificed for the sake of a misguided relativism, or out of a mis-
placed concern for those who might not yet be aware of its strengths and weaknesses."[54] Behind much of this is a tension over 'the other.' Thus, racial discourse is often the absent presence behind such positions, a fact that is very
visible in the United States in particular,[55] and increasingly visible in Britain,
France, Germany, and elsewhere. The Hillgate pamphlet thus works both to
acknowledge difference and to defuse its potential challenge to the prevailing
social order. Given its influence on government policies at the time the Reform
Act was being finalized, the reading of those policies with which we flirted earlier—seeing them as a reflection of the sort of postmodern society which celebrates heterogeneity and difference—becomes even more questionable. There is
clearly within the discourse of the Hillgate Group a master narrative that differ-
entiates cultures on a hierarchical basis, and which sees social progress largely
in terms of assimilation into European culture.

A further aspect of the National Curriculum arrangements that is likely to
arrange schools and students on a linear scale is the combination of locally
maintained schools, competition amongst schools for students, and the publication of assessment scores. This could well leave the most disadvantaged students concentrated in schools with low aggregate test scores and declining resources and morale.

Alternative Responses

The combination of policies that characterized the Thatcher government's approach to education in Britain is well-captured in the paradoxical concept of

'conservative modernisation,'[56] a term that also emphasizes its links with other aspects of modernity, rather than something distinctively anti-modern or post-modern. Despite the development of new forms of accumulation and changes in the state's mode of regulation, together with some limited changes in patterns of social and cultural differentiation in contemporary Britain, the continuities seem just as striking as the discontinuities. In theoretical terms, this seems to offer support for those who deny that there has been any radical rupture with modernity, but it is also consistent with a view that argues for a dialectic of continuity and discontinuity.[57]

Thus, while there may have been no postmodernist 'break,' recent conservative policies may well have been more responsive than others to those subtle social and cultural shifts that have been taking place in modern societies. Even though social class divisions remain an important challenge to our education system, traditional social democratic approaches to education which favor the idea of a common school and, indeed, usually some version of a common curriculum,[58] will themselves have to respond to the increasing social diversity of contemporary societies. Just as current discussions on the Left about citizenship are seeking ways of "creating unity without denying specificity,"[59] so will this be a challenge for future education policy. James Donald has called for approaches based on "participation and distributive justice rather than simple egalitarianism—and on cultural heterogeneity rather than a shared humanity."[60] Donald himself argues that this puts a question mark against the very idea of comprehensive education. While we are not convinced that is necessarily the case, it certainly requires some rethinking of the notion of comprehensive education and indicates the need for the Left to rethink old orthodoxies. What it decidedly does not do, however, is require us either to fully reject 'older' ways of understanding the social world in general and education policy in particular or to fully accept 'newer' 'post' understandings and assumptions unquestioningly. Indeed, such a view expressly contradicts itself, since oddly enough it assumes a linear view of progress that is (supposedly) rejected within postmodern approaches themselves.

Conclusion

In this chapter, we have acknowledged that many of the postmodern and post-structural emphases now emerging in critical educational studies have had a number of positive effects. They have increased the number of voices that need to be made public. They have helped legitimate and/or generate a welcome return to the concrete analysis of particular ideological and discursive formations, as well as the multiple sites of their elaboration and legitimation in policy documents, social movements, and institutions such as schools.[61] This focus on the complexities of the concrete historical instance, without always having to search for the hidden set of determinations, in part does free us to understand the local and the contingent.

Yet, this said—and it should be—there are many dangers here as well, especially involving the loss of collective memory, the loss of the gains in understanding that accompanied more structural analyses of the generation, circulation, and legitimation of educational policies within the economic, political, and cultural spheres. In many ways, there are the same silences within too many postmodern approaches that are found in one of the major figures from whom these theories have often borrowed their emphases—Michel Foucault. As Hall reminds us, it has often proven too easy to accept Foucault's epistemological position whole and uncritically. There is a world of difference (and no pun is intended here) between emphasizing the local, the contingent, and the non-correspondent and ignoring any determinacy or any structural relationship among practices. Too often, important questions surrounding the state and social formation are simply evacuated and the difficult problem of simultaneously thinking about the specificity of different practices and the forms of articulated unity they constitute are assumed out of existence as if nothing existed in structural ways.[62] Or, as has been the case of some of the material we have examined, relatively reductive relations of 'correspondence' between the economy and education are posited, as if we have learned nothing since the days of Bowles and Gintis.[63]

Yet, our analysis of educational policies demonstrates the importance of just such 'thinking through' simultaneously. Rhetorical flights into fragmentation, diversity, 'difference,' the supposed break with both 'modernity' and its grand narratives, and so on, do represent certain transformations in education and the larger society. But, it is just as possible that they construct a 'story' of the world that is overstated, that misrecognizes patterns of cause and effect, and in the process causes many people to forget who and what may be at stake as the conservative restoration litters the landscape of education with the effects of its aggressive policies. [64]

Notes

1. See Michael W. Apple, *Official Knowledge: Democratic Education in a Conservative Age* (New York: Routledge, 1993) and *Cultural Politics and Education* (New York: Teachers College Press, 1996).
2. R. Herrnstein and C. Murray, *The Bell Curve* (New York: Free Press, 1994).
3. See Apple, *Cultural Politics*.
4. S. Best and D. Kellner, *Postmodern Theory: Critical Interrogations* (Basingstoke, U.K.: Macmillan, 1991).
5. Stanley Aronowitz, *The Politics of Identity* (New York: Routledge, 1992).
6. Philip Wexler, *Becoming Somebody* (Lewes, U.K.: Falmer, 1992).
7. Nancy Fraser and Linda Gordon, "A Genealogy of Dependency," *Signs*, 19 (1994): 309–336; Michael W. Apple, *Education and Power* (New York: Routledge, 1995).
8. Apple, *Cultural Politics*.

9. L. Zipin, "Emphasising 'Discourse' and Bracketing People" in *Governmentality through Education*, ed. T. Popkewitz and M. Brennan (New York: Teachers College Press, 1998).

10. Stephen Ball, *Politics and Policymaking in Education: Explorations in Policy Sociology* (London: Routledge, 1990).

11. See, for example, Sam Bowles and Herb Gintis, *Schooling in Capitalist America* (New York: Basic Books, 1976), and *Bowles and Gintis Revisited*, ed. Mike Cole (Lewes, U.K.: Falmer Press, 1988).

12. Geoff Whitty, T. Edwards and S. Gewirtz, *Specialisation and Choice in Urban Education* (London: Routledge, 1993), 173–174.

13. Whitty et al., *Specialisation*, 180–181.

14. Edward Said, *Culture and Imperialism* (New York: Vintage, 1993).

15. See especially I. Hunter, *Rethinking the School* (Boston: Allen & Unwin, 1994).

16. L. Roman and Michael W. Apple, "Is Naturalism a Move beyond Positivism?" in *Qualitative Inquiry in Education*, ed. E. Eisner and A. Peshkin (New York: Teachers College Press, 1990), also A. Gitlin, ed., *Power and Method* (New York: Routledge, 1994).

17. C. McCarthy and W. Crichlow, eds., *Race, Identity, and Representation in Education* (New York: Routledge, 1993).

18. T. Green and Geoff Whitty, "The Legacy of the New Sociology of Education" (unpublished paper presented at the American Educational Research Association, New Orleans, 1994), 21.

19. Bruce Curtis, *True Government by Choice Men?* (Toronto: University of Toronto Press, 1992), 175.

20. Curtis, *True Government*, 8.

21. Curtis, *True Government*, 121.

22. Curtis, *True Government*, 102.

23. See Apple, *Cultural Politics*.

24. Stephen Ball, *Education Policy* (Lewes, U.K.: Falmer Press, 1994), 13.

25. Ball, *Education Policy*, 10.

26. Apple, *Official Knowledge*.

27. Apple, *Cultural Politics*.

28. Ball, *Education Policy*, 6–7.

29. Green and Whitty, "The Legacy," 22.

30. Curtis, *True Government*, 3.

31. Geoff Whitty, "Education Policy and the Inner Cities" in *The Contemporary British City*, ed. P. Lawless and C. Raban (London: Harper and Row, 1986).

32. Geoff Whitty, "Creating Quasi-Markets in Education," in "Review of Research," ed. Michael W. Apple, *Education* 22 (Washington, D.C.: American Educational Research Association, 1997).

33. Kenneth Baker, "A Bright New Term for London's Children," *Evening Standard*, March 30, 1990, 7.

34. Geoff Whitty and I. Menter, "Lessons of Thatcherism: Education Policy in England and Wales, 1979–88," *Journal of Law and Society* 16, no. 1 (1989), and Geoff Whitty, "The New Right and the National Curriculum—State Control or Market Forces?" *Journal of Education Policy* 4, no. 4 (1989), 329–341.

35. Ray Dunning, quoted in *Education*, July 8, 1988.

36. John E. Chubb and Terry M. Moe, *Politics, Markets, and America's Schools* (Washington, D.C.: Brookings Institution, 1990), and C. Glenn, *The Myth of the Common School* (Amherst: University of Massachusetts Press, 1987).

37. Stuart Hall and Martin Jacques, eds., *New Times: The Changing Face of Politics in the 1990s* (London: Lawrence & Wishart, 1989).

38. Richard Boyne and Ali Rattansi, eds., *Postmodernism and Society* (London: Macmillan, 1990).

39. Chubb and Moe, *Politics, Markets*.

40. Michael Stephens, *Japan and Education* (London: Macmillan, 1991), 148.

41. Gerald Grace, "Welfare Labourism and the New Right: The Struggle in New Zealand's Education Policy," *International Studies in Sociology of Education* 1 (1991), 25–42.

42. Boyne and Rattansi, *Postmodernism, Society*.

43. Melanie Phillips, "Why Black People Are Backing Baker," *The Guardian*, September 9, 1988.

44. Phillip Walkling and Chris Brannigan, "Anti-sexist/Anti-racist Education: A Possible Dilemma," *Journal of Moral Education* 15, no. 1 (1986).

45. Edward Said, *Orientalism* (London: Routledge, 1978); Pratibha Parmar, "Young Asian Women: A Critique of the Pathological Approach," *Multiracial Education* 9, no. 5, 1981; J. M. Halstead, *The Case for Muslim Voluntary-Aided Schools* (Cambridge, U.K.: The Islamic Academy, 1986).

46. Henry Giroux, ed., *Postmodernism, Feminism, and Cultural Politics* (New York: State University of New York Press, 1990).

47. David Harvey, *The Condition of Postmodernity* (Oxford, U.K.: Basil Blackwell, 1989).

48. Jennifer Ozga, "Policy Research and Policy Theory," *Journal of Education Policy* 5, no. 4 (October–December 1989), 359–362.

49. Olive Banks, *Parity and Prestige in English Secondary Education* (London: Routledge, 1955).

50. Geoffrey Walford and Henry Miller, *City Technology Colleges* (Milton Keynes, U.K.: Open University Press, 1991).

51. Scott Lash, *Sociology of Postmodernism* (London: Routledge, 1990).

52. Geoff Whitty, "The New Right and the National Curriculum—State Control or Market Forces?" *Journal of Education Policy* 4, no. 4 (October–December 1989): 329–341 and *Sociology and School Knowledge: Curriculum Theory, Research and Politics* (London: Methuen, 1985).

53. Apple, *Cultural Politics*.

54. Hillgate Group, *The Reform of British Education* (London: Claridge Press, 1987).

55. See Michael W. Apple, *Cultural Politics*, and "Power, Meaning, and Identity," *British Journal of Sociology of Education* 17 (June 1996), 125–144.

56. Roger Dale, "The Thatcherite Project in Education," *Critical Social Policy* 9, no. 3 (1989).

57. Best and Kellner, *Postmodern Theory*.

58. Dennis Lawton, *Class, Culture and the Curriculum* (London: Routledge, 1975).

59. Chantal Mouffe, quoted in Giroux, ed., *Postmodernism, Feminism*.

60. James Donald, "Interesting Times," *Critical Social Policy* 9, no. 3 (1989): 39–55.

61. Stuart Hall, "Cultural Studies: Two Paradigms," in *Cultural Studies*, ed. L. Grossberg, C. Nelson and P. Treichler (New York: Routledge, 1992), 537.

62. Hall, "Cultural Studies," 537–538.

63. See Bowles and Gintis, *Schooling, Capitalist America*.

64. Parts of this chapter appear in Apple, *Education, Power, Cultural Politics* and "Power, Meaning." Geoff Whitty presented other parts to the Conference on Reproduc-

tion, Social Inequality and Resistance: New Directions in the Theory of Education, at the University of Bielefeld, Germany, October 1–4, 1991. Although there have subsequently been a number of modifications to the specific policies discussed here, the major substantive and theoretical issues raised in the chapter remain the same. For further discussion of these issues, see Whitty et al. *Specialisation and Choice,* and Geoff Whitty, "Citizens or Consumers? Continuity and Change in Contemporary Education Policy," in *Power/Knowledge/Pedagogy,* ed. D. Carlson and Michael W. Apple (Boulder, Colo.: Westview Press, 1998).

Chapter 5

'Resistance Postmodernism' —Progressive Politics or Rhetorical Left Posturing?

Mike Cole and Dave Hill

Introduction

In this chapter, we begin by considering whether there are, in fact, two types of postmodernism, described, inter alia as 'postmodernism of reaction' and 'postmodernism of resistance.'[1] We argue that, while there are clear differences in intention and in emphasis between the two postmodernisms, they have too much in common to be thought of as separate discourses. It is more accurate, we suggest, to think of a continuum, with 'postmodernism of reaction' at one end and 'postmodernism of resistance' at the other. While one end of the continuum is peopled by reactionaries, engrossed in 'games of despair,' the other is composed of defeatist ex-socialists, engaged in a rhetoric of left posturing. Precisely because they claim to promote a progressive politics, we concentrate our critique on those who identify with the 'resistance' end of the continuum. Contra the postmodern rejection of the metanarrative, a Marxist analysis, we argue, still has most purchase in explaining economic, political, social and cultural changes and developments in capitalist societies, such as, for example, the Radical Right Conservative and the New Labour restructuring of education systems. We argue that postmodernist analyses, in general, marginalize and/or neglect the determining effects of the relations of production. In particular, we suggest that postmodernism, albeit unwittingly for 'resistance postmodernists,' serves to disempower the oppressed, by denying the notion of 'emancipation in a general sense.' We argue that major processes of restructuring social, welfare and educational provision, and regulating labor, are underpinned by market-led strategies, and are in line with the current requirements of capitalist states. This is either ignored or underplayed in the discourse of postmodernism, or else the

changes are designated as 'postmodern,' as reflecting or being part of postmodernity.

We suggest that, in rejecting the determining effects of capital, or in neutralizing capitalism itself, postmodernism serves to uphold the current capitalist project. Ideologically, this project involves the privileging of individualism, consumerism and greed. Economically, at state levels, it entails a privatization program, incorporating the creation of a hierarchy of provision in the 'public' services. Such a hierarchy has been intensified in the education system with respect to England and Wales[2] and in the similar 'marketization' and hierarchicalization of schooling across the globe[3]—for example, in Australasia[4] and in the United States.

'Postmodernism of Reaction' and 'Postmodernism of Resistance'

The case for the existence of two postmodernisms, one reactionary and one progressive, has been made with passion by postmodern feminist Patti Lather. Postmodernism of reaction is described as neo-Nietzschean, concerned with the collapse of meaning, with nihilism, and with cynicism. The conception of the individual is of a fractured schizoid consumer, existing in what Lather describes as "a cultural whirlpool of Baudrillardian simulcra."[5] Postmodernism of resistance, on the other hand, is defined as participatory and dialogic and as encompassing pluralistic structures of authority. It is non-dualistic and anti-hierarchical and celebrates multiple sites from which the word is spoken.[6] (More recently, Lather has taken multivocality to its logical conclusion. In adopting Jacques Derrida's concept of the "ordeal of the undecidable," where "one cannot define, finish or close," she advocates "a praxis of not being so sure"[7]—see later).

For postmodernists of resistance, the subject is 'in-process' and capable of agency. Unlike the postmodernists of reaction, who stress increased normalization and regulation, the postmodernists of resistance, Lather claims, see difference without opposition, personal autonomy and social relatedness. Whereas the former accept the inevitability of multinational hyperspace, the "latter are into ecopolitics." Postmodern feminism is somewhat immodestly described by Lather, following Arthur Kroker and David Cook, as "the quantum physics of postmodernism."[8] Postmodern feminism, on the contrary, we would argue, serves to disempower women (see Jane Kelly in chapter 10).[9]

We would like to evaluate Lather's three claims for a separate and progressive role for postmodernism of resistance, one by one. First, she states that it is "participatory and dialogic," encompasses "pluralistic structures of authority," is "anti-hierarchical" and "celebrates multiple sites from which the word is spoken."[10] Our comment would be that, while the celebration of multiple voices, as a methodology, has its strengths, it also has its weaknesses, and that there is nothing inherently 'resistant' or progressive about it. Given Lather's postmodernist preference for "multi-voiced, multi-centred discourse," and her adoption of Derrida's "ordeal of the undecidable," a valid question that must be asked is, "assuming that these voices will at least sometimes conflict," must we "confront the status and validity of these multiple views—or simply assume they are all equally true (or false), equally revealing (or opaque)?"[11] Landon E. Beyer and Daniel P. Liston conclude that postmodern theory, at least of this type, does not provide an answer. In addition, an emphasis on making sure that the voices of "the other" become heard has made some postmodernists even suspicious of or hostile to "community," which is seen as "necessarily oppressive, patriarchal and limiting." Writers such as Elizabeth Ellsworth have expressed the fear that "multiple voices" will be lost or silenced in communities and have therefore suggested that the most that might be hoped for is a gathering of voices within increasingly small and homogenous groups.[12] Arguing against this position, Beyer and Liston suggest, with considerable efficacy and clarity (although, to the oppressions of patriarchy, racism and social class, we would add sexuality and disability) that:

> personal and social conditions need to be continually created, recreated, and reinforced that will encourage, respect, and value expressions of difference. Yet if the valorization of otherness precludes the search for some common good that can engender solidarity even while it recognizes and respects that difference, we will be left with a cacophony of voices that disallow political and social action that is morally compelling. If a concern for otherness precludes community in any form, how can political action be undertaken, aimed at establishing a common good that disarms patriarchy, racism and social class oppression? What difference can difference then make in the public space?[13]

Second, postmodernism of resistance is "non-dualistic" and sees "difference without opposition, personal autonomy and social relatedness." That Lather includes "personal autonomy" here is indicative of the contradictory nature of postmodernism, since this is a concept clearly associated with the Enlightenment, an enterprise considered by the postmodernists, to have been superceded by postmodernism (see later). As far as non-dualism and 'difference without opposition' and 'social relatedness' are concerned, these are, of course, general features of postmodernism and represent, as we will argue, some of its major problems. Postmodernism is unable and unwilling to recognize a major duality in capitalist societies, that of social class (see Dave Hill, Mike Sanders and Ted Hankin in chapter 8, and Peter McLaren and Ramin Farahmandpur in chapter 11). This has, we believe, profoundly reactionary implications.

Third, the subject is 'in process' and 'capable of agency.' While 'agency' has progressive implications, the fact that the agency advocated by the postmodernists of resistance relates to localized action only,[14] renders it, over all, reactionary. This argument is developed later.

We take issue with Lather's argument that postmodernism can so neatly divide into two. We concur that the well-intentioned project of some (feminist and other) postmodernists of resistance stands in stark contrast both in analysis and approach to the nihilistic and lighthearted desperation of the Baudrillardian gameplayers. However, we would argue that ultimately, the 'two' postmodernisms lie, in fact, on one continuum. In our critique of postmodernism as a whole, we will highlight any differences as they occur. Overall, however, we believe that postmodernism does not deserve the duality afforded to it by these writers.

The Trouble with Postmodernism

We have dealt at length elsewhere with what we perceive to be the central problems with postmodernism.[15] Briefly, we take issue with its anti-foundationalism, its rejection of the metanarrative, its denial of any 'totalizing' system of thought like Marxism, liberalism or feminism. In short, we challenge its self-proclaimed inability to make general statements about society. This point has been made, inter alia, by a number of other writers.[16] We suggest that the motor of the class struggle is still determinant and that the Enlightenment metanarratives of Marxism and neo-Marxism, and their analysis of capital and power, best explain current and ongoing economic, political, social, educational, cultural and labor market developments, worldwide. In addition, we are in agreement with the arguments of Jurgen Habermas, with respect to the neo-Conservative implications of postmodernist 'theory.'[17] Postmodernism, we believe, albeit unintentionally for many postmodernists, serves the interests of capital's current hegemonic project, particularly with respect to its interrelated attempts to discredit mass ideologies, such as socialism, to disempower mass groups who are structurally oppressed, and to privilege consumption and greed over production and solidarity. An acceptance of postmodernist ideas, then, should be a cause for celebration for capital. If there are no other ways of living, and no alternatives to unbridled market-led economic strategies, if no alternative fundamental structural changes in society are possible, then the Left has indeed become an anachronism. There is another factor, which makes postmodernism inherently reactionary. Given postmodernists' insistence on anti-representationalism (the rejection of the view that reality is directly given, without mediation, to subjects), and their consequent reliance on 'textualism' (seeing the text as the only source of meaning), it would seem that the possibility of structural analysis and structural change is further removed from the agenda.[18]

For those at the reactionary end of the continuum, the future seems to consist of some kind of extension, albeit perhaps accelerated, of 'the present,' a present in which we are resigned to survive among the remnants. In *The Illusion of the End*, Jean Baudrillard argues that the 'present' will be continually recycled, the future is merely the effects of this recycling process. This, of course, implies the eternalization of capitalism—with its attendant horrors, inequalities and class-based conflicts.

At the postmodernism of resistance end of the continuum, the future is either an open book or a rhetorical 'future' of 'social justice,' of 'emancipation' (local only) and, that catchword which is all things to all people, 'democracy.' On the first page of the preface of *Getting Smart*, Patti Lather declares her "longtime interest in how to turn critical thought into emancipatory action."[19] However, after over two hundred pages of text, in which indications are made of the need for emancipatory research and praxis, in which proclamations are made of how the goals of research should be to understand the maldistribution of power and resources in society with a view to societal change, we are left wondering how all this is to come about. As other critics have pointed out, the precise nature of this maldistribution and its implications are never made clear. "How," ask Beyer and Liston, "does one identify, locate, and explain structures of oppression, much less structural contradictions?" How, wonders Mary Maynard, can "inequalities" be "made known through a research process which encourages us to see the social world as a text?"[20]

Just how close postmodernism of reaction (despair and despondency) is to postmodernism of resistance (rhetorics of resistance) is most clearly demonstrated in Lather's more recent writing. Although she adopts Derrida's 'ordeal of the undecidable' with its obligations to openness, passage and non-mastery, she nevertheless claims to be interested in "deconstructing the position of intellectuals in struggles for social justice toward *something more than academic heroics*."[21] She then tells us that she is in favor of a "post-dialectical praxis" which is about "ontological stammering, concepts with a lower ontological weight, a praxis without guaranteed subjects or objects, oriented toward the as-yet-incompletely thinkable conditions and potentials of given arrangements." Lather concludes, "we move toward an experience of the promise that is unforeseeable from the perspective of our present conceptual frameworks." Her academic efforts are informed by Alison Jones, who concludes "with a call for a 'politics of disappointment', a practice of 'failure, loss, confusion, unease, limitation for dominant ethnic groups.'" Lather is claiming to be anti-colonialist in supporting Maori students in their wish to break up into "discussion groups based on ethnic sameness."[22] However, since she believes that "all oppositional knowledge is drawn into the order against which it intends to rebel," it is difficult to see what possible progressive potential her overall project has, either for women, for minority ethnic groups or for the working class in general. Just how is her aim of deconstructing Marxist intellectuals in any way progressive?[23]

Any supporter of the capitalist order who had any belief in the efficacy of academic writing would surely be delighted to hear that Patti Lather, like so many of her postmodern contemporaries, was arguing in the 1980s that "feminism and Marxism need each other" and that "the revolution is within each and every one of us and it will come about,"[24] but is now so confused that she thinks the future is an open book, with some progressive potential and in which all opposition is drawn into the dominant order! This is essentially pro-capitalist confusion. It is one of the ways that postmodernism acts as an ideological support for national and global capital. In similar vein, Myra Hird argues:

Political struggle based on the universalisation of any particular difference (be that gender, social class, age and so on) will always be tenuous as (1) it relies on the effective silencing of inner diversity. (2) While this may signal the end of striving for a fixed notion of liberation, (3) it opens up a wider range of possibilities for coalition around short-term goals...(4) Such a reformulation of social struggle offers a tangible praxis through which critical pedagogy might operate.[25]

With respect to the point made at (1), we would suggest that women can struggle as women in localized and general struggle, workers as workers, youth as youth, without silencing other identities or other aspects of their own identity. With respect to point (2), we fail to see how a recognition of multifaceted subjectivity or of the multifaceted nature of capitalist oppression and exploitation should necessarily imply the end of striving for a generalized struggle against capitalism (see, for example, Jane Kelly, chapter 10; Dave Hill, Mike Sanders and Ted Hankin in chapter 8). With respect to (3), as stated elsewhere, we recognize the importance of coalitional struggles around short-term goals, but would make the same point as in relation to point (2). And in connection with point (4), we have to ask why coalitional struggle around short-term goals is more tangible than generalized and long-term struggle. We would presume that critical pedagogy would need to link the short-term and the long-term, the local and the general, microanalysis with macroanalysis, small-scale action with national and global action. To take the example of institutional and societal racism, governments do not amend laws and reconsider policy in the face of localized outrage—at the police execution of black immigrants in New York, of black men in Cincinnati, at aboriginal deaths in custody in Australia, or at police inaction over the racist slaying of Stephen Lawrence in southeast London in 1993. But they do when the little movements join into a big/mass movement on the streets, and when the little particularistic picture is seen as part of the big picture—of racism and of societal and institutional oppression of the black working classes and of the working classes in general (see Jenny Bourne, chapter 9). Again, we argue that this (Hird's position) is essentially anti-solidaristic, pro-capitalist confusion. Again, we argue that it is one of the ways that postmodernism acts as an ideological support for national and global capital.

Alex Callinicos has described postmodernism as "the product of a socially mobile intelligentsia in a climate dominated by the retreat of the Western labor movement and the 'overconsumptionist' dynamic of capitalism in the Reagan-Thatcher era."[26] Dowling views postmodernism as "the opiate of the intelligentsia."[27] Callinicos concludes that from this perspective, "the term 'postmodern' has sought to articulate its political disillusionment and its aspiration to a consumption orientated lifestyle."[28]

The Restructuring of Capitalist States:
Postmodernism or Neoliberalism?

Current changes in education (marketization, differentiation, pseudo consumer-choice, so-called quality control data, performance and test results, a proliferation of new routes into teaching and of new types of school) might well appear to postmodernists to be a vindication and indeed manifestation of postmodern fragmentation, consumerization and heterogeneity, of the end of mass production, mass control and uniformity in education. But such developments are not free-floating. Current 'reforms' in these areas can be seen as part of the *Ideological and Repressive Juridico-Legal Apparatuses* of the state, and are rigidly bounded by strengthened central control (see Mike Apple and Geoff Whitty, chapter 4).[29] Addressing the issue of whether we live in postcapitalist societies, Geoff Whitty argues that "to regard the espousal of heterogeneity, pluralism and local narratives as indicative of a new social order may be to mistake phenomenal forms for structural relations," while David Harvey suggests it may be more appropriate to see postmodernist cultural forms and more flexible modes of capital accumulation "more as shifts in surface appearance rather than as signs of the emergence of some entirely new post-capitalist or even post-industrial society."[30]

It is important to recognize that (1) some post-Fordist developments in the organization of production and consumption have taken and are taking place; (2) the changes, while developmental, are geographically and sectorally limited and specific; (3) such changes are not fundamentally altering workers' relations to the means of production; (4) post-Fordist developments, where they exist, should be conflated neither with postcapitalism nor postmodernism; (5) postmodernist analysis can be seen to be an ideological and theoretical product of those restricted economic change sectors; (6) postmodernist analysis, with its stress on segmentation, differentiation, collective disempowerment and its telos of individuated desire, serves well the purpose of justifying and adumbrating marketized projects of capital.

To deny that we live in a postcapitalist society is not of course to refute that capitalism is a dynamic and constantly adapting mode of production. Indeed, Marx, and particularly Gramsci, were acutely aware of this fact. The 'corporatist' and 'market' strategies that were vying for position in Western Europe between the mid-1970s and the 1980s as alternatives to traditional Social Democratic and Christian Democratic consensual 'one nation' policies both demanded, in varying degrees, that the workers pay for the crisis. So, too, in Western Europe at the beginning of the twenty-first century, has 'the Third Way' of Blair (and of former U.S. President Clinton). While 'the Third Way' may not be hegemonic, both it and the more neo-Keynesian 'Old Labor'/traditional Social Democratic policies and rhetorics of the European Union states are still manifestly predicated on the capitalist market imperative.

We (1) recognize contextual, historical, social and economic differences between different capitalist economies,[31] we (2) acknowledge tensions in the wars of position within and between different class fractions and strata, and (3) accept 'significant variations,' for example, low skill, low wage, U.K., U.S. strategies and recent West German and Japanese high skill, high wage strategies.[32] We also (4) recognize historical developments of the late 1990s in Western Europe, such as the victories of interventionist traditional social democratic-type governments and policies in Germany, France and Sweden. But we do consider that these are different ways out, different strategies of responding to national and international crises of capital accumulation, different ways of 'niching' into world and regional economies. Both 'one nation' and 'two nation' strategies[33] demand that some subaltern groups, especially the working classes, have to be yanked into ideological conformity (as noted in chapter 8).[34] They require greater ideological restructuring, greater vilification and suppression of liberal and socialist opposition, and greater state control over civil society. The major break of Thatcherism and Reaganism with the formerly hegemonic 'one nation' project, the major break with the postwar social democratic consensus continues, to a considerable extent, under Blair and Bush (Junior) (as it did, in a modified form, under Clinton). On the one hand, the 'New Labour' employment, economic and social policies in Britain, for example, continue to exacerbate the growth of social class inequalities, while at the same time the government's major social policy is dedicated to combating social exclusion, through the well-funded and multi-agency Social Exclusion Unit. We do see this twin-pronged policy, however, as a 'carrot and stick' twin policy, accompanied, as it is, by the introduction of the workfare style 'New Deal' (see Hill, Sanders and Hankin in chapter 8).

Clearly, there are rhetorical, presentational and representational differences between Blair/Clinton and their predecessors. The stark differences between the brightly and multicolored and multigendered and multisexualitied Democrat 'Congressmen' as compared to the besuited, squeaky clean, whey faced, white, male appearance of their Republican opponents has important symbolic political effects. This symbolic and representational difference is mirrored, to an extent, in the differences between the Labour and Conservative M.P.s in the House of Commons elected in May 1997 and in June 2001. This is reflected in the minuscule black votes for the Republicans in 2000 in the United States, for the Conservatives in June 2001 in Britain. Clearly, too, there are some policy differences between the parties. In some aspects of policy, such as labor law and expenditure on some social and educational services, the ratchet has been turned one notch back from unmitigated neoliberalism. Yet this is a tepid response to the neoliberal tightening of the ratchet by several notches over the previous twenty years, which exalts consumption, denigrates social expenditure and conditions of work, and eschews solidarity.

Indeed, in many policy respects—such as the part-privatization of the British air traffic control, the New Labour government intention to privatize the London Underground ('the Tube') in 2001 and (at a time of foot and mouth disease) to privatize the inspection of meat slaughtering, and in the extension of private involvement, and selection and competition in schools and in further and higher education in England and Wales—New Labour has intensified neo-liberal policies. We see the promotion of individualism, consumerism and mar-ketized 'choice' as an ideological mask for a crisis in capitalism. This mask can be implicit[35] or it can be explicit, but we refute any notion that it is all part of 'the postmodern condition.' Indeed, it is one of our main contentions that post-modernism acts as an academic support system for these material and ideologi-cal developments.

The Politics of Postmodernism

As far as the possibilities for political action are concerned, for those at the postmodernism of reaction end of the continuum, there is, as we have seen, little more to do than "survive among the remnants."[36] In contrast, for those at the postmodernism of resistance end of the continuum, as we have also seen, despite the contradictions and the confusion, the subject is claimed to be capa-ble of agency.[37] The contentious issue, however, resides in just what the project of that agency consists. For postmodern feminists, for example, what should be the task of politics? Consistent with the premises of postmodern 'theory', Judith Butler has stressed the need for an "antifoundationalist approach to coalitional politics," which assumes neither that "identity is a premise nor that the shape or meaning of a coalitional assemblage can be known prior to its achievement."[38] Butler asks what "political possibilities" are

> the consequences of a radical critique of the categories of identity? What new shape of politics emerges when identity as a common ground no longer con-strains the discourse on feminist politics? And to what extent does the effort to locate a common identity as the foundation (*sic*) for a feminist politics pre-clude a radical inquiry into the political construction and regulation of iden-tity itself?[39]

In order to "denaturalize gender as such," Butler proposes "a strategy to denatu-ralize and resignify bodily categories," which she describes as "a set of parodic practices based in a performative theory of gender acts that disrupt the catego-ries of the body, sex, gender, and sexuality and occasion their subversive resig-nification and proliferation beyond the binary frame."[40] Her primary political aim, resulting from her (unexceptional) suggestion that "multiple identifications can constitute a non-hierarchical configuration of shifting and overlapping identifications that call into question the primacy of any univocal gender attri-bution" is "to make gender trouble."[41] In more detail, her text is

> an effort to think through the possibility of subverting and displacing those naturalized and reified notions of gender that support masculine hegemony and heterosexist power, to make gender trouble, not through strategies that

figure a utopian beyond, but through the mobilisation, subversive confusion, and proliferation of precisely those constitutive categories that seek to keep gender in its place by posturing as the foundational illusions of identity.[42]

However much fun this might be, we have to ask just how much difference it would make to the class nature of economic and political power relationships if the "gender parody," drag acts and widespread denaturalization of sex and gender became anti-heterosexistly coherent?[43]

To extend the parodic activity to social class behavior, we would also have to question the extent to which workers and the ruling class mimicking each other would shake the foundations of capitalism and inequality. Surrealism and other art forms performed and continue to perform similar functions, as do, for example, certain alternative comedians. However subversive these may be, they do not provide directions for change. Satirists can mock, can work with counter-hegemonic forces to destabilise. But satire does not organize. Nor does ultra-relativism, where 'anything goes.' In such a scheme of things, 'anything' can be oppressive as well as progressive.

Butler herself notes that "parody by itself is not subversive" and suggests that there must be a way to understand what makes certain kinds of parodic repetitions effectively disruptive, truly troubling. Again, we have to ask, how far does it get us in developing and involving large numbers of individuals in a political project to understand that gender "is an identity tenuously constituted in time, instituted in an exterior space through a stylized repetition of acts," or that it is "a constructed identity, a performative accomplishment."[44] In fact, transgression of (traditional) gender roles and identities is happening contemporaneously in the material realities of the labor market as more and more women return to work and 'male' work is feminized.[45] It is also happening contemporaneously, to a certain degree, in fashion, clothing, and sexual practice. It is not clear that the more widespread existence of transvestitism, transsexualism and sado-masochistic fetishism in clothing, clubbing and erotica (apparent in the heavy sales figures of *Skin Two* magazine and fetish web pages) is rocking the capitalist class at all: "Fetishism as personal practice does not bring with it change or revolution."[46] On the contrary, being massive growth industries, eroticism and pornography are, in many ways, sustaining capitalism and, of course, providing capitalists with considerable profits. Nor does it as group practice protest, such as the Spanner protest (for the decriminalization of consenting 'hard' S&M practice) and S&M Pride, or Gay Pride, mass marches and festivals. In its dominant neoliberal form, even if less so in its neoconservative form, capitalism can cope with, and profit from, sex drugs and rock'n'roll by commodifying them. The 'pink pound' and the fetish consumer market, for example, are grist to the mill of late capitalism. What it usually finds harder to deal with is solidaristic class opposition such as in industrial action (though capitalism does, at times, use industrial action for its own ends), and such as coalitional politics with a class perspective, as in the (successful) Anti-Poll Tax movement of the late 1980s and early 1990s in Britain.

Postmodernism, Social Justice and Social Change

Vociferous claims have been more recently made by leading British educational postmodernist, Elizabeth Atkinson, that postmodernism is a powerful force for social justice and social change. Addressing herself to some of the work of Jane Kelly, Peter McLaren, Glenn Rikowski and ourselves,[47] she concentrates on our claims that the greatest faults of postmodernism are that it lacks an agenda for social change and that it is incompatible with social justice. Her argument is that, "through the acceptance of uncertainty, the acknowledgement of diversity and the refusal to see concepts such as 'justice' or society as 'fixed' or as governed by unassailable truths," postmodernism, far from lacking such an agenda, is, in fact, a powerful force for social change and social justice. Atkinson is becoming one of the fiercest and most prolific British defenders of postmodernism as such a force,[48] so her arguments merit scrutiny.

Referring specifically to the concept of justice, Atkinson states that "postmodern theorists . . . invite us to consider concepts such as 'justice' as 'effects of power.'" She implies that "social justice agendas" need to be deconstructed in order to reveal "their own underlying assumptions and beliefs." No Marxist would, of course, disagree with this (something which Atkinson acknowledges).[49] The underlying assumptions and beliefs in the concept of justice, as employed by, for example, George W. Bush or Tony Blair, are very different from those employed by, say, Che Guevara or Leon Trotsky.[50]

The problem with postmodernism, however, is that whereas postmodernists engage in an endless and relatively ahistorical process of deconstruction, Marxists look to history to understand both underlying assumptions with respect to social justice and solutions to social injustice. A very basic tenet of Marxism is that from the dissolution of primitive communism to the overthrow of capitalism, there is no social contract that capitalists or their representatives will enter into with the working class, except as a result of a defeat in the class struggle or as a tactical and temporary retreat to preserve long-term interests. For example, Marx would say that no aristocracy would voluntarily reduce feudal obligations, no capitalist would reduce the length or pace of the working day, except in the face of revolt or other mass action, or to gain a short-term advantage. Allied to this, no peasantry or proletariat has accepted an economic arrangement for long without challenging it. Accordingly, improvements in the relative position of the working class cannot, for Marxists, be brought about by appeals to any universal sense of justice.[51] In addition:

> Even when such a sense exists, no appropriate consensus can be achieved as to whether the demands of justice have in fact been fulfilled. For instance, capitalists, as a class, have always insisted that a proposed reduction of the working day . . . would do immeasurable harm to workers by destroying the capitalist economy on whose existence workers' welfare depends. [52]

A second fundamental premise of Marxism is the notion that the capitalist class is a class whose interests are served by all the major institutions in society. While the role of the state in capitalist societies has been a vigorously debated issue within Marxist theory,[53] there is a consensus among Marxists that the state is a complex of institutions, rather than just central government, and that both apparatuses of the state, the ideological and the repressive[54] are not neutral, but act, to varying degrees, albeit with some disarticulations, in the interests of capitalism. For these reasons, the creation of true social justice within capitalism is, for Marxists, not viable. If, within Marxism, there is, as we have seen, some dispute about the validity and efficacy of the concept of social justice, there is no ambiguity with respect to social change. According to Atkinson, postmodernists "do not rule out the possibility of social change altogether" but postmodernism "does not have, and could not have, a single project for social justice."[55] Socialism then, if not social change, is ruled out in a stroke. Atkinson rehearses the familiar postmodern position on multiple projects: for postmodernists, because of the rejection of grand narratives, this means by necessity localized projects only,[56] and the replacement of "emancipation in a general sense" by "emancipation in a particularist sense."[57]

Despite Atkinson's claims that postmodernism views "the local as the product of the global and vice versa" and that postmodernism should not be interpreted as limiting its scope of enquiry to the local, since postmodernism rejects the metanarrative and since it rejects universal struggle, it can, by definition, concentrate only on the local. Furthermore, "as regards aims, the concern with autonomy, in terms of organization," postmodernism comprises "a tendency toward network forms, and, in terms of mentality, a tendency toward self-limitation."[58] While networking can aid in the promotion of solidarity, it cannot replace mass action. Indeed, the postmodern depiction of mass action as totalitarian negates or renders illicit such action.

Allied to its localism is postmodernism's nondualism.[59] This does have the advantage of recognizing the struggles of groups oppressed on grounds in addition to or other than those of class. This is especially true, given the fact that recent history in the noncapitalist world has been characterized by monolithic relationships between the state, the party and the people, and where, for example, lesbian and gay struggle has been suppressed (former Stalinist states, for example). However, nondualism prevents the recognition of two major dualities in capitalist societies, those of social class[60] and of gender.[61] This has, we believe, profoundly reactionary implications, in that it negates any notion of class struggle or struggles against patriarchy.

Whereas for her Marxist opponents, the possibility of postmodernism leading to social change is a non sequitur, for Atkinson, postmodernism is "an inevitable agent for change," in that "it challenges the educator, the researcher, the social activist or the politician not only to deconstruct the certainties around which they might see as standing in need of change, but also to deconstruct their own certainties as to why they hold this view."[62] This sounds fine, but what do these constituencies actually do to effect meaningful societal change once their views have been challenged? What is constructed after the deconstruction proc-

ess? Atkinson provides no answer. Deconstruction without reconstruction typifies the divorce of the academy from the reality of struggle on the ground.
Postmodernism cannot provide strategies to achieve a different social order and
hence, in buttressing capitalist exploitation, it is essentially reactionary. This is
precisely what Marxists (and others) mean by the assertion that postmodernism
serves to disempower the oppressed.[63]

Atkinson's main argument seems to be that the strength of postmodernism
is that it "comes as something of a shock" and reveals subtexts and textual silences.[64] Well, so does Marxism on both counts. The difference is that with the
former, after our shock, there is not much else to do, except at the local level.
One of the great strengths of Marxism is that it allows us to move beyond appearances and to look beneath the surface and to move forward. The *Labour
Theory of Value*, for example, represents a massive deconstruction of taken-for-
granted notions about the capitalist labor process, revealing major subtexts. It
explains most concisely why capitalism is objectively a system of exploitation,
whether the exploited realize or not, or indeed whether they care or not. It also,
however, provides a solution to this exploitation.[65] Such praxis is outside the
remit of postmodernism.

Postmodernism is clearly capable of asking questions, but, by its own ad-
mission, has no answers. As Glenn Rikowski has put it, this leads one to ask:
Just what is the postmodernist attitude to explanation?

> Truly political strategies require explanation (of what went wrong, why the
> analysis and/or tactics failed etc.) so that improvements can be made. Do
> postmodernists have a notion of improvement (of society, of political strate-
> gies)? If they do, then they need explanation. I don't think they are interested
> in either, and hence can't have a political strategy for human betterment.[66]

Marxism allows a future to be envisioned and worked—toward a democratic
socialist world. This vision can and has been extended beyond the 'brotherhood
of man' concept of early socialists, to include the complex subjectivities of all
(subjectivities which the postmodernists are so keen to bring center stage). Socialism can and should be conceived of as a project where subjective identities,
such as gender, 'race,' ability, non-exploitative sexual preference and age, are
equally valid.

Democratic socialism involves more than the rhetoric of social justice and
democracy so prevalent in the work of the postmodernists of resistance. The
fact that historically, 'socialism' has less purchase in North America than
Europe is, we consider, a reason for its North American advocates to accentuate
and develop the concept, rather than to ditch it.

We reject the arguments of academics that have espoused postmodernism
as a new emancipatory politics. Contrary to the claims and hopes of its advocates, we believe that resistance postmodernism is essentially flawed. While we
fully support and encourage the need to organize around and struggle for various equalities, we believe that there is a common enemy and that ultimately

there is a need to contest, in a united way, the horrors of global capitalism. Postmodernism negates or deflects that ultimate struggle.

Notes

1. Others have used different formulations. For an analysis, see Darryl S. L. Jarvis, "Postmodernism: A Critical Typology," *Politics and Society* 26, no.1 (March, 1998): 95–142. He cites, inter alia, 'affirmative' and 'skeptical' postmodernism—see Pauline Marie Rosenau, *Postmodernism and the Social Sciences: Insights, Inroads and Intrusions* (Princeton, N.J.: Princeton University Press, 1992)—'deconstructionist' and 'bourgeois' postmodernism—Richard Rorty, *Philosophy and the Mirror of Nature* (Princeton, N.J.: Princeton University Press, 1980)—and 'neo-conservative' and 'poststructuralist' varieties—Hal Foster, *Recordings: Art, Spectacle, Cultural Politics* (Port Townsend, Wash.: Bay Press, 1985).

2. Sharon Gewirtz, Stephen J. Ball and Richard Bowe, *Markets, Choice and Equity in Education* (Buckingham, U.K.: Open University Press, 1995); David Gillborn and Deborah Youdell, *Rationing Education: Policy, Practice, Reform and Equity* (Buckingham, U.K.: Open University Press, 2000); Geoff Whitty, Sally Power and David Halpin, *Devolution and Choice in Education: The School, the State and the Market* (Buckingham, U.K.: Open University Press, 1998); Dave Hill, "Global Capital, Neo-liberalism, and Privatization: The Growth of Educational and Economic Inequality," in *Schooling and Equality: Fact, Concept and Policy*, ed. Dave Hill and Mike Cole (London: Kogan Page, 2001).

3. Dave Hill, *Education, Education, Education: Capitalism, Socialism and the Third Way* (Brighton, U.K.: Institute for Education Policy Studies, 2001).

4. Jill Blackmore, "Breaking Out of Masculinist Politics in Education," in *Gender and Changing Education Management*, ed. B. Limerick and Bob Lingard (Rydalmere, NSW: Hodder, 1995); Hugh Lauder, David Hughes, Sietske Waslander, Martin Thrupp, Sue Watson, Ibrahim Simiya, Rob Strathdee, Ann Depuis, Jim McGlinn and Jennie Hamlin, *Trading in Futures: The Nature of Choice in Educational Markets in New Zealand* (Wellington: Victoria University of Wellington, 1995); Martin Thrupp, *Schools Making a Difference: Let's Be Realistic!* (Buckingham, U.K.: Open University Press, 1999).

5. Patti Lather, *Getting Smart: Feminist Research and Pedagogy with/in the Postmodern* (New York: Routledge, 1991), 160–161. This vortex is captured perfectly by Jean Baudrillard himself in *Baudrillard Live: Selected Interviews*, ed. Mike Gane (London: Routledge, 1993), 95, when he describes postmodernism as "a game with the vestiges of what has been destroyed," in which we must move

> as though it were a kind of circular gravity. . . . I have the impression with postmodernism that there is an attempt to rediscover a certain pleasure in the irony of things, in the game of things. Right now one can tumble into total hopelessness—all the definitions, everything, it's all been done. What can one do? What can one become? And postmodernity is the attempt—perhaps it's desperate, I don't know—to reach a point where one can live with what is left. It is more a survival among the remnants than anything else. (Laughter).

6. Lather, *Getting Smart*, 160.

7. Patti Lather, "Critical Pedagogy and Its Complicities: A Praxis of Stuck Places," *Educational Theory* 48, no. 4 (fall 1998): 487–497.

8. Lather, *Getting Smart*, 160–161.

9. See also Jane Kelly, "Postmodernism and Feminism," *International Marxist*

Review 14 (winter 1992) (Paris: Presse-Edition-Communication, 1992) and "Gender and Equality: One Hand Tied behind Us," in *Education, Equality and Human Rights; Issues of Gender, 'Race,' Sexuality, Special Needs and Social Class,* ed. Mike Cole (London: Routledge/Falmer, 2000).

10. Lather, *Getting Smart,* 112.

11. Landon E. Beyer and Daniel P. Liston, "Discourse or Moral Action? A Critique of Postmodernism," *Educational Theory* 42, no. 4 (fall 1992): 371–393.

12. Beyer and Liston, "Discourse," 380.

13. Beyer and Liston, "Discourse," 380–381.

14. J. Flax, "Postmodernism and Gender Relations in Feminist Theory," *Signs* 12 (1987): 621–643; Myra J. Hird, "Theorising Student Identity as Fragmented: Some Implications for Feminist Critical Pedagogy," *British Journal of Sociology of Education* 19, no. 4 (December 1998): 517–527; Anna Yeatman, "A Feminist Theory of Social Differentiation" in *Feminism/ Postmodernism,* ed. Linda Nicholson (New York: Routledge, 1990).

15. Mike Cole and Dave Hill, "Games of Despair and Rhetorics of Resistance: Postmodernism, Education and Reaction," *British Journal of Sociology of Education* 16, no. 2 (June 1995): 165–168, "Resistance Postmodernism: Emancipatory Politics for a New Era or Academic Chic for a Defeatist Intelligentsia?" in *Information Society: New Media, Ethics and Postmodernism,* ed. Karamjit S. Gill (London: Springer-Verlag, 1996) and "Into the Hands of Capital: The Deluge of Postmodernism and the Delusions of Resistance Postmodernism," in *Postmodernism and Educational Theory: Education and the Politics of Human Resistance,* ed. Dave Hill, Peter McLaren, Mike Cole and Glenn Rikowski (London: Tufnell Press, 1999). Also Mike Cole, Dave Hill and Glenn Rikowski, "Between Postmodernism and Nowhere: The Predicament of the Postmodernist," *British Journal of Education Studies* 45, no. 2 (1997): 187–200; Mike Cole et al., *Red Chalk: On Schooling, Capitalism and Politics,* Brighton, U.K.: Institute for Education Policy Studies, 2001).

16. Alex Callinicos, *Against Postmodernism: A Marxist Critique* (Cambridge, U.K.: Polity Press, 1989); Stephen Crook, "The End of Radical Social Theory? Notes on Radicalism, Modernism and Postmodernism" in *Postmodernism and Society,* ed. Roy Boyne and Ali Rattansi (London: Macmillan, 1990); Pat Ainley, *Class and Skill: Changing Divisions of Knowledge and Labour* (London: Cassell, 1993); Marsha Hewitt, "Illusions of Freedom: The Regressive Implications of 'Postmodernism,'" in *Real Problems, False Solutions,* ed. Ralph. Miliband and Leo Panitch (London: Merlin Press, 1993); Mary Maynard, "Feminism and the Possibilities of a Postmodern Research Practice," *British Journal of Sociology of Education* 14, no. 3 (autumn 1993): 327–331; Peter McLaren, "Revolutionary Pedagogy in Post-Revolutionary Times: Rethinking the Political Economy of Critical Education" *Educational Theory* 48, no. 4 (fall 1998) and "The Pedagogy of Che Guevara: Critical Pedagogy and Globalization Thirty Years After Che," *Cultural Circles* 3, (1998): 29–93. Also, in their pre–postmodern phase, Stanley Aronowitz and Henry Giroux, *Education under Siege: The Conservative, Liberal and Radical Debate over Schooling* (London: Routledge and Kegan Paul, 1986) and Darryl S. L. Jarvis "Postmodernism: A Critical Typology," *Politics and Society* 26, no. 1 (March 1998): 95–142.

17. Jurgen Habermas, "Modernity vs Postmodernity," *New German Critique* 2 (1981): 3–14, "Modernity—an Incomplete Project" in *The Anti-Aesthetic: Essays on Postmodern Culture,* ed. Hal Foster (Port Townsend, Wash.: Bay Press, 1983): 3–15, and *The Philosophical Discourse of Modernity* (Cambridge, Mass.: MIT Press, 1987).

18. See, for example, Madan Sarup, *Marxism Structuralism Education* (Lewes,

U.K.: Falmer Press), 101–102, 153, 157–159) and Bob Jessop, *State Theory: Putting Capitalist States in Their Place* (Cambridge, U.K.: Polity, 1990), 288–301 for a critique of the textualism of Ernesto Laclau and Chantal Mouffe. Jarvis' "Postmodernism" is concise on this, as is Peter McLaren's critique of 'ludic postmodernism' in "Multiculturalism and the Postmodernism Critique: Toward a Pedagogy of Resistance and Transformation," in *Between Borders: Pedagogy and the Politics of Cultural Studies*, ed. Henry Giroux and Peter McLaren (London: Routledge, 1994). See also Richard Hatcher and Barry Troyna, "The Policy Cycle: A Ball by Ball Account," *Journal of Education Policy* 9, no. 2 (March–April 1994): 155–170; John Evans and Dawn Penney, "The Politics of Pedagogy: Making a National Curriculum Physical Education," *Journal of Education Policy* 10, no. 1 (January–February 1994): 27–44 and Cole et al., *Red Chalk* and "Global Capital" for a critique of Foucauldian and Derridean aspects within recent work by Stephen Ball and his co-writers. Examples of this work are Stephen Ball, *Politics and Policy Making in Education: Explorations in Policy Sociology* (London: Routledge, 1990), *Education Reform: A Critical and Post-Structural Approach* (Buckingham, U.K.: Open University Press, 1994), also Richard Bowe and Stephen Ball with Ann Gold, *Reforming Education and Changing Schools* (London: Routledge, 1992) and "The Policy Process and the Processes of Policy," in *Diversity and Change: Education, Policy and Selection*, ed. John Ahier, Ben Cosin and Margaret Hales (London: Routledge, 1996). We suggest that Ball underestimates the role and power of the state, and overestimates Foucauldian notions of the dispersion of power, in particular, the power of Radical Right discourse. Ball, we argue, overestimates the relative autonomy of (education) state apparatuses—that is, the ability, power and freedom to contest and subvert the intention of government regulation and legislation. Such work, in its overconcentration on text and discourse, and on the local and contingent, renders the state too 'invisible' and power too 'dispersed,' thereby failing to acknowledge sufficiently the material power of the ruling coalition of capital. This work we have identified as 'quasi-postmodernist' in Dave Hill and Mike Cole "Marxist State Theory and State Autonomy Theory: The Case of 'Race' Education in Initial Teacher Education," *Journal of Education Policy* 10, no. 2 (1995): 221, and Dave Hill, "State Theory and the Neo-Liberal Reconstruction of Schooling and Teacher Education: A Structuralist Neo-Marxist Critique of Postmodernist, Quasi-Postmodernist, and Culturalist Neo-Marxist Theory," *British Journal of Sociology of Education* 22, no. 1 (March 2001): 141–145.

19. Lather, *Getting Smart*, xv.

20. Beyer and Liston, "Discourse," 385; Maynard, "Feminism," 330.

21. Lather, "Critical Pedagogy," 488, 490 (emphasis added).

22. Lather, "Critical Pedagogy," 495, 497, 496.

23. Lather, "Critical Pedagogy," 493, 490.

24. Patti Lather, "Critical Theory, Curricular Transformation, and Feminist Mainstreaming," *Journal of Education* 166, no. 1 (March 1984): 49–62.

25. Hird, "Theorising," 526 (the numbering 1–4 is added).

26. Callinicos, *Against Postmodernism*, 115. See also Andy Green, "Postmodernism and State Education," *Journal of Education Policy* 9, no. 1 (January–February 1994): 67–83 and Beverley Skeggs, "Postmodernism: What Is All the Fuss About?" *British Journal of Sociology of Education* 12, no. 2 (June 1991): 255–267.

27. See Lather, *Getting Smart*, 37.

28. Callinicos, *Against Postmodernism*, 115.

29. Also Dave Hill, *Something Old, Something New, Something Borrowed, Something Blue: Schooling, Teacher Education and the Radical Right in Britain and the USA* (London: Tufnell Press, 1990), "Global Capital," *Education*, "State Theory" and "The

National Curriculum, the Hidden Curriculum and Inequality in Schooling" in *Schooling and Equality: Fact, Concept and Policy*, ed. Dave Hill and Mike Cole (London: Kogan Page, 2001); David Hartley, "Confusion in Teacher Education: A Postmodern Condition?" in *International Analyses of Teacher Education*, ed. Peter Gilroy and Michael Smith (London: Carfax, 1993), 83–93; Geoff Whitty, "Education Reform and Teacher Education in England in the 1990s," in *International Analyses of Teacher Education*, ed. Peter Gilroy and Michael Smith (London: Carfax, 1993) and "Marketization, the State, and the Re-Formation of the Teaching Profession," in *Education, Culture and Economy*, ed. A. H. Halsey et al. (Oxford, U.K.: Oxford University Press, 1997); Michael W. Apple, *Official Knowledge: Democratic Education in a Conservative Age* (London: Routledge, 1994); Andy Hargreaves, "Restructuring Restructuring: Postmodernism and the Prospects for Educational Change," *Journal of Education Policy* 9, no. 1 (January–February 1994): 47–66; Cole and Hill, "Games of Despair;" Hill and Cole, "Marxist State Theory."

30. In Whitty, "Marketization," 301. David Harvey, however, is somewhat inconsistent: his endorsement of the transition to post-Fordist capitalism in *The Condition of Postmodernity* (Oxford, U.K.: Basil Blackwell, 1989), 121–197, indicates more than a mere 'surface change.'

31. Hill, *Something Old*, 1–6.

32. Phillip Brown and Hugh Lauder, "Education, Economy and Social Change," *International Studies in the Sociology of Education* 1 (1991): 3–24.

33. Jessop, *State Theory*.

34. The move away from the rhetoric that we are all part of 'one nation', to a rhetoric that accepts a notion of an undeserving, malignant and anti-social 'underclass,' which threatens the 'rest of us' (the 'two nation' project), is functional to the economic interests of the ruling class at this particular crisis in capital accumulation, since it justifies the replacement of universal benefits with targeted benefits and further justifies a reduction or withdrawal of these benefits from 'the undeserving.' This project entails the scapegoating and vilification of these 'enemies within,' unlike the 'one nation' project, which implies that 'we are all in it together.' (See Hill, "State Theory," 136).

35. See Dave Hill, *New Labor and Education: Policy, Ideology and the Third Way* (London: Tufnell Press, 1999), "Global Capital," and "Equality, Ideology and Education Policy" in *Schooling and Equality*, ed. Hill and Cole, c.f. Whitty, "Marketization."

36. In Gane, ed., *Baudrillard Live*, 95.

37. Lather, *Getting Smart*, 160. See also Stanley Aronowitz and Henry Giroux, *Postmodern Education: Politics, Culture and Social Criticism* (Minneapolis: University of Minnesota Press, 1991); Henry Giroux, *Border Crossings* (London: Routledge, 1992); Peter McLaren, "Multiculturalism and the Postmodernism Critique: Toward a Pedagogy of Resistance and Transformation" in *Between Borders: Pedagogy and the Politics of Cultural Studies*, ed. Henry Giroux and Peter McLaren (London: Routledge, 1994).

38. Judith Butler, *Gender Trouble: Gender and the Subversion of Identity* (London: Routledge, 1990), 15, and "Merely Cultural," *New Left Review* 227 (1998): 33–44.

39. Butler, *Gender Trouble*, xi.

40. Butler, *Gender Trouble*, 149, xii.

41. Butler, *Gender Trouble*, 66, 34.

42. Butler, *Gender Trouble*, 34.

43. Butler, *Gender Trouble*, 138.

44. Butler, *Gender Trouble*, 139, 140–141.

45. Kelly, "Postmodernism and Feminism," "Gender and Equality;" Ainley, *Class*

and Skill; Kate Hirom, "Gender" in Cole and Hill, eds., *Schooling and Equality.*

46. Linda Gamman and Merrja Makinen, *Female Fetishism* (New York: New York University Press, 1994), 221.

47. Cole and Hill, "Games of Despair;" Cole et al., "Between Postmodernism and Nowhere;" Dave Hill, Peter McLaren, Mike Cole and Glenn Rikowski, eds., *Postmodernism in Educational Theory: Education and the Politics of Human Resistance* (London: Tufnell Press, 1999); Kelly, "Postmodernism and Feminism."

48. See Elizabeth Atkinson, "The Responsible Anarchist: Postmodernism and Social Change," (paper presented to British Educational Research Association Conference 2000, University of Cardiff, Wales, September, 7–9). For her full argument, see Elizabeth Atkinson, "What Can Postmodern Thinking Do for Educational Research?" (paper presented at the Annual Conference of the American Educational Research Association, New Orleans, April 2000); "The Promise of Uncertainty: Education, Postmodernism and the Politics of Possibility," *International Studies in Sociology of Education* 10, no. 1 (2000); "In Defence of Ideas, or Why 'What Works' Is Not Enough," *British Journal of Sociology of Education* 21 (September 2000); "Behind the Enquiring Mind: Exploring the Transition from External to Internal Enquiry," *Reflective Practice* 1, no. 2 (2000); "The National Literacy Strategy as Cultural Performance: Some Reflections on the Meaning(s) of Literacy in English Primary Classrooms" (paper presented at the Joint Meeting of the European Council for Educational Research and the Scottish Educational Research Association, Edinburgh, September 2000); "Critical Dissonance and Critical Schizophrenia: The Struggle between Policy Delivery and Policy Critique," *Research Intelligence*, no. 73 (November 2000):14–17; "Deconstructing Boundaries: Out on the Inside?" *International Journal of Qualitative Studies in Education* 14, no. 3 (May–June 2001).

49. Atkinson, "Responsible Anarchist," 5, 49.

50. It is necessary to point out at this stage that whether or not Marx had a theory of justice has been an issue of great controversy and has generated an enormous literature, particularly among North American philosophers. Norman Geras, for example, has a whole page of footnotes citing writings by those for and against the notion that Marx criticized capitalism as unjust (see Geras, "The Controversy about Marx and Justice" in *Marxist Theory*, edited by Alex Callinicos, on pages 212–213). The crux of the matter is that, as Callinicos has put it, on some occasions Marx eschews ethical judgements, and, on others, apparently makes them (in Callinicos, ed., *Marxist Theory*, 13). This was because he was confused about justice, as G. A. Cohen states in "A Review of A. W. Wood, Karl Marx," *Mind* 92 (1983): 444, or, to put it another way, "Marx did think capitalism was unjust but he did not think he thought so." See Geras, "Controversy," 245; Alex Callinicos, *Equality* (Cambridge, U.K.: Polity, 2000).

51. Richard Miller, "Rawls and Marxism" in *Reading Rawls: Critical Studies on Rawls' 'A Theory of Justice,'* ed. N. Daniels (Palo Alto, Calif.: Stanford University Press, 1989), 209–210.

52. Miller, "Rawls," 210. This is reminiscent of the argument of the British Conservative Party prior to the 1997 general election that adopting the European minimum wage in Britain would ultimately be detrimental to workers' interests. The general Marxist position advanced does not preclude the fact that social democrats and socialists in capitalist parliaments are, at times, able to force issues that are in workers' interests, the European minimum wage being one such example. In addition, there have, of course, been rare historical exceptions among the ruling class—philanthropic capitalists, for example.

53. For an overview, see Jessop, "State Theory." For a brief summary, see Mike

Cole, "Racism, History and Educational Policy: From the Origins of the Welfare State to the Rise of the Radical Right" (unpublished Ph.D. thesis, University of Essex, U.K.: 1992), 33–35; Hill and Cole, "Marxist State Theory;" Hill, "State Theory, Neoliberal Reconstruction."

54. Louis Althusser, *Lenin and Philosophy and Other Essays* (London: New Left Books, 1971), 121–173.

55. Atkinson, "Responsible Anarchist," 5a.

56. For example, Flax, "Postmodernism, Gender Relations;" Yeatman, "A Feminist Theory;" Hird, "Theorising."

57. Jan Nederveen Pieterse, *Emancipations, Modern and Postmodern* (London: Sage, 1992).

58. Atkinson, "Responsible Anarchist," 17; Nederveen Pieterse, *Emancipations.*

59. For example, Lather, *Getting Smart,* "Critical Pedagogy;" also Patti Lather, "Ten Years Later, Yet Again: Critical Pedagogy and Its Complicities," in *Feminist Engagements:Rreading, Resisting and Revisioning Male Theorists in Education and Cultural Studies,* ed. Kathleen Weiler (London: Routledge, 2001); Gert Biesta, "Say You Want A Revolution . . . Suggestions for the Impossible Future of Critical Pedagogy," *Educational Theory* 48, no. 4 (fall 1998): 499–510; Atkinson, "Promise of Uncertainty" and "Responsible Anarchist."

60. See also Cole and Hill, "Games of Despair," 166–168.

61. See also Kelly, "Postmodernism and Feminism" and "Gender and Equality."

62. Atkinson, "Responsible Anarchist," 5–6a.

63. On our trip to South Africa in 1995, one of us (Mike Cole) was asked to present a Marxist critique of postmodernism at a seminar attended by some leading (South African) postmodernists. Having spent considerable time in the townships and squatter camps, he asked what postmodernists could do for their inhabitants. This was met with stony silence.

64. Atkinson, "Responsible Anarchist," 10a, 12.

65. Dave Hill and Mike Cole, "Social Class" in *Schooling and Equality: Fact, Concept and Policy,* ed. Dave Hill and Mike Cole (London: Kogan Page, 2001).

66. Glenn Rikowski, verbal comment on this chapter (2001).

Part III

Human Resistance against Postmodernism

Chapter 6

Education, Capital and the Transhuman

Glenn Rikowski

There is . . . no need to search for alien intelligent life since it is already deep within us.[1]

Capital is presented as if it were an extra-human thing and labor a human thing, rather than labor as an extra-human thing and capital as what humans are . . . [For] . . . in a society dominated by money, *I am money.* I am an embodied manifestation of money in all its contradictory manifestations.[2]

Prelude

The development of capitalism coincides with the capitalization of humanity. Humans increasingly become something 'Other' than human; a new life-form, a 'new species.'[3] This is because capital is a progressive movement toward totality, and its development on this basis "consists precisely in subordinating all elements of society to itself," for "this is historically how it becomes a totality." This includes the 'human;' with the deepening of capitalist social relations, and hence capital as a social force, we evolve into a new life-form: human-capital. As capital globalizes, integrates and flows with increasing speeds and strength into its constantly expanding universe, then what was our 'humanity' becomes increasingly primordial and distant. There is no 'essence' of the human to 'recover,' and 'going back to where we once belonged' is impossible and unsustainable; our 'needs' have been redefined and integrated into the expansion of capital throughout the social universe.[4] As the capitalization of humanity deepens and strengthens, we become a life-form that increasingly incorporates the *contradictions* of capital. Capital assumes a number of *forms*—value, money, commodity, state and other forms. The capitalization of humanity implies that, as capital, these forms take on real existence within us and within our everyday lives as human-capital. Furthermore, as this process gathers pace, there is increasingly no 'individual' or 'society' duality, no 'outside' or 'inside' and no 'beyond' the realm of capital: capital progressively and exponentially becomes *all that there is*.

Our form of life changes too. We become a life-form invaded by an 'alien' force that is variegated, riven and contradictory in its motions, effects and outcomes. And our mode of existence is expressed increasingly through capital as a set of *living contradictions*. Our lives—our whole mode of existence—therefore, increasingly spin(s) out of control through successive generations as the force of capital within us gains strength; we progressively come to live, drink, sleep and exist through the contradictions of ourselves as capitalized life-form. In this historical process, capital starts out as the 'horror within,' the 'alien force;' but as it gathers hold *it is the human element* that is marginalized. Erasure of the 'human' exists as possibility in this historical development as each new generation is faced with ever stronger processes (expressed in institutional and organizational forms) of capitalization.

It follows then, that with the development of capital toward totality, the *becoming* of capital,[5] human-capital comes to take on an increasingly *real existence* as new life-form. Thus, as we increasingly become less 'human' and take on the existence of capital, we are also increasingly subjected to the *contradictions* of capital, living our lives through it as a series of contradictions. Our lives really do have less *coherence*, less 'meaning,' as we are torn between competing drives and subject to conflicting forces—within and beyond our reconfigured personhoods—on a progressive scale. In this way, however, capital *uncovers* and *reveals* itself as social force within our lives. The stronger capital becomes within us, and as capitalist social relations (and capital as social force flowing through these relations) expand toward totality—then the *speed of life*[6] increases. In the process, our lives become more fractured, battered and pressurized, even though the productive forces are ever more capable of wealth production.

The range of contradictions within human-capital as life-form, expressed through and manifested within 'everyday life,' are further compounded and extended upon the basis of *labor against capital*.[7] As laborers (potential, actual, future) we are forced, by our relation to capital, to become antagonistic toward it and its personal representatives (capitalists and functionaries of capital). Our needs derived from labor are oppositional to our constitution as capital. We labor against capital (as well as within it), and are consequently divided *within* ourselves and between ourselves, on this basis. Furthermore, our needs, desires and aspirations *as labor* continually clash with the drives of capital as social force, even though these are *constituted* by the capital relation. Hence, as labor, we are divided *within* and against ourselves as *capital*.[8] The class struggle, therefore, is not just 'out there'—on picket lines, demonstrations and other forms of confrontation—but is everywhere, including *within* human-capital as life-form constituted *by* capital.

Main street postmodernists have grasped all this, though they play out this drama at the level of 'discourse,' language and the indeterminacy of 'meaning.' The 'de-centered self' of postmodernist folklore mirrors our lives and personhoods fractured by capital, while we are simultaneously subject to, and *centered by*, capital. The key point, however, is that the increasing and deepening colonization of the 'human' by capital is becoming more susceptible to analysis as its 'obviousness' is exposed *by its own developing intensity*. Hence, the less 'human' we become, then, paradoxically, the greater is the potential for starting to grasp our real predicament. Our capacity for *awareness* of our situation as capitalized life-form *increases* as our 'humanity' is left behind. The process of capitalization of humanity includes our 'consciousness' too; our sentient powers of thought, reflection, deliberation and capacity for 'reflexivity' (much beloved by some postmodern and liberal Left thinkers) are also incorporated within capital.

It appears, then, that we 'become' the machine; we progressively become subordinated by, and incorporated within, capital in *all* respects.[9] It further appears that capital, as developing totality, as enveloping force, constructs the social universe in its own image. And this includes us as *individuals*, as nodes within the totality of social forces and relations. As Karl Marx notes: "The individual *is the social being*";[10] there is no 'society' in abstraction from 'individuals.'

However, as a 'new species' our consciousness does indeed become subordinated, *but is always open* and never *entirely determined*. This is because our fragmented existences and contradictory lives force us to think through, to live and to work through, the contradictions, tensions, dilemmas and *conflicts* generated by capital as a conglomeration of contradictory drives and forces. As capitalized life-forms we cannot avoid this: *capital forces us to think and live its contradictions*. When we think these contradictions, as and through ourselves as capital, it is only then that *capital reflects itself as consciousness of itself* in the forms that it has invaded and incorporated the human. It is through this process that capital exposes and uncovers itself within us *as it thinks itself through us*. At this moment, it reveals its weaknesses. Hence, another paradox is that the more we think *as capital*, the more clearly we can view 'its' (which are simultaneously 'our' own) problems and pathologies, and our capacity to think as capital *increases historically* as we progressively become capital. Marx was able to think from the 'standpoint of capital,' and to articulate its contradictions and unfolding, only because he *was capital*, capital thinking itself. Today, we can think as capital more easily than Marx could in his day—as our incorporation and subordination by capital has deepened through its historical development since Marx's death.

As our thought, action and practices are driven on by the need to seek 'solutions' to the lived tensions arising from ourselves as capitalized life-forms, there comes a point, for Marx, when these pressures build up to such an extent, and the effort to think through (nonexistent) solutions becomes so great that the *dissolution* of these tensions and contradictions asserts itself as the only real solution. For Marx, possibilities for this response to lives lived increasingly through and as capital expand with the historical development of capitalism. The historical drive toward communist thought, practice, organization and *praxis* is *immanent* within the unfolding of capital itself, and takes on increasing significance as human possession by capital deepens. The becoming of capital opens up possibilities for us to *think communism* and to put communist thought into action. Communism is grounded historically in "its thinking consciousness, the *comprehended* and *known* process of its *becoming*."[11] The greatest paradox perhaps, is that to the extent that we *are* capital, we are capable of *thinking* communism—and dissolving capital through *praxis* and thence to give ourselves, as post-human, and *post-capitalist* life-forms, an alternative, and *open*, future.

Marx's *Capital* can be viewed as an articulation of the horror of capital, as social life made horrific by capital. We labor for, we exist as, and we are capital.[12] Through our own labor, we create an "animated monster,"[13] a social force which then comes to dominate us.[14]

This chapter aims to expand awareness of our contemporary situation vis-à-vis capital through expressing the capitalization of humanity, ourselves as capital, 'human capital' as the flip-side of labor-power. Secondly, it shows where education and training—through the social production of labor-power—enter into processes of the capitalization of humanity. Thirdly, the chapter shows how theories of the post/trans-human typically become encumbered with some old problems—such as technological determinism, teleology and romanticism—in the absence of any explanatory and dynamic framework, which the chapter will start to develop. The key difference between the analysis presented here and postmodern post/trans-human positions is that the analysis argues that the 'transhuman' is an effect of the development of capital (not something which has only just arrived, or will arrive in the future); the postmodern positions tend to take technology (forcibly abstracted from social relations) as the germ of the transhuman.

The first section provides a brief outline of some of the problems associated with postmodernized versions of contemporary and futurized human-technology relations. The following five sections make the difficult arguments involved in exploring and explaining how we become, and in what sense, we are capital. These arguments rest upon an examination of labor-power, that abominable commodity on which the whole capitalist system rests. Elsewhere, I have indicated the importance of labor-power as the starting point for rebuilding and re-energizing Marxist educational theory.[15] These sections can be viewed as some opening shots in the *repositioning* of Marxist educational theory onto the ground of a labor-power theory that articulates the social production of labor-power in capitalism. The conclusion pulls the various strands of the chapter together and points toward the significance of critical pedagogy as one of the prerequisites for emancipation from the social domination of capital.

The Post/Trans-human

Postmodernism is an excessive intellectual phenomenon. In its de(con)structive frenzy—with the brakes off—postmodern theory runs into one or more of the dead ends of relativism, nihilism, solipsism and despair. It then occasionally splatters out into false hopes, nostalgia, romanticism or (typically vague) visions of 'new politics,' as shown in 1996 by Nigel Blake in his article "Between Postmodernism and Anti-modernism."[16] Pointing all this out (as we subsequently did in "Between Postmodernism and Nowhere,")[17] yields predictable indignation (as in Blake's "A Postmodernism Worth Bothering About: A Rejoinder to Cole, Hill and Rikowski.")[18] Postmodern excess leads to de-centered selves, shattered metanarratives and the capacity for judgment frozen (through trepidation brought on by the abnegation of 'truth' and 'knowledge' engendered by a corrosive skepticism)—with terrible consequences for stirring up any worthwhile 'politics.' Mimi Ormer, Janet Miller and Elizabeth Ellsworth show that one way of attempting to 'justify' this excess is by arguing that it is a symptom of repression;[19] excessiveness—in social and educational theory, or any other sphere of social life—is that "which exceeds the *norms* proposed as *proper* and *natural* by those with social control." Hence, "excessiveness" is:

> meaning out of control, meaning that exceeds the norms of ideological control or the requirements of any specific text. Excess is overflowing semiosis, the excessive sign performs the work of the dominant ideology, but then exceeds and overspills it, leaving excess meaning that escapes ideological control and is free to be used to resist or evade it. . . . Norms that are exceeded lose their invisibility, lose their status as natural common sense and are brought out into the open.[20]

But when meaning is really out of control, the spinners of 'discourse' seek to detach it from specific aspects of social reality which are never lost absolutely; meaning appears to 'escape,' but rather enters a trajectory on which it *never escapes beyond* (the universe of capital) and morphs into idealist form.[21] David Harvey pinpoints an effect of postmodernist excess that is the opposite to the one charted by Ormer, Miller and Ellsworth. He argues that the loss of confidence in "previously established categories,"[22] brought about by postmodernist and poststructuralist theory, has resulted in the re-location of theory onto the terrain of the body. With all referents destabilized, there "still remains one referent apart from all the other destabilized referents, whose presence cannot be denied, and that is the body referent, our very own lived body."[23] The problem with this, argues Harvey, is that the body—"as the measure of all things"—has also been de-stabilized through the writings of the post-human theorists.

For example, Robert Pepperell and Max More argue that post-human persons of the future will "overcome the biological, neurological, and psychological constraints evolved into humans." Post-humans are posited as beings of "unprecedented physical, intellectual, and psychological ability, self-programming and self-defining, potentially immortal, unlimited individuals." Thus, not only is 'the body' in question but the 'human' is too. The development of post-human life-forms can be viewed as the *practical deconstruction* of the 'human' body, which parallels the text-mediated deconstruction of postmodern theory. In the post-human future, the cyborg (fused and hybrid human-machine entity) stalks planet Earth. The "transhuman" is active engagement with such a future, for:

> We are transhuman to the extent that we *seek* to become post-human and take action to prepare for a posthuman future. This involves learning about and making use of new technologies that can increase our capacities and life expectancy, questioning common assumptions, and transforming ourselves ready for the future.

The "transhuman," for More, then, is a "politics of the post-human"; humans actively striving to *become* post-humans. It is a politics of "rising above outmoded human beliefs and behaviours."[24] In *Viroid Life*, however, Keith Ansell-Pearson attempts to establish the "transhuman condition" as supersession of the 'human.' Here, the "transhuman" is viewed similarly to Max More's post-human condition, and as constituting an entity (situated within a techno-social habitat) that is decidedly beyond the 'human.' For Ansell-Pearson, the transhuman condition can be understood as the "human as a site of contamination by alien forces." Virtual reality machines, genetic and biochemical engineering, performance-enhancing drugs and advanced human-computer/machine interaction and symbiosis constitute the collective "alien within." Ansell-Pearson dramatizes his prognosis for a transhuman future by talking in terms of "alien abduction" by the collective powers of the techno-biochemical invasive forces. While signaling that he does not wish to reduce the "transhuman" to crass empirical developments, which herald a "biological" or "technological" condition for humanity, he also makes the point that the "transhuman" should not be conceived as a "paranoid and phobic anthropocentrism that is bent on imperialistically and entropically colonizing the entire known and unknown universe, for the sake of immortal life."[25] Yet in stating that *Viroid Life* is about the "future of the human" and that he wishes to avoid writing teleologically regarding human development, Ansell-Pearson sets himself a tall order. In the event, he tends to lapse into teleology and forms of technological determinism (these criticisms of his heroic efforts to *say* something about the "future of the human" are expounded elsewhere).[26] Yet his work draws attention to several of the pitfalls and dangers lurking within post/transhuman theories.

These include a number of weaknesses, critical aporias and manic vistas embedded within post/trans-human discourses. First, the concept of '*post-human*' appears to be premised upon some naturalistic conception of the 'human,' which implies an unwarranted essentialism. Of course, different conceptions of the human subject have been proposed down the centuries (as charted by Brian Morris),[27] and ideas of human nature have changed substantially throughout history, from Plato to Wittgenstein and beyond,[28] but the post-human points toward a fundamental surpassing of the 'human.' As 'humans' are technologized, invaded, taken over, shaped and molded by biochemical manipulation, computer-tech implants and human-computer interaction, then they *become something else*—post-human. However, unless the 'human' has been fixed beforehand—perhaps resting on some biological or genetic bottom-line—then the post-human theorists are never ever in a position to say whether the *post-* has really arrived, that the 'human' is history. Hence, an assessment of the actuality of surpassing logically rests upon essentializing the 'human.'

A second danger within some discourses on the post/trans-human, as Ansell-Pearson notes, is that they can induce a kind of romanticism; revulsion in the face of our Fate as cyborgs, 'humans without organs' or some sci-fi fusion of brain, flesh and hyper-technology, can engender a yearning to reclaim our 'humanity' and our mastery over all the new technologies *as humans*. The problem here is that as 'the human' evolves through technologization of persons, then we increasingly lose our capacity to realize the myth of a 'Golden Age of Humanity.' Backward-looking authoritarian political structures could be organized in order to spawn a phase of state- and extra-state global Luddism. But this involves putting a limit to what we can become, as well as calling forth repression on a monumental scale and sowing seeds that may evolve into a Fascism fired by an attempt to freeze history. The major weakness of the romantic position is that as the concept of 'the human' is so contested and open (as, argues Ansell-Pearson, is the future of the human),[29] then there can be no sure resting place for the species.

The third problem results from attempting to solve the previous two. Say, as in Michael Crichton's *The Lost World* (the 1995 sequel to his *Jurassic Park of 1991*),[30] that *something survives* in the evolution of the 'human'; that 'the human' is literally the chain of development from *homo sapiens* to what it eventually becomes, and onwards. The 'human' as an eternalized form of transhumanity, in whatever form the future 'humans'—as represented by this evolutionary chain—survive. On this basis, though, we are amoebae (as amoebae became human), or even the primordial slime from whence they emerged. Worse, this perspective enlists the anthropomorphism where human-species immortality is guaranteed at the cost of sacrificing the universe to this development. This only makes sense, argues Ansell-Pearson, if 'the human' is placed at the center of the universe (one more time) by fiat, whereas "it is necessary to free the logic of life from anthropocentric naivete and blindness."[31]

Fourth, and finally, many of the cyber-eulogies to human-machine fusion rest on technological determinist foundations. Paul Virilio, for example, views the concept of the 'transhuman' as a form of post-Darwinism. In an age, and for a future, of human-machine integration, symbiosis and fusion, it is artificial (not natural) selection that will determine survival of types. Although there is some latitude for shaping a future from this starting point, nevertheless this perspective rests upon a technological determinism allied to an eternalization of the rule of capital.[32] Technology and biochemical inventions, innovations and products invade human bodies for consumption (or consumption aids), or for enhancing the productivity of labor. These technological developments, abstracted from capitalist social relations and the structuring elements of capitalist society (value, commodity, labor-power, abstract labor, capital),[33] form the backdrop to the most horrific of vistas and science fiction nightmares. The machine preys upon humanity, which heralds the end of (human) history, accompanied by new Luddite calls to 'control the machine.' Post/trans-human theorists who terrorize today's humanity with prognoses of genetically designed bodies, microchips in the brain and the rest, typically lack an explanatory dynamic which underpins such developments and projections. If free-floating technology were a reality, if it really had a 'life of its own,' then it would not be the powerful enemy it appears for those fearful of the future for 'the human.' Its externality to humans heralds our ability to halt its entry into our bodies, which at least opens up the possibilities for terminating its menace. But technology is an expression of capitalist social relations, and these cannot just be sent to the breaker's yard; they require fundamental forms of social destruction.

Following from this, the real challenge is not to pinpoint weaknesses within post/trans-human positions, but to show how it is *capital* that is the 'alien within.' We are extra-human as we are capital.[34] This is the deep possession (with no outward signs) which is our reality. In starting to express this reality, the argument turns toward that most abominable of commodities: labor-power.

Labor-Power: Fuel for the 'Living Fire'

"Labor is the living, form-giving fire; it is the transitoriness of things, their temporality, as their formation by living time."[35] It well known that Marx begins his analysis of capital and critique of political economy by considering the commodity. Capitalist wealth "presents itself as an immense accumulation of commodities," which *in toto* comprise a single commodity.[36] For Marx, the commodity was the "economic cell-form"[37] of capitalist society. It incorporated the basic structuring elements of this social formation: value, use-value and exchange-value posited on the basis of abstract labor as measured by labor time.[38] The commodity was a perfect starting point for analysis as it was the condensed "general form of the product" in capitalist society,[39] the "most elementary form of bourgeois wealth"[40] and hence the "formation and premiss of capitalist production."[41] Commodities were also "the *first result* of the immediate process of capitalist production, its product."[42]

What is less well known is that Marx held that there were "two great classes" of commodities: labor-power and "commodities as distinct from labor-power itself," or "commodities themselves."[43] While the "two great classes" of commodities had certain similarities, they also differed in two key respects.

First, the similarities. For Marx, in relation to "commodities themselves" (i.e., excluding labor-power) productive labor is labor exchanged against capital, labor which "produces commodities, material products, whose production has cost a definite quantity of labor or labor-time."[44] Two points are required for understanding here, notes Marx. The first is that it is not the case that these commodities had to be literally "material" products, such as bricks or sugar, for:

> When we speak of the commodity as a materialisation of labour—in the sense of its exchange-value—this is only an imaginary, that is to say, a purely *social mode* of existence of the commodity *which has nothing to do with its corporeal reality*; it is conceived as a definite quantity of social labour or of money.[45]

Marx chides Adam Smith for holding that productive labor only referred to "hard" products; those products occupying physical space for a duration and detectable by the senses. Yet, argued Marx, the production of value (and surplus-value) did not depend on this base empiricism, and, in turn, whether the labor engaged was un/productive. What was important was that unpaid labor time resulted in (and took the form of) surplus-value, and this could include examples where the product was synonymous with the labor performed (as in the case of drama performances), or in those cases where there were no physical changes in the product themselves (as in the transportation of products).[46] Another point of similarity occurs when, having fixed productive labor in terms of the "general class of commodities," Marx goes on to argue that it also refers to "such labor as produces commodities or directly produces, trains, develops, maintains or reproduces labor-power itself."[47] The social production of labor-power is also a form of productive labor, for Marx.[48] In summary, labor-power is a commodity "neither more nor less than sugar."[49]

Turning now to the differences between "general commodities" and labor-power, the first difference flows from Marx's definition of "general commodities." The "commodity is, first of all, an external object, a thing which through its qualities satisfies human needs of whatever kind."[50] Also, "a *commodity*—as distinguished from labor-power itself—is a material thing confronting man, a thing of a certain utility, in which a definite quantity of labor is fixed or materialized."[51] Labor-power, however, does "not exist apart from him [the laborer] at all,"[52] it is not an *external object* (to the person). This observation inclines Marx to make the distinction between "general commodities" and labor-power, and he notes the "uniqueness" of labor-power in this respect.[53] The second crucial difference between the class of "general commodities" and labor-power is that the latter—incorporated within the person of the laborer—is an aspect of a conscious, sentient and living being. Labor-power is incorporated within personhood (unlike commodities such as bricks) and is under the sway of a potentially hostile will internal to itself (unlike sugar). Thus, internality and consciousness differentiate labor-power from "general commodities."

These two key differences determine the need for a separate, but complementary (i.e., still based on the value-form of labor), analysis of labor-power, to go along with Marx's analysis of the "general commodity" in *Capital*. Marx did not provide such an analysis. Labor-power largely figures in Marx's work when he explores the value of labor-power in relation to the production of value and surplus-value, on the ground of "general commodities." Indeed, in the second volume of *Capital*, Marx explained that in the first two volumes he had assumed that labor-power is "always on hand."[54] Hence, there was no need to provide an account of how labor-power was socially produced through education and training. This was reasonable since, at the time Marx was writing, what I will later outline as the 'social production of labor-power in capitalism,' did not exist in a clear form. The rise of mass state education unfolded this form of production, education as production.[55]

It is important to acknowledge some key features of this weird, living commodity: labor-power. First, to expand upon a point made earlier, the "basis for the development of capitalist production" is that "*labor-power*, as the commodity belonging to the workers, confronts the conditions of labor as commodities maintained in the form of capital and existing independently of the workers."[56] Although labor-power is bought (by the capitalist) and sold (by the worker) beyond the process of production "it yet forms the absolute foundation of capitalist production and it is an integral moment within it," for "money cannot become capital [in the exchange movement M-C-M] unless it is exchanged for labor-power."[57] Labor-power is that commodity "whose *use-value* possesses the peculiar property of being a *source of value*," and being a source of "more value than it has itself," surplus-value.[58]

Secondly, although labor-power is a commodity,[59] it only exists as a commodity within the labor market or, more accurately, the market in labor-power.[60] Both "general commodities" and labor-power exist as commodities "only on the market." At the level of the market, labor-power exists "only in potentiality," as a "capacity"—the "capacity to labor."[61] Marx notes that one of the chief failings of classical political economy was that it confused the sale of labor-power with its purchase and "absorption in the labor process."[62] As will become clear, this point is not only crucial for an understanding of labor-power but also for grasping the transformation of labor-power into capital *and vice versa*. In selling herself, the worker sells her abilities and talents[63] as the basis of a capacity for value-creation. The use-value entailed in the sale of labor-power "exists only as an ability, a capacity of his [the worker's] bodily existence," and the worker sells a "temporary disposition over his laboring capacity."[64]

Thirdly, just because the laborer sells his laboring capacity as a commodity in exchange for a wage does not make him a capitalist, argues Marx. This is the case for a number of reasons. Labor-power "is a *commodity* in the hands of the workers and *not capital*" and only "becomes capital"—is transformed into, and realized as capital—"when in the hands of the capitalist, to whom falls its temporary use."[65] This is because to become capital, labor-power has first to be transformed into labor in the labor process, and the resulting value produced must exceed that as represented in the wage; that is, emerge as surplus-value. Surplus-value is the lifeblood of capital. It is the basis of subsequent production cycles and of profit. These considerations point toward a process of labor-power *becoming* capital, through labor in the labor process resulting in surplus-value. Thus, although laborers sell their labor-powers as commodities, there is no guarantee that their labor will result in surplus-value, and hence labor-power is bought by representatives of capital as a *variable* commodity; workers will work more or less hard, effectively or productively. The capitalist does not pay for labor but "only for labour capacity."[66] The basis of capital is that workers are so organized, disciplined, skilled and so on, in order to labor sufficiently for capitalists and make their labor productive; that is, as labor which produces surplus-value. Hence, when capitalists shell out on labor-power through wages, the money represents *variable capital*, so that "During the labour process, the capitalist has the variable capital in his hands as *self-activating*, value-creating labour-power, but not as value of a given magnitude."[67] And the magnitude of real import is reached when surplus-value arises from the transformation of labor-power into labor and into "general commodities," which incorporate value and finally surplus-value. At the end of the process surplus-value is appropriated by representatives of capital, and this is another reason why it is erroneous to view workers as capitalists just because they sell labor-power as their commodity. They sell their commodity (labor-power) for wages (which represents the value necessary to maintain and reproduce them as workers), but they *create* capital in the form of surplus-value (in the labor process), value over-and-above that represented in the wage.

Fourthly, once workers sell their labor-powers and enter the capitalist labor process these labor-powers are transformed from commodities with the *potential* for value-creation into a real, active *force*. Labor-power is transformed from a capacity into a force which really "exists in [the worker's] vitality."[68] Labor-power as "value-creating force" and as active "force-expenditure"[69] within the labor process, attains social reality and is realized as *social* force; as collectivity of labor-powers integrated through division of labor. Throughout his mature corpus, Marx reiterates that, as social force, labor-power "exists only as a power"[70] within the labor process. He explains at a number of points that it is crucial to grasp the difference between the sale and purchase of labor-power (as commodity, potentiality and capacity for labor) and its actual consumption within the labor process (as value-creating power and as social force for value-production).[71] Its consumption (as human energy and force) as use-value for capital within the labor process is simultaneously (through the application of this force, this power, within the immediate process of production) a process of value-creation, flowing into (through surplus-value) the formation of capital. However, what follows from this is that labor-power preserves "its property of producing value only so long as it is employed and materialized in the labour process."[72] It 'comes alive' as active value-creating force only when consumed by capital in the labor process. This is an aspect of the 'tragedy of labor' in capitalism, as the active and creative powers incorporated as labor-power within sentient human beings are expressed as labor in a form—the value-form—that breathes life into a force that comes to dominate the laborers: capital.[73]

The notion of labor-power as social force that exists within individuals as the life-force, or vitality, of individual laborers, underpins Marx's conception of labor-power as "the aggregate of those mental and physical capabilities existing in a human being, which he exercises whenever he produces a use-value of any description."[74] Hence, the life-force of individuals as labor-power is expressed through, and as, those "mental and physical capabilities" activated by the laborer when producing use-values, which, within the capitalist labor process, is also value. The capitalist labor process is also valorization process. Labor-power, as noted previously, "becomes a reality only when it has been solicited by capital, is set in motion"[75]—that is, it exists only through its transformation into labor within the labor process.

However, there is also a process of inversion, where capital—as social force created by the transformation of labor-power into value-creating labor—is incorporated within the laborer through labor-power development within the labor-process. Thus, although labor-power is "fuel for the living fire" (labor), it can also be viewed as a particular *form* of fuel for a historically specific *form* of labor; the value-form of labor—which, in turn, is grounded upon capital as emergent form and result. Showing this also opens a window on the processes through which we become extra-human, humans capitalized. The next section approaches this result.

Labor-Power into Labor: Transformation, Sacrifice and Loss

On the perspective of the previous section, labor-power is transformed into labor within the labor process when the laborer enters this domain, this lair of capital. Labor-power is activated by the laborer organizing her mental and physical capabilities (by acts of will) into a coherent force, which sets her labor in motion in conjunction with instruments of labor or machines and raw materials (where applicable), to produce commodities which incorporate value and surplus-value. Labor is the "temporary manifestation" of labor-power,[76] and can be viewed as the "activity of labour-power," labor-power expressed "in action."[77] Labor-power flits in and out of existence as it is activated by the will of the laborer within the labor process. It "becomes a reality only through its exercise" and "it sets itself in motion only by working." On the market, it is mere capacity, potential. Value-production rests on the transformation of labor-power into labor, and the capitalist pays for labor-power as owned by the worker when it has "taken effect" and "materialized itself in a product."[78] The transformation of labor-power into labor is simultaneously an active process of self-transformation on the part of the worker and an act of production (of commodities which incorporate value). Hence, labor-power is *"self-activating capacity*, a labour-power *that expresses itself* purposively by converting the means of production into the material objects of its activity, *transforming* them from their original form into a new form of the product."[79]

The self-activating nature of labor-power indicates that it is under the sway of a potentially hostile will within the person of the laborer. This is a huge problem for capital; its existence depends on workers *activating* their labor-powers. The will-determined activity of the laborer expressed as labor-power "*objectifies*" itself in the course of production and so becomes *value*,"[80] and surplus-value as capital in its emergent form. Marx views this process as an instance of loss and sacrifice on the part of the laborer. Living labor appears as alien, argues Marx, in relation to labor-power "whose labour it is, whose own life expression it is," as it has been "surrendered to capital."[81] In his early work, especially the *Economic and Philosophical Manuscripts* of 1844, Marx indicated that he viewed labor as a sacrifice, pace Adam Smith, and elaborates this view in the *Grundrisse*, too.[82] In the *Manuscripts*, Marx saw work within capitalism as self-denial, as ruination of mind and body; labor as "self-sacrifice, as mortification." On this basis, labor in capitalism is "activity as suffering, strength as weakness, begetting as emasculating, the worker's own physical and mental energy, his personal life . . . as an activity which is turned against him, independent of him and not belonging to him."[83] In this process, man (not labor-power—as Marx had not divined the significance of this concept at the time of writing the *Manuscripts*) is produced as a commodity, as a dehumanized being. Furthermore, the worker's activity is under the sway of "*inhuman* power."[84] In this process of dehumanization, the worker's life-force, her activity, is not spontaneous; this constitutes "loss of self."[85] Political economy, noted Marx in the *Manuscripts*, was a "true moral science" of "self-renunciation."[86]

This view of labor as loss and as sacrifice in the *Manuscripts* is developed by Marx in a more sophisticated way, and in relation to labor-power, in the *Grundrisse*. There, Marx views "all powers of labour" as being "transposed into powers of capital."[87] Later on (in the *Resultate*), Marx argues that the vampiric capitalist "devours the labour-power of the worker" or "appropriates his living being as the life-blood of capitalism."[88] The worker "expends [his abilities], uses them up in the act of production."[89] On the analysis here, labor-power becomes a real active force within the capitalist labor process. It is transformed into labor as its constituent items—mental and physical capabilities—are organized through the will of the laborer. Labor-power as force is transferred into labor and thence into value, surplus-value and capital. This entails a loss of human energy deriving from the utilization of physical and mental capabilities as labor-power. For Marx,[90] this energy and power is made good through the laborer exchanging the wage for the 'bundle of necessities' that are consumed by herself and her family, thus socially reproducing herself as laborer—and hence labor-power—and providing necessities and conditions for laborers of the future through rearing children. Workers are drained during labor in the labor process. Their labor-powers are replenished and re-energized as potential force through consumption.

Finally, there is a theory of dehumanization at work here—especially in the *Economic and Philosophical Manuscripts*. This emptying-out and loss of self occasioned by the alienation of the active powers of workers, which confront them as powers of capital, points toward 'the human' free from these social conditions and demonic forces. There is a certain romanticism, or philosophical anthropology, which has the 'essential human being' as its basis. Recovery of the 'human essence' resolves itself into the destruction of alienating labor, which is underscored by capitalist social relations. Therefore, this entails the annihilation of capitalist social relations, and hence capital. In this view, capital is a relation, and an *externality*. Social relations and external forces can be destroyed without destroying our 'selves.' But if we are capital then the destruction of capital implies terminating the 'monster within,' self-destruction and transformation. We must become someone else, destroy our (capitalized) 'selves' as we destroy capital. The working class, as partially capitalized humanity, must dissolve itself, as well as capital and the social relations (of worker to capitalist) its labor engenders. The argument that follows expands these perspectives.

Capital as Social Force

The conventional way to view the relationship between capital and labor is either as an externality or as ideological relation. In the latter case, *The German Ideology* (by Marx and Engels, 1846) summarizes the situation, with its notion of 'the ruling ideas' being the ideas of the ruling class, which come to permeate workers' consciousness in various ways.[91] This chapter is concerned with the former perspective, to develop the argument that capital is not just a social, external relation, but is also a social force internal to labor as labor-power, yielding an internality (to personhood) of capital as social relation too. Furthermore, the perspective on capital determines the expressed relation between capital and labor. Marx stressed this a number of times in his insistence that capital *is* a social relation, as opposed to commodities as "things" or means of production.[92] Some of these issues can be unraveled through considering aspects of the work of Moishe Postone, in particular his *Time, Labour and Social Domination*, of 1996.

First, Postone notes that the conventional way of viewing the relationship between capital and labor is to see it as a *class relation*: an antagonistic relation between those who own the means of production (the capitalist class) and those who have no means of production themselves and are therefore forced to sell themselves as labor-power (the working class). As owners of the means of production, the former are driven to maximize surplus-value in the form of profit, while working-class interests are served through driving up wages, enhancing working conditions and driving down working hours to gain more 'free' time as leisure. These antipathetic drives form the basis of class conflict. Working-class emancipation, on this view, entails appropriating the means of production from the capitalist class, abolishing private property and establishing a society based on meeting human needs. Postone's *Time, Labour and Social Domination* can be viewed as a running critique of this approach to socialist grand strategy. His key point is that the abolition of the capitalist class does not entail abolition of capital as the value-form of production. He also argues that capital cannot be understood as "the social relation between the capitalist and working classes, structured by private ownership of the means of production and mediated by the market."[93] It is not necessary to go into his critique of the class conflict view of the capital-labor relation here.[94] Rather, Postone's positive account of capital as a social relation is of more use for understanding capital as social force.

Following Marx, Postone emphasizes that capital is not a thing (material objects as products) but a social relation,[95] for "Capital is not a thing, any more than money is a thing. In capital, as in money, certain specific social relations of production between people appear as relations of things to people, or else certain social relations appear as natural properties of things in society."[96] To view capital as a "thing" is the basis of the commodity fetishism explored by Marx in the first volume of *Capital*. For Marx, the result of the process of production is "above all, the reproduction and new production of the relation of capital and labour, of capitalist and worker," and "This social relation, production relation, appears in fact as an even more important result of the process than its material manifestation [products as commodities: GR]."[97] In this process, individual capitalists are personifications of capital. As personifications of capital, the "relation of every capitalist to his own workers is the relation as such of capital and labour."[98] For Postone too, "the category of capital refers to a peculiar sort of social relation, to a dynamic, totalistic, and contradictory social form that is constituted by labor in its duality as an activity mediating people's relations with each other and with nature."[99]

Marx's *Capital* is an unfolding of capital as a constantly moving entity brought to 'life' through "socially general powers" (which includes science and knowledge, as well as labor), according to Postone. However, "these productive powers serve to reinforce the abstract compulsions exerted on the producers; they heighten the degree of exertion and intensity of exertion required, as well as the fragmentation of labor."[100] Postone notes that capital (like the commodity) has a double nature: an abstract dimension (as self-valorizing value, in the movement M-C-M), and a concrete dimension (labor as productive activity). Capital is the 'alienated form' of both these dimensions of social labor in capitalist society, and confronts individuals as "an alien, totalistic Other." In sum: capital can be viewed as "an alienated structure of labor-mediated relations of production," which "promotes the development of socially general forces of production while incorporating them as its attributes."[101] For Postone, capital as social relation takes on a real existence as the subject of history within capitalism; its existence is constituted by labor, and its various metamorphoses and transformations—into the value, money and state forms—are effected and mediated by labor. The 'tragedy of labor' is that this mediation, which produces an "enormous increase in the productive powers of the use value of labor,"[102] is the conduit for the establishment of capital as an independent power, as social force and as social relation, which oppresses individuals throughout the social formation (not just within the labor process); all forms of human activity are subordinated to the value-form of social production.

This account is interesting in that there seems to be an externality to the relation between capital and labor. Labor *confronts* capital as 'Other.' Capital as social force compels the individuals to labor through its form of mediation, which rests on labor-power having to transform itself into labor in order to reap the wage reward. Of course, powers of the state, law and other institutions (such as schools) also have their effects on forcing labor to assume the value-form of wealth creation, but Postone insists that this harsh compulsion is inscribed within the core elements of capital itself, as an unfolding, moving (but ego-less) entity constituted by labor. Aspects of the use-value dimension of labor "also function structurally to reinforce and reconstitute this framework," for they "function as attributes of capital,"[103] a point which will not be pursued here.

Also in this account, capital—as constituted and mediated by labor— appears as a vast, global oppressive social force, which, although *we* bring it to 'life,' we are nevertheless enthralled by. There is no escape; capital, in its various forms is everywhere, as social force pressing us into the service of its many-faceted forms of 'life' and reincarnations (value, money, commodity, state, law and so on). Moreover, in this account capital appears as an *external* social force to individuals, oppressing them from without their personhoods as a *structure* of social relations, with similarities to standard sociological accounts of 'social structures' as limits to human 'agency.' There is something of this in Marx, too. On numerous occasions he refers to capital, the "objective, self-sufficient indifference," as constituting the conditions within which workers labor and these conditions confront them as alien property. These conditions take on a "personality" toward labor, they assume the form of "objective powers, even of overpowering objects—of things independent of the relations among individuals themselves."[104] In the *Resultate*, Marx notes that in the capitalist labor process, labor is objectified "in opposition to living labour-power." The conditions of production and its results (commodities) seem to be "endowed with a will and a soul of their own."[105]

For both Postone and Marx, on this account, capital is an oppressive Other, independent of labor, a force which dominates labor by pressing it to expend its own force or power (labor-power) in the service of its own self-expansion. But the externality involved here, capital as an oppressive social relation 'out there,' beyond the personhood of the laborer, is only half the picture. Things are much worse; capital is also within personhood. Hence, capital as social relation is *internal* to personhood, not as a 'thing,' but as a social force. This other perspective on capital can be found in Marx (and to some extent in Postone), but the relation is invariably veiled through viewing capital as externality first and foremost.

In *Capital*—or at least the first two volumes—Marx unfolds capital as a social relation constituted by labor on the basis of *equal exchange*. For Marx, the laborer is not simply tricked in production through attaining a wage below its value; the wage is equal to the value of the laborer's labor-power. However, the argument here is that, within the labor process, there is also an exchange of social *force*. In the previous section, it was argued that labor-power is a social force that is transformed, through self-organizing acts of will on the part of laborers, into labor and thence into all the various forms of capital as self-expanding value. In this process of emptying out, loss and sacrifice, there is also a reciprocal process of self-constitution by capital as negative social force. An exchange of social force occurs where the expenditure of labor-power is paralleled by an influx of an 'alien' force, which becomes incorporated within individuals: capital as social force, through the social relation of labor to capital. Hence, on this perspective, the social relation of capital to labor is *internal* (as well as external) to labor; capital is an invasive social force as the capital relation is shot through laborers as persons. 'Human capital' is not just a bourgeois abstraction that can be safely ridiculed; it expresses the process of humans being capitalized, the capitalization of humanity. According to John Holloway, such a position is central to Marxism, for Marxism "distinguishes itself from other varieties of radical theory" in its claim to "dissolve all externality." For Holloway, it is precisely because "capital is *not* external to labor, that we can understand the vulnerability of capitalist domination" and, in turn, grasp the "*fragility* of oppression." But I would wish to press Holloway's point further, to drive him toward the most radical of conclusions: that capital is also incorporated within *labor-power*, and as labor-power is "inseparable from the worker" and exists as the "bodiliness of the worker" and is an aspect of her "living vitality,"[107] then capital exists as social force within the person.

This claim can be substantiated, to a considerable extent, by reconsidering labor-power. For Marx, although labor-power is a transhistorical concept,[108] it assumes a specific form in capitalism, and hence becomes *historical*. This is based on the fact that labor is 'free' within capitalism in a double sense. First, in terms of the laborer having control over her own body, and hence being free to sell her labor-power on the best possible terms, and where the capitalist buys labor-power as commodity for a duration which is established as free exchange between worker and capitalist (labor-power for the wage), so laborers have control over their persons. Second, labor is free in the negative sense of not owning means of production that would allow laborers to reproduce their own labor-powers, and hence having to obtain the means of consumption through commodity exchange.[109] When the laborer sells her labor-power to the capitalist, as witnessed earlier, within the labor process she is actively engaged in transforming her force, energy and living vitality into labor through self-organizing of her skills, knowledges, strength and all the other attributes necessary for effective labor. However, this force expenditure is accompanied by an inflow of capital as social force *into labor-power as it sets itself in motion.*

In the capitalist labor process, labor-power becomes part of capital, it is *capitalized*, becomes human capital. As Marx notes, "the worker functions here as a special natural form of this capital, as distinct from the elements of capital that exist in the natural form of means of production."[110] Furthermore, laborers *develop themselves* as labor-power within the labor process, but as labor-power of a specific kind: human capital, as the form that labor-power takes in capitalism. Marx notes the two-fold process going on when laborers labor within the capitalist labor process, when "the individual not only develops his abilities in production but also expends them, uses them up in the act of production."[111] Hence, "Universal prostitution appears as a necessary phase in the development of the social character of personal talents, capacities, abilities, activities."[112] There is force-expenditure (of human labor-power), but also development of this labor-power on the basis of capital, labor-power capitalized—and as labor-power is inseparable from the person, then we have *personhood capitalized, humans capitalized, human capital.* Capital becomes a living social force within the human and internal and internalized social relation within individuals—*and this is the basis of the transhuman; it is this that makes us 'extra-human.'* Capital is not just 'out there'; we are it, it is us.

Invasive Force: Deep Possession of Laborers by Capital

> I'm having the most perfect hallucination;
> Green and blue goblins are crawling all over me—
> Like a deck of cards . . .
> I don't feel I'll ever be the same again.
> Please help me . . .
> Please help me . . .
>
> Ash Ra Tempel (1996)[113]

Capital is a *social force*, as well as a social relation through which it is expressed and manifested *as* social force. Unlike demon possession, as portrayed in *The Exorcist*, there are 'no outward signs.' Or, rather, no such signs that are immediately verificatory. The demon-possessed victim in *The Exorcist* levitates, speaks in ancient languages and with facial dis/contortions, yet with capital there is nothing to immediately witness on the surface.

The natural force analogous to capital as social force is gravity. Like gravity, it cannot be immediately sensed, but exists with accompanying real effects. The effects of such *deep possession* of humans by capital as social force can be observed—as can the effects of gravity as natural force—but only on *presupposition* of the pertinent force. Marx hints at several points that we are capital, humanity capitalized, and that this is a form of deep possession of the human by capital as social force. In *The German Ideology*, for example, he and Engels argue that "As individuals express their life, so they are. What they are, therefore, coincides with their production, both *what* they produce and *how* they produce. Hence what individuals are depends on the material conditions of their production."[114] And when the material conditions of their production are forms of capital, then it follows those individuals *are capital*; they are socially produced as individuals on the basis of capital. In the immediate process of production, "the worker produces himself as labour capacity,"[115] and labor-power is incorporated within the person—as noted earlier. Capital, however, is a *negative* social force. Marx notes that labor-power produces capital as its negation, through producing the product as alien,[116] but fails to grasp that—connected to the social production of labor-power—capital also becomes a social force within the human. It is a deep invasive force; humans are deeply possessed by capital as negative force. But why capital is a negative social force requires explanation.

The fact that capital is an *alien* force cannot be the whole answer, though the thought that we are possessed by something 'Other'—as in horror and science fiction films—is not immediately appealing. No, capital's negativity arises from the fact that it is, first of all, a *limiting social force*. It drives us as internal compulsive force, reinforcing itself as external compulsive social relation configured as a set of social structures, to *submit to the value-form of labor*. What is required to explicate this is a *critical psychology of labor in capitalism*, a psychology that is yet to be written, but to which the work of Lucien Seve, in 1975, gives first expression.[117]

As well as being a limiting social force within the human, capital is also a containing social force. Labor-power is the most explosive commodity within capitalism, not just because the whole capitalist systems rests upon it—as witnessed earlier—but because it has a capacity to *go beyond capital, the latent power to expand its force beyond the control of capital through being utilized in non- and anti-capitalist forms of social production.* Labor-power has the potential to become a social force for the abolition of capitalism through being the power behind (really) post-capitalist productive forms. Hence, capital as force internal to labor-power, and the person, contains and restrains labor-power as creative and dynamic force, while limiting its expression as force for value-creation labor. Limiting, constraining-restraining within labor-power, and hence within the vitality and consciousness of the person: in these ways, capital is a *negative* social force.

Marx ascribes to capital the quality of determining "the specific gravity of every being which is materialized within it." In arguing this, he views all sentient beings, not just humans, as life-forms constituted by capital; for capital is the "all-dominating economic power of bourgeois society."[118] However, in the *Manuscripts*, Marx argued for a different position to that being expressed in this chapter: he pointed toward estrangement as the "inaccessible possession" of another, though he acknowledges there that "everything is itself something different from itself," and that the worker's activity was under the sway of "inhuman power."[119] Even in the *Grundrisse*, Marx acknowledges that living labor can penetrate "dead labour" (means of production) with "an animating soul," but nevertheless ends up losing "its own soul to it."[120] There are only hints that capital comes to possess individuals as a negative force, which limits and restrains the human soul in turn.[121] The analysis of this chapter has taken Marx's fleeting insights on the capitalization of the human to a deeper and more radical level of analysis.

On the analysis expounded, the transhuman is a specific form of humanity: humanity within capitalism and capital within humanity. The transhuman, on this account, is not something only just beginning or an effect of new technologies and biochemical engineering, whose searing development is located in the future. Rather, the transhuman is a relatively old phenomenon, as old as capitalism itself.

The 'Logic' of Capitalized Humanity at Work
Within the Labor Process

As we are capitalized as humans within the labor process, where an exchange of forces (human labor-power with capital) takes place, then we are also subject to a vicious unfolding of the dynamic of the labor process, as partially explicated by Marx in *Capital*. The capitalist labor process is the key social space where the *practical* development of labor-power on the basis of capital takes place. The development of the capitalist labor process can, therefore, also be viewed as a deepening and complexification of the transhuman in the form of human capital. In unfolding the 'logic' of this development we are not 'predicting' the future, but pointing toward what certain elements of the future could become *if* capitalism is not terminated. In this section, the explication of this unfolding of the labor process as it relates to labor and labor-power is necessarily fragmentary; it is a first shot and will be developed in future work. It is based on the fact that Marx did not unfold *all logical possibilities* for surplus-value production within the labor process.

The capitalist labor process is the immediate process of production, the social site where value is first created through laborers transforming their labor-powers into labor, which forms commodities incorporating value, thence surplus-value and capital (which then spirals off into its various forms within a huge cycle of reproduction). In *Capital*, Marx outlined two main forms of surplus-value production: absolute and relative. Absolute surplus-value production is where the laborers are made to work longer, through extending the working day; in this (inefficient) way, surplus-value is increased. With relative surplus-value production—the form "most adequate"[122] to mature capitalist production, and the form that finally fixes capitalist production as the dominant form of production in society—machinery is utilized on an increasing scale. The effect of this is that the labor-time represented by the value of the wage is reduced, leaving an increased proportion of labor-time devoted to surplus-value production.

However, Marx was not fully aware of the different forms of relative surplus-value. First, he was aware of the effect that *work intensity* could have on value production, though in *Capital* he was ambivalent about where this figured in relation to absolute/relative forms. The position here is that work intensity—allied to forms of management control that attained complexity after the rise of 'scientific' management in the early twentieth century—has functioned as a means to raise the productivity of workers through minimizing labor-time constituting the wage. Hence, it can be viewed as another form of relative surplus-value production.

A further form of relative surplus-value production is given by the possibility that *labor-power itself* can be worked upon—through education and training. This is the topic of the next section, so only the basic point will be outlined here. This is that, as capital comes to take over the whole of society, old institutions are recast in its image and new ones are established to enhance value-production. Forms of the social production of labor-power have been established in almost all societies. These social forms are characterized by their relation to the enhancement of the *quality of labor-power* in a number of respects, so that the transformation of labor-power into labor is maximized, and hence relative surplus-value is increased as workers work with greater commitment and effectiveness.

However, there is a fourth form of relative surplus-value production. This involves *fusion* of all the other forms, and could express itself in the fusion of humans and machines: the cyborg as laborer. This is no longer science fiction. Brain implants have recently been developed which "allow a computer to be

operated by thought."[123] It is early days, but this is one of the
'logic' of development underpinning the capitalist labor p
social dynamic, as opposed to a technological determinism,
could end up as cyborg workers; it provides an explanat
development of capitalist production. Of course, capit
provides a further dynamic for calling forth the human-mach
dealt with here. The strength of the account is that it enables a̤n ᴄᵡᵖˡ˯˷˷˷˷˷ ᴏ˻ ᴀ
cyborg future, while denying that this is *identical to the transhuman.* On this
view, the post/trans-human theorists see only effects, not (pre)conditions. They
also have no explanatory framework or dynamic for their prognostications.
Let's raise the game once more; in the next section, education and training enter
in.

Forcing Process:
Education and the Social Production of Labor-Power

The capitalist labor process encapsulates a logic of development that unfolds the
transhuman within, and as, capital; and the capitalization of humanity continues
within the sphere of consumption (though in the previous section, the dynamic
pushing forward this development of capitalist transhumanity was not
addressed). This indicates that there are processes through which we are
capitalized *beyond* the labor process. This section focuses on an element within
the social processes implicated in the capitalization of humanity. In developed
capitalism, as noted in the previous section, *labor-power* increasingly comes to
be the focus of forms and processes of *social production*, reproduction and
maintenance. Labor-power theory can be viewed as the attempt to understand
the social dynamics, empirical manifestation and histories of these forms and
processes pertaining to labor-power development. A subset of these processes
explored in this section is the *social production of labor-power* in capitalism;
this is where education and training make their greatest impact in the
capitalization of humans in contemporary society.

As a starting point for approaching an understanding of the nature and
significance of the social production of labor-power in capitalism, it is
necessary to revisit the section on labor-power as the fuel for the 'living fire.'
There, it was argued that Marx held that "two great classes of commodities"
existed; the "general class" and labor-power. The latter was elaborated as a
"unique" commodity in some respects. It follows from this that, although Marx
examined the production of the first class of commodities, he did not explore
the social production of labor-power in any depth; Michael Lebowitz[124] makes a
similar point. Marx did, however, distinguish these two interrelated forms of
social production at a number of key points, though he sometimes confused or
conflated them as forms of commodity production with aspects in common—
for, as we saw earlier, "general commodities" and labor-power indeed shared
some aspects.[125]

The social production of labor-power is the conglomeration of the social processes involved in producing the unique, or 'thinking' commodity. Although there are some general and elementary forms of the social production of labor-power,[126] the fragmented forms in which labor-power is socially produced in capitalism, with its institutional splits in contemporary capitalist societies makes for great difficulties—theoretically, and in terms of empirical work. Listing institutional forms involved in labor-power production we have schooling; on/off-the-job training; further and higher education; character and attitude training; the development of abilities in the labor process—as *some* of the elements. Empirical and historical research and analysis is necessary to ascertain the productive forms for particular categories of labor. The last in the list—developing labor-power in production—links up the production of "general commodities" and labor-power production; at this nodal point, labor-power and "general commodities" are produced simultaneously, through acts of labor in the labor process. The task of this section, however, is not to explore the social production of labor-power in depth, but to explicate its role in the capitalization of humanity. There are three key points here.

First, to reiterate, laboring in the labor process is an element within the process of socially producing labor-power. The attributes of labor-power (attitudes, skills, knowledges, physical strength and dexterity, apposite personality traits and aspects) are socially produced in different ways and to varying extents, depending upon the type of industry, occupation, level of expression of labor-power, work discipline regimes and so on—*within the labor process*. As argued earlier, the development of labor-power in the labor process —as exchange of social force—simultaneously involves the capitalization of the human, as labor-power (developed on the basis of capital) becomes *capitalized*.

Second, a far stronger claim could be made. This is that we do not just exist as virtual labor-power/capitalized humanity when outside the labor process, but *we are capital wherever we may be*. The processes of consumption (re-energizing, revitalizing and refreshing labor-power), and all the social processes making for the reproduction, social production and maintenance of labor-power *also* constitute labor-power (and hence the person as capital). To show this would require a colossal exploration and vast explication; the hint must be sufficient here. However, an example can be used to illustrate the more general point; the social production of labor-power, and this takes us to the next point.

Third, the social production of labor-power can be viewed as just one set of social processes involved in the *capitalization of the human beyond the labor process* (though, as witnessed above, part of the process is *internal* to the labor process). To consider education and training—key elements within most contemporary forms of labor-power production—as implicated in socially producing labor-power, reveals that attributes of the person are being developed, enhanced and formed, which then figure as labor-power, the life-force which gives 'life' to capital as social force, within the labor process. There are two aspects to this: the development of labor-power *potential*, the capacity to labor effectively within the labor process; and the development of the willingness of workers to utilize their laboring power, to expend themselves within the labor process as value-creating force. This is manifested in studies that pinpoint work attitudes as the most sought-after and significant attribute of workers in recruitment studies,[127] and the exhortations of employers that schools must produce 'well-motivated' young people with sound attitudes to work, and recruits who are 'work-ready' and embody 'employability'—though these points would need to driven home through focused empirical and historical studies. This amounts to a process of the *capitalization* of youth and adults, of developing persons as labor-power (and hence human capital) *beyond* the labor process.

There is, of course, an issue of *intentionality* here. The social actors (teachers, trainers and so on) might (and fortunately many do) have alternative perspectives and work from a different basis and outlook. They might not intentionally set about producing labor-power, or, if they are aware that this is a practice within which they are implicated, they might try to subvert or ameliorate it. Students themselves might not view 'learning' as capitalist social form, or, when they do, might resist it as such. However, these points miss the mark. Although empirical forms of the social production of labor-power are amorphous and relatively 'weak' in terms of intentionality—they are poorly defined as productive forms—nevertheless, education and policy in the United Kingdom has, since the mid-1970s, set to harden the intentionality and enhance the policy framework that develop persons as human capital (labor-power). Education and training policies of the New Labour Government are based as firmly on human capital formation as were the 1979–1997 Conservative administrations.[128] Furthermore, it might be possible to point to a long-term historical trend toward incorporating education and training as forms of labor-power enhancement within an ideology and process of human capital formation as the capitalization of humanity.

Such an outlook builds upon what Marx says in the *Grundrisse*, since in capitalism, "development to its totality consists precisely in subordinating all elements of society to itself, or in creating out of it organs which it still lacks. This is historically how it becomes a totality." Marx points toward the tendency of capital to conquer all other modes of production in all respects, and to "bring them under the rule of capital."[129] In this process, the law of value and "its abstract forms of alienated capitalist power: money, the law and the state" are just as important as the exploitation of labor in the labor process.[130] Marx also notes that "Competition is the mode generally in which capital secures the victory of its mode of production," and the increasing competition, fragmentation and marketization of education (quintessentially, further education in the U.K.) can be viewed as a mode of *subordinating educational and training institutions to the rule of capital through energizing them as sites of labor-power enhancement*, through both competitive pressures and encompassing policy constraints (state activity also as a form of capital). Marx notes, caustically, that the "severe discipline of capital, acting on succeeding generations, has developed general industriousness as the general property of the new species."[131] Hence, in modern industrial conditions, where all ȷnificant institutions have morphed into capital, then it can be expected that ṵ.e social production of labor-power, as a definite organization of the formation and enhancement of labor-power, becomes increasingly stronger. On this 'logic,' the state-form of capital comes increasingly to express education and training policy as *labor-power* policy—or human capital policy, which is the same thing. The *intentionality* of the process is tightened at the level of the capitalist state. Globalization and competitiveness, as ideologies and real process, strengthen the social *definition* of a process of labor-power production still further. (The strengthening of the *social* intentionality requires historical description and analysis, not pursued here). A narrow focus on the intentionality of individuals engaged within the social production of labor-power misses the mark in another respect. In the recruitment of labor-power, and within the labor process, representatives of capital are concerned with using and utilizing labor-power. In terms of the skills, knowledges, attitudes, aspects of personality and the rest which constitute items, or attributes, of labor-power (which are reified by employers, and in educational research which takes the constituents of labor-power as 'things'), the question is their utilization. Thus, it is logically possible—and likely—that teachers and students may develop all kinds of attributes within educational and training institutions on the basis of motivations, goals and visions *irrespective* of the labor-power 'needs' of capital. Yet these can still figure as labor-power attributes.

In the social production of labor-power, we are humanized (civilized) as capital and capitalized as humans. Transhumanization in its capitalist form 'catches 'em young,' from birth, and goes on beyond death (death *made money* through the funeral process, and perhaps survival as virtual humans). In concrete terms, this involves forcing self-formation through a specific social form; to *become* for capital (alienation), and to engage in fixing 'being' as capitalized life-form. This invasive process affects all aspects of consciousness and body. It simultaneously shatters and unifies the soul on the basis of a social force that flows into the 'human' through the capital relation.

The effectivity of processes of labor-power production is limited on the basis of a contradiction: that the social production of labor-power in capitalism is premised upon the objectification of subjectivity. Practical attempts to 'fix' labor-power attributes within personhood, which, in toto, would constitute the formation of our 'being' as capital, are limited on the following considerations:

- the contradictory drives incorporated within ourselves as capital;
- the fact that these drives are infinite—there are no limits to them as drives, but their expression is limited by the *clash* of contradictory drives;
- the process of labor-power production has no 'logical' end point (unto death), as the quality of labor-power can always be enhanced, and it can also deteriorate the further it gets away from practical expression within the labor process (a factor which studies of the unemployed reflect)—and therefore labor-power is never *finally* 'produced';

- the contradictions resulting from ourselves, our existence, as *labor against capital* (as opposed to labor within and as capital);
- our attempts to 'solve' these contradictions opens possibilities for dissolving them through subversion;
- our capacity for reflexivity, to attain awareness of the existence and practical application of processes of the production of ourselves as labor-power, raises the issue of a politics of human resistance to these processes.

The social production of labor-power has, up to the present, been a relatively 'weak' form of production (though its 'strength' is growing). Its 'weakness' rests partly on the contradictory nature of the process, partly on historical liberal Left or religious values within some sections of educational elites, states and governments, which have effects for educational policy and organization running *counter* to viewing education and training as human capital development. Furthermore, the alternative perspectives of teachers and students also have effects. Finally, the compounding of all the factors listed above, their inter-relations and political expressions, is also pertinent. Hence, there are limits to the process of capital invading (abducting) the 'human.' If there were not, humans would be automatons, and the social domination of the whole human and human-related (nature as human resource) universe would dance to the hyperdetermination by capital and its forms (money, value and so on).[132] The importance of human consciousness is the potential for awareness of the creeping possession it yields. Our ability to think can unravel the dread.

But this is a problem for capital: education and training have the potential for opening, developing and increasing an awareness of ourselves as labor-power, as human-capital, humans *capitalized*. Hence, social control (through National Curricula, 'new managerialism') of the process is crucial. This great educational fear—education as subversion, education as uncovering what we have become—is chronic and endemic within the social universe of capital. The second fear relates to the fact that, as competition—which entrenches the rule of capital—flourishes, then wage competition increases economic and social inequalities. For these two fears, our booster therapy must be a critical pedagogy that makes representatives of capital even more afraid, very afraid, through uncovering their worst fear through educational programs which 'think the—really—unthinkable.' Fortunately, the horror works both ways.

Conclusion

In this chapter, the 'transhuman' has been presented as the capitalization of humanity. Rather than viewing the transhuman in a transhistorical manner, or as some just-about-to-be or futurized technologization of the human (the reign of the cyborg), the argument here is that we are already extra-human as *capital*. The 'transhuman' has existed since the rise of capitalism; it is nothing new. The cybernauts have attempted to think a future where the 'machine' dominates the human, but without being able to provide an explanation of this development. In unfolding the 'logic' of the labor process as valorization process, it is clear that some of the futures suggested by the cybernauts (science-centered post-human theorists) and transhumanists are incorporated within this unfolding. The key to understanding the form of transhumanization explored here (historical, specific to capitalism) is that labor-power becomes capital in the process of its social production, becomes human capital. This is attained through an exchange of social force; labor-power for capital and vice versa as each constitutes the other—simultaneously—within the labor process. As labor-power is inseparable from the laborer, it cannot be isolated; as it is a power or force flowing throughout personhood, then, by default, humans are capitalized too. We *are* capital. But the capitalization of the 'human' also exists beyond the labor process. The social production of labor-power is one of the processes involved. As education and training are elements within most forms of the social production of labor-power, they are implicated in the process of the transformation of humans into human capital, the capitalization of the 'human.'

However, processes of the capitalization of humanity are never complete, since labor-power, although incorporated within personhood, is also under the sway of a potentially hostile (for capital) will. Individual and collective consciousness *exceeds* the processes of capitalization. Furthermore, through alerting individuals to what they have become, through enhancing awareness[133] of their situation as constituted by capital, a double-loop fueled by anger yields possibilities for the formation of collective strategies, modes of subversion and politics of human resistance aimed at smashing the social relations through which capital as social force invades the 'human.'

Capitalist education is a contradictory phenomenon. On the one hand, it is enmeshed in the capitalization of 'humans;' on the other, it can function as a basis for exposure and awareness of this state of being. How this might be done—the actual pedagogics—is best explained elsewhere. But the importance of a viable critical pedagogy, which has this exposure of the 'horror' as a pedagogic aim, is crucial. As Peter McLaren and Ramin Farahmandpur indicate, there is an urgent need to rescue critical pedagogy from a neo-Kantian Left liberalism where it becomes just another classroom technique. Critical pedagogy needs to place liberation on the agenda of history again, to make it useful for the task of devising a transition beyond capitalism.[134] Through a series of recent publications and conference papers, Peter McLaren has embarked on a process of reclaiming critical pedagogy from liberalism for the urgent task of increasing our awareness of our social condition, as a first step toward changing it vis-à-vis capital and the social injustices thrown up by its world domination.[135] As McLaren and his colleagues note, awareness or consciousness of our plight is "not enough to guarantee personal or collective praxis."[136] A commitment to social justice is necessary for providing the spark within individuals and collectivities if awareness is to be transformed into action. We need to educate for this too. I would add that an appreciation of capital as the 'horror within' provides an additional argument for leaving capitalism as a form of social life in the rearview mirror of history. So, let us scare ourselves: read *Capital*—with no need to wait until capitalism's midnight!

Notes

Ruth Rikowski read the first draft and made a number of criticisms, which led to some rethinking and rewriting. Mike Neary's criticisms of the first draft, and our conversations over the last three years, played a significant part in both developing and sharpening up some of the ideas and their expression. Mike's urgings to 'go the extra mile' and develop some of the ideas further than I had originally intended has had significant impact on the form and content of the chapter. But the responsibility for the final outcome is mine.

1. Keith Ansell-Pearson, "Viroid Life: On Machines, Technics and Evolution," in *Deleuze and Philosophy: The Difference Engineer*, ed. Keith Ansell-Pearson (London: Routledge, 1997), 182.

2. Michael Neary and Graham Taylor, *Money and the Human Condition* (London: Macmillan, 1998), 130, 128 (original emphasis).

3. Karl Marx, *Economic and Philosophical Manuscripts of 1844*. Moscow: Progress Publishers).

4. Karl Marx, *Grundrisse: Foundations of the Critique of Political Economy (Rough Draft)* [1858], trans. M. Nicolaus (Harmondsworth, U.K.: Penguin, 1973).

5. Marx, *Grundrisse*, 729.

6.Tim Luke, "'Moving at the Speed of Life?' A Cultural Kinematics of Telematic Times and Corporate Values," in *Time and Value*, ed. S. Lash, A. Quick and R. Roberts (Oxford: Blackwell, 1998).

7. See Michael Neary, *Youth, Training and the Training State: The Real History of Youth Training in the Twentieth Century* (Basingstoke, U.K.: Macmillan, 1997).

8. See John Holloway, "From Scream of Refusal to Scream of Power: The Centrality of Work," in *Emancipating Marx: Open Marxism, Volume III*, ed. Werner Bonefeld, Richard Gunn, John Holloway and Kosmas Psychopedis (London: Pluto Press, 1995), 151–181; also Neary, *Youth, Training*.

9. See Neary and Taylor, *Money*.

10. Marx, *Economic and Philosophical*, 99 (original emphasis).

11. Marx, *Economic and Philosophical*, 97 (original emphasis).

12. Neary and Taylor, *Money*, 130.

13. Frances Callard, "The Body in Theory," *Environment and Planning D: Society and Space* 16 (1998): 396.

14. Moishe Postone, *Time, Labour and Social Domination: A Reinterpretation of Marx's Critical Theory* (Cambridge: Cambridge University Press, 1993).

15. Glenn Rikowski, "Education Markets and Missing Products" (paper presented to the Conference of Socialist Economists, University of Northumbria at Newcastle, July 7–9, 1995); "Left Alone: End Time for Marxist Educational Theory?" *British Journal of Sociology of Education* 17, no. 4 (December 1996): 415–451, and "Scorched Earth: Prelude to Rebuilding Marxist Educational Theory," *British Journal of Sociology of Education* 18, no. 4 (December 1997): 551–574.

16. Nigel Blake, "Between Postmodernism and Anti-modernism: The Predicament of Educational Theory," *British Journal of Educational Studies* 44, no. 1 (March 1996): 42–65.

17. Mike Cole, Dave Hill and Glenn Rikowski, "Between Postmodernism and Nowhere: The Predicament of the Postmodernist," *British Journal of Educational Studies* 45, no. 2 (1997): 187–200.

18. Nigel Blake, "A Postmodernism Worth Bothering About: A Rejoinder to Cole, Hill and Rikowski," *British Journal of Educational Studies* 45, no. 3 (September 1997): 293–305.

19. Mimi Ormer, Janet Miller and Elizabeth Ellsworth, "Excessive Moments and Educational Discourses That Try to Contain Them," *Educational Theory* 46, no. 1 (spring 1996): 71–91.

20. James Fiske, *Understanding Popular Culture* (London: Routledge, 1991), 17, cited in Ormer et al., "Excessive Moments," 72.

21. There is no 'escape;' no matter what the velocity, and even given infinite generation and proliferation of meaning, the hottest of hot air can be sucked to ground. Idealism is the attempt to attain the unattainable, to seek to cast adrift from the real universe of capital through ideas as excess meaning, as shown by Karl Marx and Freidrich Engels early on in *The German Ideology* of 1846 (Moscow: Progress Publishers, 1976).

22. David Harvey, "The Body as an Accumulation Strategy", *Environment and Planning D: Society and Space* 16 (1998): 401–421.

23. In Harvey, "The Body," 401.

24. Max More, "The Post Human Sub-page," cited by Robert Pepperell, *The Post-Human Condition* (Exeter, U.K.: Intellect Books, 1997), 174–175. See also <http://www.acm.usl.edu/~dca6381/c2_mirror/xi/entropy> (June 2001).

25. Keith Ansell-Pearson, *Viroid Life: Perspectives on Nietzsche and the Trans-human Condition* (London: Routledge, 1997), 1–2.

26. A critique of Ansell-Pearson appears in Michael Neary and Glenn Rikowski, "Deep Possession: Marx, Labor and the Transhuman" (forthcoming, 2002), which also deepens and develops some of the arguments of this chapter.

27. As charted by Brian Morris, *Western Conceptions of the Individual* (Oxford, U.K.: Berg, 1991).

28. See Roger Trigg, *Ideas of Human Nature: An Historical Introduction* (Oxford, U.K.: Blackwell, 1988).

29. In Ansell-Pearson, *Viroid Life, Nietzsche*.

30. Michael Crichton, *The Lost World* (London: Century, 1995) and *Jurassic Park* (London: Arrow, 1991).

31. Ansell-Pearson, *Viroid Life, Nietzsche*, 115.

32. See Paul Virilio, *The Art of the Motor*, trans. Julie Rose (Minneapolis: University of Minnesota Press, 1995). The critique of post-Darwinism and technological determinism appears in Ansell-Pearson, *Viroid Life, Nietzsche*.

33. See Postone, *Time, Labour*.

34. Neary and Taylor, *Money*.

35. Marx, *Grundrisse*, 361.

36. Karl Marx, *A Contribution to the Critique of Political Economy* [1859] (Moscow: Progress Publishers, 1977), 27; also, in *Capital: A Critique of Political Economy—Volume I* [1867] (London: Lawrence & Wishart, 1977), 43.

37. Karl Marx, *Preface to the First German Edition of Capital (Volume 1)* [1867] (London: Lawrence & Wishart, 1977), 19.

38. Postone, *Time, Labour*, 127–128.

39. Postone, *Time, Labour*, 148.

40. Karl Marx, *Theories of Surplus Value—Part 1* [1863] (London: Lawrence & Wishart, 1969), 173.

41. Karl Marx, *Results of the Immediate Process of Production* [1866] (addendum to *Capital, Vol. I*) (Harmondsworth, U.K.: Penguin, 1979), 1004.

42. Marx, *Results*, 974 (my emphasis).

43. Marx, *Surplus Value 1*, 167, 171.

44. Marx, *Surplus Value 1*, 172.

45. Marx, *Surplus Value 1*, 171 (my emphases).

46. Marx, *Surplus Value 1*, 171–172.

47. This time Marx is a little more charitable to Adam Smith. He noted that although Smith excluded the social production of labor-power through education and training from his category of productive labor arbitrarily, he had done this "with a certain correct instinct," believing that if he included it then it would have opened the "flood gates for false pretensions to the title of productive labor." Marx, *Surplus Value 1*, 172.

48. Contemporary Marxist theorists have invariably ignored the crucial differences between "general commodities" and labor-power. Postone, in *Time, Labour*, for example, typically ignores these differences in his reinterpretation of Marx's theory. In contrast, Michael Lebowitz in *Beyond Capital: Marx's Political Economy of the Working Class* (Basingstoke, U.K.: Macmillan, 1992), notes that Marx's *Capital* was an incomplete enterprise, which called for a further analysis of wage-labor—something that Marx saw the need for but did not get around to writing. However, Lebowitz's analysis does not start from the key social form which structures wage-labor, labor-power as commodity, but jumps straight in to an analysis of wage-labor. His analysis starts from a level too concrete. Marx, after all, did not start his analysis in *Capital* with capital, but set out from the commodity: he realized that the value-form of labor grounded the development, or becoming, of capital and this could be best explicated through unfolding the contents of the commodity as the 'economic cell-form' of the whole capitalist system.

49. Karl Marx, *Wage-Labour and Capital* [1847], in *Selected Works Volume I*, ed. Institute of Marxism-Leninism under the Committee of the Communist Party of the Soviet Union (Moscow: Progress Publishers, 1977), 152.

50. Marx, *Grundrisse*, 125.

51. Marx, *Surplus Value 1*, 164 (original emphasis).

52. Marx, *Grundrisse*, 267.

53. Marx, *Surplus Value 1*, 45.

54. Karl Marx, *Capital: A Critique of Political Economy—Volume II* [1878] (Harmondsworth, U.K.: Penguin, 1978), 577.

55. Education could most obviously coincide with the general form of productive labor in the case of private schools. Such profit-making schools aim to produce value over and above the value as represented in teachers wages, the product being 'educated youth' (see Marx, *Surplus Value 1*). In this case, there is no difference in the form of productive labor as between general commodities and labor-power, and hence no special and separate analysis of the latter is called for on this basis. Where state education becomes dominant—a situation Marx did not face in the 1850s and 1860s when writing his various drafts of *Capital*—the fact that education for profit does not pertain alters nothing, if the state is taken as a form of capital, the state-form of capital. This point clearly requires expansion elsewhere.

56. Marx, *Surplus Value 1*, 45 (original emphases).

57. Marx, *Results*, 1005–1006.

58. Karl Marx, *Capital: A Critique of Political Economy—Volume III* [1865] (London: Lawrence & Wishart, 1977), 164 (original emphases); 188.

59. Marx, *Grundrisse*, 674; *Surplus Value 1*, 51; *Capital Vol. 2*, 121.

60. See David McNally, *Against the Market: Political Economy, Market Socialism and the Marxist Critique* (London: Verso, 1993).

61. Marx, *Grundrisse*, 282, also 672; *Capital, Vol. 3*, 167; *Results*, 1066.

62. Marx, *Results,* 1009.

63. Marx, *Capital, Vol. 2*, 285.

64. Marx, *Grundrisse*, 282, 293.

65. Marx, *Capital, Vol. 2*, 121, 285, 515; 456-457; 121.

66. Marx, *Grundrisse*, 593.

67. Marx, *Capital, Vol. 2, 523.*

68. Marx, Grundrisse, 323; in *Wages, Price and Profit* [1865], in *Selected Works —Volume 2* (Moscow: Progress Publishers, 1976), 56.

69. Marx, *Grundrisse*, 674, 464.

70. Marx, *Surplus Value 1*, 393.

71. For example, see Marx, *Results*, 1009 and 1017–1019, also *Capital, Volume 1*, 164–166. Only on the market is a commodity a commodity (Marx, *Grundrisse, 534*)— and this applies to labor-power too.

72. Marx, *Capital, Vol. 3*, 381.

73. See Postone, *Time, Labour.*

74. Marx, *Capital, Vol. 1*, 164.

75. Marx, *Grundrisse*, 267.

76. Marx, *Surplus Value 1*, 171.

77. Marx, *Results*, 1016, 1043.

78. Marx, *Capital, Vol. 1*, 188.

79. Marx, *Results*, 980 (original emphases).

80. Marx, *Results*, 1016 (original emphases).

81. Marx, *Grundrisse*, 462. see also *Grundrisse*, 462 where Marx notes that "Labour capacity relates to its labour as to an alien."

82. Marx, *Grundrisse*, 614.

83. Marx, *Economic and Philosophical*, 71.

84. Marx, *Economic and Philosophical*, 82; 118 (original emphasis).

85. Marx, *Economic and Philosophical*, 71; also, the *Excerpts from James Mill's Elements of Political Economy* [1844], in *Karl Marx: Early Writings* (London: Penguin Classics-New Left Review, 1992), 266.

86. Marx, *Economic and Philosophical*, 112.

87. Marx, *Grundrisse*, 701.

88. Marx, *Results*, 1008.

89. Karl Marx in *General Introduction* [1857], trans. M. Nicolaus (Harmondsworth, U.K.: Penguin, 1973), 90.

90. See Marx, *Capital, Vol. 1*, 90.

91. Giving force to such notions as 'false consciousness,' the Althusserian stress on ideology and Gramscian hegemony. These 'cultural' Marxist positions at least have the merit of posing 'capital within the human' as a real possibility—though typically at the level of ideas, thus melding easily into Left sociological and liberal Left political perspectives; where the task is to unmask the effects of the media, schools and so on, as a step in banishing capitalist hegemony for a redistributive social justice.

92. Karl Marx, cited in Postone, *Time, Labour,* 351.

93. Postone, *Time, Labour*, 349.

94. For more on Postone's critique of the conventional view of the social relations of production, and his wider critique of 'traditional' Marxism, see chapters 1 and 2 of his *Time, Labour*. For Michael Neary, "The law of value is undermined by itself, in the very act of production. While it is true that this opposition [within value itself] expresses itself

in the form of working-class organization, it is not its organization that has provided the dynamic for the antagonism in the first place" (see chapter 7). Marx noted in *Grundrisse*, 303, that "Of course, socialists sometimes say we need capital, but not the capitalist. Then capital appears as a pure thing, not as a relation of production, which, reflected in itself, is precisely the capitalist," for "capital is indeed separable from an individual capitalist, but not from *the* capitalist, who, as such confronts *the* worker" (original emphases). On Postone's and Neary's accounts—following Marx in *Grundrisse*—the basic antagonism within capitalism is not between capitalist and worker, but is internal to, and immanent within, the unfolding of capital expressed as the value-form of labor, as the "value-expansion" process. See Michael Neary, "Situating the Situationists: the Most Modern Discourse," *Radical Chains* 5 (1998): 31. Class struggle is an effect or result of this basic antagonism.

95. As Marx noted in *Theories of Surplus Value—Part 2* [1863] (London: Lawrence & Wishart, 1969), 400, "Instead of *labour*, Ricardo should have discussed labour-*power*. But had he done so, *capital* would also have been revealed as the material conditions of labour, confronting the labourer as power that had acquired an independent existence and capital would at once have been revealed as a *definite social relationship*" (original emphases). He also criticized Adam Smith (*Grundrisse*, 257–258) for holding the view that capital is objectified labor, which also results in it being viewed as a 'thing.'

96. Marx, *Results*, 1005.

97. Marx, *Grundrisse*, 458.

98. Marx, *Grundrisse*, 420.

99. Postone, *Time, Labour*, 349.

100. Postone, *Time, Labour*, 350.

101. Postone, *Time, Labour*, 351.

102. Postone, *Time, Labour*, 350.

103. Postone, *Time, Labour*, 354.

104. Marx, *Grundrisse*, 452; 512; 652.

105. Marx, *Results*, 1016; 1004.

106. Holloway, "Scream," 159 (original emphasis).

107. Marx, *Grundrisse*, 282–323.

108. See Marx, *Economic and Philosophical*, also *Grundrisse*.

109. Postone, *Time, Labour*, 270. In *Excerpts from James Mill*, 269, Marx points toward "the determination of the labourer by social needs alien to him and which act upon him with compulsive force. He must submit to this force from egoistic need, from necessity . . . his actual labours serve only as means to this end. He thus activates his life to acquire the means of *life*" (original emphases). The laborer is driven by his separation from the means of production to undertake labor. Again, the "compulsive force" driving the laborer seems to be entirely external in nature.

110. Marx, *Capital, Vol. 2*, 163.

111. Marx, *General Introduction*, 90.

112. Marx, *Grundrisse*, 163.

113. Ash Ra Tempel, Dutch Radio broadcast, November 1996.

114. Marx and Engels, *The German Ideology*, 37 (original emphases).

115. Marx, *Grundrisse*, 458.

116. Marx, *Grundrisse*, 458.

117. Lucien Seve, *Marxism and the Theory of Human Personality* (London: Lawrence & Wishart, 1975). Michael Neary, in *Youth, Training*, and Neary and Taylor in *Money*, have gone furthest along this route, building upon the pioneering work of Seve.

118. Marx, *General Introduction*, 107.

142   *Glenn Rikowski*

119. Marx, *Economic and Philosophical*, 118.
120. Marx, *Grundrisse*, 461.
121. Hints such as "viewing capital as the 'thing' that 'subjectifies itself in the person'"—alluding to possession of individuals by capital (Marx, *General Introduction*, 89); also, identifying where the worker's human qualities "only exist insofar as they exist for capital *alien* to him" (Marx, *Economic and Philosophical*, 5)—but even here the alien appears as purely external; political economy being an expression of an anti-human perspective (Marx, *Economic and Philosophical*, 90); and that the worker is estranged from himself in capitalism (in Marx, *Economic and Philosophical*).
122. See Marx, *Results*.
123. "Brain Implants Allow Patients to Work Computer by Thought-Power," *Guardian*, October 15, 1998, 7.
124. See Lebowitz, *Beyond Capital*.
125. In *Theories of Surplus Value-Part 3* [1863] (London: Lawrence & Wishart, 1975), 148, Marx most clearly refers to labor-power undergoing a process of social production when he states

> What does the labour required for its [labor-power's] production consist of? Apart from the labour involved in developing a person's labour-power, his *education*, his apprenticeship—and this hardly arises in relation to unskilled labour—its reproduction costs no more labour apart from that involved in the reproduction of the means of subsistence which the labourer consumes (original emphasis).

Two points here: first, education—as a key element in the social production of labor-power—is now a multibillion dollar enterprise in contemporary leading capitalist nations. The U.K. education budget alone is £50 billion. Thus, it is no longer the case (as it was in Marx's day) that relatively little labor enters into the development of a person's labor-power. Secondly, Marx is here viewing labor-power as a set of skills and knowledge-related attributes. I have argued, in the paper "The Recruitment Process and Labor Power" (Division of Humanities and Modern Languages, Epping Forest, Essex, U.K., 1990), for a wider conception of labor-power, taking in attitudes, personality traits and all those personal attributes incorporated within labor-power in acts of production. Other instances of Marx referring to the social production of labor-power can be found in *Wage-Labor*, 158; *Grundrisse*, 527, 575; *Surplus Value 1*, 167; *Capital, Vol. 3*, 292; *Wages, Price*, 56; *Results*, 1032, 1066; *Capital, Vol. 1*, 168. As Marx noted in *Surplus Value 1*, 210, "education produces labour-power."
126. In unpublished work, I have explored the 'amoebic,' elementary and complex forms of labor-power production as part of a method for understanding and explaining the fragmentary nature of the social production of labor-power, i.e., the myriad of empirical institutional forms and processes involved in this heterogeneous productive form. The relation between the abstract (but nevertheless real) and general forms, and their concrete, empirical manifestations, constitutes the basis of an empirical and historical research program. Given the bias against 'Marxist research' in contemporary research funding priorities, it is doubtful whether such a program could be undertaken in my lifetime.
127. In "Work Experience Schemes and Part-Time Jobs in a Recruitment Context," *British Journal of Education and Work* 5, no. 1 (1992): 19–46, I summarize these studies. A recent example of a study that places work attitudes and personality traits making for 'employability' at the top of employers shopping lists of desirable labor-power attributes, is Nigel Meagher's work on Tyneside, England, in "What Do Employers Require from Their Young Recruits?" (Department of Education, University of Newcastle, St. Thomas Street, Newcastle-upon-Tyne, U.K., 1998).

128. See Richard Hatcher, "Labour, Official School Improvement and Equality," *Journal of Education Policy* 13, no. 4 (July–August 1998): 486–490.

129. Marx, *Grundrisse*, 278, 729–730.

130. Neary, *Youth, Training*, 22.

131. Marx, *Grundrisse*, 730, 325.

132. In Glenn Rikowski, "Labour-Power Once More" (unpublished paper, Division of Humanities and Modern Languages, Epping Forest College, Loughton, Essex, U.K., 1990).

133. Marx, *Grundrisse*.

134. See Marx, *Grundrisse*.

135. See Peter McLaren, *Critical Pedagogy and Predatory Culture: Oppositional Politics in a Postmodern Age* (London: Routledge, 1995), *Revolutionary Multiculturalism: Pedagogies of Dissent for the New Millennium* (Boulder, Colo.: Westview Press, 1997), "Revolutionary Pedagogy in Post-Revolutionary Times: Rethinking the Political Economy of Critical Education," *Educational Theory* 48, no. 4 (fall 1998); also Peter McLaren, Gustavo Fischman, Silvia Serra and Estanislao Antelo, "The Specters of Gramsci: Revolutionary Praxis and the Committed Intellectual," *Journal of Thought* (fall 1998): 9–41, and Peter McLaren and Ramin Farahmandpur, chapter 11.

136. Peter McLaren et al., "The Specters of Gramsci," 9–14.

Chapter 7

Youth, Training and the Politics of 'Cool'

Michael Neary

"culture is . . . a mere training to act as the machine."[1]

In the second half of the twentieth century, youth emerged as a distinctive and dramatic form of human sociability. At first reinvented as a precious resource for the reconstructed postwar labor markets, youth quickly degenerated into delinquency, an offense against the moral conscience of the modern world and a threat to the social order. The critical reappraisal of social life that youth expressed in this period was reflected in a radical sociology, inspired by the subversive ideas that appeared to rescue a discredited orthodox Marxism from its economism and dialectic materialism by extending its critical capacity to include, among other things, race, gender and the powerful discursive practices of continental philosophy.[2] Paramount among these new energies was the recognition of culture as a site for the reappraisal of a radical critique of everyday life.

In Britain this cultural preoccupation within radical sociology was given greater emphasis by the setting up of the Birmingham Centre for Contemporary Cultural Studies (BCCCS), with a clear focus on youth. For these researchers, youth was the metaphor for social change.[3] This analysis located the resistances of youth in the material experience of working-class cultures. Its importance was that it identified these oppositions as symbolic deconstructions of middle-class values and norms that made up the dominant ideology. This metaphorical symbolism gave youthful antagonisms a radical edge that had previously been denied in the sociology of youth. Its appeal lay in the fact that it took the explanations for youthful resistances beyond the dysfunctions of a functional society and formulated it in terms of a political threat to a political order—that is, as part of a political crisis. However, the very success attributed to these subcultural strategies—by which young people were able to redefine themselves within, rather than against, massive social upheavals—undermined the radicality that the theory purported to represent. By solving their dilemmas through strategies of subcultural resistance, young people were transforming their own condition to exist within the cultural, economic and political logics of capital. Human resistance was reduced to the status of ritual opposition within which any radicality was more imaginary than real.

However, despite this disability, the 1980s spawned a rash of subcultural and cultural studies of young people as the political crisis deepened and the 'problem of youth' refused to go away—indeed, intensified after the 1981 urban riots. While the new work was critical of early cultural studies or the theoretical assumptions that underpinned it, the criticism was contained within the framework of a cultural paradigm.[4] The effect was to consolidate the position of the work as a radical alternative and to ritualize cultural studies as the basis for alternative study and a theory of human resistance.

In recent years the uncritical presuppositions of cultural studies, energized by the work of Baudrillard and Bourdieu, have asserted themselves as the distinctiveness of youth as a radical form of sociability has dissolved.[5] Whatever critical capacity subcultural studies claimed to represent has been replaced by work that mirrors the affirmative nature of club, drug and cyber cultures,[6] presents an uncritical celebration of counter cultures,[7] or frames the youth question as a problem of integrating excluded young people into social democratic models of citizenship.[8] The result is that any attempt to suggest a theory of human resistance through a radical sociology of youth has been abandoned.

This chapter suggests a theory of human resistance through critical exposition of the concept of youth.[9] I will explain this through a logical and historical account inspired by advances in Marxist science. This approach is derived from the subterranean Marxisms that were re-established in the 1970s through the Conference of Socialist Economists, which subjected the closed categories of orthodox and traditional Marxisms to the subversions found within the work of Marx himself. This approach has coalesced around the term 'Open Marxism.'[10] Central to this critique is the awareness of the real and actually existing subjectivity of capital; also, the centrality of human practice—work, in the constitution of the social world and the immanence of the relation between capital and labor, within which labor exists as a form of capital, wage-labor, in and against capital.

My intention is not to attempt to go beyond Marx but, rather, to use Marx's method in hitherto unexplored areas and to drive Marx toward his own radical conclusions.[11] By developing areas for critical enquiry outside of the limits of political economy, but based within Marx's theory of the law of value, I hope to open up new areas for critical Marxist research while at the same time undermining the claims of radical sociologists. In doing this I accept, of course, the empirical reality of the new critical categories on which this research agenda for a radical sociology is based—for example, gender, race, generation and culture; but I want to argue that the critical capacity of these categories is disabled by the unexplained presuppositions on which they are based. By concentrating on the process out of which these categories are derived, I aim to resist these presuppositions and provide a real theory of human resistance.

A Theory of Human Resistance

The theoretical significance of Marxism for a study of human resistance is that class struggle is the history of all hitherto existing societies. However, the content of class struggle for Marx is not just the struggle between capitalists and workers but, rather, that class struggle is derived out of the inner contradiction within the capital relation: "Capitalist society does not just develop through class struggle. Rather class struggle is a constituted moment of the capital relation because of labor within the concept of capital."[12] For Marx:

> The worker is the subjective manifestation of the fact that capital is man completely lost to himself, just as capital is the objective manifestation of the fact that labour is man lost to himself. But the worker has the misfortune to be a living capital, and hence a capital with needs, which forfeits its interest and hence its existence. . . . The worker produces capital and capital produces him, which means that he produces himself; man as a worker, as a commodity is the product of this entire cycle. . . . The worker exists as a worker only when he exists for himself as capital, and he exists as capital only when capital exists for him. The existence of capital is his existence, his life, for it determines the content of his life in a manner *indifferent* to him.[13]

This focus on the derivation of class struggle forces us to consider the abstract condition of human life. This explanation for the existence of human life as abstract labor is not metaphysical, even though it may appear so. It is the result of the specific way in which unpaid surplus labor is pumped out of direct producers determining the relationship between capital and labor and labor to itself. An understanding of this process reveals the innermost secret, the basis for the way in which modern human life is constituted.[14]

Marx developed the philosophical categories of his earlier work through an explanation of the processes within which human life is constituted. Working directly from the most simple determination in modern society: the commodity form, Marx unpacked the contradictory value relations through which the commodity form was determined, as use-value and exchange-value, to reveal the social form of labor in capitalist society. Labor takes the form of and is socially realized through the commodity. The commodity is a contradictory social form owing to the way it expresses the contradiction between use-value and exchange-value. In this condition concrete (useful) labor is mediated by and becomes socially realized through its opposite: abstract labor.

The substance of abstract labor is not labor embodied in the commodity but, rather, the labor-time socially necessary to produce the commodity. Socially necessary labor-time is the labor-time required to produce any use-value under the conditions of production normal for a given society, and with the average degree of skill and intensity of labor prevalent in society. What exclusively determines the magnitude of the value of an article is therefore the amount of labor socially necessary, or the labor-time socially necessary for its production.[15] Socially necessary labor-time is not simply a chronological measurement of time but the imposition of a particular form of existence on labor: abstract labor.

Values, then, are not established by reference to the intrinsic or concrete qualities of the direct producer, but by reference to the total labor expended in the generalized commodity producing system understood as labor in general, or abstract labor. Human labor exists only to the extent that it is recognized as a component part of this homogeneous and global substance. This recognition has nothing to do with the "corporeal reality" of human labor,[16] but is a purely social mode of existence. In this mode, each human life exists as a moment of the expanding social universe: a unique configuration of time and space within the process by which time and space are reconstituted. As existence is only possible through the formal recognition of the commodity itself in the process of exchange, the commodity comes to dominate the labor that produced it. This attribution of exchange-value takes place without participants being aware of what is actually being recognized.[17] It is assumed, because of the way in which revenues are accrued to the owners of particular commodities, that value is an intrinsic quality of the commodity itself, rather than a substance derived from a particular social relation.[18] This is the basis of commodity fetishism:

> The mysterious character of the commodity-form consists therefore simply in the fact that the commodity reflects the social characteristics of men's own labour as objective characteristics of the products of labour themselves, as the socio-natural properties of these things. Hence it also reflects the social relation of the producers to the sum total of labour as a social relation between objects, a relation which exists apart from and outside the producers. Through this substitution, the products of labour become commodities, sensuous things which are at the same time suprasensible or social.[19]

The significance of this is that in the moment when abstract labor is materialized, in the recognized form of a commodity, human life is disembodied or dematerialized, and "All that is solid melts into air."[20] Its recognition as abstract labor is confirmed by its recognition as a form of value: money in the human form as wage-labor. The content of this arrangement is obscured by the fact that abstract labor, although immaterial, needs to exist in a material form: as a real abstraction. In the same moment that human life is dematerialized, immaterial life is confirmed or commodified as labor and forced to exist in a virtual form: "our use-value may interest men, but it does not belong to us as objects. What does belong to us as objects however is our value. Our own intercourse as commodities proves it. We relate to each other merely as exchange-values."[21]

The dramatic conclusion to be drawn from this analysis is that capital is an impersonal form of social domination generated by labor itself which, in the form of abstract labor, mediates its own existence. Abstract labor is not a mental generalization of various sorts of concrete labor but the real expression of something real.[22] It becomes the identity of value in motion as it expands through itself. Labor in capital is not mediated by social relations; rather it constitutes the mediation and is a form of the mediation. The domination of labor is self-domination.[23] As a real abstraction humanity exists as forms of self-expanding value. This suggests that the real subject of social life is not labor, but capital:

> Its [value] is constantly changing from one into another without becoming lost in this movement: it thus transforms itself into an automatic subject...In truth, however, value is here the subject of a process in which, while constantly assuming the form in turn of money and commodities, it changes its own magnitude . . . and thus valorises itself. . . . For the movement in the course of which it adds surplus value is its own movement, its valorisation is therefore self valorisation. . . . [Value] suddenly presents itself as a self-moving substance which passes through a process of its own, and for which the commodity and money are both mere forms.[24]

But the subjectivity of capital is peculiar: the subject is an unknowing, unconscious subject without an ego, historically determinate and blind;[25] and whose existence demands the denial of its self-generating, or self-valorizing negative capacity, that is, itself.

From this account capital cannot produce itself. Value is not produced by capital.[26] Capital is the expanded form of abstract labor. Abstract labor is the presupposition of capital but it is also the immediate result of the capitalist process of production.[27] Capital and labor then do not simply oppose each other as discrete factors of production, "capital exists only in and through labor."[28] What this means is that the capital relation contains the substance for a revolutionary critique and the possibility for social transformation. In the form of abstract labor, human life exists as the constitutive power of social labor in the form of being denied.[29] This is a peculiar and perverse arrangement within which the real process of the social world is inverted, forming the basis for "the unrealism of the real world. . . . Human life as proxy. . . . The autonomous movement of the non-living. . . . The concrete inversion of life. . . . In a world that really is topsy turvy the true is a moment of the false. . . . A negation of life which has become visible."[30]

This relation is, therefore, deeply and irreconcilably antagonistic. Human life exists in a form that is oppositional not only to the institutions within which, and through which, it is constantly recomposed: money and the state,[31] but in and against itself. The consequence of this condition is that there is no aspect of essential human life to which it can rely to rescue itself as an "alien being."[32] The positive and transforming nature of the relationship is that, as a being that is alien to itself, abstract labor contains the possibility of its own negation, to be not-capital, to dissolve itself and the relation within which it exists and to recompose the relation without negating the constitutive power of labor as the creative force of the social world.[33] This formulation does not suggest an essential humanism as an alternative to capital, but provides the basis for an existential reality not yet constituted, within which human life is the project rather than a resource.[34]

In the next section, I illustrate this theory of human resistance through an historical account of the production of a specific form of human sociability—youth, through a particular form of regulation—training. I concentrate on an

important piece of legislation—the Employment and Training Act 1948, ignored by the sociology of youth—to reveal how the modern category of youth
was constructed. According to my account, the postwar youth phenomenon is
not the result of changes in patterns of consumption and communication;
rather, it derives from the intensification and restructuring of the processes of
production and, within these processes, the recomposition of youth as the imposition of work through the commodity-form—abstract labor.

Youth Training

The modern condition of 'youth' was invented in 1948, as part of the Employment and Training Act 1948 (ETA). The act was intended to support the drive
for productivity that formed the basis for British economic recovery and political importance in the reconstructed postwar world.

The class relations of the postwar period were formalized within this productivity drive as capital sought to reconstruct the conditions for sustained accumulation within an efficient and stable national regime.[35] Productivity, however, is not simply a technical problem to be overcome, based on the mutual
recognition of natural advantage between workers and employers, regulated
through market rationalities; but is, as Marx showed through his exposition of
the law of value, an antagonistic and contradictory process derived from the fact
that in modern society social reproduction is subordinate to the production, accumulation and appropriation of surplus value: a process which depends on the
cooperation of the producers it subordinates. The social relations of capital are
therefore the social relations of struggle between capital and the subordinate
class: labor.

The concrete expression of productivity appeared at this time as increasing
state intervention—at the international level, through currency adjustments,
GATT, IMF and Marshall Aid; nationally through social insurance and administration, rising wages, credit, full employment and a system of industrial relations modeled around the new 'Americanized' methods of mass production that
developed new models of work intensification and a new form of mass
worker.[36] In Britain, this period marks the culmination of a process within which
the working class is finally subsumed within the relations of capitalist production.[37] The place for young people in this new fully integrated form of regulation was prepared by the Employment and Training Act 1948.

The Act of 1948: A Revolution in Social Progress

The Employment and Training Act (ETA) of 1948 lacked the spectacular provisions associated with the socialization of consumption and the intoxicating
wish-fulfillment of the policy of full employment. The ETA 1948 was a significant moment in the history of vocational education and training in the U.K.,
representing the first coordinated response by the state to the disequilibrium, as

it was portrayed, in the labor market and, as such, it did not lack passionate advocates. Lord Hewerson, the First Lord of the Admiralty, was in no doubt about the importance of the act: "From the days of Kier Hardie," he said, "men of vision have had this ideal before them," forming part of "a revolution in social progress."[38] Charles Tennyson, president of the British Association of Commercial and Industrial Education (BACIE), addressing its national conference in July 1948, articulated these sentiments: "The conditions confronting the country are so new, and so little original thought has been given in the past to the subject" of training "that it is practically a new subject." Therefore, it was felt that young people should be connected more intimately to the capitalist labor process. The device through which this could be achieved was "national training schemes which would be made compulsory in law in all industry," within the context of manpower planning and full employment.[39]

The purpose of the act was to consolidate existing labor legislation in a way that recognized the final subsumption of labor within the capital relation and provide an effective labor market across all sectors, skills and age ranges. The first part of the act dealt with general matters to facilitate this process. The second part of the act, deemed "more interesting" by *The Economist*[40] was designed "to create a more effective organisation for giving young people advice and assistance in choosing their careers," and to end the confusion between what "some regard as an education service and others more closely aligned to the world of employments."[41] It was hoped that this clarification would allow for better labor market planning, to make for higher quality and common standards and to address the chronic labor shortage of young people—"rare and precious creatures"—the seriousness of which demanded "a revolution in thought about the training of the young."[42] All this would be achieved by centralizing schemes for young people under a Central Juvenile Employment Executive, staffed by the Minister of Labor and the Minister of Education and advised by a National Juvenile Employment Council, consisting of teachers, employers, trade unionists, local authority representatives and five independent persons.[43]

The scheme was marketed as a structure to ease the transition from school to work for all "boys and girls," a vital component for "their future development and happiness" and a "sympathetic and practical guide" to those "boys and girls" who had ideas for work but "are too shy to talk about them," or whom "their teachers were not experienced to deal with." Provision was to be made, "where appropriate, for a grant to be given to young people with a special aptitude for a particular occupation, but with no local outlet, so as to be able to leave home and be placed with an employer in another area as an apprentice or learner."[44]

The area of most dispute centered on the question of compulsion. Such was the shortage of young people that it was originally felt that attachment to the scheme should be mandatory: parents and children should be required to attend Employment Exchanges in order that they might receive advice and be made aware of the opportunities available. It was, however, eventually decided that persuasion as to the benefits of the scheme would be more appropriate.[45]

The drafters of the Employment and Training Act, therefore, paid a good deal of attention to 'propaganda', that is, how the world of capitalist work could be made attractive to the young working class. Much of that discussion centered on what to call the new employment scheme for the young working class and, more particularly, what to call the young working class.

This is a fascinating and critical moment in the creation of modern youth and yet it has been completely ignored by the sociology of youth. The debate focused on what to call young workers. This problem was discussed at length by Members of Parliament (MPs) in debates on the floor of the House and in Committee. The problem was that, as Issacs (the Minister of Labour) pointed out, there is no English word that properly describes those between the ages of 15 and 18. Other MPs (Dumpleton, Langford-Holt, Lindsay) argued that the former title of "juvenile" was too offensive, suggesting delinquency and likely to dissuade young people from approaching the new employment service. However, as Issacs made clear, there were real practical difficulties in replacing "juvenile" as it was carved on the headings outside employment exchanges. Suggestions for a new title included the serious and the not so serious. Maitland's suggestion "careerist advisee" was rejected for its "bourgeois, middle-class snobbishness;" the term "young people" suggested by Dumpleton, a self-proclaimed expert on such matters, was refused as being "patronising and priggish;" and "adultry," recommended by Orr-Ewing, was not taken seriously. In the end the title "youth," suggested by Lindsay, was agreed on despite the fact that Dumpleton felt it to be "too abstract and refer to young people en mass." And so the Juvenile Employment Service became the Youth Employment Service.[46]

Youth: A Real Abstraction

At first reading this might seem like a trivial amendment, but I want to suggest that it reflects a significant recomposition that occurred in the world of work through the recomposition of youthful labor. This discussion among MPs is, in fact, a spectacular example of the way in which the real process, by which labor is recomposed as abstract labor, is reflected by its definition as a real abstraction. The term 'youth' is chosen precisely because of its abstract and depersonalized character and its ability to convey the characteristic of immaterial life. The category 'youth' was a recognition of the new condition of massified and intensified labor as it was to apply to the young working class.

It is precisely because 'youth' was an abstract term and did not apply to young body in particular that it was felt to be so appropriate. The status of youth does not refer to any person in particular nor is it based on the particular attributes of any young person, but is a status attributed to the young working class based entirely on their capacity to become the commodity labor power: to exist as abstract labor. As such it marks the culmination of a process by which the young working class were fully and really subsumed within the capital relation as commodity labor power. The recognition of this new status by MPs is not a conscious decision but is the outcome of a process that occurs 'behind the backs' of the politicians. While recognition occurs in the minds of the legislators, it is not the product of the mind but is derived from the real status of young people in the production of the social relations of capitalist society.[47] By recognizing modern youth as a real abstraction it is possible to reformulate the way in which youth can be understood in this period, while at the same time undermining and overcoming the sociology of youth. As a real abstraction, youth is understood not simply as an empirical reality that is defined by its consumptive characteristics, but as a productive energy within the social relations of capitalist society. The condition of youth is not defined by physical attributes but is a status attributed to youth as a result of its position within the productive relations of capital. In this form it is possible to explain the conformity of modern youth: as abstract labor, youth exists as a form of capital, and its antagonism: as a form of abstract labor, youth exists in the form of being denied, a form that is antagonistic not only to the institutions within which it is maintained but also to itself. Youth is a being that is alien to itself. The theory of human resistance derived from this condition is that as a being that is alien to itself, youth as a form of abstract labor contains the possibility of its own negation, to be not-capital, to dissolve itself and the relation within which it exists and to recompose the relation without negating the constitutive power of labor as the creative force of the social world.

Training Culture: Against Human Resistance

Utilizing this methodology, it is possible to invert the critical devices of cultural studies of youth and provide a much richer and fuller account of the development of postwar youth, its conformity, its radicality and its eventual demise. Through an examination of the dynamic principle contained within the production of the commodity-form, it is possible to argue that young people were not accommodating themselves to the social upheavals caused by massive economic and political upheavals; but, rather, as a result of the productive negativity of abstract labor, capital and its institutions are forced to recompose themselves into institutional forms that exist to contain the power of labor.

By recognizing the significance of this struggle, rather than accepting the cultural logics of the capitalist machine, it is possible to reassess the institutional forms of the state. Confronted by the resistance of the working class, it was capital that was forced to find solutions to the uncompromising character of the form of sociability that they had produced. From this line of argument it is possible to reconsider the training legislation of the period. Rather than understanding postwar training regimes—for example, Industrial Training Boards—as a rational response to the 'white hot' capacities of the new technologies, or as instruments to resolve labor market inefficiencies—for example, the Employment and Training Act, 1972—or, even more critically, as functional agents of social control—for example, the Manpower Services Commission—this analysis allows us to understand that:

every innovation, new body, tribunal or commission originates either directly or at one removed from working class resistance to the formal conditions of its life. Just as machinery is the product of labour which then confronts its producer as an alien force, so [training] administration is the appropriation of the revolutionary will by the state, and its transformation into a counter-revolutionary force.48

The training regimes of the period are a dramatic demonstration of an attempt by capital to recompose young labor into an appropriate form. These solutions are not imaginary, but neither are they convincing. This lack of conviction leads to further recomposition and intensification of struggle and resistance.

Human Resistance and the Politics of 'Cool'

This account also allows us to theorize resistance beyond the orthodox account of working class struggle: to conceive of a theory of human resistance that does not derive its radicality from its attachment to a dramatic category of human sociability, nor gain its radical credibility through attempts to affirm these categories. Instead, the critical purpose of this theory is to reveal the dynamic principle out of which those critical categories are derived so as to dissolve the categorical way in which human life is constructed. From this account young people are not simply struggling in and against the alienated institutional power of capital in the form of money and the state, they are also struggling in and against the institutional form of human sociability through which their own existence is determined. Youth is struggling in and against itself. The distinct forms of sociability that young people adopted in this period are not accommodating solutions to the problem of enormous social, political and economic restructuring; they are, rather, the outcome of a very developed form of labor (abstract labor) within which all identity has been destroyed. The dramatic and distinctive styles that young people produce are not based on attachments to working-class history (e.g., skinheads), or the aspirations for a higher class status (e.g., mods). In fact, they derive from the destruction of class categories, the lack of any defining particularity of work and the need for abstract labor to take on a specific human identity. The defining characteristic of this arrangement is indifference, or 'cool.'

Although this most youthful condition appears as a mental event or attitude, it is not a product of the mind. Cool indifference corresponds to the world of abstract labor, where individuals can with ease transfer from one labor to another, or one style to another and where the specific kind of labor, or style, is a matter of chance or indifference to its demonstrators. But 'cool' is not simply a matter of fashion: as an expression of abstract labor, 'cool' also contains the possibility of its own negation, to exist as 'not youth.'[49] In this significant way, indifference carries within it the logic of human indiscipline and resistance. 'Cool' is not only the actuality of a revolt into style,[50] but also carries within it the possibility of a revolt into *revolt*.

In the current moment, the form of youthful labor created in 1948 and the life and culture that was associated with it is being destroyed. Young workers have been redesigned not as a trained and integral parts of a dynamic productive process, but as cheap labor.[51] In this condition, the irresponsibility and indifference that characterized the postwar generation is denied, and young people are forced to exist as responsible citizens. For the moment, the politics of resistance are elsewhere, but from Marx's theory of human resistance and from the modern history of human struggle, we know it cannot be contained.

Notes

1. Karl Marx and Friedrich Engels, *The Communist Manifesto* [1848] (Harmondsworth, U.K.: Penguin Classics, 1985), 99.

2. This approach was inspired by proponents of Western Marxism (e.g., Gramsci, Poulantzas), writers from the Frankfurt school (e.g., Adorno), British Marxist history (e.g., E. P. Thompson) and various types of French structuralism and poststructuralism (Levi-Strauss, Foucault), amongst others.

3. See Stuart Hall and Tony Jefferson, eds., *Resistance through Rituals: Youth Subculture in Post-War Britain* (London: Hutchinson, 1975).

4. See Dick Hebdige, *Subculture: The Meaning of Style* (London: Methuen, 1979) and *Hiding in the Light* (London: Routledge, 1988); Mike Cole and Bob Skelton, eds., *Blind Alley: Youth in a Crisis of Capital* (Ormskirk, U.K.: G. W. & A. Hesketh, 1980); Phil Cohen, *Rethinking the Youth Question, Education, Labour and Cultural Studies* (Basingstoke, U.K.: Macmillan, 1997); Dan Finn, *Training without Jobs, New Deals and Broken Promises* (London: Macmillan, 1987); Simon Frith, *Sound Effects: Youth, Leisure, and the Politics of Rock* (London: Constable, 1983); Simon Clarke, *Marx, Marginalism and Modern Sociology* (London: Macmillan, 1991); Robert Hollands, *The Long Transition* (London: Macmillan, 1990); Paul Willis, *Consuming Passions* (Milton Keynes, U.K.: Open University Press, 1990) and *Moving Culture* (London: Calouste Gulbenkian Foundation, 1990); Angela McRobbie, *Postmodern and Popular Culture* (London: Routledge, 1994).

5. It has become commonplace to mourn the loss of youth culture. This approach is more prevalent in journalistic accounts than in radical sociological perspectives, which seem intent on keeping the category alive. See *The Modern Review*, March 1998, on the transition of adolescence into adultescence.

6. See Willis, *Consuming Passions*; McRobbie, *Postmodern and Popular*; Steven Redhead, *Rave Off* (Aldershot, U.K.: Avebury, 1993).

7. Paul Gilroy, *Black Atlantic: Modernity and Double Consciousness* (London: Verso, 1993); George McKay, *Senseless Acts of Beauty: Cultures of Resistance since the Sixties* (London: Verso, 1996).

8. Cohen, *Rethinking*; Johanna Wyn and Robert White, *Rethinking Youth* (London: Sage, 1997).

9. I have chosen this category for the radicality it seemed to offer to sociology. I do not mean to privilege youth above any other critical concept. Indeed, the basis of my argument is that my critical approach toward the sociology of youth is generalizable to all other critical categories of radical sociology.

10. See volumes 1 and 2 of Werner Bonefeld, Richard Gunn, and Kosmas Psychopedis, eds., *Open Marxism* (London: Pluto, 1992); also, Werner Bonefeld, Richard

Gunn, John Holloway and Kosmas Psychopedis, eds., *Open Marxism Vol. 3* (London: Pluto, 1995).

11. Alfred Sohn-Rethel, *Intellectual and Manual Labour: A Critique of Epistemology* (London: Macmillan, 1978).

12. Werner Bonefeld, "Capital as Subject and the Existence of Labour," in *Open Marxism 3*, 182–212.

13. Karl Marx, *Economic and Philosophical Manuscripts of 1844*, in *Early Writings* (London: Penguin Classics, 1992); emphasis added.

14. For this point, see Karl Marx, *Capital: A Critique of Political Economy—Volume 1* (Harmondsworth, U.K.: Penguin, 1986), 163, and Karl Marx, *Capital: A Critique of Political Economy—Volume.3*, (Harmonsdsworth, U.K.: Penguin, 1981), 799.

15. Marx, *Capital Vol. 1*, 129.

16. Karl Marx, *Theories of Surplus Value—Part 1* (Moscow: Progress Publishers, 1975), 167.

17. Marx, *Capital, Vol. 1*, 166.

18. Clarke, *Marx, Marginalism*, 126.

19. Marx, *Capital, Vol. 1*, 164–165.

20. Marx and Engels, *Manifesto*, 83.

21. Marx, *Capital, Vol. 1*, 176–177.

22. Moishe Postone, *Time, Labour and Social Domination: A Reinterpretation of Marx's Critical Theory* (Cambridge: Cambridge University Press, 1993), 146.

23. Postone, *Time, Labour*, 172–173.

24. Marx, *Capital, Vol. 1*, 255–256.

25. Postone, *Time, Labour*, 77.

26. See John Holloway, "From Scream of Refusal to Scream of Power: The Centrality of work," in Bonefeld et al., *Open Marxism 3*.

27. Marx, *Capital, Vol. 1*, 949.

28. Bonefeld et al., *Open Marxism 3*, 189.

29. See Bonefeld et al., *Open Marxism Vols. 1 and 2*. The same point is developed by Geoffrey Kay and James Mott in *Political Order and the Law of Labour* (London: Macmillan, 1982), 96, where they state:

> Administration is working-class power post festum; working class political victories captured and formalised at their moment of triumph. . . . The development of administration and the advance of technology both appear in the same light, as rationalisations which unfold themselves, each moment forward seeming to arise from a logical development of the previous one, but in both cases the appearance is false. In capitalist society technology has always developed in response to specific conditions as a means of overcoming working class opposition to existing methods of production, and in this sense, of being precipitated by working class struggles, new techniques can be seen as their obituary.

30. Guy Debord, *The Society of the Spectacle* (Detroit: Black and Red, 1977), extracts from Theses 1–10.

31. See Simon Clarke, *Keynesianism, Monetarism and the Crisis of the State* (Aldershot, U.K.: Edward Elgar, 1988).

32. Bonefeld et al., *Open Marxism 3*, 199.

33. Holloway, "Scream," 172.

34. See Bonefeld, *Open Marxism 3*.

35. Clarke, *Keynesianism*, 244–286.

36. See Antonio Negri, *Revolution Retrieved, Selected Writings on Marx, Keynes, Capitalist Crisis and New Social Subjects 1967–1983* (London: Red Notes, 1988).

37. See Kay and Mott, *Political Order*.

38. The notes from a Ministry of Labour speech in June 1948, *Employment and Training Bill, 8/1507Y* (London: National Record Office, 1948).

39. Trades Union Congress Report, 1948. See Michael Neary, *Youth, Training and the Training State: The Real History of Youth Training in the Twentieth Century* (London: Macmillan, 1997).

40. *The Economist*, April 3, 1947.

41. *Ministry of Labour Papers 8/1508* (London: National Record Office, 1948), and see Neary, *Youth, Training.*

42. *The Economist*, April 3, 1948 and *The Economist*, November 29, 1946.

43. *Ministry of Labour Papers, 8/1508* (London: National Record Office, 1948).

44. "Notes on First Reading of the Employment and Training Bill," *Ministry of Labour Papers* (London: National Record Office, 1948).

45. Trades Union Congress Report, 1948, 224. See Neary, *Youth, Training.*

46. These extracts are from "Employment and Training Bill, 16th April 1948," in *Hansard* (1948), 1379–1386; and from "Employment and Training Bill Committee, 4 May 1948," in *Hansard Vol. III* (1948), 486–549. For a full account of this debate see Neary, *Youth, Training.*

47. For a theoretical exposition of the relationship between consciousness and human actions, see Sohn-Rethel, *Intellectual and Manual.*

48. Kay and Mott, *Political Order*, 96.

49. The most dramatic form of youth being not youth was demonstrated by Punk. This extraordinary phenomenon appeared in the moment when the world for which youth had been created in 1948 collapsed, and the process of the recomposition of youth began. Punk was a refusal by young people to accept their new condition.

50. See Hebdige, *Subculture.*

51. See Glenn Rikowski and Michael Neary, "Working Schoolchildren in Britain Today," *Capital and Class* 63 (1997): 25–35.

Chapter 8

Marxism, Class Analysis and Postmodernism

Dave Hill, Mike Sanders and Ted Hankin

Introduction: A Class-Divided Society

The overall economic context in which educational, social, economic and political inequalities are reproduced is a class-based capitalist mode of production. In this chapter we challenge the analyses and pronouncements that 'class is dead;' 'we live in a classless society;' 'class identity and affiliation are archaic formulae;' 'relations of production have been superseded in political, educational and social importance by relations of consumption;' 'we live in a postmodern and post-Fordist society and economy;' 'there is no class struggle;' and the notion that 'political and educational practices and theories of class struggle are totalitarian, oppressive of other social groups, and doomed to failure.'

Postmodern academics at one level, and a range of politicians and political theorists at another, have attempted to consign Marxist analysis and socialist egalitarian educational and political programs to the dustbin of history. In addition to postmodernist academics, political groups seeking to inter Marxism include both Radical Right Thatcherites/Reaganites and their neoliberal/ neoconservative successors, and 'Third Way' politicians such as Bill Clinton, Tony Blair and Gerhardt Schroeder.[1] However, the perspective forwarded in this chapter is that a Marxist analysis and understanding of social class is crucially significant for an understanding of contemporary capitalism, and for a grasping of the restructuring of education that has been occurring since the 1980s in many of the advanced capitalist industrial states. It is also argued that an understanding of social class is essential for developing and constructing economic, political and education systems based on social justice and egalitarianism.

Social Class: What Are the Facts?

Despite proclamations from politicians and pundits that we now inhabit a class-less society, or that "we are all middle class now,"[2] the simple truth is that for the last two decades class divisions and class-based forms of inequality have increased. The degree to which the United Kingdom is class-divided society is apparent from following statistics:

- "Looking at the very poorest, 8.75 million people were in households with less than 40 per cent of average income. This is half a million higher than in 1996/97 and four times the level of the early 1980s."[3]

- "As of 1998/99 . . . there were 4.5 million children in households with below half-average income after housing costs. This represents a three-fold rise over the last twenty years. Around two million children live in households where there is no adult in paid employment."[4] Child poverty is almost 50 percent higher in 2001 than in 1979, the last year Labour was in office, "despite falling levels of unemployment since 1997 and a massive growth in the wealth of the country since 1979."[5]

- Differences in health between the different social classes "remains striking: children in the manual social classes are twice as likely to die in an accident as those in the non-manual classes, and girls in the manual social classes are around five times as likely to become mothers as those in non-manual classes."[6]

- "Lone parents and households with an unemployed head are twice as likely to get burgled as the average, and much less likely to have any household insurance. And one in six of the poorest households do not have any type of bank or building society account, compared with one in twenty households on average incomes,"[7] living poorly, running out of money for food and fares before the next payday or the next welfare check.

- "Based on a survey in September 1999 . . . more than two-fifths of [lone parents] with one child said they had incomes below £163 ($261) a week, the amount needed to buy the goods and services that most people regarded as essentials," and "More than half lone parents with two or more children had incomes below . . . £227 ($363) a week."[8]

- A Social Trends survey "found that the distribution of income became more unequal in the 80s, stabilised in the early 90s and began to widen again in 1997. In 1997–98 the income of the richest 10% rose 4% cent to £559.70 ($896) a week while for the poorest it rose only 1.8% to £136.10 ($218)."[9]

- As regards the distribution of wealth, the poorest half of the population owns only 5–6 percent of the total national wealth. The most wealthy 1 percent on the other hand, owned around a quarter of all wealth.[10]

At the same time as salaries and wages have risen at the top end of the scale, there has been an accompanying shift from such labor income to property income. In 1995 while wages and salaries rose by 4 percent before tax, income from dividends and interest is estimated to have grown by 38 percent in money terms before tax. In the period from 1992 to 1995 there was a redistribution of around £24 billion ($38 billion) each year from British wages and salaries to gross profits.

In *A Class Act, The Myth of Britain's Classless Society* (1997), further evidence shows the extent to which Britain is still a deeply divided society, characterized by class distinctions. In particular, this account by Andrew Adonis and Stephen Pollard focuses on the system of secondary education, which is rigidly separated into a flourishing, lavishly funded private sector, and a demoralized, underfinanced public sector. They point out that those who benefit from private education are almost invariably from privileged backgrounds: the fact that they attend the best schools in the country merely entrenches their privileges and enhances their prospects still further.[11]

Poverty—low income and the lack of wealth—is overwhelmingly a function of social class position. While there are certainly examples of distressed gentlefolk who have attended the most prestigious and expensive private schools (such as Eton or Roedean), and while there are many highly paid professionals and senior managers whose weekly income is less than their weekly expenditure, poverty is not the typical characteristic of graduates of Eton or Roedean, nor of senior managers or media moguls. Poverty is, however, the typical characteristic of the unemployed and the unskilled white-collar and blue-collar working classes. The increasing inequalities in Britain, the impoverishment and creation of a substantial underclass have been well documented. For example, in Britain the ratio of chief executives' pay to average worker's pay stands at 35 to 1. In the United States it has climbed to 450 to 1 (from around 35 to 1 in the mid-1980s).[12] Inequalities both between states and within states have increased dramatically during the era of global neoliberalism. In the United States, for example, the economic apartheid nature of capitalism has been widely exposed in the work of Peter McLaren.[13] In July 2000, in a speech to the NAACP, Ralph Nader depicted the growing inequalities in California:

> I just bring to you a little fact from California. For those of you who are skeptical of people who tell you that things are getting better but we got to make them even better, try child poverty in California. In 1980, it was 15.2 percent; today it is 25.1 per cent. And if you take near poverty—the children who are near poverty, who I would consider in poverty because I think the official levels of poverty are absurd, how can anyone support a four-member family on $17,200 a year—before deductions, before the cost of getting to work, et cetera? If you add the near poverty, 46 per cent of all the children in

California are in the category. This is not just a badge of shame for our country, the richest country in the world, it's a reflection of our inability to focus
on the signal phenomena that is blocking justice, and that is the concentration
of power and wealth in too few hands...And to give you a further illustration,
the top 1 per cent of the richest people in our country have wealth—financial
wealth—equal to the bottom 95 percent.[14]

To take another example, Chile, hailed as a beacon of neoliberal policies,

boasts one of the most unequal economies in the world . . . in which only 10
per cent of the Chilean population earns almost half the wealth and in which
the richest 100 people earn more than the state spends on social services. Real
salaries have declined 10 per cent since 1986 and they are still 18 per cent
lower than when Allende was in power.[15]

In this context, postmodernism's celebration of consumerism, consumption and
'lifestyle choices' seems a hollow, if not an obscene, mockery. What, we might
ask, does postmodernism have to say about poverty and inequality? The answer
is very little. Indeed, it is difficult to see how postmodernism can address these
issues. After all, where Marxism sees structural inequality, postmodernism sees
'social difference.' Similarly, when Marxism argues that poverty is an offense
against the notion of a just social order it betrays (at least to postmodern opponents) its nostalgic, if not reactionary, commitment to those metanarratives of
the Enlightenment that postmodernism rejects.

Postmodernism and Social Class

Given the decisive role played by class as a structuring factor in people's lives,
the question which arises is this: Why have so many ostensibly, and often self-
proclaimed, 'radical' critics and theorists enlisted under the banner of postmodernism and abandoned class as a category of analysis? For there can be no doubt
that class has been abandoned by many critics who would describe themselves
as committed to a progressive politics, for example, as 'resistance postmodernists.'[16]

In the following paragraphs, we identify the cultural-historical factors that
underpin the abandonment of class by sections of the radical intelligentsia.
These are grouped under two main headings, which for convenience we might
term extrinsic problems with class analysis and intrinsic problems of class
analysis. This distinction is necessary because it is important to disentangle
those wider cultural and historical factors informing the retreat from class and
the internal problems of inadequate theorization within class-based analyses that
allow the retreat from class to cover itself with a veneer of intellectual sophistication. It is also vital that class-based analyses address their own theoretical
weaknesses, as these have contributed to the way the concept of class lost purchase within the academy.

Extrinsic Problems with Class Analysis

We begin with the briefest of sketches of changing intellectual trends within the Western academy. During the sixties and seventies Marxism became fashionable in academia, although in the latter decade it was increasingly contested by a variety of poststructuralisms which, cumulatively, contributed to the formation of postmodernism. The timing, extent and success of this challenge to Marxism varied across disciplines but, generally speaking, by the mid-eighties postmodernism had installed itself as the fashionable, and thereafter dominant, intellectual trend. In order to understand the reasons for postmodernism's dominance within the academy we must situate that rise within the wider historical and social context that produced it. As Aijaz Ahmad observes, in *In Theory: Classes, Nations, Literatures*, a Marxist analysis of theory must engage with the following questions:

> the issue of the institutional sites from which that theory emanates; the actual class practices and concrete social locations, in systems of power and powerlessness, of the agents who produce it; the circuits through which it circulates and the class fractions who endow it with whatever power it gains; hence the objective determination of the theory itself by these material co-ordinates of its production, regardless of the individual agent's personal stance toward these locations and co-ordinates. . . . The characteristic feature of contemporary literary radicalism is that it rarely addresses the question of its own determination by the conditions of its production and the class location of its agents.[17]

It is precisely this absence that Ahmad seeks to interrogate, by asking how and why poststructuralism and then postmodernism came to dominate the Western academy. Although Ahmad is immediately concerned with developments within literary studies, we would argue that his analysis is applicable generally.

Ahmad argues that poststructuralism is conditioned by the contradictory experiences of, on the one hand the anti-imperialist struggles, student radicalism and labor militancy of the late 1960s to early 1970s, and on the other hand their containment by the mid-1970s and the subsequent capitalist counter-offensive of the 1980s. The class background of many of the students who participated in this "revolutionary wave" meant that most lacked any previous connection with the organized labor movement and few developed a lasting commitment to it. Almost by definition, Ahmad suggests, those students who completed a Ph.D. and became academics were those who were least involved in the political movements:

> It was, in other words, mostly the survivors of the 'movement' who later became so successful in the profession. Radicalism had been, for most of them, a state of mind, brought about by an intellectual identification with the revolutionary wave that had gripped so much of the world when they were truly young; of the day-to-day drudgeries of, say, a political party or a trade union they had been (and were to remain) largely innocent.[18]

Many critics of postmodernism, including us, have insisted that it is the product of a very particular historical conjuncture. Alex Callinicos, for example, has described postmodernism as "the product of a socially mobile intelligentsia in a climate dominated by the retreat of the Western labor movement and the 'overconsumptionist' dynamic of capitalism in the Reagan-Thatcher era." Callinicos also suggests that postmodernism allows that same intelligentsia "to articulate its political disillusionment and its aspiration to a consumption orientated lifestyle." While the attractions of a consumerist lifestyle are obvious, the claim of "political disillusionment" requires closer attention.[19]

On one level, postmodernist political disillusion appears to replicate a well-established cultural pattern whereby young radicals become old conservatives. Yet unlike earlier examples (for example, Wordsworth and Coleridge, or many 'Marxist' intellectuals of the 1930s), conversion to postmodernism is usually accompanied by declarations of an increased, rather than abandoned, radicalism. These claims have generally been accepted by the rising generation of academic 'resistance postmodernists,' who proudly insist on the ultraradicalism of their postmodernist affiliations and denounce the conservatism of Marxism with its 'reactionary' attachment to a range of discredited, 'totalitarian' metanarratives.[20]

Amongst the attractions of postmodernism is the way in which it harmonizes with the career needs of a rising generation of professional intellectuals. Postmodernism, with its rejection of 'foundationalist' modes of thought, provides the theoretical underpinning for an assault on the established academic order. In this respect, postmodernism was able to posit itself as standing in the same relation to Marxism as (academic) Marxism had to 'Liberal Humanism.' Moreover, postmodernism had the added attraction of promising something entirely new, and in this respect it fully deserves its characterization (by Frederic Jameson) as "the cultural logic of late capitalism."[21] For in representing itself as 'new,' it was simultaneously laying claim to the epithet—which always accompanies newness in contemporary advertising—of 'improved.' There is an interesting homology here between commodity production and theoretical production. Just as under late capitalism any change to a product leads to its being advertised as 'new and improved' (even when, as in the case of a certain soap-powder, this improvement actually entailed the more rapid degradation and destruction of your clothing), so in the realm of academia the new theoretical paradigm pronounced itself to be 'new and improved' (with similarly corrosive and destructive results as regards the 'fabric' of progressive action as the aforementioned soap-powder).

Postmodernism, however, offered a rather different account of its relationship to late capitalism. It had emerged (so it was claimed) precisely because the old paradigms were no longer capable of explaining the new social and cultural order which, postmodernists also claimed, had recently arisen. There is a sense in which postmodernism can be seen as the latest in a long line of theories which have proclaimed the transformation of capitalism into something qualitatively different, the latest incarnation of the type of revisionist and class-collaborationist politics associated with the social democracy of Edward Bernstein in the late nineteenth and early twentieth century. In conformity to this tradition, postmodernists also have "the obvious ideological mission of demonstrating, to their own relief, that the new social formation in question no longer obeys the laws of classical capitalism, namely, the primacy of industrial production and the omnipresence of class struggle."[22] As such, postmodernism is likely to founder on the same rocks that have shattered all of its ancestors—economic crisis, rising class antagonism, interimperialist rivalry.

Postmodernists, no doubt, would reject the charge of class collaboration. After all, a key part of their analysis denies that there are such things as social classes. It is this part of the theoretical project of postmodernism—its jettison of class analysis as something which is no longer relevant in the postmodern world—that we want to examine in greater depth. We want to begin with what is perhaps the most frequent 'common sense' rejection of class, which holds that it is an anachronistic category no longer relevant in the context of a (postmodern) society, which has become 'classless'—as claimed by the former Conservative British Prime Minister, John Major, for example.

The basic thesis of classlessness comes (appropriately enough, considering postmodernism's emphasis on the importance of consumer choice) in a wide range of models with varying degrees of theoretical sophistication and varying accounts of how this state of affairs was produced. For the most part, theorists of classlessness agree that class has only disappeared relatively recently from the historical stage (i.e., in the postwar period and, for many, not until the collapse of Soviet style 'communism' in the 1980s and 1990s). They also argue that the disappearance of class has resulted from cultural changes occurring as a result of the transition from a 'Fordist' to a 'post-Fordist' economy. Champions of this position point to the destruction, variously, of 'traditional' class signifiers (in Britain, the decline of flat caps and whippets), class institutions (such as Trades Unions, the Co-op, the Workers Educational Association), class locations (such as the mining village, the steel town, factory area), and therefore of class consciousness (evidenced by four successive Conservative electoral victories between 1979 and 1997, and by New Labour's 'classless' appeal in its 1997 and 2001 general election campaigns). The social and cultural order organized around class has been replaced, they assert, by a 'new order' based on individual rights, mobility, choice (of consumption and lifestyle in particular), and freedom.

It needs to be acknowledged, however, that the 'autonomous consumer' account of recent cultural changes has convinced many people and that its appeal is based on its *apparent* accuracy—it does appear to offer a convincing explanation of recent history. Our contention, however, is that this account is only *superficially* accurate: homelessness and unemployment, for example, have rapidly expanded but to accept this as a feature of autonomy is predicated on an ideological surrender to neoliberalism. In other words, the acceptance of this account of recent changes depends on a prior acceptance of its ideological assumptions.

A willingness to be convinced by postmodernism is influenced to a considerable extent by class position and/or affiliation. This assertion will no doubt provoke outrage from those postmodernists who are happy to demonstrate the ways in which the theoretical preferences of particular individuals are always already determined by wider networks of power, but who are far less willing to accept that their own position (by their own logic) is generated by and serves 'power' beyond themselves.[23]

In response to this account of the disappearance of class, we must draw attention to the way in which it depends on an account of class that is not so much a theory as a caricature. Consider, for example, John Urry's summary of the conventional Marxist account of class:

> Marxism has traditionally held that social classes are generated by the economic base of societies, in particular by their dominant form of exploitation; that such classes have a relatively unambiguous 'interest,' either to preserve or to destroy existing social relations; that there is a once-and-for-all establishment of classes-for-themselves which are nationally (or even internationally) unified and which have a clear class interest; that such classes generate forms of politics and culture which, except at the point of revolutionary transformation, cannot reflect back upon the class structure; and that the only social forces of real significance within capitalism are the bourgeoisie and the proletariat, meaning that other social classes and forces do not possess significant transformative powers. [24]

Outside the Marxist tradition, it is clear that many critics of class analysis (such as Jan Pakulski, referred to later) confound (whether deliberately or accidentally) class consciousness with the fact of class—and tend to deduce the nonexistence of the latter from the 'absence' of the former.[25]

As noted earlier, the collapse of many traditional signifiers of 'working-classness' has led many to pronounce the demise of class. Our first response to this is to observe with Beverley Skeggs that:

> To abandon class as a theoretical tool does not mean that it does not exist any more; only that some theorists do not value it. It does not mean . . . [working-class people] experience inequality any differently; rather, it would make it more difficult for them to identify and challenge the basis of the inequality which they experience. *Class inequality exists beyond its theoretical representation.*[26]

To this we might add that the structural effects of class persist, and are in fact more pernicious in their operation and effects, precisely because of the difficulties of finding adequate cultural (as well as theoretical) representations of 'working-classness.' To extend the military metaphor of the 'class war,' we might say that while the class war still rages[27] the working class in general has been culturally—and, more importantly, politically—demobilized and only the capitalist class knows itself to be in uniform. It always does. In this context the denial of the relevance of a class analysis by postmodernism has contributed to the ideological disarming of the working-class movement.

Class Struggle from Above and Below

The arguments concerning the disappearance of class might appear to possess a certain purchase when the focus is placed exclusively on the 'working class,' but are far less persuasive if we turn our attention to the question of the existence of a capitalist class. Is there, we wonder, anyone amongst the postmodernists who would dispute the existence of a relatively small group of people owning tremendous amounts of material wealth, wielding immense power, sharing similar cultural backgrounds and aspirations often reinforced by close family and other personal ties, who are adept at defending and promoting their interests?

In contrast, at first sight it may appear that the wealthiest 500 individuals in the United States are acting in opposition to their class interests by signing a petition and lobbying against President George W. Bush's proposed cuts on estate duty. This reflects a robust cultural difference with Britain, where persons who have inherited wealth are still held in high social esteem and indeed fawned upon. The notion that there are 'no free lunches' in America, which is widely upheld as a major ideological legitimation for the various 'Welfare to Work' programs, is merely being exhibited, albeit in a different format, by this superrich grouping. Members of this group are much more perceptive than the president in upholding their long-term hegemony: much better for their offspring to be perceived by the mass of the population as having to earn a living and progress on merit—even if in reality the life chances available to them (of which education is a major one) mean that they start near the top of the ladder—than to be identified as effortless purveyors of inherited wealth.

The view of these 500 richest has not gone unregarded: by a vote of 35 to 65 the U.S. Senate in early April 2001 substantially cut Bush's proposed tax cuts from $1.62 trillion over a ten-year period to $1.18 trillion and, as importantly, substantially raised spending by billions of dollars on education and agriculture (as well as on that Bush favorite, defense). Expenditure on a Medicare drug program was also doubled to $300 billion over a ten-year period. However, this needs to be contextualized: the United States remains immensely undertaxed, in comparison to Western European levels. Accordingly, social, welfare and health provision, and the differences in wealth and income between the ruling capitalist class and the working class in the United States, are far more marked and visible than in Western Europe as a whole.

In *Divided Societies*, Ralph Miliband makes the analytical distinction between "class struggle from below" (waged by the working class) and "class struggle from above" (in which the "crucial protagonists are usually those who own or control the main means of domination in capitalist society").[28] This distinction seems particularly appropriate when considering the history of the last twenty-five years or so. In Britain, we could describe the period between 1970 and 1985 as one of intense class struggle from below, as well as from above, marked by a series of major industrial actions: strikes by miners, dockers and construction workers in the early 1970s, the Grunwick photo development workers strike of the late 1970s, the so-called 'Winter of Discontent' which preceded the defeat of the Callaghan Labor government in 1979, the Great Miners' Strike of 1984–1985 and the Wapping printworkers' strike against the Murdoch Press, which marked the end of this sequence.[29]

In contrast, the period during and after the Great Miners' Strike of 1984–1985 can be described as one of class struggle from above, waged against a disorientated, divided and, let us not forget, an effectively criminalized working-class movement.[30] With the changed balance of forces between the classes, consequent on the defeat of the miners, a whole series of anti-Trade Union laws, and a series of fines and sequestrations against Trade Union assets were passed by the Thatcher government. Mass picketing had been criminalized prior to the miners' strike, with the number of pickets limited to six (although during the miners' strike this was not enforced). Widespread and violent policing against strike action took place during the strike, epitomized by the baton–wielding horseback police and the occupation of the coal-mining village of Orgreave. Following the Thatcher government's victory over the miners, sympathetic strikes were banned, cooling-off periods and compulsory postal ballots prior to strike action were enforced and widescale union derecognition occurred.[31]

One of the crucial differences between these two forms of class struggle is the relative invisibility of many aspects of the class struggle from above (such as, for example, anti-union legislation, changes to the taxation system, privatization, quango-ization). After 1985, the intensification of (invisible) class struggle from above, combined with the decline of visible resistance from below, led many commentators to announce, both complacently and erroneously, the end of class society. Jan Pakulski provides a model example: "The key assumption of class analysis—that all important social conflicts have a class basis and class character because class represents the key social dimension of modern (capitalist) society—does not withstand critical scrutiny."[32]

We are suggesting that most of the 'evidence' demonstrating the disappearance of class is in fact highly trumpeted and orchestrated evidence of the disappearance of traditional working-class consciousness and working-class action as traditionally conceived. It is simply incorrect to suggest that there is no 'human resistance,' whether individual or collective, to capitalism: strong resistance is evident, for example, to the intensification of work demanded of workers by capital, both nationally and internationally.

Moreover, it could be argued that the decline in 'traditional' forms of working-class action, such as strikes, has been exaggerated as the result of a 'changed' media agenda. The decline in working-class protest strikes during the 1990s involved a decline in the number of days lost through strikes accompanied by a wider decline in media coverage of such action. The media, amongst the most important of ideological state apparatuses,[33] clearly play a censorship role here which tends to reinforce positions such as that of Pakulski. For example, through the mid-1990s and up to the present time there has been a constant series of *illegal* strikes by London Underground ('Tube') workers, which has hit the news headlines because of the obvious impact of the strikes on millions of Londoners. But there have also been others, such as the series of *illegal* stoppages by Royal Mail employees which have either been under-reported or never reported at all, possibly because they have not led to any sanctions against these workers, and reporting them may give other groups of workers ideas. Again, the strikes that have occurred in Britain since the late 1990s—by the Magnet workers, the Liverpool dockworkers, the Hillingdon Hospital workers, the London underground ('Tube') workers and by teachers, for example—have been defensive, usually against redundancies or attacks or threatened attacks on working conditions.

From the perspective of the socialist Left, it is not enough simply to demonstrate the shoddy conceptualizations of much postmodernist orthodoxy. To demonstrate the flaws in many postmodern arguments can be of little comfort while the working class in Britain has continued to experience political defeat after political defeat by the conservative state and the capitalist class, whether under the Conservative governments from 1979 to 1997 or under the New Labour government, elected on May Day 1997 and re-elected in June 2001.

Intrinsic Problems with Class Analysis

So far, we have outlined the historical, cultural and ideological forces conditioning postmodernism's rise to a position of theoretical orthodoxy within the academy, and we have criticized the ways in which postmodernism has theorized class. We will now focus on what we have termed the 'intrinsic problems with class analysis.' Our reason for doing this is, as we noted earlier, that the inadequate theorization of class within Marxism constitutes a fundamental intellectual weakness, which is vital for Marxism to address. We intend, here, to recover that sense of social class as simultaneously a category of analysis and a theoretical and political problem, which is always in process and never finally resolved. This is to say that analysis needs to recover *a sense of the complexity of social class as a multidimensional category of analysis, which seeks to negotiate the relationships between class as a category of economic analysis, cultural analysis, individual identification, and political mobilization.* This, we feel, is one of the most important theoretical legacies left by Marx, one which has exercised many subsequent Marxist theoreticians. It is through a brief summary of this tradition that we hope to demonstrate the problematic yet sophisticated theorization of class within Marxism, and to suggest ways in which a non-reductive understanding of class must play an important role in any project of liberation.

The Relationship between Economic and Social Class

Marx provided an 'objective' definition of class. He argued that an individual's class position is determined by relationship to the means of production and exists independently of an individual's subjective evaluation of her or his own class position. A condensed definition is that,

> Classes are large groups of people differing from each other by the place they
> occupy in a historically determined system of social production, by their rela-
> tion (in most cases fixed and formulated by law) to the means of production,
> by their role in the social organisation of labour, by the dimensions of the
> share of the social wealth of which they dispose and their mode of acquiring
> it.[34]

This notion of 'objective class position' has always been subject to two major objections. Either it is condemned as 'reductive' precisely because it refuses to consider the question of how social actors understand and make sense of class (at which point the Weberian tradition with its notion of 'status' is usually mobilized); or, and this has been the more recent phenomenon, under the influence of various perspectivist schools of thought (which usually derive from Nietzsche) the possibility of their being any such thing as an 'objective' definition of class is denied or even ridiculed as being, at best, a positivist illusion or, at worst, an example of oppressive, totalizing Enlightenment rationalism.[35]

It seems to us that we cannot afford to jettison the notion of objective class position because it allows us to identify and understand a number of inter-related, significant social truths. Firstly, it enables us to identify and account for the massive inequality in material wealth that exists in Britain. Class allows us to see such inequalities not as the chance result of some cosmic lottery game, 'the luck of the draw,' but as the determinate result of existing property relations. Beyond this, class (in combination with the *labor theory of value*) allows us to understand why the economic relationship between the owners and non-owners is necessarily antagonistic. 'Supermarkets Inc.' profits arise out of the difference between the value (wages) that they pay their workers and the value that those workers produce as a result of their labor. This is not a 'win-win' game: more for 'Supermarkets Inc.' means less for their workforce and vice-versa. The antagonism also explains the daily struggle (familiar to all workers) to control the working day which is usually fought over such things as start/finish times, length of breaks, frequency of toilet breaks. Attempts by line managers to 'persuade' their subordinates to start work five minutes early or finish five minutes late are not just arbitrary displays of local authority: they are intended to increase surplus value and ultimately profit and point to the permanent presence of class struggle waged at the point of production. The technical term for this is 'class exploitation.' Such a concept has no place in the vocabulary of leading postmodernist philosophers such as Lyotard and Baudrillard, and appears to be of little consequence to others who follow Foucault. Various 're-sistance postmodernists' such as Henry Giroux and Peter McLaren in their postmodern phases (arguably, 1992 to the present and from 1992 to 1997, respectively) would accept the concept of class exploitation but dispute its salience vis-à-vis other forms of exploitation.

The same pattern is repeated in the political sphere. Governments do not take neutral decisions based on the 'national interest': politics is about the allocation of scarce resources in society. It is about who gets what and who doesn't, who wins and who loses, who is empowered and who is disempowered, who gets the gravy and who has to make it. It is also about how this system is organized, legitimated and resisted. And it is about how ideological state apparatuses (such as the education system and the mass media) and the repressive state apparatuses (such as the police, the law, and the army) seek to ensure the continuation and enforcement of the current system.

Every single decision and policy made in the realms of taxation and expenditure (in particular) has the effect of moving material resources from one class to another. When the government reduces corporation tax it redistributes wealth in favor of the owners. Similarly, when it increases value added tax (national sales tax), it redistributes wealth away from the non-owners. Privatization and the burgeoning of quangos (Quasi-official non-governmental organizations) divert state finances from public into private hands, thereby returning us to the world of 'old corruption' as practiced in the late-eighteenth and early-nineteenth centuries, whereby the state served as a conduit through which revenue raised by taxing the working population was diverted into the pockets of those closely connected with the political elites at both national and local levels.[36]

This outline analysis, of economic exploitation compounded by political expropriation, can be (and historically has been) used by the socialist Left to try and persuade all wage-laborers that they have a common interest in seeking the end of capitalism. Postmodernists have objected to this project on the grounds that it denies or suppresses the facts of 'social difference.' David Harvey succinctly summarizes this postmodernist critique:

> Concentration on class alone is seen to hide, marginalize, disempower, repress and perhaps even oppress all kinds of 'others' precisely because it cannot and does not acknowledge explicitly the existence of heterogeneities and differences based on, for example, race, gender, age, ability, culture, locality, ethnicity, religion, community, consumer preferences, group affiliation, and the like.[37]

And there can be no doubt that at times in the history of the socialist project the white, male, heterosexual worker was represented as the exclusive (or at least the most significant) model of the interpellated wage-laborer, and that criticism of this project on these grounds is both well founded and has needed to be acknowledged and acted upon by the Left. However, many institutions within the labor movement—particularly the trade unions—have responded and are continuing to respond, with varying degrees of effectiveness, to this challenge through the creation of equal opportunities committees, advisories and officers. Lynne Segal has noted that in those countries with stronger trade union and social-democratic traditions than exist in the United States, "there is far less pay-differential and occupational segregation (both vertical and horizontal) between women and men, and far greater expansion of welfare services." Even more pertinently, Segal contends that at a time when the advances of some women are overshadowed by the increasing poverty of others, "it seems perverse to pose women's specific interests against rather than alongside more traditional socialist goals."[38]

In the light of this, it is interesting to note the renewed interest in class analysis within British feminism, exemplified by Beverly Skeggs in 1997 with

Formations of Class and Gender, and by *Class Matters*, the first of a proposed new series on women and social class edited by Pat Mahony and Christine Zmroczek.[39] Of course, for socialist feminists such as Jane Kelly[40] this class analysis never went away! (See Jane Kelly, chapter 10). Socialists such as Segal and Kelly call for a reaffirmation of the value of traditional socialist goals, a call we fully support. In particular, we would suggest that classical Marxism's emphasis on the ethical necessity of greater social equality, its conception of individual liberty as something which can only be realized collectively, and its quest for an alternative basis for social relations to that offered by the 'cash nexus' (encapsulated in the two memorable maxims, 'from each according to their ability; to each according to their need' and 'the free development of each is the condition for the free development of all') provide the outline of a transformative social program that is politically more radical, and ethically far superior, to that offered by postmodernism.

At its best, the socialist project is not about denying the fact of social difference but about the need to construct solidarity. This, we argue, is as important to the socialist project as 'choice' is to the neoliberal one. Historically, the socialist movement has worked to establish solidarity as both a normative value ('an injury to one is an injury to all'), and a practical prerequisite for successful struggle (based on an achieved understanding that it is through collective self-organization and alliance formation that relatively disempowered social groups have improved their conditions). We argue that implicit in the notion of 'solidarity' is respect for difference. As David Harvey observes, "to discover the basis of similarity (rather than to presume sameness) is to uncover the basis for alliance formation between seemingly disparate groups."[41] This is exactly what happened in the British Miner's Strike of 1984 to 1985, which was supported by a disparate array of gay and lesbian, Irish Republican, environmental, black and women's groups. It is also, to an extent, what happened during the years of (Left-wing) Labor Party control of the Greater London Council and the Inner London Education Authority, until their abolition by the Conservative government in the late 1980s. Both were supported by an array—a coalition—of socialist, working-class and trade union, minority ethnic group, women's movement and gay and lesbian movement groups.[42] And it is what happened in Labor groups (of Councilors) virtually wherever the Left within the party held local control.

Harvey continues by arguing that in contemporary society those similarities which are capable of grounding alliances (and thereby engendering solidarity) are generated by the prevailing economic conditions (and, therefore, the objective class positions) which 'we' share. In defending the notion of objective class position, we do not claim it as anything other than the starting point for a Marxist class analysis. It is important that analysis is not arrested at this level, because the point after all is not merely to describe the world but to change it. And at the risk of simplification we might propose that *economic class describes the world, social classes (conscious of their exploitation and of the possibility of ending it) transform it*. In moving from a concept of 'economic class' to that of 'social class' we are trying to define a category capable of dealing with the specificities of class as it exists and operates at a particular historical moment and within a determinate social formation. This involves those questions of class consciousness and subjective identification as well as the interaction of gender, race, sexuality, religious and spatial (nation, region, locality) factors in the construction of what we might term a concrete class identity. Again at this point we would like to emphasize that we remain firmly within the 'problematic' of classical Marxism. In the third volume of *Capital*, Marx offers us a tantalizing glimpse of the more complete theorization of class on which he was engaged:

> What constitutes a class ?—and the reply to this follows naturally from the reply to another question, namely: What makes wage-labourers, capitalists and landlords constitute the three great social classes? At first glance—the identity of revenues and sources of revenue. There are three great social groups whose members, the individuals forming them, live on wages, profit and ground-rent respectively, on the realisation of their labour power, their capital, and their landed property. However, from this standpoint, physicians and officials, e.g., would also constitute two classes, for they belong to two distinct social groups, the members of each of these groups receiving their revenue from one and the same source. The same would also be true of the infinite fragmentation of interest and rank into which the division of social labour splits laborers as well as capitalists and landlords—the latter, e.g., into owners of vineyards, farm owners, owners of forests, mine owners and owners of fisheries.[43]

Class as Internally Differentiated

This statement by Marx has a number of important implications for our theorization of class. In the first place, it conceives of classes as internally differentiated entities. Class, for Marx, is neither simply monolithic nor static. Under capitalist economic laws of motion, the working class in particular is constantly decomposed and reconstituted due to changes in the forces of production—forces of which members of the working class are themselves a part.[44] Furthermore, Marx had taken great pains to stress that social class as distinct from economic class necessarily includes a political dimension, which is in the broadest sense of the term 'culturally' rather than 'economically' determined. Class-consciousness does not follow automatically or inevitably from the fact of class position. The *Poverty of Philosophy* [1847] distinguishes between a 'class in itself' (class position) and a 'class for itself' (class consciousness); *The Communist Manifesto* [1848] explicitly identifies the formation of the proletariat into a class as the key political task facing the communists. In *The Eighteenth Brumaire of Louis Napoleon* [1852] Marx observes,

> In so far as millions of families live under economic conditions of existence that divide their mode of life, their interests and their cultural formation from those of the other classes and bring them into conflict with those classes, they form a class. In so far as these small peasant proprietors are merely connected

on a local basis, and the identity of their interests fails to produce a feeling of community, national links, or a political organisation, they do not form a class. [45]

The major consequence of this formulation is that *social class exists in a contingent rather than a necessary relation to economic class. The process (and conceptual category) which links economic and social class is that of 'class consciousness.'* This is arguably the most contentious and problematic term in the debate over class. (A cogent summary of the arguments within the Marxist tradition is provided by Richard Johnson's essay "Three Problematics: Elements of a Theory of Working-Class Culture.")[46]

Re-Building Class Identity as a Political Task

To reiterate our earlier point, demonstrating the weaknesses and errors in postmodern analysis does not prove the superiority of our own class-based analysis. Beyond that, there is a gulf between, firstly, demonstrating the theoretical validity of our own analysis and, secondly, translating that into an effective political strategy. For the latter to occur, we have to find a register in which we can make a class analysis relevant to those in whose name and on whose behalf we claim to perform our theorizing. In short, we have to find a way of developing class consciousness in the altered political circumstances of the period from the 1990s to the beginning of the new century/millennium.

It is necessary to find ways of articulating and representing a class analysis as part of the process of rebuilding class consciousness. This form of class consciousness must recognize practically and theoretically the heterogeneous nature of the working class, as well as its common experience—of being in exploited wage labor. In particular, it must address the problematic relationship between class, gender, 'race,' religion, sexuality, disability and other aspects of subjectivity, and seek to build solidarity on the basis of respect and toleration for difference rather than its obliteration. In order to achieve this it is necessary to develop an understanding of class as a political identity capable of uniting the largest amount of people for the purposes of progressive change. Most of the necessary work will be (and is being) done in the sphere of practical politics at a variety of levels, from the grass roots to the international. There are, however, a number of specific contributions that can be made by workers in the sphere of intellectual production—there is, as always, a battle of ideas contributing to the war of the classes.

One of the most influential contributions made by postmodernist and poststructuralist thinking has been in the area of 'identity.' It is not inaccurate to say that poststructuralist accounts of fragmented, decentered subjectivity are intellectually dominant. In some respects, we recognize this as an advance on former, monolithic 'vulgar Marxist' accounts of social class, which substantially ignored questions of ethnicity, sex and sexuality in both theoretical terms and in terms of political action and mobilization. However, as argued earlier, Marxist theory and practice have recognized the complexity of subjectivity. Thus, we support the concept of decanted subjectivity as both correct and possessing useful explanatory power when we come to confront the question of declining class consciousness. While recognizing the utility of this concept of decentering, we challenge arguments and theories proclaiming 'the death of class,' and those proclaiming that there is a qualitative equality, a sameness, between oppression and exploitation based on 'race,' gender, and social class. Our contention is that class exploitation is fundamental to capitalist economy, as opposed to the (admittedly near universal) sex or 'race' exploitation. We see social class exploitation as fundamental to the continuation of capitalism. Capitalism can (and may) survive with sex and 'race' equality—indeed, for neo-liberals, these are desirable attributes of an economy and education or training system—but to conceive of social class equality and the continuance of capitalism is a contradiction in terms.

This is not to trivialize the issue of identity and of identity politics, either in the microsphere of day-to-day personal existence, delight and dismissal, or in the macrosphere of structural forms of positive and negative discrimination and positioning. However, we wish to point out that the notion of an essential, unitary self was rejected, over a century and a half ago, by Marx in his sixth thesis on Feuerbach, where he states "But the human essence is no abstraction inherent in each single individual. In its reality it is the ensemble of the social relations."[47] Social class is clearly only one of a range of possible identifications and one which is, *on various occasions*, less immediately 'obvious' than, for example, those of gender or 'race' or religion. It is useful to compare the term 'worker' with 'man/woman,' 'black/white,' 'Muslim, Christian, Jew or non-believer,' 'gay/straight' (not to mention partner, wife, mother, daughter, son, father, husband), so that its relatively abstract quality can become apparent. For many, though by no means all, people in today's society the first label, 'worker,' describes something that they do—all the other labels, to a greater or lesser extent, describe what they are.

However, for millions, the duality 'worker/boss' (or 'worker/guvner' or 'worker/gaffer') is not at all abstract. Postmodernism stresses that we need to learn that a class identity is only one possible identity and that identification with it will frequently be hard-won. Yet on other occasions, it is a ready and automatic self-identifier. Where postmodernism must be resisted is by enabling and encouraging people to conceptualize in terms of class identities and identifications—and, indeed, by recognizing that people do so both in their daily lives and, more specifically, at certain conjunctures.[48] By postmodernism's own internal logic, class remains a possible and valid identity (given that no identity is 'essential' and all are constructed). In systematically denigrating class and encouraging people to think in terms of other identifications, postmodernism is engaging in class struggle (at the level of ideas). Furthermore, it is engaged on the side of the more powerful classes—those that wish to obstruct the development of working-class consciousness. In this respect, postmodernism is, whatever its intentions and/or proclamations, objectively reactionary (a point made by Mike Cole and Dave Hill in chapter 5).[49] The absence of class in postmodern theory actively contributes to the ideological disarmament of the working-class movement.

Social Class Analysis and Education

To combat the ideological disarmament of the working class and of progressive political forces, it is necessary for socialists within schools, further education colleges and universities and other higher education institutions to strive to rein-scribe social class and social class awareness and consciousness wherever possible in the system, to address issues of educational 'structures' as well as of overall 'standards.' This means promoting comprehensive education from the ages of three to nineteen years, as well as addressing questions and patterns of teacher expectation. It demands critiquing and developing inclusive, critical and egalitarian curriculum content as well as paying attention to patterns and standards of academic attainment. It is not enough for Tony Blair's New Labour government to repeat and repeat the mantra of 'standards not structures' when it is those very structures, selective and marketized, that are divisive, competitive, anti-egalitarian, and hierarchicalizing, and thereby penalizing and suppressing the educational attainment of working-class children and school students, whatever their gender and whatever their ethnicity.

Social Class and Education: What Are the Facts?

The stark relationship between social class and education success is shown in England and Wales by the annually published 'league tables' of schools and their assessment and examination results, which in overall effect re-present the social map of England and Wales, the social map of each town and city. Some secondary schools manage a 98 percent pass rate for school students to achieve five or more subject GCSE passes at grade C or above (the national average for these tests taken by sixteen-year-olds in British schools is around 45 percent)—other schools manage a 2 percent pass rate. This, of course, is reflected in figures showing the percentage of each social class gaining entry into higher education (table 8.1).[50]

Table 8.1 Comparative Participation Rates in Higher Education by Social Class (England and Wales)

Social Class	1991–1992	1998–1999
Professional	55%	72%
Intermediate	36%	45%
Skilled Non-Manual	22%	29%
Skilled Manual	11%	17%

Table 8.1 (Continued)

Partly Skilled	12%	17%
Unskilled	6%	13%

Source: Claire Sanders, Tony Tysome and Olga Wojtas, "Is a Return to Grants Really the Answer?" *Times Higher Education Supplement*, March 9, 2001.

Schools play a major role in reproducing educational, social, cultural and economic inequality. Sam Bowles and Herb Gintis, in their *Correspondence Principle*, suggest:

> The educational system helps integrate youth into the economic system . . . through a structural correspondence between its social relations and those of production. The structure of social relations in education not only inures the student to the discipline of the work place, but also develops the types of personal demeanor, modes of self-presentation, self-image, and social-class identifications that are the crucial ingredients of job adequacy. Specifically, the social relationships of education—the relationships between administrators and teachers, teachers and students, students and students, and students and their work—replicate the hierarchical division of labour. . . . By attuning young people to a set of social relationships similar to those of the work place, schooling attempts to gear the development of personal needs to its requirements. . . . Different levels of education feed workers into different levels within the occupational structure.[51]

For Bowles and Gintis, pace the need to incorporate a selection of the most able into supervisory and some leadership levels in the state and economic apparatuses, the raison d'être of the capitalist system of schooling is working-class failure, the reproduction of the economic, social, cultural and ideological status quo.

The work of Bowles and Gintis, as with other 'reproduction theorists' such as Althusser and Bourdieu, has been the subject of a considerable debate, since the publication of *Schooling in Capitalist America* in 1976, most of it from within a Marxist perspective.[52] One of the main criticisms has identified the seeming lack of space for resistance to the reproduction of the capitalist system as described by Bowles and Gintis. Although Marxist in intent, and even though Bowles and Gintis do provide a chapter on how to resist and ultimately replace capitalism by socialism, their theoretical line of argument has been widely perceived as functional in effect, in the way it centralizes the 'inevitable' reproduction of the capitalist system within education.

However, for neo-Marxists critical of reproduction theory, as well as those such as Mike Cole and Dave Hill who consider that by the late 1990s the neo-Marxist pendulum had swung too far in the culturalist direction and too far away from the structuralist,[53] there has remained an acute awareness of 'what schools do to working-class kids.' Individuals in classrooms and school corridors bring with them and exhibit different sets of linguistic and cultural competencies. As Giroux wrote in 1983 (in fact in his seminal critique of reproduction theory), individuals

> inherit by way of the class-located boundaries of their family. A child inherits from his or her family those sets of meanings, qualities of style, modes of thinking, and types of dispositions that are assigned a certain social value and status in accordance with what the dominant class(es) label as the most valued cultural capital. Schools play a particularly important role in legitimating and reproducing dominant cultural capital. They tend to legitimize certain forms of knowledge, ways of speaking, and ways of relating to the world that capitalize on the type of familiarity and skills that only certain students have received from their family backgrounds and class relations. Students whose families have only a tenuous connection to the dominant cultural capital are at a decided disadvantage.[54]

How does the school function as an ideological apparatus of the state? Louis Althusser suggests that what children learn at school is "know-how." But besides techniques and knowledges, and in the course of learning them, children at school also learn the 'rules' of good behavior, "rules of respect for the sociotechnical division of labour and ultimately the rules of the order established by class domination." The school

> takes children from every class at infant-school age, and then for years in which the child is most 'vulnerable,' squeezed between the family state apparatus and the educational state apparatus, it drums into them, whether it uses new or old methods, a certain amount of "know-how" wrapped in the ruling ideology in its pure state.[55]

As Madan Sarup summarizes, "in this system each mass of children ejected en route is practically provided with the ideology which suits the role it has to fulfil in class society."[56]

It is worth noting that though the ideological state apparatuses function predominantly by ideology, there is no such thing as a purely ideological apparatus: they also function secondarily by discipline, coercion, demotion or non-promotion, penalties and, ultimately, repression: they have a material base. Changes to, the curtailing of, schooling and initial teacher education have been effected through the repressive as well as ideological means available to the state.[57] As Althusser suggests, every *ideological* state apparatus is also in part a *repressive* state apparatus, punishing those who dissent, so that "There is no such thing as a purely ideological apparatus. . . . Schools and Churches use suitable methods of punishment, expulsion, selection etc., to 'discipline' not only their shepherds, but also their flocks."[58]

Ideological state apparatuses have internal coercive practices, for example, forms of punishment, non-promotion, displacement, being 'out of favor.' Similarly, repressive state apparatuses attempt to secure significant internal unity and wider social authority through ideology (for example, through ideologies of patriotism and national integrity). For Althusser, the difference between an ideological and a repressive apparatus of state is one of degree, a matter of whether force or idea predominates in the functioning of particular apparatus.[59]

It is no coincidence that trade union activists are often top of the list when school or college redundancies are about; or that schools clinging to what OFSTED (the Office for Standards in Education, the national inspectorate of schools in England and Wales) now regards as 'outdated' (mixed ability) methods, are likely to be 'failed' at their OFSTED inspection; or that schools, such as the Earl Marshall Comprehensive school in Sheffield, can have the headteacher removed for refusing to stick to the National Curriculum (the official curriculum laid down nationally by the Department for Education and Employment).[60]

In contrast, a number of writers stress the crucial role, actual and potential, for teachers and students to play in resisting the reproduction of capitalism and agitating for progressive social change. Within this critique, a number of writers (particularly Henry Giroux, Peter McLaren and Dave Hill)[61] have developed the concept of teachers (and other cultural workers) as 'critical transformative intellectuals,' using a neo-Gramscian understanding and model of critically using spaces to develop and reinforce counter-hegemonic ideologies, of developing class consciousness and an understanding and commitment to egalitarian change for social justice.[62]

Why Class Is Still a Classroom Issue

In Britain, Marxist analysis throughout the 1970s, 1980s and 1990s was derided as 'Neanderthal, as 'loony Left' dogma, as Cold War style 'oldspeak.' But the same truths are ever new—as is the witch-hunting and suppression and sidelining of those who speak and act such Marxist/radical Left analysis and commitment. The truth is that children and teenagers bring their social class backgrounds into school with them (as well, of course, as other aspects of their subjectivities). In so doing, they tend to meet with socially differentiated (social-class related) teacher expectations. This is primarily through 'the hidden curriculum'—the values and attitudes and desired social and work behaviors expected of them. Teenagers attending schools with very low standards of academic achievement (such as Hackney Downs School in inner city London, or Ramsgate Secondary Modern in a run-down corner of Kent, or The Ridings Secondary School in Halifax) tend to have different expectations, and labeling, and stereotyped work futures than those attending schools that are far more prestigious and selective, on either financial or academic grounds (such as the selective London Oratory School or the most prestigious of private schools, Benenden or Eton).

As part of this social-class based differentiation between schools via the hidden curriculum, there is ample evidence that the pedagogies—the teaching and learning methods used by teachers and pupils—vary according to a pupil's social class. Sally Brown, Sheila Riddell and Jill Duffield base numerous articles on research conducted in schools. For example, "Classroom Approaches to Learning and Teaching: The Social Class Dimension" (1997) is based on following two classes in each of four schools through their first two years of secondary education, observing 204 lessons. This shows that children in two working-class schools spent between 3 and 6 percent of their time in discussion, compared with 17 to 25 percent in the middle-class schools. Pupils in predominantly working-class secondary schools appear to be given many more time-consuming reading and writing tasks than children in middle-class schools, and have less opportunity for classroom discussions. A two-year study by Brown, Riddell and Duffield of four schools in a Scottish education authority demonstrates that teachers of English in the two middle-class schools were more likely to give a reading or writing assignment as homework, leaving time in class for feedback and redrafting written work. The long writing tasks were very much associated with control; the lack of discussion was, the writers suggest, also related to assumptions by teachers that the children could not really manage to discuss things among themselves.[63]

Capitalist Knowledge and the National Curriculum

The National Curriculum, compulsory for schools in England and Wales since 1988, is part of the concern to revamp school education in line with a capitalist society in decay.[64] Obviously, any curriculum that is enforced nationally takes autonomy away from potentially 'unreliable' teachers; also, by insisting on the prioritized inclusion of (for example) Shakespeare and British history,[65] it may very well allow the exclusion of subjects viewed not only as nonutilitarian but potentially critical of the status quo. Dave Hill observes how the opportunity has also been taken to influence the cultural content of the National Curriculum and reinforce some of the ideological positions held by the Right—through testing procedures, for example, and the fetishizing of 'standard' English,' a literary canon, 'traditional' grammar and spelling. The National Curriculum asserts the centrality of particular definitions of 'national' culture in opposition to the increasing tendencies to both ethnic and social class pluralism that were at work in schools. It is driven more, now, by a project of cultural homogeneity than by the rhetoric of equal opportunity. It is now more and more plainly the embodiment of a Conservative vision of a national culture. As Hill indicates, an unashamedly culturally elitist view of the curriculum is clearly put forward by Nicholas Tate, the chief curriculum adviser to both Conservative and 'New Labour' governments.[66] In suggesting that schools must introduce their pupils to high culture, Tate regularly attacks 'cultural relativism' and warns that the British heritage, and with it the notion of strong communities and shared values, is in danger of disintegrating unless teachers actively transmit it. Children should learn which works of art, music and literature are better than others. (The National Curriculum revision of 1995 already insists, for example, that children should read two Shakespeare plays before the age of fourteen and learn mainly British history.) At a conference in 1996 entitled "Curriculum, Culture and Society," Tate proposed a series of ideas to clarify the purpose of the national curriculum. He proclaimed that the fundamental purpose of the school curriculum is to transmit an appreciation of and commitment to the best of the culture we have inherited. We need a more active sense of education as preserving and transmitting, but in a way that is forward looking, the best of what we have inherited from the past.[67]

Challenging what he described as the growing trend toward multimedia study, Tate asserted that books must remain the medium of the future. In addition, the curriculum should be grounded in ancient Greece and Rome, Christianity and European civilization, and "English English" should be taught, not "some watered-down modern version."[68]

Far from being a haven of diversity and creativity, the educational system is now under tighter managerial control and assessment, from top to bottom, than it has been for many years, with a strong concentration on business values and instrumental procedures. This can be seen in the British government's fascination with the 'School Effectiveness Movement,' a fairly mechanistic and management-focused organizational perspective that concentrates on factors internal to the school and ignores questions of curriculum selection and social class intake into a school.[69] It remains to be seen whether, regardless of intentionality, the changes implemented throughout the education system will tend to attenuate or diminish social inequalities in particular respects. As far as the schooling system is concerned, Dave Hill argues that while the National Curriculum may have some positive influence on gender differences, it will "increase social class differentiation," and indeed this is an explicit aim.[70] There is overwhelming evidence that the increase in selection within education systems, and the accompanying increased competitive marketization in education through policies of 'diversity in schooling,' including 'parental choice,' have increased the hierarchical nature of schooling.[71] Inequalities between schools have increased because in many cases the 'parental' choice of schools has become the "school's choice" of the most desirable parents and children—and rejection of others. "Sink schools" have become more "sink-like" as more favored schools have picked the children they think are likely to be "the cream of the crop," so that "'Where you have selection, the sink schools just sink further and the privileged schools just become more privileged.'"[72]

The changes in the organization and content of the curriculum are, more or less, the opposite of what Michael W. Apple has defined as the 'advocacy' position on education:

> Among the most important 'internal' stances would be that of support for student rights (and the democratic rights of teachers, oppressed groups and others). Since curriculum as a field has as one of its primary concerns the task of creating access to knowledge and tradition, especially those areas that have been victims of selective tradition, the question of a student's right to have free access to politically and culturally honest information and to public expression based on this cannot be divorced from our own pursuit of just educative environments.[73]

It is important to note that the relationship between the education system and wider social control is highly mediated, and far from the mechanical response envisaged by some of the more rigid schemas of reproduction theory. This is hardly surprising because, as Kevin Harris puts it,

> Eventually one has to face a realistic and unfortunately, pessimistic conclusion: education, as provided by capitalist liberal democracies, will not change from providing structured systematic distortions of reality by bringing people non-misrepresentative knowledge of the world.

As reasoning for this conclusion, Harris lists two basic Marxist concerns:

> To begin with, education is an instrument of the state. Its job is to maintain and stabilize the social order . . . second, change in education requires initial recognition that something is wrong followed by a long process of demystification; and it is difficult to imagine how either of these could occur.[74]

Harris is attempting, here, to combat the naïve view that education is a 'thing in itself,' somewhat autonomous from capitalist society and possessing the power of change (an impetus also pertaining in some media studies). Education is the handmaiden of capitalism and not vice versa. Far from recent changes providing additional diversity, and augmenting opportunity for individual fulfilment,[75] the educational system across the spectrum has become increasingly geared toward instrumental industrial interests. In terms of access and student contextual choices, particularly, the educational system has moved backwards. Of course, the ruling-class demand to maintain an ideological hegemony ensures the restriction of access to education (a process which is anyway incrementally protracted and thereby lacking strong moments of focus for oppositional activity),[76] while the policing of its content marks an attempt to set an agenda of 'realism,' to develop an educational system fit for a capitalist twenty-first century.

   Changes in the capitalist economy at the level of forces of production exhibit resonances at the level of the relationships of production. While these are many and varied, one of the most important for the education system is the creation, due to technological innovations in the forces of production, of a layer of the working class, particularly of male youth, who by tradition would have entered unskilled/semi-skilled manual work but who are simply no longer needed. This is nothing new. As long ago as 1982, anxieties were raised about the potential effects of youth unemployment, in relation to social control, when work socialization is nullified:

> The problem of youth unemployment is connected with many fears that are not usually explicitly stated. There is, for example, an underlying fear of social and political unrest. First, could the young unemployed become so disaffected that they become a threat to existing authority structures. . . . There is an anxiety about future employability. If young people begin to lose their 'motivation' their desire to be good, responsible workers, what is going to happen when jobs eventually become available? . . . Could the culture of wagelessness amongst youth develop into a refusal of all work?[77]

Youth subcultures could form a "cultural response, a form of resistance to the conditions young people face."[78] It is hardly very useful for the hard-pressed teacher to threaten recalcitrant pupils with 'not getting the qualifications for a job' when the lived experience of the pupil is one of unemployment. Here, education, at least in any formal sense, is simply irrelevant. While for some this has led to a situation of demoralization, drug dependency or crime, for others, albeit a small minority, there has developed an alternative lifestyle with a distinct critical edge in relation to environmental and animal rights issues. These provide the (sometimes full-time) personnel for the various protests against projects such as new road building.

New Labour's 'New Deal': From Welfare to Work

Aware that repression, the traditional Conservative response, can only get one so far, the New Labour government quickly attempted to assert a different form of hegemony over the unemployed. A 'windfall tax' on the recently privatized energy sector provided the finance for the Welfare to Work program, of which the 'New Deal' is a core component. There *is* a level of repression inherent in New Deal: refusal to attend after a 'Gateway' period of interrogations results, for the vast majority of people, in a total loss of Job Seekers Allowance. At a political-theoretical level the New Deal purports to assert a link between a low level of educational attainment and a low skills level by the workforce and unemployed, especially the young unemployed, and low levels of labor productivity.[79] However, even a cursory look at the practical options offered by New Deal shows a radical divorce of the supposed theoretical legitimations from the actual practice.[80]

The New Deal is almost totally about social control, as exemplified by the constant refrain that staying on the dole is not an option. Typically, New Labour's program attempts to hide any contradiction between capital and labor. At the top end of the scale, university education is geared to processing large numbers of people with limited resources (this numerical factor itself helps to minimize the nominal level of unemployment); at the other end, the ideological concern is to achieve hegemony over a section of the working class via the tyranny of training, which the etymological conflation simply reflects:

> Clearly, under the prevailing economic conditions it is necessary for the ruling class to foster ideological control by means of an intensification of constant vocational training. Not only does this shift responsibility for unemployment onto the individual, it reinforces the alliance of 'class factions' necessary to maintain hegemonic control.[81]

It does appear, then, that an orthodox Marxist view of education, which emphasizes it as a mechanism of social control, and a considerable influence on the reproduction of capitalist relations of production, is borne out by empirical developments, however 'crude' and 'instrumentalist' the approach may appear. In short, Marxism is optimistic regarding the possibility of change in the human condition. This is in stark contrast to some of the perpetrators of postmodernism who see no other possibility but to "survive amongst the remnants," and have by

.ccount "nothing positive to offer educational theory, or those at-
 ɔ effect radical change in education, or finally, those attempting to
 ucational politics."[82]

 divergence between postmodernism and those promulgating a Marxist
p.̵ ̲ ive is simply a reconfiguration in different terms of a tension, which has
existed since the origins of mass education within capitalism. As Madan Sarup
observes, the "educational system is a site of struggle, exemplifying the tension
between those who wish to transform it as part of a revolutionary process and
those for whom the school is largely an agency of social reproduction and control."[83] Postmodernism is the contemporary form in which a pluralist view of
education and the state is expressed.

Conclusion: The Way Forward

So far, we have been very critical of the way in which schools and education
systems are run. We would like to finish on a positive and creative note. We
believe that students in schools, in further education and in higher education,
should be made aware of all the major possible ways that have been suggested
to run local, national and international economies and societies. But we believe
more than that. We are not proposing or representing a liberal pluralist or a
postmodernist pluralist perspective (critique and policy program) for education.
The Marxist tradition challenges the restrictive ethos of current conservative
developments in schools (whatever the name of the government in power), and
replaces it with one that encourages rather than obstructs critical thinking. Furthermore, Marxism sets out an analysis and program based on an understanding
of the salience of social class reproduction in capitalist schools (as well as recognizing the specific oppressions of 'race,' gender, sexuality and disability).

We are not suggesting that only socialist/Marxist/radical Left theories be
given critical attention in schools. This would amount to propaganda, just as we
believe that in Britain and the United States, and in capitalist systems in general,
the present 'curricula and hidden curricula' system amounts to systematic,
long-standing, and deep-reaching bias. Instead, we are suggesting that
schools—and education and cultural workers in general—should encourage
critical thinking and critical reflection, based on and predicated on a metanarrative of social justice and a morality and ethic of egalitarianism. We share the
concerns of tens of thousands of teachers, student teachers, and others involved
in education that, in terms of the consideration of alternatives, and in terms of
the development of 'critical thinking,'[84] British schooling, and, indeed, further
and higher education, is in danger of being 'dumbed down.' Although there are
some discernible differences in policy, we see New Labour's education policy
as being essentially the same as that of the Conservative government.

At present, the ongoing education revolution in England and Wales,[85] initiated by Margaret Thatcher and continued with a vengeance by New Labour,[86]
accords very much with the theoretical tenets of functionalism. This accord is
realized not only in terms of educational policy (globalized capitalism is taken

as given, and schools and teachers are required to function efficiently to prepare pupils/students for their future roles in the division of labor in capitalist Britain),[87] but also in terms of content (again the free market economy is taken as given and debate about alternatives is stifled). Through the hidden curriculum, via the expectations of teachers and other school staff and by the respective roles of staff in the schools, schooling reflects and reinforces the social class hierarchy of the wider society.

As Dave Hill and Mike Cole suggest, schools and other parts of the education system do not have to be places where students are encouraged to think uncritically and unidimensionally.[88] Schools, and further and higher education, can and should be arenas for the encouragement of critical thought, where young people engage with a number of ways of interpreting the world, not just the dominant forms. We are doing young people and societal futures a serious disservice if, through our teaching, market capitalism—with its hierarchies of social class, of gender, of 'race' and ethnicity, of able-bodied and able-mindedness, and of sexuality—is presented as God-given, natural and uncontested; if, for example, possible alternative systems, such as socialism (e.g., 'state interventionist' on the one hand, and 'democratic workers' control' on the other) are not fully addressed, then school students are being denied an effective, meaningful choice, while alternative social, political and economic systems are being, in effect, hidden from history. All students have a right to know that market capitalism is simply one way, albeit the globally dominant one, of running economies, nationally and globally. In order to begin to understand the changes occurring in industry and in the economy and society in general in any meaningful way, students need a thorough awareness of the significance—conceptually, empirically and programmatically—of social class.

Notes

This is to acknowledge with thanks the comments on various drafts of this chapter by Mike Cole, Jane Kelly, David Limond, Jane Martin, Ann Monroe, Glenn Rikowski and Tim Waller.

1. For expositions of the 'Third Way' in politics, 'beyond socialism and capitalism,' see Tony Blair, *The Third Way* (London: Fabian Society, 1998); Anthony Giddens, *The Third Way* (Cambridge: Polity Press, 1998), *The Third Way and Its Critics* (Cambridge: Polity Press, 2000), *The Global Third Way Debate* (Cambridge: Polity Press, 2001). For critical commentaries, see Mike Cole and Dave Hill, "'New Labour,' Old Policies: Tony Blair's 'Vision' for Education in Britain," *Education Australia* 37 (1997); Mike Cole, "Globalisation, Modernisation and Competitiveness: A Critique of the New Labour Project in Education," *International Studies in the Sociology of Education* 8, no. 3 (1998): 315–332; Stuart Hall, "The Great Moving Nowhere Show: Blair Has Failed to Break with Neo-liberalism and thereby Squandered a Golden Opportunity," *Marxism Today* (November–December 1998), 9–14; Eric Hobsbawm, "The Death of Neo-Liberalism: The Present Global Crisis Marks the End of Market Fundamentalism," *Marxism Today* (November–December 1998), 4–8; Martin Jacques, "Leader: As we Move into a New Era, New Labour remains Firmly Stuck in the Old One," *Marxism Today* (November–December 1998); Dave Hill, *New Labour and Education: Policy,*

Ideology and the Third Way (London: Tufnell Press, 1999), "Equality, Ideology and Education Policy," in *Schooling and Equality: Fact, Concept and Policy*, ed. Dave Hill and Mike Cole (London: Kogan Page) and Dave Hill, ed., *Education, Education, Education: Capitalism, Socialism and the Third Way* (Brighton, U.K.: Institute for Education Policy Studies, 2002).

2. Michael White, "Blair Hails Middle Class Revolution," *Guardian*, January 15, 1999.

3. Mohibur Rahman, Guy Palmer, Peter Kenway and Catherine Howarth, *Monitoring Poverty and Social Exclusion 2000* (York, U.K.: Joseph Rowntree Foundation, 2001), 3.

4. Rahman et al., *Monitoring Poverty*, 5.

5. Clare Fermont, "Four Years Hard Labour," *Socialist Review* 251 (2001): 10.

6. Fermont, "Four Years," 6.

7. Fermont, "Four Years," 6–7.

8. David Gordon and Peter Townsend, eds., *Breadline Europe: The Measurement of Poverty* (Bristol, U.K.: Policy Press, 2001). For a report of this, see John Carvel, "5m Britons Living on the Breadline," *Guardian*, March 8, 2001.

9. Her Majesty's Stationery Office, "Social Trends," *Social Trends* 31 (London: Stationery Office, 2001).

10. "Distribution of Wealth in the United Kingdom 1976 and 1998," *Social Trends* 31 (2001): 109 and the "Appendix," Part 5.

11. Andrew Adonis and Stephen Pollard, *A Class Act, the Myth of Britain's Classless Society* (London: Hamish Hamilton, 1997).

12. For data on social class inequalities in income, wealth and educational attainment in Britain, and on how much inequality has increased since 1979, see Hill and Cole, "Social Class," in *Schooling and Equality*; publications by the Joseph Rowntree Foundation (<http://www.jrf.org.uk>), such as Rahman et al., *Monitoring Poverty*; Gordon and Townsend, eds., *Breadline Europe*. For detail on executive pay, see Will Hutton, "The Rich Aren't Cleverer, Just Richer," *Observer*, April 1, 2001.

13. For example, see Peter McLaren, *Che Guevara, Paolo Freire and the Pedagogy of Revolution* (Lanham, Md.: Rowman & Littlefield, 2000).

14. "Presidential candidate Ralph Nader's Speech to the NAACP, Tuesday, July 11, 2000," <http:// www.washingtonpost.com/wp-srv/onpolitics/elections/nader.htm> November 7, 2000.

15. McLaren, *Che Guevara*, 27.

16. For criticisms of 'resistance postmodernism,' see Mike Cole and Dave Hill, "Games of Despair and Rhetorics of Resistance: Postmodernism, Education and Reaction," *British Journal of Sociology of Education* 16, no. 2 (1995): 165–182, "'Resistance Postmodernism': Emancipatory Politics for a New Era or Academic Chic for a Defeatist Intelligentsia?" in *Information Society: New Media, Ethics and Postmodernism*, ed. Karamjit S. Gill (London: Springer-Verlag, 1996), "Postmodernism, Education and Contemporary Capitalism: A Materialist Critique," in *Teacher Training and Values in Education*, ed. Maria Odette Valente, Amalia Barrios, Alberto Gaspar and V. D. Teodoro (Lisbon: Association for Teacher Education in Europe in association with Departamento de Educacao da Faculdade de Ciencias da Universidade de Lisboa, 1996), and chapter 5 of this volume. Also Dave Hill and Mike Cole, "Materialism and the Postmodern Fallacy: The Case of Education," in *Proceedings of the Second International Conference of Sociology of Education in Portugal*, ed. Joao Viegas Fernandes (Faro, Portugal: Escola Superior de Educacao da Universidade do Algarve, 1996), 5–20; Mike Cole, Dave Hill and Glenn Rikowski, "Between Postmodernism and Nowhere: the Predicament of the Postmodernist," *British Journal of Education Studies* 45, no. 2 (1997): 187–200; Glenn Rikowski, "Left Alone: End Time for Marxist Educational Theory?" *British*

Journal of Sociology of Education 17, no. 4 (December 1996); Jane Kelly, chapter 10 of this volume.

17. Aijaz Ahmad, *In Theory: Classes, Nations, Literatures* (London: Verso, 1992), 5–6.

18. Ahmad, *In Theory*, 66.

19. See Alex Callinicos, *Against Postmodernism: A Marxist Critique* (Cambridge, U.K.: Polity Press, 1989), 115.

20. See also the criticism of postmodern feminism and its leading writers such as Patti Lather, Valerie Walkerdine and Judith Butler, in Mike Cole and Dave Hill, "Games of Despair," "Resistance Postmodernism," and "Postmodernism, Education"; Dave Hill and Mike Cole, "Materialism, Postmodern Fallacy," and chapter 5 in this volume. See also McLaren and Farahmandpur in chapter 11, with reference to United States feminist critics of postmodern feminism, and Jane Kelly, chapter 10.

21. Frederic Jameson, "Postmodernism and the Cultural Logic of Late Capitalism," *New Left Review* 146 (1984): 59–92.

22. Frederic Jameson, *Postmodernism* (London: Verso, 1992), 3.

23. Ahmad's *In Theory* offers a cogent analysis of this particular postmodernist aporia, particularly his "Introduction" and opening chapter.

24. John Urry, "Rethinking Class," in *Social Movements and Social Classes*, ed. L. Maheu (London: Sage, 1995).

25. Caution, however, needs to be exercised regarding the veracity of this claim. For example, B. Deer in "Still Struggling after All These Years," *New Statesman*, August 23, 1996, 12–13, observes that "the proportion of [British] voters believing there is a 'class struggle' in Britain rose from around 48% in early 1964 to 81% in 1995, according to Gallup." Similarly, a *New York Times* poll in 1996 "found that 55% of Americans now defined themselves as working class," as reported by Colin Leys and Leo Panitch, "The Political Legacy of the Manifesto," in *Socialist Register*, ed. Leo Panitch and Colin Leys (Rendlesham, U.K.: Merlin, 1998): 20–21.

26. Beverley Skeggs, *Formations of Class and Gender* (London: Sage, 1997), 6 (our emphasis added).

27. It is pertinent to note that in the United States, often given as an example of a nation with a proletariat who have a low level of class-consciousness, a major successful strike by the Teamsters at United Parcel Services in 1997 won permanent status for many temporary staff. In mid-1998, the most significant strike to hit General Motors since the Great Flint Sit Down Strike of 1937 took place under the auspices of the United Auto Workers union, bringing one of the world's largest corporations to a standstill. Coverage of these not insignificant events in the British media was absolutely minimal (information from *Workers Vanguard*, Box 1377, GPO, N.Y. 10116). See Sheila Cohen and Kim Moody, "Unions, Strikes and Class Consciousness Today," in *Socialist Register*, ed. Leo Panitch and Colin Leys (Rendlesham: Merlin, 1998), for an analytical description of these struggles.

28. Ralph Miliband, *Divided Societies* (Oxford: Oxford University Press, 1991), 56, 117.

29. The Left press in Britain has catalogued and highlighted such struggles on a weekly basis. *Militant* (now *The Socialist*), *Socialist Worker* and *Tribune* throughout the period have been the highest circulation socialist weeklies, and the (formerly Soviet subsidized) *Morning Star*, the only socialist daily newspaper.

30. As Chris Harman, Socialist Workers Party, states in *In the Heat of the Struggle: 25 Years of Socialist Worker* (London: Socialist Worker and Bookmarks, 1993), 177–178:

> the early and mid 1980s were the grimmest years the working-class movement had known since the 1930s. The Thatcher government introduced new

anti-union laws, allowed the recession to destroy about a third of manufacturing jobs until the real level of unemployment was close to four million, began to slash social benefits, and began a carefully thought out strategy of isolating and then defeating key sections of workers—first the steel workers, then the rail workers, then the miners, then the printers.

31. For a Left description and analysis of these struggles, see Ken Livingstone, *If Voting Changed Anything, They'd Abolish It* (London: Collins, 1987); Tony Cliff and Donny Gluckstein, *The Labour Party: A Marxist History* (London: Bookmarks, 1996); Derek Hatton, *Inside Left, the Story So Far* (London: Bloomsbury Publishing, 1988); Peter Taaffe and Tony Mulhearn, *Liverpool: A City That Dared to Fight* (London: Fortress Books, 1988); Chris Harman/Socialist Worker, *In the Heat*; Tony Benn, *The Benn Diaries* (London: Arrow Books, 1996); Tony Wright and Matt Carter, *The People's Party: The History of the Labour Party* (London: Thames and Hudson, 1997). Tony Cliff, Donny Gluckstein and Chris Harman are leading members of the (Trotskyist) Socialist Workers Party; Derek Hatton, Peter Taaffe and Tony Mulhearn were leading members of Militant (renamed The Socialist Party following its expulsion from the Labour Party in the late 1980s). It was, during the eighties, one of the two most significant Trotskyist groups in Britain, having two of its members elected as Members of Parliament, controlling dozens of Constituency Labour Parties, and controlling Liverpool City Council through the mid-1980s. Tony Benn and Ken Livingstone can be depicted as two of the leaders of the democratic socialist (or 'hard') left through the 1980s and 1990s. As 'Blairite' loyalists, Tony Wright and Matt Carter supported Blair's 'Third Way.'

32. Jan Pakulski, "Social Movements and Class: The Decline of the Marxist Paradigm," in *Social Movements and Social Classes*, ed. L. Maheu (London: Sage, 1995), 75.

33. Our use of Althusserian concepts here does not imply an uncritical acceptance of his theoretical and party political trajectory and corpus of actions. The same applies to others cited in this chapter.

34. Vladimir Ilyich Lenin, "A Great Beginning," in *Collected Works*, 29 (Moscow: Progress Publishers, 1965), 421.

35. Perspectivism is defined as "The view that the external world is to be interpreted through different alternative concepts and systems of beliefs and that there is no authoritative independent criterion for determining that one such system is more valid than another" in *Dictionary of Philosophy* (London: Pan, 1979), 247.

36. John Saville, *The Consolidation of the Capitalist State 1800–1850* (London: Pluto Press, 1994), 41–50.

37. David Harvey, "Class Relations, Social Justice and the Politics of Difference," in *Principled Positions*, ed. J. Squires (London: Lawrence & Wishart, 1993), 101.

38. Lynne Segal, *New Sexual Agendas* (London: Macmillan, 1997), 90–91.

39. Skeggs, *Formations*; Pat Mahony and Christine Zmroczek, eds., *Class Matters: 'Working-Class' Women's Perspectives on Social Class* (London: Taylor and Francis, 1997).

40. See also Jane Kelly, "Postmodernism and Feminism," *International Marxist Review* 14 (1992): 39–55 and "Gender and Equality: One Hand Tied behind Us," in *Education, Equality and Human Rights: Issues of Gender, 'Race,' Sexuality, Special Needs and Social Class*, ed. Mike Cole (New York: Routledge, 2000).

41. Harvey, "Class Relations," 114.

42. See Cole, Hill and Rikowski, "Between Postmodernism and Nowhere" and Rikowski, "Left Alone," for evidence of such alliances accepted by and participated in by the radical and Marxist Left. See the account of Ken Livingstone, the 'hard Left' leader of the Greater London Council in the 1980s, in Livingstone, *If Voting Changed Anything, They'd Abolish It*. Which is precisely what Margaret Thatcher did. She abolished

the Greater London Council in March 1986. The Inner London Education Authority followed into oblivion as part of the Education Reform Act of 1988. What they had in common was that they were both enormously popular with Londoners, that they were well funded and mounted anti-Conservative government campaigns, and that they were both controlled by 'the hard Left,' the socialist wing of the Labour Party.

43. Karl Marx [1894], cited in *The Marx-Engels Reader*, ed. Robert C. Tucker (New York: W. W. Norton, 1978), 441–442.

44. The most obvious and profound consequence in Britain of a modification in the social composition of the workforce is the vast numerical diminishment of the manual working class in line with the collapse of manufacturing industries such as steel, ship-building and coal—the proletariat, and the substantial increase in the professional and managerial strata. In making this internal distinction it is important to note that the designation of 'proletarian' identifies only that section of the working class who are directly involved in the production of surplus value. Members of the proletariat are by definition part of the working class while most working-class people in Britain are no longer proletarians. See F. Gordon, "Workers and Masses," *Open Polemic* (March 11, 1995): 36. (Contact P.O. Box 1169, London, W3 9OF.) There are manifestly different layers, or strata, among the working classes. Skilled workers (if in work, and particularly in full-time, long-term work) generally have a higher standard of living than semiskilled or unskilled, or unemployed workers. Their weekly and annual income is likely to be considerably higher. And their wealth is likely to be higher. They are more likely, for example to have equity, or surplus value, on an owner-occupied home. In contrast, poorer families, in poorer sections of the working class, may have no wealth whatsoever, and are far more likely to live in private rented accommodation or in rented Council housing (what, in the United States, are termed 'the Projects'). Another important 'internal' class distinction, and one which is inevitable as many workers no longer directly produce surplus value, is the growth of a professional and managerial stratum. That is, those who are 'between capital and labor' in the sense that while being entirely dependent on capital, often in the shape of the national or local state, they exercise supervisory functions over the working class—see Pat Walker, ed., *Between Labour and Capital* (Brighton, U.K.: Harvester Press, 1979), 5, and *Subversion* (June 23, 1998) (Dept. 10, 1 Newton Street, Manchester, M1 1HW, U.K.). Examples of this category would be social workers, teachers, lecturers in further and higher education, probation officers, employment service workers and so forth. Many of them have a consciousness of status in which they place themselves above other, especially manual, sectors of the working class. (Indeed, the Ehrenreich's talk of a professional and managerial class: see Walker, *Between Labour and Capital*, 5.) Some, of course, though not many, retain a working-class consciousness, family, social and political affiliations while, pace casualization and proletarianization of many managerial and professional jobs, at the same time benefiting from superior income, conditions of work, and wealth. Of course, while class positional location might allow one to make broad generalizations it does not automatically determine individual consciousness and activity. For example, workers on a temporary contract can do the work on a minimalist basis and get out, or attempt to curry favor with management as being 'reliable' in the hope of being offered secure employment.

45. Karl Marx, cited in *Surveys from Exile* (New York: Vintage Books, 1974), 239.

46. Richard Johnson, "Three Problematics: Elements of a Theory of Working-Class Culture," in *Working Class Culture*, ed. John Clarke, Charles Critcher and Richard Johnson (London: Hutchinson, 1979).

47. Robert C. Tucker, ed., *The Marx-Engels Reader* (New York: W. W. Norton, 1978), 145.

48. See Cohen and Moody, "Unions, Strikes."

49. Christopher Norris, *Uncritical Theory* (London: Lawrence & Wishart, 1992); Cole and Hill, chapter 5, "Games of Despair" and "'Resistance Postmodernism'"; Cole, Hill and Rikowski, "Between Postmodernism and Nowhere"; Mike Cole, Dave Hill, Peter McLaren and Glenn Rikowski, *Red Chalk: On Schooling, Capitalism and Politics* (Brighton, U.K.: Institute for Education Policy Studies, 2001) and Dave Hill, "State Theory and the Neo-Liberal Reconstruction of Teacher Education: A Structuralist Neo-Marxist Critique of Postmodernist, Quasi-Postmodernist, and Culturalist Neo-Marxist Theory," *British Journal of Sociology of Education* 22, no. 1 (2001): 137–157.

50. Claire Sanders, Tony Tysome and Olga Wojtas, "Is a Return to Grants Really the Answer?" *Times Higher Education Supplement*, March 9, 2001.

51. Mike Cole, ed., *Bowles and Gintis Revisited: Correspondence and Contradiction in Educational Theory* (Lewes: Falmer Press, 1988), 2–3. It should be mentioned that since the publication of *Schooling in Capitalist America* (New York: Basic Books, 1996), Bowles and Gintis have moved their position theoretically from revolutionary socialism to one they describe as post-liberal democracy (for a discussion, see Mike Cole, "From Reductionist Marxism and Revolutionary Socialism to Post-Liberal Democracy and Ambiguity: Some Comments on the Changing Political Philosophy of Bowles and Gintis," *British Journal of Sociology* 34, no. 3 (September 1988): 452–462.

52. For the United States during the 1980s, see, for example, Michael W. Apple, *Official Knowledge: Democratic Education in a Conservative Age* (London: Routledge, 1993); Henry Giroux, "Theories of Reproduction and Resistance in the New Sociology of Education: A Critical Analysis," *Harvard Education Review* 53, no. 3 (1983), *Teachers as Intellectuals: Toward a Critical Pedagogy of Learning* (Granby, Mass.: Bergin and Garvey, 1988) and Henry Giroux and Peter McLaren, *Critical Pedagogy, the State and Cultural Struggle* (New York: State University of New York Press, 1988). For the 1980s in Britain, see Madan Sarup, *Education, State and Crisis* (London: RKP, 1982) and *Marxism/Structuralism/Education: Theoretical Developments in the Sociology of Education* (Lewes, U.K.: Falmer Press, 1983). See also, in North America, Ira Shor, *Culture Wars: School and Society in the Conservative Restoration 1969–1984* (London: Routledge Kegan Paul, 1986); Daniel Liston, *Capitalist Schools: Explanation and Ethics in Radical Studies of Schooling* (London: Routledge, 1988); Peter McLaren, "Revolutionary Pedagogy in Post-Revolutionary Times: Rethinking the Political Economy of Critical Education," *Education Theory* (fall 1998). Also in Britain, Cole, "From Reductionist Marxism" and "Globalisation, Modernisation;" Dave Hill, *Something Old, Something New, Something Borrowed, Something Blue: Schooling, Teacher Education, and the Radical Right in Britain and the USA* (London: Tufnell Press, 1990); David Livingstone, "Searching for the Missing Links: Neo-Marxist Theories of Education," *British Journal of Sociology of Education* 16 (1995); Rikowski, "Left Alone"; Cole, Hill and Rikowski, "Between Postmodernism and Nowhere", Dave Hill, "Social Class," in *An Introduction to the Study of Education*, ed. David Matheson and Ian Grosvenor (London: David Fulton, 1999), also "State Theory" and "The National Curriculum, the Hidden Curriculum and Equality," in *Schooling and Equality: Fact, Concept and Policy,* ed. D. Hill and M. Cole (London: Kogan Page, 2001).

53. Dave Hill and Mike Cole, "Marxist State Theory and State Autonomy Theory: The Case of 'Race' Education in Initial Teacher Education," *Journal of Education Policy* 10, no. 2 (1995): 221–232; Cole and Hill, "Postmodernism, Education"; Cole, Hill and Rikowski, "Between Postmodernism and Nowhere"; Hill, *New Labour and Education* and "State Theory."

54. Giroux, "Theories of Reproduction," 268.

55. Louis Althusser, "Ideology and Ideological State Apparatuses," in *Lenin and Philosophy and Other Essays* (London: New Left Books, 1971), 147. See also Sarup's synopsis and critique of Althusser in *Marxism/Structuralism*; Giroux, "Theories of Re-

production"; Geoff Whitty, *Sociology and School Knowledge: Curriculum Theory, Research and Policy* (London: Methuen, 1985); Cole, "From Reductionist Marxism."

56. Sarup, *Marxism/Structuralism*, 13. See note 55, and particularly the discussion and extension of Althusser in Hill, "State Theory."

57. Hill, "State Theory." See also Althusser, "Ideology;" Nicos Poulantzas, "Problems of the Capitalist State," in *Ideology and Social Science*, ed. Robin Blackburn (London: Fontana, 1972); Dave Hill, *Charge of the Right Brigade: The Radical Right's Attack on Teacher Education* (Brighton, U.K.: Institute for Education Policy Studies, 1989), <http.www. ieps.org.uk.html> (May 1, 2001) and *Something Old.*

58. Althusser, "Ideology," 138.

59. See Ted Benton, *The Rise and Fall of Structural Marxism: Althusser and His Influence* (London: Macmillan, 1984), 101–102 and cited in Hill, "State Theory."

60. Chris Searle, "OFSTEDed, Blunketted and Permanently Excluded: An Experience of English Education," *Race and Class* 38, no. 1 (July–September, 1996), 21–38 and *Living Community, Living School* (London: Tufnell Press, 1997).

61. See Giroux, "Theories of Reproduction" and Giroux and McLaren, *Critical Pedagogy*; Peter McLaren, *Life in Schools: An Introduction to Critical Pedagogy in the Foundations of Education* (Harlow, U.K.: Longman, 1998); Dave Hill, *Something Old*, also "Cultural Diversity and Initial Teacher Education," in *Cultural Diversity and the Curriculum Volume 4: Cross-Curricular Contexts, Themes and Dimensions in Primary Schools*, ed. Gajendra Verma and Peter Pumfrey (London: Falmer Press, 1994), 218–241 and "Reflection in Teacher Education," in *Educational Dilemmas: Debate and Diversity, Volume 1: Teacher Education and Training*, ed. K. Watson, S. Modgil and C. Modgil (London: Cassell, 1997), 193–208.

62. See Mike Cole, Dave Hill and Sharanjeet Shan, eds., *Promoting Equality in Primary Schools* (London: Cassell, 1997) and Dave Hill and Mike Cole, eds., *Promoting Equality in Secondary Schools* (London: Cassell, 1999) for detail on how curricular subjects within the English/Welsh National Curriculum can be used for egalitarian purposes and to reinscribe class within the curriculum. See also the two Hillcole Group books, *Changing the Future: Redprint for Education*, ed. Clyde Chitty (London: Tufnell Press, 1991) and *Rethinking Education and Democracy: A Socialist Alternative for the Twenty-first Century* (London: Tufnell Press, 1997).

63. Sally Brown, Jill Duffield and Sheila Riddell, "School Effectiveness Research: The Policy Makers' Tool for School Improvement?" *European Educational Research Association Bulletin* (March 1995): 6–15 and "Classroom Approaches to Learning and Teaching: The Social Class Dimension" (paper presented to the European Educational Research Association Annual Conference, Seville, Spain, 1997). See also Jill Duffield, "School Support for Lower Achieving Pupils," *British Journal of Special Education* 25, no. 3 (February 1998): 126–134, "Unequal Opportunities or Don't Mention the (Class) War" (paper presented at the Scottish Educational Research Association (SERA) Conference, Dundee, Scotland, 1998) and "Learning Experiences, Effective Schools and Social Context," *Support for Learning* 13, no. 1 (February 1998): 3–8.

64. Hill, "Social Class" and "The National Curriculum." See also Sarup, *Education, State, Crisis*, 74. Some people still do think that social goals can be won within capitalism, and to some extent and for some individuals they can, but the long-term social prognosis for capitalism is decay. In this sense, 'decay' is economic decline along with the corollaries of persistent unemployment, an increase in 'flexible' working conditions, cuts in the social wage (which impact disproportionately on the poorer sections of the population), increasingly repressive measures to maintain social control, the increasing militarization of society, a gradual degradation in the level of popular culture leading to the paradox of mass ignorance in an information-rich society.

65. Hill, "Social Class", "State Theory" and "The National Curriculum."

66. See *Schooling and Equality*, 101.

67. Tate, quoted in David Charter, "Schools Must Not Blur Boundary of Culture, Says Curriculum Chief," *Times*, February 8, 1996.

68. Tate continued:

The final big idea is that we should aim to develop in young people a sense that some works of art, music, literature or architecture are more valuable than others...by the post-modern view there are no differences in value between, say, Schubert's Ave Maria and the latest Blur release, or between Milton and Mills & Boon. . . . The final big idea therefore is that a key purpose of the curriculum is to introduce young people to some of the characteristics of what traditionally has been known as 'high culture,' the pursuit of knowledge for its own sake. I am not saying that young people should spend all their time studying Jane Austen and Shakespeare or listening to Bach and Mozart. What I am suggesting is that we, their educators, should give these things their proper value as, in the words of Matthew Arnold, "the best that has been known and thought."

See Charter, "Schools Must Not Blur."

69. Brown et al., "School Effectiveness"; Clyde Chitty, "The School Effectiveness Movement: Origins, Shortcomings and Future Possibilities," *The Curriculum Journal* 8, no. 1 (spring 1997): 45–62; Richard Hatcher, "Social Justice and the Politics of School Effectiveness and Improvement," *Race, Ethnicity and Education* 1, no. 2 (October 1998): 267–289; Hill, "The National Curriculum."

70. See Dave Hill's argument in "Equality in British Schooling: The Policy Context of the Reforms," in *Promoting Equality in Primary Schools*, ed. Cole et al.; also *New Labour and Education*; "Global Capital, Neo-Liberalism and Privatisation: The Growth of Educational and Economic Inequality," in *Schooling and Equality: Fact, Concept and Policy*, ed. D. Hill and M. Cole (London: Kogan Page, 2001) and "The National Curriculum."

71. Sharon Gewirtz, Stephen Ball and Richard Bowe, *Markets, Choice and Equity in Education* (Buckingham, U.K.: Open University Press, 1995); Hill, "Equality in British Schooling"; Geoff Whitty, "New Labour, Education and Social Justice," *Socialist Teacher* 65 (1998); Geoff Whitty, Sally Power and David Halpin, *Devolution and Choice in Education: The School, the State and the Market* (Buckingham, U.K.: Open University Press, 1998); Martin Thrupp, *Schools Making a Difference: Let's Be Realistic!* (Buckingham, U.K.: Open University Press, 1999) and "Compensating for Class: Are School Improvement Researchers Being Realistic?" *Education and Social Justice* 2, no. 2 (summer 2000): 2–11.

72. Dave Hill, from an interview cited in Rupert Haymer, "How 11-Plus Divided Twin Brothers with the Same IQ," *Sunday Mirror*, February 18, 2001. See also Dave Hill, "The Third Way Ideology of New Labour's Educational Policy in England and Wales," in *Combating Social Exclusion through Education: Laissez faire, Authoritarianism or Third Way?* ed. Guido Walraven, Chris Day, Carl Parsons and Dolf Van Deen (Leuven-Apeldoon, Belgium: Garant, 2000), and Hill, ed., *Education, Education, Education.*

73. Michael W. Apple, *Ideology and Curriculum* (London: Routledge and Kegan Paul, 1979), 164.

74. Kevin Harris, *Education and Knowledge* (London: RKP, 1979), 182–183. For more rigid schemas of reproduction theory, see Philip G. Altbach, "Professors and Politics: An International Perspective," in *The Politics of Educators Work and Lives*, ed. Mark B. Ginsburg (New York: Garland Publishing, 1995), 235; Robert Connell, "Trans-

formative Labor: Theorizing the Politics of Teachers Work," in *The Politics of Educators Work*, 93.

75. A fulfillment which in some cases can be profound. John McVicar was a notorious armed robber and at one period held the distinction of being Britain's 'most wanted man.' In *By Himself* (London: Arrow, 1979), 205, his account of serving his prison sentence, he states:

When I was paroled in 1978, the Prison Department described me as one of the most remarkable cases of 'conversion' that it had ever witnessed. From recapture until release I did virtually nothing except study—through 'O' and 'A' levels, a Social Science Certificate, a sociology degree. I was paroled, in fact, to take up a place at Leicester University to continue with the postgraduate degree, an M.Phil. which I'd begun a year earlier.

76. There have been protests regarding such impositions as cutting student grants or implementing tuition fees for higher education. See the web site of the Campaign for Free Education, a Left pressure group opposed to tuition fees, at <http://www. members.nbci.com.nus_cfe>. However, to some extent, these protests carried an air of ritualism rather than real expectation, even of forcing concessions. 'There is no alternative' (TINA) seems to be as powerful an ideological tool for New Labour, to promote pragmatic acceptance, as it was under the Thatcher regime.

77. Sarup, *Education, State, Crisis*, 30.

78. Sarup, *Education, State, Crisis*, 31.

79. Clara Donnelly, Matthew Nimmo and Paul Convery, *The New Deal Handbook* (London: Unemployment Unit and Youthaid, 1998), xi.

80. The New Deal is an adaptation of U.S. 'Welfare to Work' schemes especially as practiced in New York and Wisconsin. Apart from self-employment, which was added to the New Deal at a very late stage, there are four options. These are (1) *A subsidized job:* depending on the hours worked the employer will receive from £40 to £60 weekly. This must be every capitalist's dream: they receive payment for allowing a worker to work for them! See Donnelly et al., *New Deal*, 53; (2) *Environmental task force:* this is the heavy manual work option on the New Deal—past projects (on the Project Work pilots) included tree planting, restoring canal towpaths, etc. Employers are to be encouraged to pay a wage, but if not, the unemployed worker (if that is not a contradiction in terms) receives just over £15 weekly in addition to benefit plus some traveling expenses. See Donnelly et al., *New Deal*, 60–67. Essentially, the unemployed person will do work previously carried out by volunteers concerned for the environment. The whole notion of 'volunteer' is degraded; (3) *Work in the voluntary sector:* on Project Work, this involved people working as sales assistants in various charity shops (Barnardo's, the British Heart Foundation, etc.), which obviously saw no contradiction between concern for their particular clientele and their exploitation of British workers. The financial arrangements for this option are similar to those for (2), and similarly negate the very notion of altruistic behavior inherent in some voluntary work. Both of these options emphasize control at work via a concentration on such aspects as teamwork and time management. See Donnelly et al., *New Deal*, 61; (4) *Full-time education and training:* this is an option, but only up to the extremely basic level of NVQ level 2, whatever the abilities or aspirations of the student. The intention here appears to be to train people to a standard where they may be of use in an operational capacity to capitalism, without giving them any of the intellectual tools required to make a critical analysis of their situation. In reality, there is no genuine educational opportunity available on the New Deal and an etymological transformation has been enacted whereby education is deliberately conflated with vocational training. There is no extra £15 available on the training option. See Donnelly et al., *New Deal*, 50.

81. Andrew Davies, "The Cheapening of Education," in *Fight Racism, Fight Imperialism!* 143 (June–July 1998): 11. (Contact BM Box 5909, London, WCIN 3XX.)

82. Cole and Hill, "Games of Despair," 171; Cole, Hill and Rikowski, "Between Postmodernism and Nowhere."

83. Sarup, *Education, State, Crisis*, 74.

84. For an elaboration of the concept and practice of critical thinking, see Kenneth Zeichner and Daniel Liston, "Teaching Student Teachers to Reflect," *Harvard Educational Review* 57, no. 1 (1987); Dave Hill, "Seven Ideological Perspectives on Teacher Education Today and the Development of a Radical Left Discourse," *Australian Journal of Teacher Education* 16, no. 2 (1991): 5–29; Hill, "Cultural Diversity," "Reflection in Teacher Education"; Hill and Cole, "Social Class." See also the works of Giroux and of McLaren through the 1980s and 1990s, such as Giroux, *Teachers as Intellectuals*; Giroux and McLaren, *Critical Pedagogy*; McLaren, *Life in Schools*. For a radical Left program for education, see Hillcole Group, *Changing the Future* and *Rethinking Education*; Mike Cole and Dave Hill, "Capitalism, Education and Equality: A Way Forward," in Hill et al., eds., *Schooling and Equality*.

85. By this we mean the establishment of a competitive market in schooling, and its strengthening through increased selection of students by schools, the marked increase in 'setting and streaming' (tracking) in both secondary and primary schools (see David Gillborn, "Articulating the Relationship between EAL, Bilingualism, African Caribbean Pupil Achievement and Race Equality," *NALDIC News*, March 23, 2001: 4–6), by the imposition of ever more prescriptive curriculum guidelines for the National Curriculum core subjects (Numeracy Hour and Literacy Hour) and through what New Labour, in emulation of the Conservatives, insists on calling 'Teacher Training' (rather than Teacher Education).

86. See Cole and Hill, "'New Labour,' Old Policies"; Hatcher, "Social Injustice"; Whitty, "New Labour"; Hill, *New Labour and Education*, "Global Capital" and "Equality, Ideology." See also Hall, "The Great Moving Nowhere"; Hobsbawm, "Death of Neo-Liberalism" and Jacques, "Leader," for a wider analysis.

87. Cole, "Globalisation."

88. Hill and Cole, *Promoting Equality*.

Chapter 9

Racism, Postmodernism and the Flight from Class

Jenny Bourne

In the same week that we learnt how, in Britain, young Stephen Lawrence's racist murderers had gone free because of the 'benign neglect' of the police force and how, in the United States, a young black man was tied to the back of a truck and bounced to a dismembered death, Routledge announced the publication of a learned journal, *Interventions*, which would carry articles such as "The Veil: Postcolonialism and the Politics of Dress." In the United States, the revamped *Social Identities: Journal for the Study of Race, Nation and Culture* advertised itself as "a forum for contesting ideas and debates concerning the formations of, and transformations in, socially significant identities, their attendant forms of material exclusion and power, as well as the political and cultural possibilities opened up by these identifications."[1]

On the one hand, we have palpable, violent, crushing racism. On the other, we have an academy retreating further and further into esoteric sophistry and rarefied language. How has this massive gap between the impact of racism on the ground and its theorizing developed?

Radicalizing the Study of Race

The theorization of race in Britain has always been highly contested—not least in the struggles, over a quarter of a century ago, to transform the Institute of Race Relations (IRR), from where I now write. That struggle at the IRR, examined in detail by Ambalavaner Sivanandan in *Race and Resistance*, was important for articulating, for the first time in Britain, a radical approach to 'race relations' and the role that academics could play. (Till then, 'race relations' studies had been divided between trained anthropologists now studying 'natives' in a British habitat and a bevy of lay social analysts advising government on how to assimilate the said natives into British society.)[2] The impetus for transforming the production of knowledge at the IRR came from the radical Left, which was already challenging every aspect of learning in the universities, from curriculum to examination. Robin Jenkins, himself a researcher in the international unit of the IRR, in his address to the 'Race and Neo-imperialism Section' of the British Sociological Association in January 1971, denounced the IRR's widely acclaimed race relations bible, *Colour and Citizenship*, as helping to make the power elite more powerful and the subject (immigrant) population relatively more impotent and ignorant.[3] In future, when IRR's researchers came knocking on black people's doors, they should be told to 'fuck off.'[4] Already, in 1970, two London School of Economics researchers had attacked the book's ideological bias. In particular, they condemned its 'social problem' framework, its emphasis on studying prejudiced attitudes, and its suggested solutions, which took as given an economic system based on exploitation in which blacks played the part of an oppressed international proletariat.[5]

Bourgeois interpretations of 'race relations' came increasingly under attack, and Marxists began to analyze racism itself within the overall context of capitalist accumulation in western economies. Marios Nikolinakos, professor of economics at the Free University in Berlin, looking at the position of migrant labor, declared that:

> the migratory mechanism of late capitalism in Western Europe is supported by an institutionalised system of discrimination which is anchored in legislation regarding foreigners and in inter-state agreements. . . . Discrimination raises the rate of exploitation. Capital succeeds in maximising surplus value through dividing the working class and granting privileges to a section of it.[6]

Sivanandan, in his seminal *Race, Class and the State*, produced the first analysis of the black presence in Britain in terms of Britain's labor needs, on the one hand, and the cost of social control, on the other. He also explained how immigration laws, by turning black people into second-class citizens, had put the state's imprimatur on racism, and how administrative edicts and court rulings, taking their cue from such laws, helped to *institutionalize* racism.[7]

The impetus to change race theory might have come from 'traditional' Marxist academics and those who, like Nikolinakos and Sivanandan, were strongly influenced by militant trade union organizing among Europe's migrant workers[8] but they would have made little impact had they not resonated with the immediate experiences of black working-class communities in Britain. Police brutality, Paki-bashing, ESN-schooling, criminalization of young people were everyday occurrences for black families. Yet the old-school race academics and the IRR 'experts,' prompted by government concerns, continued researching on how 'they' could be taught to 'adjust' or be made to 'disperse.'[9] And it is in that context that the battle to transform the IRR in 1972 by rank and file staff became significant: it fired the first broadside against institutional racism and declared that racism, not race relations, was the field of study. It was not black people who should be examined, but white society; it was not a question of educating blacks and whites for integration, but of fighting institutional racism, and that was not about changing attitudes but taking on state power.

The IRR's struggle and change had a salutary effect on the academy. Gone was the genteel 'let's hold a coffee-morning' approach to racial understanding; gone were the psychological tolerance scales and attitude surveys; gone was the innocence that social scientists were somehow objective and impartial. Academics had been put on their mettle, and those on the Left, seeing how racism affected black people's lives, decided to fight that racism both as individuals and as academics.[10] That is where we were in the mid-1970s. But many of today's academics, influenced by poststructuralism and postmodernism, would take issue with most of the central themes of the last three paragraphs. First, they would probably contest the concept of institutional racism, putting *racialized discourse* in its place as the key concept of study. Second, they would object to the term black people (because it is 'essentialist') and replace it with *ethnic identities*. Third, they would consider the idea of engaging in a political fight against racism passé. Fourth, they would object to the use of the term anti-racism and indeed the anti-racist project, calling instead for the acceptance of *difference*.

The whole of race thinking has been turned on its head—depoliticized, while keeping the trappings of politics. Every aspect of Left race theorizing: the relationship of race to class, the fact of institutional racism, the importance of black struggle, the emphasis on the structural as opposed to the individual, has been overturned.

The Path to Postmodernism

Discontent with orthodox Left analyses, however, began long before postmodernism gained ascendancy. Already, in the 1970s, black activists were taking issue with a Marxism that relegated racism to the superstructure, and demanded affiliation to a party which would deal with 'their' problems after the class war had been won.[11] At the same time, feminists (and, later, gay activists) were resisting the macho definition of blackness emanating from black political parties. The growth of the black feminist movement in Britain and networks like the Organization of Women of Asian and African Descent (OWAAD) attested to the limitations to be found within both black theorizing and black practice.

But what was significant then was that, by and large, critics who saw limitations in the orthodox Marxist position of subsuming race to class, or the traditional black position of subsuming gender to race, chose not to ditch Marxism or black struggle but to try to change or augment them. Hence, black activists tried to 'blacken' Marxism and, to some extent, managed to get changes (such as the fight against immigration controls) on to the Marxist agenda. And black feminists, while forming their own groupings to discuss their own issues, expressed, simultaneously, a commitment to the struggles of the black community as a whole.[12] Marxism and black struggle had their discontents, but there was a kind of tacit understanding that contradictions were to be worked through.

The Rise of Cultural Studies

Meanwhile, elsewhere in academia, cultural studies (which had, under the influences of Richard Hoggart and Raymond Williams, been created to extend the teaching of literature and root it in the popular) was, under the influence of Stuart Hall, beginning to examine the cultural inscape and impact of race and racism. It was no longer enough to look at black workers in class terms or measure racism in terms of fascist activity. Racism was not just some kind of aberrant false consciousness. The old model, with its economic base and cultural superstructure, was wanting. Racism was, as Gramsci had indicated in his treatment of ideology, in general, being structured into society culturally, and reproduced in everyday life. And the publication of *Policing the Crisis: Mugging, the State and Law and Order* from the Centre for Cultural Studies (directed by Stuart Hall) signaled these changes in the study of racism. The book's aim was, in the words of its authors: "to examine why and how the themes of *race, crime and youth*—condensed into the image of 'mugging'— come to serve as the articulator of the crisis" that society was slipping into.[13]   Why and how was a 'moral panic' being created and used by the state, around the imported concept of mugging, to police its crisis?

But if the early work of the Centre was a necessary corrective to those on the Left who continued to ignore the autonomy of the cultural superstructure, its later oeuvres tended to emphasize the cultural to the exclusion of everything else. And Hall himself, in his subsequent writings, seems to have emerged from the shadow of Gramsci and Althusser to come under the more dubious influence of Foucault, Derrida, Laclau, Lyotard et al. (you name it and he was there) to end up a fully blown post-Marxist in the vestibule of 'New Times,' of which he himself was the supreme architect.[14]

The Hokum of New Times

Neither thesis, nor concept, nor ideology, New Times was a hall of mirrors, reflecting the moving picture show of the social and cultural upheavals of our time. Everything was in flux, making life uncertain, destroying old realities, creating new ones that were equally ephemeral. "All that is solid melts into air," declared the New Timers, citing Marx in a last ditch attempt to sound radical, and went on to describe (not analyze) how "our world is being remade by the shift from the old mass-producing Fordist economy to a new, more flexible post-Fordist order based on computers, information-technology and robotics"[15]—i.e. the technological revolution, i.e. the qualitative leap in the productive forces, i.e. the economic imperative. But they had already thrown out 'economic determinism,' cause and effect, analysis. Hence they juxtapose the social, cultural and economic changes in society without seeing them as interdependent and interactive. Hence the politics they arrive at is not structural, systemic, but cultural, personal, subjective. But then, according to Stuart Hall, "all interests, including class ones are [now] culturally and ideologically defined." And,

> far from there being no resistance to the system, there has been a proliferation of new points of antagonism, new social movements of resistance organised around them and, consequently, a generalisation of 'politics' to spheres which the Left assumed to be apolitical: a politics of the family, of health, of food, of sexuality, of the body.[16]

"Thatcherism in drag" is how Sivanandan characterized this complete break with class politics in his searing critique of New Times. Noting the influences on Marxism of linguistics, semiotics, psychoanalysis, post-structuralism and deconstruction, he showed how this section of the 'Left,' in throwing out the bath water of 'economic determinism' and 'class reductionism,' had thrown out the baby of political struggle against capital and the state. In its stead, there was now a 'cultural politics' that challenged 'social blocs' in civil society.[17]

The Personal and the Political

Eschewing collective political struggle opened the gates to a whole supermarket of different quasi-political brands of fashionable thinking on what used to be called racism. Prominent among the ideas being sold was that power itself was no longer to be conceptualized in terms of 'the state' or 'the ruling class' but as something that operated everywhere, "horizontally as much as vertically, internally as well as externally." It could therefore be taken on at a "multiplicity of points of resistance," which included creating new discourses.[18] Thus, politics was not something done 'out there' in meetings and parties but here in the person.

New Times also put its pseudo-Left seal on the feminist construct that the personal is the political. When that maxim gained currency in the race field and came to inhere as holy script in the race policies of Left-wing councils, the results turned out to be disastrous. Racism, divorced from its institutional definition,[19] was no longer to do with practices, laws or state power, but with individuals: the personal is the political personalized power, personalized the enemy. The white person was the enemy of the black person. And all whites were racist. Thus official racism was the combination of power plus prejudice. "Remove the prejudice and you remove the cutting edge of power; change the person and you change the office."[20]

This personalizing of racism, and the racism awareness training (RAT) classes that were set up to counter it, ended up by instilling guilt in white people and hampering anti-racist action.[21] Worse, where 'action' did take place, it was often at the level of language and discourse alone—taking issue with the term 'black' in nursery rhymes, having children's books revised, images reworked, streets re-named. And because such anti-racism was tokenistic and often imposed from above, it lent itself to pillorying by the Right-wing media, and provided the basis for the creation of the popular image of the loony Left and, later, for the creation of the bogey of political correctness.[22]

Identity Is All

The 'personal is the political' also helped to shift the center of gravity of struggle from the community and society to the individual. 'What has to be done?' was replaced by 'who am I?' as the blacks, feminists and gays, previously part of the pressure groups in Left parties or in social movements campaigning for rights, turned to Identity Politics. Articulating one's identity changed from being a path to political action to being the political action itself.[23] In the event, all kinds of people and groups claimed some kind of oppression, some kind of victim status which would allow them an in to an 'identity.' And some, by purloining Derrida's concept of *differance* and other currents in the emergent postmodern critique of the Enlightenment emanating from French philosophers, posited 'difference' and 'otherness' to rationalize Identity Politics.[24] "In these Postmodern times," wrote Pratibha Parmar,

> the question of identity has taken on colossal weight . . . Being cast into the role of the Other, marginalised, discriminated against and too often invisible within the 'grand narratives' of European thought, black women in particular have fought to assert . . . our sense of self.[25]

For Hall, "the play of identity and difference which constructs racism . . . fundamentally *displaces* many of our hitherto stable political categories."[26]

The politics of identity and difference were now being clearly used to justify the break with class politics and, indeed, with the concept of Left politics altogether. "Identity is a key motif of post-consensus politics because the postwar vocabulary of Left and Right and centre . . . has been shot to pieces," asserted Kobena Mercer.[27] "This 'Left' is now so diverse," agreed Jonathan Rutherford, "that its constituent parts have no underlying shared logic, values or politics." He went on, "We can use the word difference as a motif for that uprooting of certainty. It represents an experience of change, transformation and hybridity"[28]

Reclaiming Ethnicity

Although on the surface these writers appeared to be extending democracy by giving new groups a voice, what they were in fact holding out was nothing more than a debased pluralism. Theirs was a view of society that had no horizontal divisions of class, only vertical divisions of gender, sexuality, ethnicity, religion, etc.—and class did not enter into those gender or ethnicity divisions either. But pluralism as a solution to the race problem had, in effect, been rejected both by the Black Power movement and the strugglers at the IRR in the 1970s. Black writers like Sivanandan had pointed to the destructive nature of state policies that encouraged the fragmentation of black politics with ethnic programs and ethnic funding.[29] Reducing black people's problems to cultural or religious needs was, he explained, to side step both racism and poverty.

A rescue package was at hand for the Identity Politics school. In a talk on film at the ICA, London, in 1988, Stuart Hall explained how we need to recognize "the end of the innocent notion of the essential black experience" and "the extraordinary diversity of subjective positions, social experience and cultural identities which compose the category 'black.'" He predicted "a renewed contestation over the meaning of the term 'ethnicity.'" A new conception of ethnicity would emerge that would be "a new cultural politics which engages rather than suppresses *difference*." Ethnicity needed to be "decoupled" from the way it functioned in dominant discourse, so that we could "represent a non-coercive and a more diverse conception . . . a positive conception of the ethnicity of the margins . . . of the periphery . . . a recognition that we all speak from a particular place, but of a particular history, out of a particular experience, a particular culture."[30]

Cultural difference was a world apart from cultural diversity, concurred Homi Bhabha, drawing on poststructuralist thinking, psychoanalytic concepts and a critique of Western universalism. What he was attempting, he explained to an interviewer, was

> to begin to see how the notion of the West itself, or Western culture, its liberalism and relativism—these very potent mythologies of 'progress'—also contain a cutting edge, a limit. With the notion of cultural difference, I try to place myself in that position of liminality, in that productive space of the construction of culture as difference, in the spirit of alterity or otherness.[31]

The obscurantist had succeeded the wordsmith.

Full-Blown Postmodernism

Writers like Hall and Bhabha, coming from cultural studies and literature, might be expected to analyze race on a culturally rarefied level. But what is surprising is that so many sociologists, including erstwhile serious Marxists, have forsworn what might be called a political economy of race or racism in favor of culturalist interpretations using postmodern concepts.[32]

One of the most full-blown defenses of the shift can be found in the work of sociologist Ali Rattansi. In *Race, Culture and Difference, a Postmodern Anthology*, he explains with James Donald that "Getting to grips with the dynamics of 'race,' racism and anti-racism in Britain today means studying an ever-changing nexus of representation, discourse and power. And that requires a critical return to the concept *culture*." 'Critical,' for them, means taking in the impact of Saussurian semiotics, Althusserian and post-Marxist theories of ideology, Lacanian psychoanalysis, Foucault's concern with discourse and power, the British cultural studies school and "various strands of feminism"—in what appears to be a rerun of Stuart Hall's own journey, but this time as farce. Re-thinking culture means discarding "the claims and comforts" of concepts like community or "the black experience" to understand that 'race' and identity are "inherently contestable social and political categories." According to Rattansi, the new thinkers have re-posed the question "in terms of cultural authority and individual agency" to require a "careful analysis of contemporary political struggles over questions of representation, symbolic boundary formation and identification."

But he wants us to discard yet more of the old baggage. 'Racism,' 'ethnicity,' 'nationalism' are no longer part of "a viable taxonomy." For they belong to that era of creating "convincing, all-encompassing explanatory frameworks." Today, in postmodern times, there is a "loss of confidence in the West's metanarratives." Nor could he accept the European Enlightenment's confidence in 'Reason with Progress' that emanates from 'Western Man.' On the contrary, racism is connected to the subconscious and the irrational. Besides, how can we use the concepts of a modernity that has been associated with colonialism, genocide, slavery and the Holocaust? If Enlightenment-derived values of human universalism installed 'Western Man' as the norm, how can we use these same tainted values to mobilize for human rights "against racialized discrimination, inequalities and violence?"[33]

In a largely undigested and indigestible chapter of *Racism, Modernity and Identity*, which Rattansi again co-edited, this time with Sallie Westwood, he romps through the range of authors—Bauman, Giddens, Foucault, Derrida, Laclau and Mouffe—who have helped him construct his postmodern frame. The language in which he introduces his chapter conveys some of the topics he covers as well as his convoluted approach. For Rattansi, the 'postmodern' condition is

> a reflection on the nature and limits of Western modernity; an analysis of modernity which focuses on its typical dualities, for example the chronic dis-embedding and reinvention of traditions and collective identities; the marginalization of Western modernity's Others in the construction of Western identities; the impact of new forms of globalization; the decentring and de-essentialization of both subjects and the 'social'; an appreciation of temporality and spatiality as constitutive of identities and the 'social;' a consideration of the relation between the 'psychic and the 'social;' and an engagement with questions of sexuality and sexual difference.[34]

Taking Issue with Postmodernism

On Difference and Universalism

To mock the postmodernists for their pretentiousness, though, is not enough. The project reflects far more serious political dangers. Kenan Malik's first objection to the postmodernists rests on the fact that they use the very same assumptions as racists: the notion of difference and a hostility to equality. "The postmodern critique of racial discourse flows out of its hostility to universalism and in its embrace of the particular and the relative, postmodernism embodies the same notions of difference as are contained in nineteenth-century Romantic racial theories." Malik acknowledges that it is important to see identities as socially constructed and not naturally given but, he explains,

> by insisting that society is inherently and irreducibly heterogeneous and diverse and by rejecting any idea of "totality" that might allow us to see the commonalties or connections among heterogeneous and diverse elements, poststructuralist discourse has undermined its own capacity to challenge naturalistic explanations of difference.

Postmodernists deny the idea of an essential identity, stressing instead multiple social identities, which suggests that everything from color, gender, to music or clothes are matters of style. Yet difference is not a coat you choose to put on. Different, for Malik, is what society has systematically made you, if you are black in Brixton or a Jew in Nazi Germany. Blackness is a social distinction, not a personal choice.[35]

And without a human 'essence' how can one, asks Malik, call for equality between groups? Without some totalizing universal principle of equality or racial justice, how can one respect the difference of others or ask them to respect one? Most critically then, the anti-essentialism of postmodernism disables the anti-racist project. For Aijaz Ahmad, too, "no struggle against racism or any kind of collective oppression is possible without some concept of universality." Contrary to what Rattansi says, Ahmad holds that the "fact that men have historically had more rights than women does not turn us against the concept of rights. . . . Anti-imperialism itself will be merely xenophobic if it breaks with the idea of universality."[36] Asked how to grant recognition to human 'difference' without giving up the universal principles that used to underlie socialism, Ahmad concludes that, just because struggles "of both universal and particular rights" have not produced socialism, people tend to note only what they failed to achieve. "We also need to have memories of the traditions of mercy and the struggles for justice" if we are to affect a real reconciliation between the universal and the particular.[37]

Against Culturalism

Sivanandan critiques postmodernism not so much in terms of the inward-looking self-referencing type of debate, beloved of academics, as in terms of the danger it spells to anti-racist practice. First, he takes issue with those intellectuals who, at a time when racism against the black working class is getting worse, have

> retreated into culturalism and ethnicity or, worse, fled into discourse and deconstruction and representation—as though to interpret the world is more im-

portant than to change it, as though changing the interpretation is all we could do to change the world.

And in an acerbic aside he adds: "Marxists interpret the world in order to change it, postmodernists change the interpretation."

Second, Sivanandan shows how the emphasis on culturalism and ethnicism is in fact a retreat from the struggle against racism. Struggling *for* culture is not struggling *against* racism. Cultural politics

> does not have to confront economic power (including the state), only cultural power. . . . And such power can be personal, individual. Hence the personal is the political: the fight for my blackness, for my Asian-ness, as they would call it, is also my fight against racism. Granted, but the converse is not necessarily true: the political is not necessarily personal: the fight against racism does not necessarily help my Asian-ness. The one is about cultural politics as it affects some sections of society, the other is about political culture as it affects the whole of society.

Third, he shows how the postmodernists, by maintaining that experience itself is nothing till it is "linguisized, discoursed, represented," remove the ordinary person's ability to act out of the authority of her/his experience and put it in the hands of her/his discoursist interpreters. But then, for the postmodernists, "there are only processes and provisionality and ever-changing perspectives through which subjects are 'constituted,' identities are 'negotiated,' problems 'represented.' By the same token, "there is no racism in schools, only a 'racialisation process,' no ghettos but a 'racialisation of space,' no 'binary oppositions' such as old racism/new racism, but all sorts of racisms feeding off and into each other."

Fourth, Sivanandan argues, the postmodernist intellectuals, who are the real betrayers of the Left, blame modernity for having failed them, and "to justify their betrayal . . . have created a whole new language of their own which allows them to appropriate struggle without engaging in it."[38]

Applied Postmodernism in Education

Fortunately, most postmodern theorists on race are confined to the lecture theatre and so rarely contaminate 'the real world.' But when their ideas become applied more widely, by constructing a kind of postmodern pedagogy, of which Phil Cohen is the foremost proponent, the results are dangerous.

Phil Cohen was, in the 1970s, a worker with disaffected youth and, in the 1980s, a researcher in cultural studies and antiracist curricula at the Institute of Education. More recently, he has been instrumental in setting up a New Ethnicities Unit at the University of East London. Based in the heart of London's East End—an area unique in its mix of migrant communities and a breeding ground for fascist movements—the Unit boasts an interdisciplinary forum where "cultures of racism and anti-racism can be investigated" with an emphasis on "the question of identity and cultural empowerment." Cohen himself, keened to the growing concerns in Europe about organized racism within youth cultures, has targeted the study of white working-class boys' attitudes— an area which till now has been relatively neglected in British research. And his ideas, straddling as they do, the academic postmodern race arena, cultural studies and the development of educational pedagogy,[39] are becoming increasingly fashionable both in education and youth work.

In brief, Cohen's position is that all types of educational anti-racism are: a) wrong because they rest on a *theory* of racism; and b), will fail because they appeal to *reason*.

Inevitably, he rejects historical materialism because "it has proved quite incapable of grasping the micro-foundation of racist ideologies,"[40] and "offers a rationalist pedagogy which fails to engage with the structures of feeling and belief through which children relate to history and racism."[41] And he is opposed to any attempt, Marxist or otherwise, to analyze society by making "certain *a priori* assumptions about origins, causes, meaning and effect" that "correspond to particular forms of experiences of racism." He attacks the "totalisation rule," substituting instead a rule of "relative autonomy," where "different sites or forms of racism have their own conditions of existence and articulation."[42] (I have no quarrel with that if, by it, he is saying what we all know: racism is not one-dimensional or static but complex and dynamic.) For "the relationship between race, class and gender is not a fixed eternal correspondence" but "one of shifting internal articulations between specific discourses and technologies of power, producing uneven and indeed contradictory effects."[43] (Here he loses me, but I am left wondering at the sophistry that so readily transforms a common-or-garden platitude into high-faluting thought). There is no such thing as racism for Cohen, only racialized discourses. And how they are constructed is "an integral part of the power they exercise in and through material practices of discrimination."[44] Thus, his work as an educationalist is to "decode and deconstruct racist representations" and "to elicit and give expression to cultural materials which resist or are repressed by racist discourses."[45] Why, in fact, the whole of antiracist education founders is because it starts from the premise that reason can overcome racist ideas.

Antiracism, for Cohen, is a catchall term which brings together everything he dislikes—whether it is tame multiculturalism that merely teaches children about cultures, religions, artifacts, mores, etc., or the kind of radical anti-racism set up in opposition to multiculturalism to situate racism in the British history of slavery, colonialism and imperialism.[46] Indeed, he goes out of his way to destroy the philosophical foundation of the type of anti-racist education that the Institute of Race Relations (IRR) and others have battled for in schooling. He ignores the genesis of antiracist education as a response to a biased curriculum which gave all children—black and white—a partial and sanitized view of history in which racism was divorced both from the black presence in Britain and Britain's history as a colonizing power.

Cohen parodies attempts (by the IRR and others) to write an account of how racism was written into exploitation and different modes of production, terming it a "teleology of the oppressed." According to him, an account is being constructed around the oppressions faced by certain 'privileged' groups: Blacks, Irish, Jews. In other words, the producers of this kind of history, by picking their groups and their moments, write the inevitability of racism into history, producing a narrative of victimhood. His analogy is a mystery story that always has the same culprit. He mocks antiracists in an article entitled, "'It Was Racism What Dunnit,'" supposedly a real remark made to him by a white pupil.[47]

Yet, when progressive writers—usually Marxist with a black perspective—try to redress this tale of eternal victimisation,[48] they are equally derided. These "Roots Radicals," he claims, are just turning the "teleology of the oppressed" inside out and upside down to construct an over-glorifying "triumphalist narrative" of the fights against racism. (Cohen fails to see that such works of reclaiming black working-class history were necessary exercises for the struggle on the ground—and a counter, at the same time, to the dominant pedagogies which either wrote anticolonial struggles and black people's fights out of working-class history or personalized history to individual black achievers). Cohen states that he is against such antiracist narratives because of the teleology involved. Yet there is evidence that he is actually antagonistic to the emphasis on black history itself. In his early work, he queries why anti-black racism is privileged over anti-Semitism or anti-Irish racism. And he is emphatic that racist discourses do not have their roots in Britain's colonial and slave history but that "its essential idioms are generated from within certain strategic discourses in British class society," and the codes of breeding which grew up.[49]

But Cohen's niggle, today, is reserved for any antiracist education that attempts to reason young people out of their racism. For this is a practice that comes straight out of the eighteenth century's Enlightenment project, with its belief in the progress of 'Man' from barbarism to civilization. Anti-racist education, "locked into a 'civilising mission,' which is itself founded on a hidden curriculum of middle-class racism," will naturally be resisted by working-class pupils.[50] And teachers on this mission commit another cardinal sin in trying to silence racism in the classroom: "Resentments against the pedagogic form compound resistance to the ideological content." You cannot, he says, shut down racism "by order."[51] (Although he does state that serious acts of racism cannot go unpunished, he is unclear on how a teacher is to distinguish between acts to be punished and those to be allowed, or prevent one slipping into the other, or how a teacher in a mixed classroom can prevent minority group children from feeling vulnerable and open to attack.)

Why does reason fail, punishment provoke? Because, says Cohen, racism thrives in the imagination and "unless the inner workings of the racist imagination are properly understood there is little chance of challenging its 'common sense.'"[52] We ignore at our peril, "the deeper reaches of the racist imagination, the structures of feeling and fantasy which are embedded in even the most rationalized forms of racist argument and action."[53] It is "the failure of humanist arguments" to "engage with the subtle dialectics of the racist imagination," in Cohen's view, which keep young people one up on the anti-racist movement.[54] The issue, therefore, is not whether racist myths are true or not, but why an individual needs the myths. It is psychological fear over sexuality and identity, states Cohen, drawing on Foucault's work and various psychoanalytic theories, that leads the individual to find solace in racist ideas. And, today, the most insecure and identity-less is the white working-class male who "has been written out of the script" by antiracist teachers. Being a "working-class racist is something to be," because it addresses "a profound sense of dislocation." For "one of the more seductive ruses of racism, its secret pleasure principle, is the way it reduces ontological insecurity."[55]

Cohen, like others at the cultural end of the postmodern spectrum, loves his tropes, puns and word plays. Most of all, though, he relishes his iconoclasm. "Look at me!" he seems to shout out of every article, "I am really at the cutting edge of the *avant garde.*" But he is in fact one of the most defeatist of writers on racism. He has locked racism firmly in the subconscious where it cannot be reached by reasoned argument or rational analysis. He has taken racism from the structured part of society, where it could be combated, and located it solely in discourse, where it could be negotiated. He has not merely written morality out of the discussion, he has also ditched equality. And, for an anti-doctrinaire postmodernist, he is remarkably doctrinaire about his own 'theories.' He does not seem to care how many hostages he offers the enemy. Or, perhaps, he is the enemy. How else to explain his joining the New Right's cause in defining antiracists as the cause of racism and white working-class boys as its true victims?

Postmodernism has come full circle. It had its roots in the genuine shortcomings of Marxism and Left politics, especially in relation to issues of race and gender. But, in the process of pulling the rug from beneath "complacent certainties" and prying open "some paranoid totalities," it has also surrendered to "a politically paralyzing scepticism, a flashy populism and a full-blooded moral relativism."[56] It has pulled the rug from under itself too: there is no reason to resist racism; there is nothing to choose between its perpetrators and its opponents.

Notes

1. *Social Identities: Journal for the Study of Race, Nation and Culture,* <http://www.tandf.co.uk/Journals/carfax/13504630.html> (July 20, 2001).

2. Ambalavaner Sivanandan, *Race and Resistance: The IRR Story* (London: Institute of Race relations, 1974); Jenny Bourne, "Cheerleaders and Ombudsmen: the Sociology of Race Relations in Britain," *Race and Class* 21, no. 4 (spring 1980): 331–352.

3. Jim Rose et al., *Colour and Citizenship: A Report on British Race Relations* (London: Oxford University Press for the IRR, 1972).

4. Robin Jenkins, *The Production of Knowledge at the Institute of Race Relations* (London: Independent Labour Party, 1971).

5. John McGreal and Phil Corrigan, *Ideology in 'Colour and Citizenship'* (London: LSE, 1970).

6. Marios Nikolinakos, "Notes toward a General Theory of Migration in Late Capitalism," *Race and Class* 17, no. 1 (summer 1975): 12.

7. Ambalavaner Sivanandan, *Race, Class and the State* (London: IRR, 1976).

8. The Pan-European Conference of Migrant Workers (which both Nikolinakos and Sivanandan helped to organize) was held in the Netherlands on November 21, 1974. See *Race and Class* 16, no. 2 (1974): 207–213.

9. Of the studies carried out by the domestic policy wing of the IRR in the early 1970s, one was called 'The Adjustment Study' and the second was on how to encourage the dispersal of black people to the New Towns.

10. The influence of the IRR's struggle could be seen in the work of people such as Robert Moore, Lee Bridges, Anne Dummett, John Downing et al.

11. At this time numerous black papers and magazines, such as *Samaj, Mukti, Black Struggle* and *Flame,* emerged from the ranks of black socialists impatient with the blindness of the Left parties to the race issue. Socialist feminists were making similar critiques of the gender-blindness of Left parties and showing the way to new forms of organization engendered by the women's movement. See, for example, Sheila Rowbotham, Lynne Segal and Hilary Wainwright, *Beyond the fragments* (London: Merlin, 1979).

12. This dual consciousness can be seen in FOWAAD, the magazine of OWAAD and in Beverley Bryan et al., *The Heart of the Race: Black Women's Lives in Britain* (London: Virago, 1985).

13. Stuart Hall et al., *Policing the Crisis: Mugging, the State and Law and Order* (London: Macmillan, 1978), viii.

14. Stuart Hall and Martin Jacques, *New Times: The Changing Face of Politics in the 1990s* (London: Lawrence & Wishart, 1989). As Ellen Meiksins Wood points out, "Hall's theoretical statements are sufficiently ambiguous and his movements in an NTS [New True Socialism] direction are so often accompanied by qualifications and disclaimers that it is not always easy to know exactly where he stands." See Meiksins Wood, *The Retreat from Class* (London: Verso, 1986), 3 (N).

15. Martin Jacques, *Marxism Today,* Special Issue (October 1988).

16. Stuart Hall, "Brave New World," *Marxism Today* Special Issue (October 1988): 27.

17. Ambalavaner Sivanandan, "All That Melts into Air Is Solid: The Hokum of New Times," *Race and Class* 31, no. 3 (1990): 1–30.

18. Rosalind Brunt, "Bones in the Corset," *Marxism Today* (October 1988): 20–23.

19. The fact that Metropolitan Commissioner Paul Condon was able, during the Lawrence Inquiry of 1998, to deny institutionalized racism in his force (since that, he said, would be saying that all his officers were guilty of racism) is partly a legacy of the personalized definition of racism which was popularized during these times.

20. Sivanandan, "All that Melts." An example of the disastrous implementation of this as policy was the suspension of head teacher Maureen McGoldrick. See Sivanandan, "Race, Class and Brent," *Race and Class* 29, no. 1 (summer 1987): 73–77.

21. See Jenny Bourne, *Toward an Anti-racist Feminism* (London: IRR, 1987) and Ambalavaner Sivanandan, "RAT and the Degradation of Black Struggle," *Race and Class* 26, no. 4 (April 1985): 1–33.

22. Nancy Murray, "Anti-racists and Other Demons: The Press and Ideology in Thatcher's Britain," *Racism and the Press in Thatcher's Britain* (London: IRR, 1989); Jenny Bourne, "Review of S. Dunant. The War of the Words: The Political Correctness Debate," *Race and Class* 36, no. 3 (1995): 89–91.

23. Jenny Bourne, *Homelands of the Mind: Jewish Feminism and Identity Politics* (London: Institute for Race Relations, 1987).

24. Derrida's *différance* seems to derive from the combination of the verbs to defer and to differ.

25. Pratibha Parmar, "Black Feminism: The Politics of Articulation," in Identity: *Community, Culture, Difference,* ed. Jonathan Rutherford (London: Lawrence and Wishart, 1990), 106.

26. Stuart Hall, "New Ethnicities," in *'Race,' Culture and Difference,* ed. Ali Rattansi and James Donald (London: Sage, 1992), 255.

27. Kobena Mercer, "Welcome to the Jungle: Identity and Diversity in Postmodern Politics," in Rutherford, *Identity,* 50.

28. Jonathan Rutherford, "A Place Called Home: Identity and the Cultural Politics of Difference," in Rutherford, *Identity,* 10.

29. Ambalavaner Sivanandan, "Challenging Racism: Strategies for the 1980s," *Race and Class* 25, no. 2 (autumn 1983): 1–11.

30. Hall, "New Ethnicities," 253–258.

31. Homi Bhabha, "Interview with Homi Bhabha, the Third Space," in Rutherford, *Identity,* 209.

32. This is not to say that I or any others who write for the IRR's magazine, *Race and Class,* think that there is no place for examining aspects of racialized discourse or how things are represented. In fact, many of the articles already cited earlier from *Race and Class*—on race strategies, feminism, the media, antiracism, etc.—have been doing just that. But we examine discourse as just one arena where racism can be analyzed. And we look for strategies that would change racism's material operations (which might well later be reflected in discourse). For the postmodernists, however, the emphasis is quite different. They seek to change, not the world, but the word. Stuart Hall, for example, draws attention to the way that "scenarios of representation" are increasingly being given "a formative, not merely an expressive, place in the constitution of social and political life." See Hall, "New Ethnicities," 254.

33. All quotations in this section are taken from Rattansi and Donald, "Introduction," in Rattansi and Donald, *'Race,' Culture.*

34. Ali Rattansi, "Modern Racisms, Racialized Identities," in *Racism, Modernity and Identity: On the Western Front,* ed. Ali Rattansi and Sallie Westwood (Cambridge, U.K.: Polity, 1994), 4.

35. All references to Malik's argument can be found in Kenan Malik, "The Mirror of Race: Postmodernism and the Celebration of Difference," in *In Defense of History: Marxism and the Postmodern Agenda,* ed. Ellen Meiksins Wood and John Bellamy Foster (New York: Monthly Review, 1997). See also Kenan Malik, "Universalism and Difference: Race and the Postmodernists," *Race and Class* 37, no. 3 (January–March 1996): 1–17.

36. Aijaz Ahmad, "Interview I: Culture, Nationalism and the Role of Intellectuals," in Ellen Meiksins Wood and John Bellamy Foster, eds., *In Defense of History.*

37. Aijaz Ahmad, "Interview II: Issues of Class and Culture," in Ellen Meiksins Wood and John Bellamy Foster, eds., *In Defense of History.*

38. All quotations in this section are taken from Ambalavaner Sivanandan, "La trahison des clercs," *New Statesman* (July 14, 1995): 20–21.

39. He even went so far as to publish a whole paper on how Althusser and Foucault might have deconstructed the East London football supporters' chant, "We hate humans." See *Monstrous Images, Perverse Reasons* (London: Centre for Multicultural Education, University of London Institute of Education, 1991).

40. Phil Cohen, "'It's Racism What Dunnit': Hidden Narratives in Theories of Racism," in Rattansi and Donald, *'Race,' Culture,* 96.

41. Cohen, *Monstrous Images,* 38.

42. Cohen, "'It's Racism,'" 83, 95.

43. Phil Cohen, *Anti-racist Cultural Studies: A Curriculum Development Project in School and Community Education.* London: London University Institute of Education, 1986).

44. Cohen, "'It's Racism,'" 68.

45. Cohen, *Anti-racist Cultural Studies.*

46. "Just to learn about other people's cultures is not to learn about the racism of one's own. To learn about the racism of one's own culture, on the other hand, is to approach other cultures objectively," explained Amabalavaner Sivanandan in the introductions to two antiracist educational books—*Roots of Racism* and *Patterns of Racism* (London: IRR, 1982).

47. See Cohen, *Monstrous Images* and "'It's Racism.'"

48. See, for example, Ambalavaner Sivanandan, *From Resistance to Rebellion: Asian and Afro-Caribbean Struggles in Britain* (London: IRR, 1982); Peter Fryer, *Staying Power* (London: Pluto, 1984).

49. Phil Cohen, "The Perversions of Inheritance: Studies in the Making of Multi-racist Britain," in *Multi-racist Britain,* ed. Phil Cohen and Harwant Bains (London: Macmillan, 1988); also Cohen, *Monstrous Images.*

50. Cohen, "Perversions," 2.

51. Cohen, *Monstrous Images,* 49.

52. Cohen, "Perversions," 2.

53. Cohen, "'It's Racism,'" 82.

54. Cohen, *Monstrous Images,* 19.

55. Cohen, *Monstrous Images,* 19. And for a longer critique of Cohen's tendency to focus on white racist youth as the new victims, see Liz Fekete, "Let Them Eat Cake," *Race and Class* 39, no. 3 (January–March 1998): 77–82.

56. Terry Eagleton, "Where do Postmodernists Come From?" in Wood and Bellamy, *In Defense of History,* 17–25.

Chapter 10

Women, Work and the Family: Or Why Postmodernism Cannot Explain the Links

Jane Kelly

Introduction

In the last twenty years of the twentieth century, feminism was profoundly affected by postmodern and poststructuralist ideas and this influence is still pervasive. In its turn, Women's Studies also suffered from the same ideas. While taught today in most academic institutions, feminism developed during a period of the decline of the women's liberation movement (WLM), from which it had its inception. Since the middle of the 1980s, the division between theory and practice has deepened so that not only is most feminist theory now devoid of the experience of practice, but feminist campaigns and activities, while often militant in themselves, have become less and less informed by theory.

The growth in the influence of ideas described as postmodern has sidelined socialist and Marxist feminism, which in the 1970s, in a variety of forms, had dominated feminist thinking in Britain. Initially, with the shift to the right in Britain and the United States, especially after the election of Thatcher and Reagan, the attack on socialist feminism came from an influx of ideas contained in books from the United States that were essentialist in their framework. But although they used a radical feminist rhetoric—against pornography, against male-dominated language, against rape, for the celebration of motherhood— their politics was bourgeois.[1] Rather than basing themselves on mass campaigns and trying to build alliances with the organizations of the working class, as had to some degree happened in Britain in the 1970s, these writers, often using a civil rights agenda, were oriented toward the use of the state to enact legislation.[2]

With socialist feminism on the defensive in Britain in the 1980s, the ideas of these writers had some influence. But there were other changes in feminist theory too. Increasingly, the writings of the French female psychoanalysts Luce Irigaray and Julia Kristeva, who had been students of Jacques Lacan, were adopted, along with the writings of Michel Foucault, Jacques Derrida, Roland Barthes. These writers stress the instability of the subject, the negative entry of women into the conscious world, the decenteredness of power that is located within the individual, rather than emanating from the state or recognizable authority, and the impossibility of attaining knowledge or of judging truth from falsity.

Issues such as the family, raised so potently in descriptive and analytical material at the outset of the WLM of the late 1960s until the mid-1980s, have faded away. And since the work of feminists has become increasingly dominated by postmodern concerns—identity, the body, difference—the family as an object of study or critique, has been steadily ignored. After the great debates about domestic labor and the (re)discoveries of forms of gendered power in the private sphere, the early theoretical work gave rise to predominantly empirical work. While this empirical work was theoretically driven by the earlier debates, there were no new theoretical developments to nourish or challenge these studies. Meanwhile, feminist theorizing redirected attention toward other issues such as identity, sexuality, agency, the body and, of course, the thorny question of the very concept of 'Woman' and its homogenizing tendency. While initially feminist theorizing had understood 'the family' to be the core site of women's oppression, trends in theorizing by the 1990s rejected the idea that there could be such a thing as a core site of oppression, dispensed with the idea that the family could have the same significance for all women, and challenged the idea that one could speak of women as if they were a unitary category at all. Thus, what had made 'the family' so significant to feminist theorizing was swept away on a tide of criticism, from black feminists initially and then from the growing poststructuralist tendency in feminist thought.[3]

Whether you agree with the centrality of black feminists in this process, it is certainly the case that poststructuralism and postmodern theories have played a central part in the decline of serious feminist analysis of the family. It is a great pity, for many of the insights of the early WLM feminists are even more telling today than they were in the 1970s. Many of their criticisms of the nuclear family, including as a place of oppression for women and for children, are clearer today than they were when the ideas were developed. How did these insights disappear? When did socialist feminist analysis drop the issue of the family and why? Is postmodernism capable of analyzing the family, the place of women in it and its relation to women's paid work? And if it is not, what theories do we need to develop to refocus discussion on these issues?

Pessimistic attacks on what postmodern writers call Enlightenment thought, against the idea of any overarching theory by which the world could be understood, have particular significance for feminism and Women's Studies. For Women's Studies was never just another academic discipline, it always crossed constitutional boundaries and it always had implications for everyday life, and in particular how to change it. While it was set up as "another" academic discipline, Women's Studies has always been different to other subjects like English Literature, French Studies, Art History, Math or Physics. It is both broader in its remit—anything to do with women and the way we live—and, much more dangerous—this can change your life! Women, especially mature returners to education, have found it a subject that they can bring all sorts of experiences to bear upon—work, motherhood, family relations, sexuality, race, class, trade unionism, abortion, etc.—despite what they might see as a lack in their own formal education. So while the discipline of Women's Studies makes demands on women to generalize from and theorize their experiences, its evidence often rests on everyday life, on the real lives of women. In such a context, the moves to postmodernity and poststructuralism in feminist theory have profoundly negative consequences.

One such consequence is the development of theoreticism, endemic in much postmodern writing, which makes the writing inaccessible and often unreadable. Another consequence is the lack of obvious connection between much of this theory and ordinary women's lives, which makes it seem irrelevant.[4] Thirdly, and most importantly, postmodernism's refusal to think about the whole world and its relationships, to refuse to investigate the links between women's position in the family and their place in the labor market is thoroughly pessimistic when it comes to changing the lives of half the world's population—namely, women. To replace this necessary investigation by a blinkered focus on the contingent, the local, the specific, the relative, is nothing but a failure to see the wood for the trees.

The 1990s saw various developments within feminism: from the postfeminism of those who thought the battles had been won, to academic feminists who built their careers out of an engagement with theory, increasingly devoid of any practice other than theory itself,[5] and especially the development of a wide range of positions more or less critical of, but placing themselves within, postmodernism. What all these have in common is a rejection of the concepts of socialist and Marxist feminism. In this chapter, I am not going to deal with the postfeminist agenda, nor with those feminists who adopt postmodernism hook, line and sinker, for both of these are easy targets. Rather, I want to concentrate on feminist writers who take a critical stance toward postmodernism, but who try to draw out what they regard as useful to a feminist analysis and discard what is not. I hope to show that by engaging with the terms of postmodernity, albeit critically, and rejecting the possibility of any overarching theory of the oppression of women, these writers get caught up in circular arguments that tell us little of the sources of our oppression or how and where to fight it. I believe such developments do a disservice to women, including those who study the issues through Women's Studies courses, many of whom are also fighting against their oppressions, but without the help of useful knowledge and theory.

Against those who say that Marxist and socialist theory is gender- and color-blind, that it "has used the generalizing categories of production and class to delegitimize demands of women, black people, gays, lesbians, and others whose oppression cannot be reduced to economics,"[6] I want to argue for a return to the ideas of socialism and Marxism, to reject the criticism that it ignores and is ignorant of the position of women (and other oppressed groups), in order to discuss the position of women today in Britain. I think it is important to focus on the real position of women, at home, in the family, and in the paid workforce, and to relate this to the ideological offensive against women, carried out by the Tory governments since 1979 and continued by New Labour after their election in 1997. Finally, I want to sketch out some areas of fruitful campaigning activity for the development of feminism and women's liberation.

Theoretical Chaos: Postmodern Feminism— the Road to Nowhere

Many feminists who have rejected Marxism damn with faint praise. In her book, *Feminist Practice & Poststructuralist Theory*, Chris Weedon summarizes the positions of Marxist feminism quite accurately. She points to its understanding of the historically specific aspects of oppression, including the interrelationship between different forms of oppression (capitalism, patriarchy, racism); its acknowledgment that the meaning of biology is also historical and social; its recognition that the psychic dimension, too, is historically produced, and how Marxist feminists correctly argue that, "while the family is a key site of all these issues, it cannot be seen in isolation from broader social relations of work, leisure and public life, all of which require transformation."[7] Weedon then goes on to elaborate the implications for socialism of these understandings: the need to eliminate the sexual division of labor, to achieve reproductive rights, the freedom to define one's own sexuality, and so on. Later in the chapter she elaborates Marxism's contribution to an understanding of human consciousness,

> early Marxist writing decentred the sovereign, rational humanist consciousness of liberal philosophy and economics, making consciousness not the origin of social relations but their effect. As such, consciousness is always historically and culturally specific . . . determined ultimately by the conflict of interests between capital and labour. [8]

It is this linking of ideology with material interests that is, she argues, so important for feminism, for it is where in struggle these material conditions can be reproduced or transformed. So far so good. But then comes the bombshell: she continues,

However, experience for Marxism as for poststructuralism, is a linguistic construct. The dominant liberal account of the experience of capitalist relations of production is one way among others of interpreting the world and, for Marxism, a false one which helps reproduce oppressive power relations by misrepresenting the real relations of capitalist society. Marxist discourse is able to use the terms "real" and "false" because it has a concept of historical materialist science which can offer a true explanation of capitalism, guaranteed by the Marxist principle of the ultimate determining power of the relations of production. Poststructuralist discourses reject the claim that scientific theories can give access to the truth.[9]

Influenced by Althusserian Marxism, experience for Weedon "is a linguistic construct," and seeking "truth" a belief in "false" objectivity. Despite some rigorous critiques of Lacanian psychoanalysis, including the writings of Irigaray and Kristeva, which she says, "offer little space for feminist appropriation,"[10] and a sharp attack on radical feminism which she says fixes difference and "rejects the need to engage politically,"[11] she argues in her last chapter, "Feminist Critical Practice,"

From a feminist poststructuralist perspective the process of criticism is infinite since meaning can never be finally fixed. Every act of reading is a new production of meaning. Positions from which to read and the discourses with which to read are in principle infinite and constantly changing. At any particular historical moment, however, there is a finite number of discourses in circulation, discourses which are in competition for meaning. It is the conflict between these discourses which creates the possibility of new ways of thinking and new forms of subjectivity.[12]

Although Weedon admits to a limit on the possible available meanings, it is the conflict between discourses that she proposes as the motor force of change. Quite how this happens except at a level of ideas and intellectual work is unclear. For, despite her apparent understanding of Marxism, this is the complete opposite of the Marxist concept of the class struggle as the motor of change. Her ideas are founded on the Althusserian notion that theory is a political practice in itself. This is a distortion of Marx for whom praxis—the unity of theory and practice—meant that actual political activity informs and is informed by theory in a dialectical relation, neither one having precedence or priority.

Weedon combines Althusserian Marxism with the poststructural notion that 'truth' is only ever a momentary reading in a chain of meanings: "Modes of subjectivity, like theories of society or versions of history, are temporary fixings in the on-going process in which any absolute meaning or truth is constantly deferred."[13] This means that despite the final paragraph of her book, which calls on women to adopt her poststructuralist framework and "use it in the fight for change,"[14] it can only be change at the level of the individual and ideas—in the end, a liberal and idealist project.

While Weedon's work does not, ultimately, use a classical Marxist method, despite her understanding of some of its theories, many other postmodern feminist writers dismiss Marxism altogether. In "Feminism and the Politics of Postmodernism,"[15] Linda Nicholson cites Lyotard in her rejection of what she terms "foundationalist" philosophy, finding "problematic the requirement that philosophical claims be grounded in basic, or foundational, truths."[16] She continues, "Marxism's inadequacies for feminism [are] a consequence of Marxism's reliance on a single category to explain social life across history and diverse culture . . . it had become . . . politically oppressive."[17] This single category is production:

Like many feminists, I had come to see that this focus on production within Marxism provided a crucial obstacle in Marxism's abilities to explain and to help remove many forms of women's oppression. . . . While theoretically the term referred to any activity conducive to human reproduction, Marxists most frequently understood it in accord with its predominant meaning in capitalist societies: as an activity taking place outside the home in the form of wage labour. Such a use situated oppression outside the home. Moreover, since the theory claimed to account for all aspects of social life, this use constructed Marxism as not only irrelevant to explaining important aspects of women's oppression but, indeed, as an obstacle in the attempt to develop such explanations.[18]

While it may be true that some Left-wing currents have adopted such economistic and workerist politics in the past, including in Britain the Socialist Workers Party and the Socialist Party in its previous incarnation, the Militant, it is not good enough to reject a whole theory on the basis that you do not agree with some of its self-proclaimed proponents, who themselves apply only partial understandings of the ideas. Nicholson makes no reference to the writings of Engels[19] and so ignores one of the key texts of what she calls "oppressive Marxism," which deals with the position of women in the family.

Engels' analysis of the family entails a belief that the equality of bourgeois marriage is like the equality between the bourgeoisie and the proletariat: a false "equality," hiding a reality of oppression in which the woman is a proletarian and the man a bourgeois.[20] Nor is it the case that later Marxists forgot the work of Marx and Engels on these questions. Among the members of the Bolshevik Party, Alexandra Kollontai had much to say about how to overcome women's oppression after the revolution, and Trotsky too believed that socialism could not be achieved without the liberation of women from unpaid domestic labor. He wrote in 1924, "In order to change the conditions of life, we must learn to see them through women's eyes,"[21] and in his polemic against the effects of the Stalinist counter–revolution on the family, he writes:

How man enslaved woman, how the exploiter subjected them both, how the toilers have attempted at the price of blood to free themselves from slavery and have only exchanged one chain for another—history tells us much about this. In essence, it tells us nothing else. But how in reality to free the child, the woman, and the human being? For that we have as yet no reliable models. All past historical experience, wholly negative, demands of the toilers at least and first of all an implacable distrust of all privileged and uncontrolled guardians.[22]

Far from being 'gender-blind,' Marxism has a long history of interest in, theories about, and practical attempts at overcoming the oppression of women. It is true that there are problems with Engels' book on the family.[23] It fails to theorize the interrelationship between the spheres of production and reproduction, a relationship which ensures women's secondary entry into the labor market, and it underestimates capitalism's ability to structure women's oppression through production. He did not foresee the capacity for survival of the monogamous nuclear family amongst the working class. Nonetheless, his understanding of the bourgeois nuclear family both as the place of women's oppression and as a historically specific form and therefore open to change, were major insights into the recognition that women's oppression resulted not from biology but was (and is) a problem of history.

Nonetheless Marxism, along with any other so-called 'monocausal' theory, is rejected by the majority of feminists who have adopted poststructuralist or postmodern positions. Thus, Kate Nash in an article entitled "The Feminist Production of Knowledge: Is Deconstruction a Practice for Women?"[24] and Nancy Fraser and Linda Nicholson in "Social Criticism without Philosophy: An Encounter between Feminism and Postmodernism,"[25] both adopt, more or less critically, Lyotard's critique of the 'Grand Narratives' of Enlightenment thought, the central motif of all postmodern writers. In her argument for the usefulness of deconstructive theory for feminism, Nash states that "the importance given to detail and context in the theory and method of deconstruction is readily appreciated by feminists at the moment because of the way we have come to distrust the grand monocausal theories of women's oppression."[26] Fraser and Nicholson are more circumspect: while they reject, along with Lyotard and postmodernism, 'foundational' philosophy, they nonetheless want to retain some aspects of sociotheoretical analyses, and note that Lyotard "throws out the baby of large historical narrative with the bathwater of philosophical metanarrative and the baby of socio-theoretical analysis of large-scale inequalities with the bathwater of reductive Marxian class theory."[27]

Both articles reject Marxism as the basis for sociotheoretical analysis. Nash cites Michelle Barrett's *Women's Oppression Today* (1980) to confirm her statement that the attempts to ally feminism with Marxism failed because "the central categories of grand theories are simultaneously too abstract and too specific, and also too fixed in their theoretical framework, to allow the specific position of women to be considered."[28] Fraser and Nicholson paraphrase Lyotard in their caricature of Marxism. He presents it as one-dimensional and both historically and economically determinist, "and most importantly, Marx's drama of the forward march of human productive capacities via class conflict culminating in proletarian revolution."[29] Here, as in Nicholson's later article of 1994, Fraser and Nicholson do not actually deal with Marxist theory vis-à-vis feminism, and their discussion of Lyotard's dismissal of it is critical only in so far as he refuses (or is unable) to replace the "Marxian conception of capitalist society as a totality traversed by one major division and contradiction," by a "better social theory."[30] But they are caught in an impossible contradiction themselves, for they recognize that "a phenomenon as pervasive and multifaceted as male dominance simply cannot be adequately grasped with the meager critical resources to which they [the postmodernists] would limit us."[31] Indeed, when trying to construct an alternative social theory to Marxism that is adequate to the task, they catalogue a range of sociological methods, producing an incoherent and contradictory list,

> an array of different methods and genres . . . large narratives about changes in social organisation and ideology, empirical and socio-theoretical analyses of macrostructure and institutions, interactionist analyses of the micro-politics of everyday life, critical-hermeneutical and institutional analyses of cultural production, historically and culturally specific sociologies of gender. . . . The list could go on.[32]

Mainly notable for its use of long words to disguise the appalling lack of understanding of the role and place of theory, this is a sort of 'pick an' mix' method, which might be all right when choosing sweets in Woolworth's, but is hardly adequate when faced with the task of achieving the liberation of women. They seem to suggest that we can adopt one way of looking at the realm of institutions, another method to analyze everyday life (as if the two were not connected), and as for gender—"historically and culturally specific sociologies"—will be the means. We could use a bourgeois feminist framework to discuss legal rights, a radical feminist theory to analyze pornography and socialist feminism to look at women and work. Suitably postmodern in its variety it might be, but incoherent and chaotic if you are trying to link together different elements of women's oppression in order to understand them and so be in a position to develop strategies for change.

Both articles accept that feminism is, by its very nature, political and therefore inevitably about change, making strategic ideas a necessity. Yet both also adopt versions of postmodernism that, because of their adherence to the local, the contingent and the specific, disallow precisely that necessary strategic thought.

To overcome the contradiction between their recognition that feminism is political and their rejection of any totalizing theory, the two articles adopt tactics that gloss over the problems. Having dismissed Marxism from the frame, Fraser and Nicholson continue by exposing what they call the essentialist and monocausal explanations of women's oppression, in the work of Shulamith Firestone, Michelle Zimbalist Rosaldo, Nancy Chodorow, Carol Gilligan.[33] Equating essentialism with monocausality, they ignore the several different uses of this word available to feminism. Essentialism has traditionally been used to describe a radical feminist framework that proposes something essentially female about women, usually biologically determined, though sometimes developed as psychological characteristics. In British feminism, it has nearly always been opposed by a social construction theory (sometimes socialist, sometimes Marxist)[34] that rejects biology as the source of oppression whilst recognizing women's reproductive capacity as an element in the equation. In these articles, however, essentialism is used to describe any theory with what Nash terms a "monocausal" explanation of women's oppression: as such, she dumps Marxism and presumably socialist feminism as well, in with it.

This is really a sleight of hand. All but one of the writers referred to by Fraser and Nicholson are radical feminists, but theirs is an essentialism shot through with a strong dose of bourgeois politics, mostly because all are North American, where bourgeois and radical feminism have been dominant, and socialist and Marxist feminism always weaker than in Britain. But these articles neither prove nor disprove the redundancy of a socialist or Marxist feminist approach—it is just not dealt with. The inconsistencies in the article by Fraser and Nicholson are revealed in the short final section, "Toward a Postmodern Feminism." The prescription of a theory that "would be explicitly historical, attuned to the cultural specificity of different societies and periods, and to that of different groups within societies and periods,"[35] seems to me not at all at odds with a Marxist framework, which at its non-Stalinist best is coherent, consistent and flexible, has different levels of analysis, and was developed by many in the twentieth century to take account of changes that its originators could not have foreseen. However, the second part of this final section does rule out Marxism, for while the writers adopt the term class, like the 'movementist'[36] politics redolent of the 1980s and the slightly later 'identity'[37] politics of the 1990s, this is just one category among others, such as 'gender,' 'race,' 'ethnicity,' 'sexuality,' none of which has any priority over any other. Moreover, they seek a postmodern feminism that is,

> pragmatic and fallibilistic. It would tailor its methods and categories to the specific task at hand, using multiple categories when appropriate and forswearing the metaphysical comfort of a single 'feminist method' or 'feminist epistemology.' In short this theory would look more like a tapestry composed of threads of many different hues than one woven in a single color.[38]

The political purpose of such a postmodern feminism is unclear. They propose that it should be, "a practice made up of a patchwork of overlapping alliances," which would find "its theoretical expression in a postmodern-feminist form of critical inquiry."[39] But who these alliances would be with and what "postmodern-feminist critical enquiry" would be like (apart from more confused and confusing articles in academic journals) is not answered.

In some ways, however, this earlier article is a model of coherence compared with the one published in *Feminist Review* in the summer of 1994. Although they concur on their rejection of Marxism, this later article by Kate Nash goes much further down the road of dismissing all possibility of objective knowledge, adopting a Derridian deconstruction theory and arguing for its compatibility with feminism. Although the writer tries to put both sides of the argument—for and against its usefulness—and recognizes a tension between the two, it is clear she thinks this can be a productive tension. Describing deconstruction as "anti-essentialist," she argues that

> anti-essentialism, the demonstration of the inadequacy, incompletion and undecidable nature of every characterisation of 'woman,' or even 'women,' has been an important feature of second-wave feminism and deconstruction would seem to be closely related.[40]

Apart from lumping together the feminism of the 1970s with that of the 1980s as "second-wave feminism," as though those decades were identical,[41] such argumentation is clearly inadequate. Even if we accept the related interests of deconstruction, which "aims to show how every identity is contingent, provisional and incomplete"[42] with feminism, as Nash does, this only deals with half the problem, for what each may wish to do about this apparent collision of interest may be totally different. Indeed 'collision' is perhaps a clue to the whole sorry mess, for maybe deconstruction and feminism are colliding because they are coming from and going in two different directions! The 1970s feminist slogan 'the personal is political' did not imply that only personal experience was valid; on the contrary, it stressed the interconnectedness of the personal with the political. It was this tension that was so productive in developing an understanding of the causes of women's oppression and, by inference, an analysis of how to move forward against that oppression.

The acceptance by Nash and others of the theories of deconstruction, poststructuralism and postmodernism has been very damaging for feminism. Her uncritical adoption of Barthes' idea that "texts and discourses always escape their authors' intentions"[43] disregards the relation between theory and practice, which has been central for feminism in the past and was based, sometimes unconsciously, on the method of historical materialism. Indeed, the deepening division between theory and practice has proved one of the most negative features of the last two decades of the twentieth century—damaging both to feminist theory that has not been tested out in action, and to feminist campaigns and activities less and less informed by theory.[44]

Moreover, the acceptance of Foucault's notion that knowledge "positions subjects within certain discourses"[45] is always partial and incomplete and cannot be objective, leads Nash to deny the validity of anything feminists might say. Surely, this is a worse option than the use of theories which women have had to fight to be included in. For Nash, deconstruction emphasises how knowledge is always partial and incomplete, always produced from a particular perspective. In this way it helps confound a rigid distinction between subjective and objective knowledge and releases us from the burden of trying to show how knowledge produced from an overtly political position— feminism—is really more objective than (androcentric) research results achieved using neutral methods and theories.[46]

This is the theoretical equivalent of saying something and then laughing—'don't listen to me, I'm only a woman.' In any case, Marxists, better than most, are aware of the way writers and thinkers always come from a certain position or perspective which will influence what they argue—such an understanding is by no means the prerogative of deconstruction. Finally, the use of the concept of rhetoric to defend Nash's definition of knowledge tells us little:

> We can never have certain knowledge according to the theory of rhetoric but we can, and do, have good reasons for the beliefs we hold . . . knowledge consists in having, at best, good reasons for holding the beliefs one holds about the world and, at least, no good reasons for giving them up. [47]

This vague and woolly definition is followed by an implicit negation of much of the earlier argument, by assuming a *unified* feminism:

> As feminists, then, we need not scare ourselves with the prospect of falling into relativism; we have good reasons for preferring feminist to non- or anti-feminist beliefs, for preferring one feminist definition of women to another and for whatever short- or long-term political strategies we propose or support.[48]

The use of "we" not only confounds Nash's own adoption of the strategy of the contingent and partial, but also confuses the real political interests of and differences between feminists, precisely those expressed in different positions, bourgeois, radical, socialist and Marxist feminism. For these differences do matter. A bourgeois feminist analysis of, and answer to, the changing patterns of women's (un)employment will not be the same as a radical feminist analysis and answer; and they will both differ from that proposed by socialists and Marxists.

This confusion is taken a stage further in the recent work of Patti Lather. In a recent essay,[49] she adopts Derrida's notion of 'the ordeal of the undecidable' and, taking the writing of Peter McLaren, contrasts his discussion of critical pedagogy within a Marxist framework, which she characterizes as one of the "master discourses of 'liberation,'" to her interest in a "reconstruction [which] favours a sort of stammering and stuttering in terms of the constitution and protocols of knowledge." Lather advocates a "moral and political responsibility [that] can only occur in the not knowing, the not being sure."[50] This in order to oppose "the masculinist voice of abstraction, universalisation, and the rhetorical position of 'the one who knows.'"[51] She thus counterposes 'male' knowledge, the ability to theorize and to work with abstractions, which she calls "a boy thing," to a (presumably) female indecision of "not being sure." This is an essentialist framework, based on what used to be called 'radical' feminism, where women and men are seen as 'essentially' different, a framework socialist feminists refute. Since the 1970s and 1980s, socialist and Marxist feminists[52] have fought for the recognition that women are just as able as men when it comes to theorizing an understanding of the world and our place in it, not simply for understanding's sake but to develop political activities and campaigns to pursue the liberation element of the Women's Liberation Movement. In rejecting apparently 'male' practices, the fight for the acceptance of women as theorists on a par with men seems to have been jettisoned. Does Lather really believe, as she seems to suggest, it is better not to know? Is this useful theory?

Basing herself on theories of identity and difference derived from the work of Foucault, Lather underlines the impossibility of the oppressed empathizing with each other and acting together with other oppressed and exploited groups. This leads to confusion and paralysis rather than a way forward. The notion of difference between the sexes is then extended to differences between women themselves, between 'races,' sexualities and so on, until it becomes impossible to talk of any group in society at all. Not only class, as a category, but also the differently oppressed groups, disappear, to be replaced by a celebration of uncertainty, confusion and lack of knowledge. For 'postmodernists of resistance,' such as Lather, the subject is 'in-process' and incapable of agency. Quoting Alison Jones, she suggests we adopt her "call for a 'politics of disappointment,'" a "practice of failure, loss, confusion, unease, limitation for dominant ethnic groups." [53] The chapter finishes on a note of assumed innocence:

> As an arena of practice, critical pedagogy might serve as a transvaluation of praxis if it can find a way to participate in the struggle of these forces as we move toward an experience of the promise that is unforeseeable from the perspective of our present conceptual frameworks.[54]

I am reminded of the Marxist dictum that 'Those who do not learn from history are destined to repeat it,' for such lack of clarity leads us nowhere and if Lather's theories were to be put into practice, they would change nothing. Such ideas are no match for the processes set in train by the WTO and its subsidiary GATS,[55] which have the public sector and especially education and health in their sights, as the next arena in which the market and big business can blossom. Whether disguised in the garb of "raising standards, social inclusion and value for money,"[56] or expressed openly in the words of Gordon Brown, Chancellor of the Exchequer in Tony Blair's government, seeking to introduce entrepreneurship into schools so that children can be 'trained' for a future of self-employment, globalization means the intrusion of the market into public sector services on a world scale. To adopt a position of 'not knowing' in the face of this offensive is not only to disarm in the struggle against it but, worse, to be culpable in the process.

Useful Theory: Marxism, Socialism and the Liberation of Women

In order to understand the situation of women in the here and now, the real lives of women, our role in society, our position in the family and in the labor market, we have to analyze these as a whole. Postmodern theory is incapable, by its very nature, of doing this. In contrast, Marxism and the method of historical materialism can start to explain how the different aspects of women's lives are connected together. It can show the ways in which the oppression of women (as well as other oppressed groups) is linked to the exploitation of the working class by capital; that the bourgeois nuclear family, the historically specific form most appropriate to capital's needs, is also the site of women's oppression. It reveals how women's position in the workforce is structured by their assumed role in the family. It can investigate the ways in which changes in the labor market and especially changes in the employment of women, responding to the needs of capital, are linked to an ideological offensive against women and their position in the family, pursued in Britain by both Conservative and Labour governments. And, most importantly, it can suggest the alliances that have to be forged, between women and between women and men to fight these oppressions, as well as the issues on which these alliances will be brought together.

Any socialist or Marxist analysis will be based on the idea that there can be no socialism without the liberation of women and other oppressed groups, but also that there can be no such liberation without socialism. This basic premise was well understood in the 1970s, even if today it has been submerged by a welter of postmodern theory on, amongst other unhelpful notions, the unstable nature of female subjectivity. At that time, there were links made by the women's liberation movement with trade unions and other working class organizations and these had an impact far beyond the ranks of women organized in the Women's Liberation Movement.

Traditionally, the divisions between women and men in the working class have been used by capital to weaken any struggle against it, but the late 1960s and early 1970s brought changes. Women at Ford's went on strike over equal pay, night cleaners went into battle over the right to join a trade union. These and other struggles gave birth to the Women's Liberation Movement in Britain. In 1972, miners' wives organized in support of the striking miners. In 1974, a media-orchestrated demonstration of wives of workers at the Cowley car plant in Oxford, arguing for a return to work of striking car workers, was defeated by an alliance between women from Oxford Trades Council, the Oxford socialist feminist movement, women working in the trim shop at Cowley and some wives of striking car workers, in a formation called 'Women in Support of the Union.'[57] This type of alliance was evident again in the Miners' Strike of 1984–1985, where socialist feminists worked in solidarity with the relations and friends of miners to sustain the strike. Moreover, many of the tactics adopted by the Women Against Pit Closures groups had been learnt from feminists at Greenham Common in the early eighties, in the peace camp against Cruise Missiles—tactics like nonviolent direct action and sit-ins. More recently, the Liverpool Dockers' Strike (1995–1998) was supported by a women's group, Women of the Waterfront. Socialist feminism has always understood that divisions in the working class are dangerous and lead to defeats. This has been learnt by women who do not see themselves first and foremost as feminists, but who have recognized the centrality of solidarity in the working class.

Here and Now: Women, Work and the Family

The alliances built in struggles like these were ultimately based on ideas rooted in Marxist theory and it is to this that I now want to turn. Marxism has analyzed the intimate connections between women's position in society, in the family and in the paid workplace. Postmodernism, whether through lack of interest or the inadequacy of its theories, ignores analysis of these related issues. The exclusive interest in subjects cultural rather than directly political or economic, has meant that feminists using a postmodern framework, seem unaware of the major changes affecting the position of women at home and at work, as well as the population as a whole, and have little to say about the connected ideological offensive in relation to the role of women in the family as wives, mothers and sisters.

There were major changes to the shape of the family in Britain during the last fifteen or so years of the twentieth century, but the dominant voice in popular discourse is not a feminist one. Rather, in public debate these changes are isolated from other social transformations, and then "family members are admonished for their failure to stand still while the conditions that supported specific forms of family organisation in the past are demolished."[58] The idealization of a family form, which may have existed in the 1950s at best, remains a pervasive and sought-after dream, supported by a conservative ideology, with those who fail to live up to its impossible ideals blamed for society's failures.

Socialist feminists in the late 1960s and 1970s understood the centrality of the family as the site of women's oppression, and were able to combine their own specific experiences with a broader analytical framework to produce useful theory. The strength of feminist writing on these issues lay precisely in this combination of descriptive and experiential examples, within a strong theoretical understanding. Micheline Wandor, in her essay "The Family under Capitalism: The Conditions of Illusion," written in 1972 and published in 1974 in the book *Conditions of Illusion*, unites autobiographical description of first time motherhood—"I used to check that the baby was still breathing every couple of hours"[59]—with ironic comment on the unreality of social expectations, such as "female intuition, that telepathic communication between mother and baby, is born of the circumstances and the necessity to learn, rather than some inbuilt genetic trait peculiar to women."[60] Underlying her personal memories is a so-cialist feminist framework that recognizes not only the socially necessary work women perform in the home—"people must eat, have somewhere to live, clothes to wear, be looked after when they are ill"[61]—but also, by quoting Mar-garet Benston, "the amount of unpaid labour performed by women is very large and very profitable for those who own the means of production."[62] Wandor gen-eralizes from her personal experience to the position of women as a whole in capitalist society. While recognizing that men and children are oppressed in the family too, she argues nonetheless that since women are most oppressed by the family, it is from women that the impetus for change must come. "After all, we know more about it than men, and have more power than children."[63] This rec-ognition of oppression and the need to analyze and fight it is what is missing in postmodern writing.

Other writers of the earlier period put even greater stress on the importance of theory—not just to denaturalize and historicize the family, but also to stake out some intellectual ground for women and feminist ideas in what was then truly a world of theory dominated by men. Sometimes these writings appear crude to us today, but their directness in tackling what were new issues is re-freshing, when compared to the relativism of postmodern thought today. For ex-ample, Judith White writing in *Socialist Woman*:

> The nuclear family is the only institution which capitalism has been able to of-fer the worker to care for his basic wants; the only place, moreover, in which he can be master . . . the division between work and 'life' might be maintained as though it were some natural phenomenon. [64]

White also addresses the relation of women's role in the home to the role in the workplace:

> At the same time as she fulfils this function without cost to employer or state, the women remains part of a reserve pool of labour. This pool has been drawn upon in particular conditions—in the two world wars (as a result of which certain minimal concessions had to be granted to them); in conditions of high demand for labour, such as the post-war boom, lasting until recent years; and in a different context, in periods of slump, when women are forced out into menial jobs in order to provide any family income, or employers (in backward sectors of industry) replace men with cheaper women workers, as happened in the 30s.[65]

Other socialist writers of the period, such as Lee Sanders Comer, stressed the importance of the ideal family for the ruling class in producing social stability:

> The pressure of the family ideal is so pervasive that people outside it—spinsters, bachelors, unmarried mothers, the divorced and gay people—symbolise either deviancy, personal failure or abnormality. It is because the family is the only sanctioned unit for living that everything which in any way threatens it takes on the proportions of a serious social problem—that is, free contraception, 'promiscuity,' abortion, illegitimacy, 'broken homes' and homosexuality. All these things threaten the stability and, indeed, inflexibility of family life.[66]

While some of the language—"spinsters" and "bachelors"—is outdated, the list of supposed deviances that threaten the family's stability reads very much like those blamed today for society's ills—single or divorced parents, broken homes, sexual permissiveness, lesbians and gay men, latchkey kids, etc.

However, despite the similarities, the situation in which these fears are expressed today is very different from the early 1970s. Today many more people are having children outside marriage: from 8.4 percent in 1971 to 38 percent in 1999—four and a half times as many. The age at which we are having children has risen—from 23.9 years in 1971 to 30 years in 1999. Having children later also means we have fewer children—in 1971, the rate averaged at 2.37 compared to 1.72 in 1999. One of the reasons for this drop in childbirth is that we are marrying later, if at all. In 1987, nearly a quarter of 20–24 year olds were married, but a decade later in 1997 it was less than a tenth; the same figures can be seen in older age groups.[67]

Much is made by politicians and others in Britain about the growth in the number of single parents, especially single mothers. Yet the figures suggest that while this is rising, the changes are not in fact so startling. In 1971, 91 percent of families were made up of two parents with children, 8 percent of lone mothers and 1 percent of lone fathers. By 1994, these figures had changed to 85.4 percent, 13.6 percent and 1 percent respectively.[68] However much the establishment would like to isolate these changes from general social change, it is a transformation in the way we all work that is driving them, and unless we are able to link together these different aspects of women's lives—work and the family—we will not understand what is happening nor how to propose alternatives.

The percentage of women in the workforce has increased from about 40 percent in 1970 to about 50 percent today, and has altered the great imbalance between men and women in relationships, giving many women some level of economic independence. This partly accounts for the high levels of divorce and low levels of marriage in Britain, but we should not assume that this gives women total freedom from male power or excludes them from violence. Firstly, although the proportion and the actual number of working women has increased, women's average wage still hovers around 70 percent of the average male wage, with women in full-time work earning 82 percent of the average hourly rate of a male worker. This is reduced to an appalling 52 percent when we compare the average part-time female wage to that of an hourly paid full-time male employee.[69] Secondly, women are much more likely to work part-time than men. This fact is based on the belief that women's work is always secondary to that of wife and mother. Thus, most working-class women earn a good deal less than men, making separation and divorce from an unhappy and unequal relationship financially difficult. We should not be misled by the success of a small number of women executives or professionals to make generalizations about working women as a whole.

The other economic function played by the family, and noted in Comer's paper, is that "the family consumes" and is,

> at one and the same time, the dumping ground for overproduction and the pivot of the capitalist machine. The system demands that each family barricade itself in a small house or flat in order to fill it with consumer goods. Now we have the technology to collectivize and eradicate most of the menial tasks which each woman in each flat performs in isolation from every other. We have the technology for a shute in each flat which would carry everyone's dirty washing to a central automated area in the basement which would wash, dry, air and iron those clothes and return them. But the market for 80 washing machines, dryers, irons and ironing boards is eliminated at one blow and so also is the alienated labour of the women, standing mindlessly over the machine which is supposed to ease her labour. The profit system guarantees that 80 families will buy a washing machine in order for each one to stand idle for 90% of the time.[70]

The lack of socialist feminist writing today makes this extract seem an age away, but its argument was proven when, during the Miners' Strike of 1984–1985, women in the mining communities found the nuclear family form useless as they tried to help the men prosecute the strike as well as feed, clean and care for their families. Their resulting and spontaneous turn to collective care, especially in feeding the community, shows how, *in extremis*, the nuclear family form has to be overcome to avoid it holding back and threatening collective action.

In order to understand the radical changes taking place in the family today in Britain, it is necessary to locate them in the context of changes taking place in the labor market and at work. It is a commonplace that women's waged work is underpaid, occurs in poor conditions and in a segregated labor market, a market that depends on the assumed skills derived from domestic labor—caring, cleaning, repetitive tasks. Even after the introduction of the national minimum wage (by the New Labour government elected in 1997), recognized by many as a way of raising low female wages, women in full-time work were still earning £115 a week on average less than men in 2000. In addition, because looking after a family is seen as the central role carried out by women, part-time work with flexible patterns, including home working, is seen to fit in appropriately with domestic responsibilities. The same discriminatory pattern of pay is seen here, too. Despite the fact that hourly earnings for women in manual jobs rose by 7.5 percent in 2000, they still received £1.80 an hour less than men in similar work.[71]

In the last twenty years or so of the twentieth century, major changes in the workforce affected all workplaces. A combination of the closure of much heavy industry and engineering, deskilling and the introduction of new technology, led to a steep decline in traditional 'male' jobs in heavy industry, such as engineering, steel-working, mining, etc. At the same time, there was an increase in traditional 'female' work. Women now make up around half the workforce in Britain, the highest percentage ever. But there has not been a straight swap of jobs between men and women—nearly one million skilled, industrial, unionized, male jobs have been lost, while women have gained a similar number, but mainly part-time, temporary, fixed contract jobs often in the service sector, with flexible work patterns and usually nonunionized. This shift is evidenced by reports on the makeup of the labor market. According to *Labour Market Trends* in March 1997, 71 percent of women between the ages of 16 and 59 were economically active at the start of 1996, of whom 44 percent were working part-time (compared to 8 percent of men). This represents 82 percent of the 5.8 million people working part-time. In addition, women's work is confined to several key sectors, with just over half (52 percent) working in three major occupational groups—clerical/secretarial, personal and protective services, and sales—areas where only 18 percent of men worked.[72]

Along with the changes in the labor market, increasing privatizations have led to cuts in the welfare state and the public sector,[73] in provision for child care, in the National Health Service, in education, in community services for the old, the ill (including the mentally ill), the disabled, in social services. These cuts affect women twice over, first as workers in the caring professions and secondly as users. Where services have been privatized, women's wages have been reduced and their terms and conditions worsened; where they have been closed down, women have both lost their paid work and been left to pick up the pieces from a failing welfare state. It is estimated that by the mid-1990s, 6.8 million people in Britain were carers for relatives or friends: 17 percent of women are carers, saving the state an estimated £24 million.

These structural changes in the workforce and in the state provision of welfare are accompanied by an ideological offensive against women. The nuclear family, that contradictory place where love and intimacy flourish beside violence and dependency, was promoted by all postwar British governments—indeed, for Thatcher the family was more important than society, since for her, the latter did not exist. While less than 30 percent of the population now live in this type of nuclear family, it is still promoted as the ideal model and anyone living a different lifestyle, especially if there are children involved, is castigated. Single parents (predominantly women) have been scapegoated for every social evil, from petty crime to drug addiction, from truancy from school to low levels of literacy and numeracy, and what began under the Conservative governments has been continued by the Labour government. The Child Support Act, while it did not attempt to 'glue' families back together, tried to force women to identify the father of their child so that the agency could force the father to pay for the child's upkeep, thus reducing state benefits.

How are we to understand this process? In the late 1970s, several socialist feminists[74] adopted the Marxist concept of a 'Reserve Army of Labour' to analyze the ways in which women were being used by capital. According to Marx, the reserve army of labor is a pool of the unemployed, especially young people and women, characterized by its capacity to depress wages and which, through the threat of unemployment and competition in the labor market, enables capital to increase the rate of exploitation, and therefore the rate of profit. Marx notes the tendency of capital to substitute from this surplus labor the unskilled for the skilled, youth for adults and women for men. Although initially used to analyze male unemployment, this seemed a useful concept for looking at the way women had been historically used in the labor market, for example, during the early years of industrialization and in both world wars. It also goes some way to explaining why male trade unionists have seen women as a threat to their jobs—not simply because they were, and probably still are, sexist toward women, but because they knew women could be used to undermine their wage levels and even take their jobs. This antagonism exacerbated existing gender divisions in the workforce to capital's advantage.

Moreover, the whole process of women being drawn into and then expelled from the workforce, according to the needs of capital and industry, happened in the context of a gradual increase of working women throughout the twentieth century: in 1918 women made up about 30 percent of the labor force, while the figure increases to around 50 percent in 2001.[75] Although women tend to work in different sectors to men, as noted before, it does look as though women have been increasingly used as a reserve army. Whereas they were drawn into and then expelled from the workforce during and after the second world war, in the later period their cheaper labor depressed wages and helped to worsen working conditions.[76] Not only has there been a decrease of 3 percent in the number of working men, and a similar increase in the number of women, but the kinds of work and the conditions and contracts women have traditionally had to suffer—part-time, flexible, unskilled with few fringe benefits—are increasingly being applied to male employment. Right across the labor market, short-term, even zero hours contracts, compulsory overtime and draconian work practices are being introduced. The percentage of men working part-time doubled between 1986 and 1996 to 8 percent, while the number of part-time women workers went up only 1 percent in the same decade. Even more striking, the number of women in temporary jobs increased by 23 percent while the increase for men was 74 percent. We can be sure not only that these figures are an underestimate, but that the trend is continuing, despite an upturn in the economy in the late 1990s.[77]

But how is it possible to use women and their labor in this way? Why does it seem to have been relatively easy to remove women from 'male' jobs after 1945, when returning soldiers needed employment, even though women had spent the war years in munitions factories and heavy engineering plants? How has capital been able to use women to introduce widespread part-time and temporary work in the last fifteen years?

The answer lies in the fact that women, whatever their real position, are primarily seen as carers in the family and breadwinners only second. Although the term 'pin money' is now outmoded, the misconception that it described has not gone away. Despite the reality of women making up around half the workforce, of their wages being a necessary component of the family income, and of many families being headed by single mothers, whether widowed or separated, the assumption remains that the woman's earnings are an addition, secondary to the main male wage. To understand this it is useful to look again at Engels' writings on the family and women's role in it. To the centrality of production, Engels added the importance of reproduction, "the decisive element of history is pre-eminently production and reproduction of life and its material requirements."[78] Engels analyzed the position of women within these two spheres separately, noting that the role of women within the bourgeois family was part of the private sphere of reproduction, while her entry into production, into the paid labor force, into the public sphere, was a precondition for her liberation; although this was not an inevitable process. Key to this understanding was that women who took on paid work outside the home would become increasingly financially independent, with the social and collective organization experienced through paid work replacing their isolation within the family.

More recent writing on the subject by feminists[79] shows that these two spheres, production and reproduction, the private and the public, are in fact interconnected. It is precisely the position of women in the family, whose domestic labor reproduces the labor force, both daily and generationally, which determines their entry into paid labor. The concept of the 'family wage,' adopted in the late nineteenth century by the bourgeoisie and supported by the male-dominated trade union movement, still today underpins gender divisions in the workforce. The cost of reproducing the woman is deemed to be included in the male wage, so that if a woman works that cost is deducted and she receives a lower wage.

All of these changes in work are having a profound effect on many aspects of our lives, both as women and as men, including within the family, but the process also has contradictions for capital, which we need to be able to analyze and understand in order to resist capitalism's logic. These contradictions include the conflict between the need to develop the forces of production, including the paid labor of women, with the private reproduction of labor power, including fulfilling the functions once carried out by the welfare state; the conflict between women's childbearing capacity and the role as wage laborer; and the potential conflict between the tendency to remove tasks of domestic labor such as cooking, laundering, sewing, education and health care, into the profit-making sector, thus drawing more women into the workforce. Furthermore, there is an increasing mismatch between ideological assumptions about the nuclear family and lived reality. High levels of male unemployment paralleled by an increase of working women have led to some redistribution of domestic labor—men taking children to and from school is no longer an uncommon sight, especially in those areas devastated by de-industrialization. The increased participation in the public world by women also means that as the isolation of domesticity is overcome, women are more and more able to organize together and with men to fight for their rights.[80]

More specifically, the increasing number of women in the workforce conflicts with cuts in the welfare state, which depend on the unpaid work of women to replace these lost services. It is possible that once the kinds of jobs women have traditionally done have been accepted by men—including the poor conditions women have suffered—there will be attempts to cut back on women's work. The European Union Inter-Governmental Conference in Cardiff in June 1998, adopted a set of working conditions based on the flexibility achieved in Britain over the last ten years, the annualization of hours being one example of the regulations which will become mandatory across Europe. This will give employers the right to impose the working conditions on the whole workforce that so far mostly women and the young have endured. There are some examples of this happening. According to the report of the Equal Pay Task Force in 2001, there is evidence that for a sales assistant, a job that one in ten women do, relative pay fell during the 1990s, even though in 1998 women earned on average only 45 percent of the average pay of all male full-time employees. In the twenty-first century, with more men working in this sector, "gender pay equity may occur through 'levelling down.'"[81]

We must not simply accept these changes and allow women's unequal pay to be used as a norm, nor allow women to be forced back into the home to provide free labor to replace the welfare state. This suggests the areas of activities that feminists should be developing. Firstly, it is important to recruit women into trade unions so that the existing gender divisions and pay differentials can be fought. Secondly, in order to facilitate women's paid work, we should campaign for free crèches and nurseries, for both maternity and paternity leave and for women's reproductive rights. Thirdly, we should be fighting against privatizations in the public sector and cuts in the welfare state, to retain what are mainly female jobs and also to ensure that women are not forced into the role of unpaid carers.

Conclusion

These issues are distant indeed from the preoccupations of postmodernism. It may be interesting to debate how knowledge is always relative, how subjectivity is fragmented, how women's identities are formed from a multitude of different experiences, but while we do, the lives and working patterns of ordinary women and men (including those of the very people who are engaged in the debate) are radically changing, and most of us remain ignorant of it. Without the use of a theory that can link together the different aspects of the lives of women, and analyze and develop strategies to overcome elements of our oppression, we will remain commentators on the sidelines. Careers can be built from these commentaries, but progressive change will not happen. If feminism has at its core the understanding of the need for such change, then postmodernist theory has to be rejected in favor of useful theory.

For Women's Studies as an academic subject, the actual lives of women, including working-class women, have always been an impetus both to study itself and to the development of theories to understand oppression. Without that link between real experience and ways of understanding it—praxis—we are on the road to nowhere.

Notes

This chapter is indebted to the support of my companion David Packer. His knowledge of Marxism and its implications for a political practice are an inspiration.

1. Socialist feminism was never as strong in the United States as in Britain, which can partly be explained by the lack of a mass party of the working class and a less powerful trade union movement.

2. Anti-pornography campaigners Andrea Dworkin and Catherine McKinnon attempted to get states to legislate for what they called 'Porn-free zones.'

3. Carol Smart and Barry Neale, *Family Fragments?* (Cambridge, U.K.: Polity Press, 1999), 2–3.

4. I am not arguing here against theory, but against theory for its own sake, rather than theory to make a difference, to change things.

5. This is based on the notion put forward by Althusser, that theory is a practice in itself.

6. Linda J. Nicholson, ed., *Feminism/Postmodernism* (London: Routledge, 1990), 11.

7. Chris Weedon, *Feminist Practice and Poststructuralist Theory* (Oxford, U.K.: Blackwells, 1987), 18.

8. Weedon, *Feminist Practice*, 27.

9. Weedon, *Feminist Practice*, 28.

10. Weedon, *Feminist Practice*, 73.

11. Weedon, *Feminist Practice*, 135.

12. Weedon, *Feminist Practice*, 139.

13. Weedon, *Feminist Practice*, 173.

14. Weedon, *Feminist Practice*, 175.

15. Linda J. Nicholson, "Feminism and the Politics of Postmodernism," in *Feminism and Postmodernism*, ed. Margaret Ferguson and Jennifer Wicke (Durham, N.C.: Duke University Press, 1994), 69–85.

16. Nicholson, "Politics of Postmodernism," 70.

17. Nicholson, "Politics of Postmodernism," 71.

18. Nicholson, "Politics of Postmodernism," 71.

19. Nor does his name appear anywhere in Nicholson, *Feminism/Postmodernism*.

20. See Frederick Engels, *The Origin of the Family, Private Property and the State* [1884] (Peking: Foreign Language Press, 1978).

21. Leon Trotsky, *Women and the Family* (New York: Pathfinder Press, 1973), 8.

22. Leon Trotsky, "Thermidor in the Family," in Trotsky, *Women*, 73.

23. I am grateful for the ideas of Gill Lee in the following critique of Engels.

24. Kate Nash, "The Feminist Production of Knowledge: Is Deconstruction a Practice for Women?" *Feminist Review* 47 (summer 1994): 65–77.

25. Nancy Fraser and Linda J. Nicholson, "Social Criticism without Philosophy: An Encounter between Feminism and Postmodernism," in *Feminism/Postmodernism*, (London: Routledge, 1990), 19–38.

26. Nash, "Feminist Production," 68.

27. Fraser and Nicholson, "Social Criticism," 25.

28. Nash, "Feminist Production," 68.

29. Fraser and Nicholson, "Social Criticism," 22.

30. Fraser and Nicholson, "Social Criticism," 24.

31. Fraser and Nicholson, "Social Criticism," 26.

32. Fraser and Nicholson, "Social Criticism," 26.

33. Fraser and Nicholson, "Social Criticism," 27–33. The works they discuss are Shulamith Firestone, *The Dialectic of Sex* (New York: Bantam, 1970); Michelle Rosaldo, *Woman, Culture, and Society* (Palo Alto, Calif.: Stanford University Press, 1974); Nancy Chodorow, *The Reproduction of Mothering: Psychoanalysis and the Sociology of Gender* (Berkeley: University of California Press, 1978) and Carol Gilligan, *In a Different Voice: Psychological Theory and Women's Development* (Cambridge, Mass.: Harvard University Press, 1983).

34. There is some confusion between these two types of feminism. I use socialist feminism to describe feminists whose political framework is ultimately reformist, although they may often adopt Marxist terms such as class, ideology, etc. Marxist feminists, by contrast, would see women's liberation intimately tied to (but not an inevitable consequence of) the achievement of socialism, resulting from the revolutionary overthrow of capitalism. The two terms are used differently by different people at different times and so definitions are much argued over.

35. Fraser and Nicholson, "Social Criticism," 34.

36. 'Movementist' politics can be defined as a politics which aligns itself with any progressive social movement fighting the status quo on any issue (such as gay rights, antiracism, peace protesters) without trying to link the campaign to the organizations of the working class, such as trade unions. *Marxism Today*, that ill-named journal of the Communist Party in Britain, most influential during the 1980s, was a good example of movementist politics, giving, as it did, at least equal weight to the social movements of the oppressed as to the labor movement. Sometimes, as in the writing of Bea Campbell, these were even counterposed to each other. For a stimulating critique of the impact of *Marxism Today* on political ideas in Britain in the 1980s, see Alex Callinicos, *Against Postmodernism* (Cambridge, U.K.: Polity Press, 1989).

37. 'Identity' politics develops the position outlined in note 36, emphasizing difference against commonality. Thus separate analyses of lesbians, black women, older women, Irish women would be promoted as against what all women have in common. While it is of course imperative to promote the right to autonomy (each oppressed group having the right to discuss and develop demands based on their specific oppression), this does not mean that each group should fight alone for its liberation: separatism should not be the goal.

38. Nicholson, *Feminism/Postmodernism*, 35.

39. Nicholson, *Feminism/Postmodernism*, 35.

40. Nash, "Feminist Production," 75.

41. An emphasis on difference and identity is characteristic of the 1980s and early 1990s, but not of the 1970s.

42. Nash, "Feminist Production," 75.

43. Nash, "Feminist Production," 68.

44. For example, the antipornography campaigns of the 1980s, which mistakenly called for censorship without realizing the damaging impact this would have on the availability of, amongst other things, gay and lesbian material.

45. Nash, "Feminist Production," 69.

46. Nash, "Feminist Production," 69–70.

47. Nash, "Feminist Production," 72.

48. Nash, "Feminist Production," 73.

49. Patti Lather, "Ten Years Later, Yet Again: Critical Pedagogy and Its Complicities," in *Feminist Engagements: Reading, Resisting and Revisioning Male Theorists in Education and Cultural Studies*, ed. Kathleen Weiler (London: Routledge, 2001), 183–195.

50. Lather, "Ten Years Later," 187.

51. Lather, "Ten Years Later," 184.

52. See Annette Kuhn and Ann Marie Volpe, eds., *Feminism and Materialism: Women and Modes of Production* (London: Routledge and Kegan Paul, 1978); Lydia Sargent, ed., *The Unhappy Marriage of Marxism and Feminism: A Debate on Class and Patriarchy* (London: Pluto Press, 1986); Lise Vogel, *Marxism and the Oppression of Women: Towards a Unitary Theory* (London: Pluto Press, 1983) and *Woman Questions: Essays for a Materialist Feminism* (London: Pluto Press, 1995); also Veronica Beechey, *Unequal Work* (London: Verso, 1987).

53. Lather, "Ten Years Later," 191.

54. Lather, "Ten Years Later," 192.

55. WTO, the World Trade Organization, is a U.S.-dominated international organization with a neoliberal, free market, capitalist agenda. GATS, the General Agreements on Trade and Services, is also being used by the United States to open up the public sector to private enterprise and big business. Within Europe, this is being led by the New Labour government of Tony Blair.

56. Rick Hatcher, "Getting Down to Business: Schooling in the Globalised Economy," *Education and Social Justice* 3, no. 2 (spring 2001): 58.

57. This is documented in Alan Thornett, *Inside Cowley* (London: Porcupine Press, 1998), 38–55.

58. Smart and Neale, *Family*, 25.

59. Micheline Wandor, "The Family under Capitalism: The Conditions of Illusion," in *Conditions of Illusion*, ed. Sandra Allen, Lee Sanders and Jan Wallis (Leeds, U.K.: Feminist Books, 1974), 188.

60. Wandor, "Family under Capitalism," 190–191.

61. Wandor, "Family under Capitalism," 205.

62. Margaret Benston, "The Political Economy of Women's Liberation." I have so far been unable to trace this pamphlet. However, an article of the same title by Benston was published in *Monthly Review* (September 1969): 13–27.

63. Wandor, "Family under Capitalism," 205.

64. See Judith White, "The Family in Capitalist Society," *Socialist Woman*, (July–August 1971): 3.

65. White, "The Family," 3.

66. Lee Sanders Comer, "Functions of the Family under Capitalism," in *Conditions of Illusion*, 208–216.

67. All figures from *Population Trends* (London: HMSO, 1971, 1987, 1997, 1999). The proportion of 25–29 year olds who were married fell from a half in 1987 to a third in 1997; the proportion of 30–34 year olds who were married fell from three-quarters in 1987 to just over a half in 1997.

68. Figures from *General Household Survey* (London: HMSO, 1971, 1994).

69. Equal Pay Task Force, *Just Pay* (London: Equal Opportunities Commission, 2001), <http://www.eoc.org.uk> (June 20, 2001).

70. Comer, "Functions of the Family," 4.

71. Low Pay Unit, "One Small Step for Woman (and Man) Kind," *The New Review* 66 (November–December 2000): 6–8.

72. All figures from *Labour Market Trends*, (London: Government Statistical Service, March 1997).

73. Governments are attempting cuts in the public sector, welfare and benefits across Europe under the dynamic of the convergence criteria demanded by the European Monetary Union. In addition, privatizations in the education and health sectors are being pushed forward by the WTO and GATS.

74. For example, Veronica Beechey, *Unequal Work* (London: Verso, 1987); Irene Bruegel, "The Reserve Army of Labour, 1974–1979," in *Waged Work: A Reader*, ed. Feminist Review (London: Virago, 1986), 40–53.

75. Frances Sly, Alistair Price and Andrew Risdon, "Women in the Labour Market: Results from the Spring 1996 Labour Force Survey," in *Labour Market Trends*, 99–120. In March 1997, it was reported that 44 percent of the labor force was female. The discrepancy between this and the reported 50 percent is due to different reporting criteria.

76. Women still only earn about 70 percent of full-time pay. See Low Pay Unit, "Problems in Search of a Solution," *The New Review* 48 (November–December 1997): 6–9.

77. Sly, Price and Risdon, "Women in the Labour Market," 99.

78. Engels, *Origin of the Family*, 4.

79. For example, Beechey, *Unequal Work.*

80. See Lise Vogel, "Beyond Domestic Labour," in *Marxism and the Oppression of Women*, 151–175.

81. Equal Pay Task Force, "Just Pay."

Part IV

Pedagogy, Reprise and Conclusion

Chapter 11

Recentering Class:
Wither Postmodernism?
Toward a Contraband Pedagogy

Peter McLaren and Ramin Farahmandpur

Introduction

Division of labour only becomes truly such from the moment when a division of material labour appears. From this moment onwards consciousness can really flatter itself that it is something other than consciousness of existing practice, that it is really represents something without representing something real; from now on consciousness is in a position to emancipate itself from the world and to proceed to the formation of "pure" theory, theology, philosophy, ethics, etc. But even if this, theory, theology, philosophy, ethics, etc., comes into contradiction with the existing relations, this can only occur because existing social relations have come into contradiction with existing forces of production.[1]

Capitalism can not be gradually replaced or removed piecemeal; it must be transformed in its entirety or not at all.[2]

From whose point of view do you then read history? From the standpoint of capital that circulates globally, or from that of labor which is everywhere in chains?[3]

The economic anarchy of capitalist society as it exists today is, in my opinion, the real source of all evil.[4]

As we lean into the gusty winds of the new millennium, squaring our shoulders and lowering our heads against an icy unknown, we discover much to our surprise that the future has already arrived; that it has silently imploded into the singularity of the present. We are lost in a crevice in the 'wrong side' of history, in a furious calm at the end of a century-old breath, doing solitary confinement in the future anterior. Time has inhaled so hard that it has lodged us in its lungs, compressing us into shadowy, ovaloid spectres out of the horror classic, *Nosferatu*. Capitalism has authored this moment, synchronizing the heartbeat of the globe with the autocopulatory rhythms of the marketplace; deregulating history; downsizing eternity.

Contemporary global capitalism signals the revival of idolatry in the deification of the marketplace. With its new degree of mobility (yet with no fundamental change in the mode of production), its mixture of flexible accumulation and older Fordist formations, its growing mobility, its increasing autonomy of financial markets, and greater flexibility of labor markets, and its financial gutting of those regimes foolish enough to place barriers in its profit-seeking trajectories, capitalism has banalized all serious oppositions to its robust presence. Its sacerdotal power is derived, in part, from both the vulnerability of the worker within the new forces of globalization and the capitalist's unslakable thirst for power and profit. Capitalism has become a surrogate for nature and a synecdoche for progress. Having confuted the socialism and Marxian optic of the Eastern bloc nations with a triumphaliant 'end of history' mockery, capitalism has found its most exalted place in the pantheon of quintessential bourgeois virtues celebrated by the apostate of that great factory of dreams known as 'America.' The 1944 Bretton Woods conference at the now-famous Mt. Washington Hotel, Bretton Woods, New Hampshire, that created the World Bank, the International Monetary Fund, and shortly after, the General Agreement of Tariffs and Trade, established the framework and political architecture necessary for the United States to acquire free access to the markets and raw materials of the Western Hemisphere, the Far East, and the British Empire. The vision that emerged from this historical meeting laid the groundwork for the lurid transmogrification of the world economy into a global financial system overrun by speculators and "arbitrageurs" who act not in the interests of world peace and prosperity and the needs of real people but for the cause of profit at any cost.[5]

As the world's 'mentor capitalist nation,' the United States has not only become detached from the struggles of its wide-ranging communities but betrays an aggressive disregard for them. Of course, capitalism has not brought about the "end of history" as the triumphalist discourse of neoliberalism has announced. Historically, capitalism has not carried humankind closer to "the end of ideology" or "end of history." Rather, as Samir Amin comments,

> in spite of the hymns to the glory of capital, the violence of the system's real contradictions was driving history not to its end as announced in triumphalist "belle époque" proclamations, but to world wars, socialist revolutions, and the revolt of the colonized peoples. Re-established in post-First World War Europe, triumphant liberalism aggravated the chaos and paved the way for the illusionary, criminal response that fascism was to provide.[6]

As social agents within a neoliberal capitalist regime, one whose link between international competitive forces and neoliberal state policy tightens as market forces gain strength, we seem to lack substance. Capitalism's history appears to have written us out of the story, displacing human agency into the cabinet of lost memories. The world shrinks while difference swells into a forbidding colossus, bringing us face-to-face with all that is other to ourselves.[7] Global capitalism has exfoliated the branches of history, laying bare its riot of tangled possibilities, and hacking away at those roots which nourish a socialist latency. As capital reconstitutes itself á discrétion, as traditionally secure factory work is replaced by the feckless insecurity of McJobs, as the disadvantaged are cast about in the icy wind of world commodity price fluctuations, as the comprador elite expands its power base in the financial precincts of the postmodern necropolis, and as the White House redecorates itself in the forms-fits-function architectonic of neoliberalism, capitalist hegemony digs its bony talons into the structure of subjectivity itself. Communications networks—the electronic servomechanisms of the state—with their propulsions and fluxes of information that have grown apace with capitalism, make this hegemony not only a tenebrous possibility but also an inevitability as they ideologically secure forms of exploitation so furious that every vulnerability of the masses is seized and made over into a crisis. Neoliberalism is not simply an abstract term without a literal referent. The current corporate downsizing, outsourcing, deregulation, and the poverty it has left in its wake are neoliberalism in flagrante delicto. Look at the faces of the men and women who line up for food stamps in South Central and East Los Angeles, the slumped shoulders of the workers lining up the gates of the *malquiladores* in Juarez, Mexico, and the wounded smiles of children juggling tennis balls, breathing fire, and washing car windows in the midst of a traffic jam in Mexico City, and you will have come face-to-face with the destructive power of neoliberalism.

The global death rattle that announces this fin-de-siècle moment joltingly alerts lost generations whose subjectivities have been melded into capitalist forms of such pure intensity that time and history do not seem necessary. We are always already shaped by the labyrinthine circuits of capitalist desire, a desire that hides catachrestically behind the veiled dystopianism of postmodern bourgeois rhetorics. It is a desire so ruthless that it thirsts even for the tears of the poor. Accumulation in the name of profit has become the *acta sanctorum* of the age of desire.

In the United States, we have lost our yearning to know ourselves by recognizing what we are not. Investing in the singular culture we call American, by means of echoliac rhetorical proclamations that bind us together as one nation indivisible, many cling only to the familiar or the promise thereof, fearful that all acts of knowing *who* we are sooner or later become acts of destroying *what* we have become. To know who we are is, after all, to recognize the slack-jawed, low intensity democracy despoiled by the lesions of greed that now pockmark the unconquerable visage of the holiest of U.S. monuments, the Statue of Liberty. It is also to acknowledge the United States' total propinquity with inventing ways of exploiting the wealth of the globe and razing the fragile infrastructures of the most poor and powerless of nations.

The political punditocracy of that same Washington elite who boasted that the United States was the 'only remaining superpower' and who—conveniently ignoring the United States' two trillion dollar debt to the outside world and the fact that 60 percent of its population is sinking into penury—has been zealously promoting, by way of neoliberal monetary orthodoxy, the merits of deregulated markets, is now finding its triumphalist proclamations in dangerous conflict with reality. August 13, 1998 marked the sixteenth birthday of the lavish bull market of the 1980s and 1990s (decades when 'foreign' policy finally became recognized as a code word for 'trade' policy), but it was anything but sweet. Considering the collapse of the Russian, Mexican, and Asian markets, it came closer to a wake. In the face of the current 'global paroxysm' of worldwide deflation,and what has been described as the "crises of an entire economic model," the United States government continues its draconian welfare reforms, maintains its shameful and callous punishment of defenseless children (as in the repeal of the federal guarantee of Aid to Families with Dependent Children), weakens civil rights initiatives, enacts dangerously cruel legislation against immigrants, and imprisons and puts to death African-Americans and Latino/as in unprecedented numbers.[8]

Over the last several decades the social, economic, and political metamorphoses in Western industrial nations and developing Third World countries have culminated in an increasing interest in Marxist social theory within various critical traditions of educational scholarship. While some critical educators are rediscovering Marxism, recognizing its rich historical and theoretical contribution to social theory and acknowledging its invaluable insights into the role of schooling in the unequal distribution of skills, knowledge, and power in society, others are riding the fashionable currents of the postmodern soi-disant Quartier Latin.[9] Among educational scholars there has been a growing interest in melding various strands of postmodern social theory with elements of Marxist theory, a project that would be too otiose to summarize here. However, many theorists who straddle the postmodernist-Marxist divide have failed to formulate a sustained and convincing critique of the prevailing social and economic inequalities within advanced Western industrial capitalist nations.[10] Too often, such attempts have witnessed social relations of production becoming buried in the synergistic swirl of theoretical eclecticism.

We believe that the urgent task is to locate educational theory more securely within a Marxist problematic than we have done in the past, in order to explain in more convincing fashion the dynamic mechanisms that ensure the production and reproduction of capitalist social and economic relations, as well as to unravel the complex ways in which schools participate in the asymmetrical distribution of technical knowledge and skills. This is not an argument against eclecticism per se, but a cautionary reminder that much conceptual ground already covered can get lost in the laboratory of theory when trying to meld models into some grand synthesis in an attempt to reveal what has been hidden.

The intensification of international competition among multinational corporations under the flagship of neoliberal economic policies has the threatening tendency of colonizing everyday life. It has created conditions in which declining living standards and increasing wage inequalities between the poor and the wealthy have become the norm. The new global economy is regulated by the growing service and retail industry that relies significantly on the exploitation of unskilled immigrant labor in the Western industrial nations and workers in Third World countries. As a means of decreasing production costs, manufacturing jobs are exported abroad to Third World developing countries where a combination of cheap labor markets and weak labor unions create a ripe mixture for a massive accumulation of capital in a frictionless, deregulated industrial milieu. The "K-marting of the labor force" has yielded unprecedented record profitability for transnational corporations, especially in Third World countries where a combination of cheap labor markets and weak unions has created extremely ripe conditions for economic exploitation of the working class.[11] Kim Moody reminds us that today's transnational corporations "are clearly predators waging class war to expand their world-wide empires and restore the legendary profit-rates of decades ago."[12]

The replacement of the United States manufacturing industry by low wage employment in the service and retail industry has contributed in no insignificant way to the increasing social and economic inequalities and has witnessed 10 percent of the population taking ownership of more that 90 percent of the nation's wealth. Much of the recent evisceration of social programs and the vicious assaults against trade unions by the neoliberal comprador elite can be traced to the 1980s, when the capitalist class was given a dose of corporate Viagra through massive deregulation policies. According to Robert Brenner:

> Capitalists and the wealthy accumulated wealth with such success during the 1980s largely because the state intervened directly to place money in their hands—enabling them to profit from their own business failure through lucrative bailouts, offering them massive tax breaks which played no small part in the recovery of corporate balance sheets, and providing them with an unprecedented array of other politically constituted opportunities to get richer faster through fiscal, monetary, and deregulation policies—all at the expense of the great mass of the population.[13]

Of course, after the initial surge, the economy went flaccid, which put the lie to the myth of deregulation. Brenner remarks:

> If, after more than two decades of wage-cutting, tax-cutting, reductions in the growth of social expenditure, deregulation and 'sound finance,' the ever less fettered 'free market' economy is unable to perform half as well as in the 1960s, there might be some reason to question the dogma that the freer the market, the better the economic performance.[14]

Moody reports that, at a global level, we are witnessing the production of a transnational working class. He warns that "the division of labor in the production of the word's wealth is more truly international than at any time."[15] In tandem with these economic shifts has been the unceasing virulence of neoliberal attacks against social programs, educational opportunities, and the civil rights of working-class women and minorities. The globalization of national economies—something that is not really new, but as old as capitalism itself—through deregulation, free marketization, and privatization has become an open-door policy to the unrestricted movement of finance capital from national to international markets, creating flexible arrangements suitable for capitalist exploitation.[16] As globalization has dramatically intensified over the last several decades, its lack of an ethical foundation or warrant has never been so apparent. Michael Parenti writes:

> Capitalism is a system without a soul, without humanity. It tries to reduce every human activity to market profitability. It has no loyalty to democracy, family values, culture, Judeo-Christian ethics, ordinary folks, or any of the other shibboleths mouthed by its public relations representatives on special occasions. It has no loyalty to any nation; its only loyalty is to its own system of capital accumulation. It is not dedicated to 'serving the community;' it serves only itself, extracting all it can from the many so that it might give all it can to the few.[17]

The growing number of undocumented immigrants in Los Angeles and throughout the southwestern United States is being examined by the general public as the probable result of miserable social, political, and economic conditions in so-called Third World countries. What the media persistently fails to report is that the root of this situation can be traced to the downgraded manufacturing sector in the United States and the growth of new low-wage jobs in the service sector where the growth industries—finance, real estate, insurance, retail trade, and business services—come equipped with low wages, weak unions, and a high proportion of part-time and female workers. These workers are more than likely to be immigrants who are forced to work for low pay, have little employment security, possess few technical skills and little knowledge of English.[18] Of course, the growing high-income professional and managerial class in the major metropolitan centers has created a need for low-wage service workers— restaurant workers, residential building attendants, preparers of specialty and gourmet foods, dog walkers, errand runners, apartment cleaners, childcare providers and others who work in the informal economy 'off the books.'[19]

In the face of the changing dynamics of world capitalism, Moody argues the persistent continuation of three aspects of today's economic, social, and political world resembles the world of a century ago. First, there is no existing social system that competes with capitalism for the future, whether precapitalist regimes or bastions of postcapitalist, communist, bureaucratic collectives. Second, capitalism has retained its market-driven form to create uneven development on a world scale. Third, the state and institutions of capitalist politics have been captured by neoliberal/conservative movements and politicians; the objective power of international markets continue to impose severe limits on reform projects for those unwilling to struggle.[20]

Yet while much remains the same about capitalism, there does exist a profound difference. Social provisions within the working class have worsened and resistance to the regime of wage labor is much more difficult than at any other historical moment. David Harvey reminds us that the barriers to that unity are far more formidable than they were in the already complicated European context of 1848 [publication date of the Communist Manifesto]. The workforce is now far more geographically dispersed, culturally heterogeneous, ethnically and religiously diverse, racially stratified, and linguistically fragmented. The effect is to radically differentiate both the modes of resistance to capitalism and the definitions of alternatives. And while it is true that means of communication and opportunities for translation have greatly improved, this has little meaning for the billion or so workers living on less than a dollar a day possessed of quite different cultural histories, literatures and understandings (compared to international financiers and transnationals who use them all the time). Differentials (both geographical and social) in wages and social provisions within the global working class are likewise greater than they have ever been.[21]

Addicted to its own self-induced adrenaline rush, capitalism's reckless gun-slinging frontierism and goon squad financial assaults on vulnerable nations has brought itself into a naked confrontation with its own expanding limits, the ne plus ultra extremity of accumulation, turning it upon itself in a cannibalistic orgy of self-destruction. The collapse of the former Soviet Union and Eastern European state-sponsored bureaucratic socialism, following in the wake of a speeded up process of globalization and its unholy alliance with neoliberalism, has fostered hostile conditions for progressive educators who wish to create coalitions and social movements that speak to the urgent issues and needs inside and outside our urban schools.[22] These include growing poverty, racism, and jobless futures for generations of increasingly alienated youth. Confronted by the fancifully adorned avant-garde guises worn by postmodernists as they enact their wine-and-cheese-party revolution, the education Left is hard-pressed to make a case for Marx. It has become exceedingly more difficult to mobilize against capital which is conscripting the school curriculum and culture into its project of eternal accumulation.

Postmodern theory has made significant contributions to the education field by examining how schools participate in producing and reproducing asymmetrical relations of power, and how discourses, systems of intelligibility, and representational practices continue to support gender inequality, racism, and class advantage. For the most part, however, postmodernism has failed to develop alternative democratic social models. This is partly due to its failure to mount a sophisticated and coherent opposition politics against economic exploitation, political oppression, and cultural hegemony. In its celebration of the aleatory freeplay of signification, postmodernism exhibits a profound cynicism—if not sustained intellectual contempt—toward what it regards as the Eurocentric Enlightenment project of human progress, equality, justice, rationality, and truth, a project built upon patriarchal master narratives that can be traced to seventeenth-century European thinkers.[23] Perry Anderson, paraphrasing Terry Eagleton, aptly describes the phenomenon of postmodernism as follows:

> Advanced capitalism . . . requires two contradictory systems of justification: a metaphysics of abiding impersonal verities—the discourse of sovereignty and law, contract and obligation—in the political order, and a casuistic of individual preferences for perpetually shifting fashions and gratifications of consumption in the economic order. Postmodernism gives paradoxical expression to this dualism, since while its dismissal of the centered subject in favor of the erratic swarming of desire colludes with the amoral hedonism of the market, its denial of any grounded values or objective truths undermines the prevailing legitimations of the state.[24]

Challenging such ambivalence is one reason that Marxism has come under trenchant assault in recent years by postmodernist theorists of various stripe. Postmodernists have taken Marxism to task for its perceived lack of attention to issues of race and gender.[25] Leaning heavily on the idea of the incommensurability of discourses, some intellectual apostles of postmodernism such as Patti Lather offer a tired and hidebound caricature of Marxism as a patriarchal totalizing discourse, in order to reinvent the all-too-familiar assertion that Marxist educational theory is quintessentially hostile to feminist theory.[26] This is, of course, a gross overstatement, ignoring much that has gone on within Marxist theory over the last several decades.[27] For Lather, the so-called subsumption of Marxism under the superior model of deconstruction has not been a *crévecoeur*. Contrary to Lather's grievous misapprehension that links Marxism to modernism's boy's club, Marxism recognizes that the greatest threat to equality on the basis of race, class, gender, and sexual orientation is capitalism itself. As Aijaz Ahmad notes:

> Marxism is today often accused of neglecting all kinds difference, of gender, race, ethnicity, nationality, culture, and so on. But it is not Marxism that recognizes no gender differences. These differences are at once abolished by capitalism, by turning women as much as men into instruments of production. These differences are also maintained through cross-class sexual exploitation, not to speak of the differential wage rate, in which women are paid less than men for the same work, or the direct appropriation of women's labor in the domestic economy. Similarly, it is not communism that sets out to abolish nationality. It is abolished by capitalism itself, through imperialism, through circulation of finance and commodities, through the objectivity of the labor process itself, while nation-states are maintained simply as mechanisms for the management of various units of the world capitalist economy in the context of globally uneven and unequal development. Finally, the bourgeoisie is already a universal class, transnational in its operations and with a culture that also tends to be globally uniform.[28]

Bourgeois critics who condemn Marxism as too 'deterministic' often advance an ideology of unfettered capitalism that is even more deterministic. Samir Amin remarks:

> It is rather amusing to see managerial types who dismiss Marxism as unduly deterministic proffering this rather vulgar absolute kind of determinism. Moreover, the social design they seek to defend with this argument, namely

the market-based management of the world system, is utopian in the worst sense of the term, a reactionary, criminal utopia, doomed in any case to fall apart under the pressure, of its own highly explosive charge.[29]

Bourgeois liberal educational theorists in the United States have enjoyed a long-standing apostolic advantage to Marxist scholars who for the most part are characterized as political extremists, idealists, untrustworthy and intransigent intellectuals, and rogues and renegades. The works of Marx and his heirs have been placed on the librorum prohibitorum. Regrettably, too few Marxist analyses are published in U.S. education journals, and even fewer works by Marxist educators appear in the syllabuses of teacher education programs. With the exception of works by Michael Apple, Richard Brosio, Giroux, Geoff Whitty, and a handful of others, very few social and cultural theorists in the field of education appear to recognize the extent to which political economy shapes educational curriculum and policy decisions.[30] Although we acknowledge many of the inherent weaknesses in the reproduction and correspondence theories and models of schooling that surfaced in the 1970s and early 1980s, we nevertheless believe that, mutatis mutandis, schools still wittingly and unwittingly participate in reproducing social and economic inequalities in the name of freedom and democracy.[31] Further, they function in the thrall of capital more overwhelmingly today than at any time in history. Acknowledging the brute and intractable reality of capitalist schooling, Carol A. Stabile asserts that

> capitalist education is organized and has a purpose, which is held in place by a number of other institutions and their ideologies. In a word, the educational system in the United States reproduces and maintains division between capitalists and workers, thereby producing . . . capitalist relations of production. This organization and purpose are manifest in the historical link between educational institutions and industry, with the former being directed by the needs and interests of the latter.[32]

We apologize to those conservative postmodernists, neo-Nietzscheans, deconstructionists, Gallo-poststructuralists and the like, who find this observation too crude for their academic taste. We follow our apology with an historical materialist alternative.

The Naughtiness of Postmodernism

The incursion of French social theory into North American academic precincts over the last thirty years is foregrounded against a lack of Leftist political coalitions poised to effectively resist the expanding power of capital orchestrated by organized multinational corporations. Many liberals and progressive intellectuals on the Left now seek post-Marxist frameworks for explaining the current disorganization of capitalism in order to avoid the so-called reductionism of conventional Marxist theories. These Leftists are often quick to comfort themselves with the debonair gestures of avant-garde social critics that emerged from the fashionably elegant apartments of Paris during the last several decades.

During the Khruschev era, it became quite clear that the social and economic models that had been put forth by the former Soviet Union and Eastern European countries had failed to offer promising alternatives for developing democratic social life. And by the late 1980s it became clearer that Soviet-style state capitalism was doomed. Shortly thereafter, neoliberal politicians in the West pledged the demise of the welfare state to its antisocialist constituencies, while liberal politicians continued to sing the praises of humanism and envision a pluralistic democracy built on happy consensus. Marxism, however, was relegated to the dank and garbage-strewn gutters of failed revolutionary and popular struggles, often due to political fragmentation and ideological differences among its proponents, and the role played by the international capitalist cavalry—the marines and the CIA.[33] Rarely did these liberals stop to think that reforms correspond to a certain period of the capitalist mode of production, represent at best an imposed amelioration of the worst effects of capitalism, fail to challenge the basic principles or contradictions of capitalist exploitation, serve as mere state mandated accords, and fail to free the working class from complete dependence on the labor market or change the fundamental relations of ownership in society.[34]

Moody touches on a key issue of contemporary politics when he remarks that socialist thought over the last century has separated the idea of economic struggle from political struggle.[35] This dualistic counterposition of the economic and the political has posed some serious problems. For instance, traditional mass parties of the working class and the political Left are now more removed from the idea of socialism than ever before. There has rarely—if ever—been a time when the revolutionary socialist Left has been so fragmented. Many socialists were slow to realize that all aspects of social life involved both the economic and the political and that there existed no such dichotomy in the world of everyday social life. That a lack of a coherent political platform against global capitalism contributed to the increasing factionalism within the United States Left should come as little surprise to those who have lived through decades of sophisticated antisocialist cold war propaganda, a sacerdotal celebration of neoliberal free enterprise practices, and the deregulation of markets propagandized as the advance guard of democracy. James Petras and Chronis Polychroniou refer to the crisis of Marxism as a "crisis of the intellectual nerves," which "is rooted in the failure of the Left to resist the ideological pressures from the Western mass media and states (as well as their intellectuals in uniform) to amalgamate Marxism with the bureaucratic collectivist regimes and to reproduce history from an anti-socialist, anti-working-class perspective."[36] Petras and Polychroniou provide three explanations for the prevalent crisis: many intellectuals on the Left erroneously equated bureaucratic socialism with Marxism; the Left was largely subservient to the political and ideological support it received from the former Soviet Union and Eastern European socialist countries; and the mass media and intellectuals in Western capitalist countries succeeded in portraying the demise of bureaucratic socialism as the end of Marxism. Yet the crises of Marxism can also be considered a deepening intellectual malaise brought about by the disorganization of global capitalist relations. The intellectual crises is perhaps most evident in the 'post-Marxist' attack on Marxism as a decidedly modernist enterprise rooted in the imperializing project of the Western Enlightenment tradition.

Globalization binds people together through the economic-political machinery of new technology, the media, and new circuits of production, distribution, and consumption within the culture industry. Yet globalization also creates new divisions and hierarchies of difference, style, and taste. To be sure, consumer culture industries have intensified 'sign value' and exchange-value through the processes of commercialization. Following in the wake of the globalization of capital is the globalization of culture, a process that creates as many new differences as it does patterns of sameness. Noting that 60 percent of the revenues of all feature films are made in overseas mass markets, Disney has brought Henry Kissinger to Hollywood to advise on its projects in China (with all its potential moviegoers). If there is already a McDonalds near Tiananmen Square, why not envision a movie theater in the Great Hall of the People?[37]

Yet it would be a mistake to agree with the postmodernist claim that sign value has superseded use-value. Such a claim rests on a mistaken realist assumption and truncated conception of use value that argues that use values have been replaced with exchange values, meaning with money, and human needs with profit.[38] We claim that all capitalist commodity production rests upon the production and reproduction of needs and use values. Specific needs and desires have been inflected in certain directions—a process that is certainly visible in the aesthetic surfaces of everyday consumer culture. But Marx anticipated the heterogenization of needs in his commodity theory. We need to stress that sign value does not exceed use value but rather is constitutive of it. What we regard on the new postmodern empire of signs actually belongs to the material reality of use value, even though we concede, as did Marx, that the relationships between needs and use values have been historically and intersubjectively defined. While the aestheticization of everyday life gives the illusion that sign values are epiphenomena of use values, this is decidedly not the case. As Johan Fornäs has put it, "symbols and aesthetics are more than simple effects of commodification and more than a secondary aura above a firm material base."[39]

Under the impact of rapid technological innovations over the last half of the century in computers and communications devices, some ludic postmodernists have argued that the hierarchical distinctions between reality and its representations have been erased.[40] Teresa Ebert identifies two variants of postmodernism: 'ludic' and 'resistance' postmodernism.[41] Ludic postmodernism celebrates the free-floating articulation of signifiers in the construction of lifestyle discourses that are viewed for the most part as decapitated from external determinations. Resistance postmodernism draws upon poststructuralist advances in understanding signification, but views language as the product of history and links signification to class struggle through the Formalist linguistics of Mikhail Bakhtin, V. N. Volosinov, and a sociological analysis of language associated with Lev Vygotsky and G. Plekhanov. Ebert explains that while ludic postmodernism is the result of material and historical contradictions inherent within capitalist social relations of production, resistance postmodernism exposes those contradictions by linking social, political, and cultural phenomena with the existing asymmetrical social and economic relations. Resistance postmodernism and critical postmodernism reveal that the base and superstructure are not independent of one another, as ludic postmodern thinkers such as Baudrillard, Derrida, and Lyotard are wont to argue.

Jean Baudrillard's faux pas begins with the belief that a Marxist emphasis on production is no longer relevant in a consumer-driven capitalist culture. Baudrillard's 'spectral superstructuralism' privileges cultural production (i.e., images, texts, simulations) over economic production. While postmodern theory swimming in the currents of Baudrillard's renegade vanguardism dismantles meaning in brilliant and manic flashes of hypertheorizing, it too often ricochets off anticapitalist critique, angling toward a politics of representation whose progressive inertia eventually log jams in a centerless cesspool of floating signifiers.

Postmodernists refute metanarratives and participate in an unequivocal rejection of universal truths.[42] However, critics of postmodernism point out that decentering grand narratives and rejecting universalism in favor of heterogeneity and a plurality of truths is feasible only if postmodernism constitutes itself as a totalizing narrative. As Rick Joines comments:

> One of the founding principles and shibboleths of the postmodern academic left is the disavowal of totalizing master narratives (which are coded as 'totalitarian') and the conjoined belief that Marx's so-called predictions have failed as the world of class struggle becomes a world of discursive representations and linguistic play. This discourse, which cannot admit its own totalizing, has abandoned thinking about labor and exploitation in favor of textuality and body: desire is hot—economics and class struggle are not.[43]

Even journals that profess a Leftist agenda are succumbing to the lure of postmodernist perspectives. In a recent article in the journal *New Left Review*, Boris Frankel deftly exposes several post-Marxist intellectual movements as liberalism in disguise.[44] The American journal *Telos* is criticized for advocating postmodern populism as a way of confronting corporate capitalism. Frankel notes that postmodern populism falls short of developing a persuasive critique of capitalism since it remains trapped within a Keynesian welfare economics. Similarly, Frankel criticizes the British journal, *Economy and Society* for supporting a neo-Foucauldian form of realpolitik influenced by the works of Max Weber and Frederick Nietzsche, and for rejecting Marxism and socialism on the basis of its putative political romanticism. Frankel traces the roots of these contemporary postmodern and politically conservative intellectual movements in the works of early twentieth-century bourgeois classical elite theorists such as Mosca, Pareto, and Michels. Postmodernists and classical elite theorists both share a rejection of universalism and totalizing theories while failing adequately to critique class inequalities in capitalist societies. Although both journals see themselves as politically progressive, they recuperate the project of globalization and the politics of neoliberalism.

We agree with Samir Amin when he asserts that modernism has not been surpassed by the fictional period known as 'postmodernism.' Rather, modernism has yet to be finished:

> Modernity is still unfinished, and it remains so as long as the human race continues to exist. Currently, the fundamental obstacle setting its limits is still defined by the social relationships specific to capitalism. What the postmodernists refuse to see is that modernity can progress further only by going beyond capitalism.[45]

We are not suggesting that the Marxist problematic that informs our work cannot greatly benefit from criticism by postmodernists, feminists, or critical multiculturalists. We continue to advocate for feminist theory and antiracist and antihomophobic perspectives as an extension and as a deepening of many aspects of the Marxist project. This is far different, however, from abandoning the Marxist project tout court in favor of identity politics.

Surely, it is undeniably a good idea to follow anti-essentialism in disbanding, dispersing and displacing the terms that claim to represent us in a shared field of representations, premised on the mutual imbrication of 'us and them,' that we call 'Western identity.'[46] Anti-essentialism has, above all, enabled researchers to criticize the notion of the unsullied position of enunciation, the location of interpretation free of ideology, what Vincent Crapanzano refers to as a "lazy divinity . . . contemplating its creation in order to observe it, register it, and interpret it."[47] Yet identity politics grounded in an anti-essentialist position has not focused sufficiently on the material preconditions for liberated ethnic identities that have been undermined by the dramatic intensity of historical events irrupting across the landscape of advanced capitalism. While displacing our historical selves into some new fashionably renegade identity, through a frenzied spilling over of signifiers once lashed to the pillars of conventional meanings, might reap benefits and help to soften the certainty of the dominant ideological field, such postmodern maneuvers do little to threaten material relations of production that contribute to the already hierarchically-bound international division of labor.

We are not against the development of self-reflexivity directed at issues in popular culture or cultural criticism in general. We are interested in finding *common ground* between cultural criticism and the movement for a transformation of productive relations. Our position is that postmodern cultural criticism mainly addresses the specific logics of noneconomic factors and, for the most part, has not addressed the liberation of humankind from economic alienation linked to the capitalist economic logics that serve as the motor for transnational oligopolies and the reproduction of established social relations. Samir Amin sets forth a non–economic-determinist interpretation of Marxism that we find convincing.[48] In Amin's model, the capitalist mode of production is *not* reduced to the status of an economic structure. In other words, the law of value governs both the economic reproduction of capitalism *and* all the aspects of social life within capitalism. Unlike the concept of 'overdetermination,' famously articulated by Althusser, Amin counterposes the concept of 'underdetermination,' in which the determinations of economics, politics, and culture each possess their specific logic and autonomy. There is no complimentarity among logics within the systems of underdetermination; there exist only conflicts among their determining factors, conflicts which allow choice among different possible alternatives. Conflicts among logics find solutions by subordinating some logics to others. The accumulation of capital is the dominant trait of the logic of capitalism and provides the channels through which economic logic is imposed onto political, ideological, and cultural logics.

Precisely because underdetermination rather than overdetermination typifies the conflictual way in which the logics governing the various factors of social causation are interlaced, all social revolutions must of necessity be cultural revolutions. The law of value, therefore, governs not only the capitalist mode of production but also the other social determinants. In order to move beyond—to overstep—contemporary capitalism that is defined by its three basic contradictions of economic alienation, global polarization, and destruction of the natural environment, Amin charts out social transformation that would initiate through its political economy, its politics, and its cultural logics, a social evolution bent on reducing these contradictions rather than aggravating them. Amin convincingly argues that postmodern criticism for the most part capitulates to the demands of the current phase of capitalist political economy in the hope of making the system more humane. Marxists perceive the humanization of capitalism to be a contradiction in terms. Efforts such as those by Bill Clinton to create a "third way" have rightly been dismissed as "neoliberalism with a smiley face."[49]

Within the precincts of postmodern theorizing and in the absence of universal criteria for evaluating the validity of truth claims, we are forced to accept politically ambiguous positions when confronting the privileging hierarchies of capitalist social relations. In our view, concepts such as universal rights are *central* to the development of a democratic society and should not be placed in philosophical quarantine as the postmodernists believe. While we may agree with those postmodernists who claim that truth does not have a predetermined or fixed meaning, embedded as it is within the specificity of social, political, and historical contexts, this in no way implies the validity of every truth-claim, since truths-claims conceal asymmetrical social and economic relations. Teresa Ebert elaborates on this idea:

> The question of knowing the 'truth' is neither a question of describing some 'true' metaphysical or ontological 'essence' nor a matter of negotiating incommensurable language games, as Lyotard suggests. Rather it is a question of dialectical understanding of the dynamic relations between superstructure and base: between ideology—(mis)representations, signifying practices, discourses, frames of intelligibility, objectives—and the workings of the forces of production and the historical relations of production. Crucial to such a dialectical knowledge is ideology critique—a practice for developing class consciousness.[50]

Conservative postmodernism—epitomized by that *bien-aimé* of postmodern pseudo-transgressors, Jean Baudrillard—leaches attention away from the messy, conflictual and power-sensitive materiality of everyday life, by refusing to differentiate between image and reality, surface and depth, discourse and ideology, and fact and fiction. Postmodern epistemology is based not so much upon critical inquiry in which 'objectivity' is pursued, but rather is constructed in relation to the tropicity and rhetoricity of discourse. The fixed dualism of reality versus fiction does not apply. Carl Boggs captures this absence of any substantive counter-hegemonic agenda beneath conservative postmodernism's façade of avant-bohemianism:

> In politics as in the cultural and intellectual realm, a postmodern fascination with indeterminacy, ambiguity, and chaos easily supports a drift toward cynicism and passivity; the subject becomes powerless to change either itself or society. Further, the pretentious, jargon-filled, and often indecipherable discourse of postmodernism reinforces the most faddish tendencies in academia. Endless (and often pointless) attempts to deconstruct texts and narratives readily become a façade behind which professional scholars justify their own retreat from political commitment . . . the extreme postmodern assault on macro institutions severs the connections between critique and action.[51]

Similarly, Hilary Wainwright argues that postmodernism lacks

> adequate tools to answer the radical right . . . the tools of postmodernism produce only a more volatile version of the radical right. . . . Postmodernism cuts the connection between human intention and social outcome. While for the radical right the incompleteness of our knowledge means that society is the outcome of the blindfold and therefore haphazard activities of the individual, for the postmodern theorist, society is an equally haphazard plethora of solipsistic statements of various sorts.[52]

Sardar makes the cogent claim that postmodernism suffers from a "paradoxical dualism" or double coding. It claims that nothing is real, yet it also claims that reality represents something real: simulated *images*.[53] Postmodernists view history as a collection of necessarily fragmented narratives where the notion of determinate relations is made anemic by the hemorrhaging of signifiers and their bleeding into each other.[54] Historical events are too often transformed into a Disneyesque theme park of fantasy and play where the distinction between fact and fiction is barely—if at all—perceptible. History is sequestered away in a grammatologist's laboratory where it can conjure a metaphysics of disappearances and invent reality as a nightmare where all attempts at objectivity suffer the fate of Dr. Frankenstein and his monster.

And what about the postmodernist aversion to master narratives that guide global struggles for liberation? We find that the postmodernist alternative—the stress on local struggles and regional antagonisms—often subverts the anticapitalist project necessary to bring about social democracy. The development of world capitalism as an imperializing force, as a means of subjugating labor, as a system of unequal and combined development, as a means of superexploitation and the repression of democratic aspirations, needs more than monadic local efforts at improving resource allocation and warning the public against excessive consumptive practices. Local efforts fail to take advantage of reform at the level of the state. The fact that the state is more dependent on capital than ever before suggests that it could potentially serve as an instrument in reform efforts if these are organized with broad national support. According to Ahmad:

> The currently fashionable postmodern discourse has its own answer: it leaves the market fully intact while debunking the nation-state and seeking to dissolve it even further into little communities and competitive narcissisms, which sometimes gets called 'multiculturalism.' In other words, postmodernism seeks an even deeper universalization of the market, while seeking to decompose 'social humanity' even further, to the point where only the monadic individual remains, with no dream but that of, in Jean-François Lyotard's words, "the enjoyment of goods and services." Or, to put it somewhat differently: the postmodern utopia takes the form of a complementary relationship between universalization of the market and individualization of commodity fetishisms. This, of course, has been a dream of capitalism since its very inception.[55]

For Amin, postmodernism gives theoretical legitimacy to a retreat from revolutionary momentum. He further claims that

> these retreats go exactly counter to the sincere wishes of the postmodernists for a strengthening of democratic practices in the administration of everyday affairs. They give fodder to conformity and hatred, contempt for democracy, and to all sorts of chauvinisms. . . . Postmodernism, therefore, is a negative utopia (in contradistinction to positive utopias, which call for transformation of the world). At bottom, it expresses capitulation to the demands of capitalist political economy in its current phase, in the hope—the utopian hope—of 'humanly managing the system.' This position is untenable.[56]

Postmodernists rarely elevate facts from anecdote to history, a practice commensurate with following the latest top-of-the-line designer narratives. At the same time they ritualistically weave together post-Marxist and end-of-history claims into a seamless genealogy in an attempt to mummify historical agency and seal the project of liberation in a vault marked 'antiquity.' It is worth quoting Sardar again:

> In designer history any choice can be fitted with a tradition by associating it with a chosen historical pattern of ideas or events or characters that are selectively assembled. History returns not to its fictional, putative father—Herodotus—as he was constructed by nineteenth century historians, but to the spirit that moved the civilisation that produced him: history becomes mythmaking.[57]

Educational theorists working in the Marxist tradition, such as Mike Cole and Dave Hill and Glenn Rikowski, view postmodernism as altogether reactionary and serving only to reinscribe capitalist social relations.[58] They reject Leftist appropriations of postmodernism (i.e., critical postmodernism, radical postmodernism, resistance postmodernism) as basically a trompe l'oeil in which capitalism is able to masquerade as a necessary condition in order for democracy to flourish. In contrast, we are more sympathetic to limited aspects of these radical variants of postmodernism, at the very least for their ability to analyze intersecting relationships among race, class, and gender in late capitalist societies without falling prey to epistemological reductionism. Yet, as we mentioned at the beginning of this essay, some forms of postmodernism that attempt to incorporate a Marxian problematic often fall prey to an obfuscating eclecticism, in which the priority of anticapitalist struggle is subsumed under a concern with identity politics in consumer society.

An antifoundationalist cynicism surrounding the telos of human progress often leads ludic postmodernism to reject narratives about history's inevitability that have emerged out of the Marxist tradition. However, Marxism's emphasis on teleology is nonteleological; it arches toward an eradication of social injustice, poverty, racism, and sexism while recognizing that history is mutable and contingent. We must emphasize that Marx did not believe history as altogether progressive. He understood that historical progress is never secured or guaranteed, but moves in and between contradictory and conflicting social spaces and zones of engagement. Alex Callinicos explains this further by arguing that

> historical materialism is a non-teleological theory of social evolution: not only does it deny that capitalism is the final stage of historical development, but communism, the classless society which Marx believed would be the outcome of socialist revolution, is not the inevitable consequence of the contradictions of capitalism, since an alternative exists, what Marx called 'the mutual ruination of the contending classes.'[59]

Contrary to the criticism of Marxist teleology advanced by some postmodern critics, "Marx doesn't describe the overthrow of capitalism as marking the end of history but rather the end of the *prehistory* of human society."[60]

Terry Eagleton similarly confirms Marx's opinion that historical regression is more probable than historical progression, since the outcome of historical progress depends upon the development of social forces and social relations of production.[61] Moreover, he adds that the "point for Marx is not to move us toward the telos of History, but to get out from under all that so that we may make a beginning—so that histories proper, in all their wealth of difference, might get off the ground."[62] Postmodern theory too often discounts class struggle and underestimates the importance of addressing economic inequality for fear of succumbing to an implicit teleology of progress. At the same time, it continues to recite the satanic verses of capitalist ideology represented by free-market economics and political neoliberalization, which is fast becoming the governing ethos of our time.

We want to be clear that we are not trying to privilege class relations over those of gender, race, ethnicity, or sexual orientation. We remain aware, however, that the law of value under capitalism plays a formidable role in coordinating these relationships and their interrelations. We acknowledge the complex and mutual constitutiveness of race/ethnicity, gender, and sexual orientation as an ensemble of social practices that, while interconnected, to a certain extent constitute different logics. Our point is to underscore the ways that the state makes use of 'difference' and 'diversity' and the militant antagonisms that play out in the theater of identity politics in order to break up the unity of popular forces.

Postmodernism's petit-bourgeois driven movement away from a 'represented exterior' of signifying practices renders an anticapitalist project not only unlikely but firmly inadmissible. Notwithstanding the slippage between Marxist categories and some poststructuralist categories, we believe that postmodernist theories, in effectively delinking identity politics from class analysis, have damagingly relegated the category of class to the epiphenomena of race/ethnicity, gender and sexuality. Class solidarity has often been replaced by ethnic solidarity and an uncritical rehabilitation of difference that defines ethnicity and race in essentialist ways.[63] This does not mean that we take the position that history is shaped by the infallible laws of economics. Far from it. Amin rightly argues that history "is the product of social reactions to the effects of these laws, which in turn define the social relations of the framework within which economic laws operate."[64] History in this view becomes more than an effect of a specific logic inherent in the accumulation of capital; in fact it is given shape by the refusal to subordinate society to the absolute needs of economic laws. Such a politics of refusal admittedly takes many forms, including struggles involving gender, race, ethnic, and sexual liberation. Yet we believe, along with Amin, that "the postmodernist critique, pitched short of the radical perspectives attained by Marxist thought, fails to provide the tools needed to transcend capitalism."[65]

A poststructuralist focus on discourse and difference via Derrida's and Nietzsche's corps, paradoxically can have the effect of homogenizing all struggles and identities as they "proceed further into decadence (equality of all values) in the name of 'progress' in order to accelerate the process of self-destruction, which leads to the necessity of founding new modes and orders."[66] As Rick Joines has argued, Derrida is a Nietzschean and Schmittian revolutionary whose New International is "comprehensively nihilist . . . [and] . . . more threatening than any mere fascism."[67] The denunciatory cry of some Derridean inspired poststructuralists in "Ten Years Later: Yet Again" (which raises the issue of why Marxist pedagogues still work within supposedly received and exhausted masculinist categories after poststructuralists had—ten years earlier—shown them how to be less self-assured and to adopt a less transparent analysis under the theoretical advance guard of "teletechnic dislocation, rhizomatic spreading and acceleration, and new experiences of frontier and identity") should be read against another cry in the face of the barbarianized academy: "One Hundred and Fifty Years after the *Communist Manifesto:* Ruling Class Pedagogues Performing as Avant-Gardists Defending the Capitalist Class, Yet Again."[68] Here the politics of revolutionary class struggle is replaced by a jacuzzi Leftist pedagogy of unknowability and impossibility—ludicrously described as "ontological stammering." As political activist Raphael Rentiera put the issue recently: "For me, the issue surrounding people who advocate that reality is unknowable is that they have things they don't want known. . . . I think it is important to ask: Who is served by the unknowability that these people claim is liberatory?"[69]

Derridean "messianicity *without* messianism" that marks so much of postmodernist educational theorizing today, and that makes use of esotericism, sigetics, acroamatics, proleptics, and illocutionary and perlocutionary acts in the disguise of a new pedagogy of the unknowable, wasn't the answer ten years ago. Nor will it be the answer ten years hence. According to Joines, Derrida's appeal for an International whose essential basis or motivating force is not class, party, or practice of citizenship "should be read and understood as a threat to any potential international organized around such concepts."[70]

Despite postmodernism's ability to deconstruct the metaphysical nature of post-Enlightenment bourgeois discourse and socialist thought, and to reveal its economistic rationality while exposing its teleological prejudices, Amin argues that postmodernism's

> penchant for the uncritical adulation of difference and the glorification of empiricism make it quite compatible with conventional, economistic management practices designed to perpetuate capitalist practices, still considered the definitive, eternal expression of rationality. That leaves the way open for neoconservative communalist ideologies of the kind common in Anglo-Saxon traditions of social management. In extreme cases, it may also lead to nihilistic explosions. Either way, the result is an ideology compatible with the interests of the privileged.[71]

Within the United States, postmodernism's contribution to the dominance of categories of identity politics over those of class is due, in part, to the demise of the once vigorous Marxist culture that thrived in the United States before the McCarthy Era. One thinks immediately of the Critics Group of New York, the work of Granville Hicks, V. F. Calverston, Edmund Wilson, Joseph Freeman, John Reed, John Dos Passos, James T. Farrell, and others. In the 1960s the work of Michael Harrington and Norman Mailer captured national attention. Despite the fact that the works of bell hooks, Cornel West, Henry Louis Gates, Barbara Ehrenreich, Michael Parenti, Noam Chomsky and other thinkers are appearing more frequently in popular publications, contemporary Leftist intellectual life makes very little impact in public debates.

Sherry Ortner remarks that "class exists in America but cannot be talked about," that it "is 'hidden' . . . there is no language for it," but it "is 'displaced' or 'spoken through' other languages of social difference—race, ethnicity, and gender."[72] We agree with Ortner that while to a certain extent class, race, and ethnicity are separate but interacting dimensions of United States social geography, and while they operate at least in part on different logics, "*at the level of discourse*, class, race, and ethnicity are so deeply mutually implicated in American culture that it makes little sense to pull them apart."[73] And while "there is no class in America that is not always already racialized and ethnicized" or racial and ethnic categories that are not always already class categories, the salience of race and ethnicity in the United States is such that when they are introduced into the discussion, they tend to override to a considerable degree that of social class.[74] The persistent hiddenness of class means, for Ortner, that the discourse of class "is muted and often unavailable, subordinated to virtually every other kind of claim about social success and social failure."[75] Given the frenetic advance of contemporary global capitalist social relations, the disappearance of class from the public discourse presents favorable conditions for the uncontested reproduction of the social division of labor.

In these times of extreme pessimism and cynicism, the *brujos* of global capitalism and neoliberalism, with their well-orchestrated Deja Voodoo wizardry, reinvent the present in the image of a luminous past, harkening back in Panglossian fashion to an earlier period of capitalist expansion under Reagan and Thatcher. We reject *tout court* such social amnesia. Coal miners in England and air traffic controllers and General Motors factory workers in the United States—to name only a few groups sacrificed at the altar of neoliberal greed during the profligacy of Reagan and Thatcher—should put this roseate version of historical memory to rest. The aim of neoliberal economic politics is to privatize social and public institutions while socializing the risks involved in order to facilitate the frenzied accumulation of capital. Ellen Meiksins Wood argues that the

> objective of today's neoliberal politics is to 'privatize' anything that could be conceivably be run for capitalist profit—from prisons, to postal services, to old age pensions. But it has also set out to ensure that every public enterprise, every social service, that cannot be profitably privatized will still be subject to market imperatives.[76]

The cultural critique that today predominates in cultural studies and post-Marxist 'new times' critical exegesis, and that assails Marxist theory for privileging social class over race, gender, and identity, often constitutes a veiled essentialism. In contrast to such an accusation, Marxism emphasizes that racism, sexism, and heteronormativity are mutually informing relations and integrally linked to one another, yet they always need to be theorized *in relation to* social and economic inequalities. For antisexist and antiracist struggles to move beyond the rhetoric of identity politics and take on a transformative rather than reactive role within the public sphere, they need to consider beyond simple head-nodding gestures the global shifts in the social relations of production and international division of labor. For this reason, it is important to move beyond "political standpoints that view class, gender, race, and ethnicity as discrete, mutually exclusive phenomena."[77]

Furthermore, a closer examination of relations of class reveals, for example, how the feminization of poverty and the oppression of women are linked with world-consolidating forces within capitalist social relations, patriarchy, and other catechisms of the market. Carol A. Stabile illuminates the relationship between gender and class by arguing that reinstating "class as a central category of analysis for feminism emphasizes the relationality of structures of oppression in politically powerful ways." She adds that "this move does not mean relinquishing the theoretical and practical gains following from feminists analysis of gender and race; instead, it provides a much more nuanced and complicated understanding of the manner in which oppressions are structurally inter- twined."[78] The meanings that follow from socially constructed concepts of race, gender, sexuality, identity, and ethnicity are never fixed, but historically con- structed and interwoven *with* social relations of production. Martha Gimenez emphasizes this idea, arguing that in order to

> attain a fuller grasp of the relevance of gender divisions and struggles for the political future of the working class, it is necessary to leave behind the notion of gender as being primarily an individual attribute and to examine it, instead, as the observable effect of underlying social relations of physical and social reproduction.[79]

While the success of socialist and Left-wing progressive movements in Western industrial and Third World countries in forming effective anticapitalist revolu- tionary alliances has been detained (we hope only temporarily) by the onslaught of global capitalism, postmodern social theorists continue to regard themselves as the primary animateurs of a egalitarian new world order—one that will pro- vide an aesthetic education for the profanum vulgus while leaning on the ideo- logical backbone of the multinational corporations. Having dismissed Rosa Luxemburg's alternative of 'socialism or barbarianism' as a quaint blot on the horizon of social struggles, postmodern apostles are codifying in their vulgate discourses of transgression, primarily linked to an aesthetic problematic which in turn is grounded in the often ex tempore apostatizing pretensions of the me- tropolis. The conservative nature of postmodern politics has largely remained undetected, helping to keep the ideology of free enterprise, individualism, and privatization the only real game in town.

Since postmodern theorists have been unable to offer convincing accounts of existing class inequalities, a shroud of suspicion surrounds their political mo- tivation and a jaundiced eye is cast upon their social and political objectives by the Marxist Left. Postmodernists have the appearance at least of rejecting a uni- fied political commitment to social change and transformation. Samir Amin has offered a cogent description of the way in which neoliberal economics under- writes the political philosophy of postmodernism. He asserts that

> empty economics has its pale complement in the enfeebled social and philo- sophical theses of 'postmodernism,' which teach us to be happy and to cope with the system on a day-to-day basis, while closing our eyes to the ever more gigantic catastrophe which it is cooking for us. Postmodernism thus legiti- mizes, in its own way, the manipulative practices required of political manag- ers for whom democracy must be reduced to the status of "low intensity" ac- tivity even as it treats the attachment of a society to its own identity as something neurotic, empty, and impotent.[80]

The treatment of class as yet another arbitrary floating signifier among race, class, and identity, and the taboo usage of concepts such as 'base' and 'super- structure,' have led postmodernists to expunge the notions of capitalist exploi- tation and imperialism from their lexicon and replace them with more politically benign discourses of 'difference' and 'identity politics.' Even self-proclaimed progressive postmodernists fair no better in articulating a persuasive critique of capitalism. Roslyn Wallach Bologh and Leonard Mell remark that "the best that this tradition can offer is a rearrangement of the existing distribution of power—ideally, some kind of vague hope for egalitarianism or radical democracy."[81] Because postmodern politics has failed to develop a sustained critique of class inequalities, racism, sexism, and economic inequality are thus framed superficially within fragmented discourses articulated around the holy trinity of race, class, and gender. Bologh and Mell culminate their argument with the assertion that

> If postmodernism wants to confront colonization and the production of otherness, it must confront capital. If it wants to deconstruct universal categories, it might begin with the categories of political economy—as did Marx. Those are the most universal categories in which power resides.[82]

It follows that we need to critically examine and re-articulate from a Marxist perspective the dynamic mechanisms that allow capitalist social relations of exploitation to persist.

Developing and envisioning an anticapitalist pedagogy requires a common yet open-ended historical-materialist framework of equality and social justice. The meanings of equality and justice are not predetermined nor do they float freely in some effanescent semiotic ether; rather, they are embedded within the specificity of social, economic, and political relations. In fact, historical specificity of the concept of equality neither denies its universal quality nor its objective significance. Rather, it is a standard by which we are able to judge political arguments or social practices, and it is a measure by which we can objectively gauge historical and social progress.[83]

The anti-essentialism and anti-universalism of conservative postmodernism considers race, class and gender to be indeterminate and relatively unstable identities by which we represent ourselves. However, race, class, and gender are not merely fashionable costumes we wear in our daily social relations but constitute historically-grounded social practices within the material relations of production. As Ahmad explains at length:

> There is the idea of discreteness of identities, cultural, ethnic, or national; a kind of remorseless differentialism, whereby I am not permitted the claim that I may understand your identity but I am supposed to simply respect whatever you say are the requirements of your identity. In this ideology, any number of people celebrate hardened boundaries between self and other, denounce, what they understand as the 'universalism' of the enlightenment, rationalism, and so on, while also fully participating in the globalization of consumption patterns and the packaging of identities as so many exhibits. At the same time and often from the same people, we also have the propagation of the idea of infinite hybridity, migrancy, choice of alternate or multiple identities, as if new selves could be fashioned in the instant out of any clay that one could lay on one's hand on, and as if cultures had no real historical density and identi-

ties could be simply made up, sui generis, out of the global traffic and malle-ability of elements taken from all over the world.[84]

In sum, we need to fashion identities that partake of a universal commitment to social equality. This also means that an ethics of social justice must more clearly underwrite the current work being done in identity politics.[85]

We need to identify radical elements within the postmodern movement and not simply ignore postmodernism since there are conservative, liberal, and criti-cal variants of it. This does not imply, as many critics of postmodernism would prematurely argue, a defeatist or assimilationist position. On the contrary, we believe that class by itself cannot be the driving force for social change. This is not to argue that class is no longer central in developing a revolutionary praxis. What it does suggest is that we need to expand our struggles by way of culture, language, and discourse in order to contest the contemporary triad of social, economic, political oppression. And the scope of our struggle must be interna-tional. On this issue, Michael Parenti writes:

> Our task is not to wage a class war but to realize that class war is being waged against us constantly. More international cooperation between labor unions, progressive organizations, and other popular movements is necessary. The ruling classes have taken the struggle to the international level and we must meet them there to prevent our standard of living, our sovereignty, our rights, and indeed our planet, from being sacrificed to a rapaciously profit-driven, monopoly capitalism.[86]

Class analysis needs to be deepened along the lines of its Marxist predecessors, in order to explain its contemporary connections among race, class, gender and disability. This is, however, a far cry from the postmodern claim that 'class' is just one of the many identities by which people represent themselves. Douglas Kellner reminds us that "it would be wrong to ignore the centrality of class and the importance of class politics, [however] a radical politics today should be more multicultural, race and gender focused, and broad-based than the original Marxian theory."[87] This is not an endorsement of the radical democracy of La-clau and Mouffe.[88] Nor is it a call for a commitment to nonviolent negotiation at all costs. If war is being waged on the working class, we support the working class in their attempts to fight back. Our concern is to create the conditions for the defeat of capitalism and in so doing define the real stakes and challenges. Samir Amin poses one of the biggest challenges in the form of the following question: "How are we to create conditions that allow the genuine advance of universalist values beyond their formulations by historical capitalism?"[89] Cer-tainly, the answer is not to be found in the postmodernist's call for local, spe-cific struggles over more global ones. This strategy only plays into the hands of a culturalist, communalist solution resulting in political fragmentation. Rather than contributing to a resistance to exploitation, however, such culturalism itself becomes part of the problem. As Amin notes in the case of European capitalism:

> The European project itself is conceived in these terms as the communal man-agement of the market and no more, while beyond its borders maximum

fragmentation (as many Slovenias, Macedonias, Chechnyas as possible) is systematically sought. Themes of 'democracy' and 'peoples' rights' are mobilized to obtain results that cancel peoples' capacity to make use of the democracy and rights in whose name they have been manipulated. Praise of specificity and difference, ideological mobilization around ethnic or culturalist objectives, are the engine of impotent communalism, and shift the struggle onto the ground of ethnic cleansing or religious totalitarianism.[90]

In sum, class needs to be broadly theorized and class struggle needs to be reconsidered taking into consideration the complexity of its contradictory and shifting meaning within global capitalism. As Julie Graham and Katherine Gibson remark:

> Because class is understood as a process that exists in change, the class 'structure' constituted by the totality of these positions and sites is continually changing. Projects of class transformation are therefore always possible and do not necessarily involve social upheavals and hegemonic transition. Class struggles do not necessarily take place between groups of people whose identities are constituted by the objective reality and subjective consciousness of a particular location in a social structure. Rather, they take place whenever there is an attempt to change the way in which surplus labor is produced, appropriated, or distributed.[91]

If we can conceive of class as the process of producing, appropriating, and distributing surplus value (which is not to displace or deny the importance of property and power in the structure of contemporary society), and if we can also consider class as types of groupings in terms of how persons perform, appropriate, or receive distributed shares of surplus labor, we will notice that allocations of power and property follow from the different relationships one has to the production and appropriation of surplus labor.[92] If the class process defines the performers (productive laborers) and the appropriators (capitalists) of surplus value as the fundamental class process, we will also notice that there are two subsumed classes: distributors and recipients of surplus value. Nonclass processes also need consideration because such processes can at times and under certain circumstances compromise the conditions of existence of the capitalist fundamental class process.

Nonclass processes involving race and gender relations can provide the changes necessary for a transformation of the class processes of Western capitalist societies. Using gender as one example, Richard Wolff and Stephen Resnick remark that

> specific changes in social processes concerned with gender relationships would provide conditions for a change in the class processes of Western capitalists societies today. A change in popular consciousness about what 'male' and 'female' mean (i.e., a change in certain cultural processes) alongside a change in the authority distribution process within families (a change in political or power processes) might combine with a change as women sell more of their labor power as a commodity (a change in the economic process of exchange) to jeopardize capitalist class processes. With other changes in

still other social processes—which our class analysis seeks to identify—such altered gender relationships might provide the conditions of existence for a revolutionary change to a new social system including a different class structure.[93]

It follows that our agenda for revolutionary social change does not subsume gender relations or relations involving race, ethnicity, disability, or sexual orientation beneath the class process. Rather, we are trying to call attention to the possibility of using nonclass relations as part of a larger anticapitalist revolutionary project, not by analytically isolating nonclass relations, but by *bringing them into conversation* with class relations.

Critical postmodernism can generate, at best, a limited counter-hegemonic praxis to capitalism. Yet, to its credit, it can open new sites for transforming the oppressed social conditions of marginalized groups through ideology critique and consciousness-raising practices. But postmodern critique will be most effective in this regard when it centers its analysis around a critique of existing capitalist social relations. We don't want to downplay the effectiveness of, say, queer pedagogy in offering a powerful critique of capitalism through a deconstruction of the social and cultural myths pervasively at work that legitimize heteronormativity and demonize other sex/gender orientations and identities. It can challenge rather forcefully the social construction of gender/sex roles that men and women have been forced to accept by exposing how heterosexuality supports ideologies geared toward stabilizing the social division of labor. Queer pedagogy articulates a multiplicity of gender roles, identities, and desires that exist beyond the biologically regulated concepts of male and female—concepts that ensure the production and reproduction of labor in maintaining social inequality.

Conclusion

As the third millennium unfolds, leaving behind a centuries-rich legacy of social and political history, the triumphant victories and bitter failures of revolutionary struggles remain forever sketched in our memories. Yet the fight for a socialist alternative to the current capitalist reality is taking place at a time when the manufacturing of capitalist ideologies under the banner of ludic postmodernism in academia ensures, rather than impedes, the flow of capital and the uninterrupted business-as-usual economic, cultural and environmental exploitation backed by neoliberal social and economic policies.

Marxist-Leninism's success in effectively challenging capitalism has been interrupted by the market-Leninist ideologues of state capitalism. Although its exponents cry out for the abandonment of the welfare state, the deregulation of the market, and the abolition of social programs, they argue for strident state protection, in the boldest Hayekian fashion imaginable, when it comes to protecting the spontaneity of the marketplace. Today, few revolutions and revolutionary ideas escape the profit-hungry claws of predatory capitalism unscathed. Figures associated with Marxism have been reduced to fodder for advertisements: Che Guevara's revolutionary ideals are inverted by chainfood restaurants such as Taco Bell where, in a series of commercials, he is depicted as a Chihuahua wearing a beret and selling the new revolutionary "Gordita" taco to the masses. A "Cabezol Cerveza" billboard sign on Sunset Strip in Los Angeles that reads, "Is Stalin buried in a Communist plot?" periodically revives the murderous ghost of Stalin and the Communist Party as a way of discrediting anticapitalist struggles. Referring to the new anarchist anti-establishment rock band, *Chumbawamba*, which recently signed with EMI Records, Adam Bregman writes that

> multinational corporations [are] skillfully turning rebellion into profit. If the biggies can buy up leftist newspapers, black-separatist rap acts and anarchist collectives and turn them into another source of capital for themselves and their stockholders, is no-one immune to their fat checks? Is it some weird, modern form of progress when corporations sell products that endorse anarchy, or another case of their unchecked dominance over every sector of the economy?[94]

We must not forget that even an end to capitalist social relations of production does not necessarily guarantee an end to the circulation of capital. This is because, as István Mészáros explains, "capital is a command system whose mode of functioning is accumulation-oriented, and the accumulation can be secured in a number of different ways."[95] For this reason, we must also not underestimate the power of capital which possesses the capacity to temporarily absorb its internal contradictions by disarming anticapitalist ideas and socialist movements. Capitalism offers us the illusion of democracy by separating political rights from economic rights, and conceals economic inequalities by depicting itself as democratic.[96] It accomplishes this by creating a democratic political atmosphere but only up to the point where it does not threaten its economic order. Ellen Meiksins Wood argues that "Capitalism can tolerate democracy because capitalists control the labor of others not by means of exclusive political rights but by means of exclusive property." Wood goes on to argue that "in its best and most democratic forms, capitalism can, and must, confine equality to a separate political sphere which does not, and must not, intrude into the economic sphere or subvert economic inequality."[97]

Postmodernists and neoliberals alike, who have temporarily succeeded in retiring the history of class struggle to the graveyard of failed social revolutions, have become customarily blind to the pale ghost of Marx still hovering protectively over the horizon of humankind's hopes and dreams. Some harbor a desperate wish for Marx be to be disinterred and brought back to life in a commodified state, so he can participate in the ideological polarization of capital's rule, as a reincarnated threat to capitalism's social and economic order. The return of the demon seed of Marx would only ensure the progress of capital's expansion. If Marx had never existed, capital would have to invent him, for such ritual slayings are always, to borrow the words of Ian McKay, "in the interests of the mental health of each new corn-fed, rosy-cheeked bourgeois gen-

eration."[98] We believe that Marxist ideas will continue to play a crucial ro.
in the academic and political arena in the years to come.

As a counter-praxis to capital, we envision a type of social movement ι.
ionism recently discussed by Kim Moody. Social movement unionism uses the
power of organized workers to mobilize the poor, the casualized workers, and
the unemployed as well as neighborhood organizations. This is a far cry from
the old business-union service model, which is often seen as just another labor
aristocracy that remains largely circumscribed by what goes on within the factory gates. Social movement unionism attempts to mobilize the less well organized sectors of the working class. Here, the members participate in shaping the
union's agenda and democratic workplace organization, fighting to eliminate
racial and gender inequalities in job sites and struggles to ensure social justice
for the disabled. Unions must fight for common demands among workers in all
countries. In fact, common cross-border activities must be designed to destroy
transnational markets. What is important about Moody's vision of social movement unionism is its emphasis on becoming part of a transnational worker network.

Social movement unionism is an approach that significantly moves beyond
mere reformism, as in the standard reformist attempts to overcome the fragmentation of the working class through a stress on diversity, through a reform
of the old mass party system. Unions must continue to defend welfare measures,
health care provisions, employment benefits and existing public services and the
gains of women, ethnic minorities, the disabled, and gays and lesbians. At the
same time, it should be recognized that the counterforce to capital's job-
destroying tendencies is length of working time. An effective campaign for
shorter work time must be worldwide and, as Moody asserts, must resist de
facto wage cuts. Hourly wages must be increased proportionately as hours are
reduced. Moody is at pains to point out that the social movement unionism that
he endorses is critical of liberal-populist 'stakeholder' capitalism, which emphasizes a social contract between capital and 'civil society' or the 'Third Sector' of
non-governmental organizations.

We agree with Moody that Left alternatives such as stakeholder capitalism
and civil society/Third sector counterforce movements are not enough. We need
an approach that prefigures a deeper and more international socialist politics,
such as social movement unionism. The new socialism needs to be more international, as Che Guevara envisioned, and should contribute actively to the recomposition of regional groupings capable of opposing the internationalism of
people to that of capital. We need to focus on the differentiations occurring in
the process of capitalist expansion, precisely at the interface between the global
and the national aspects of this reality, and on the tension between general
struggles and particular, regional efforts.

In order to place liberation on the agenda of history again, we need to
re-enchant the project of critical educational theory. As educationalists whose
work is underwritten by critical pedagogy, we need to conscript such a rethinking into the development of a critical pedagogy that is capable of devising a
transition beyond capitalism.[99] The stakes in the debate are considerable. In or-

der to make possible the type of dialogue needed for strategizing within today's global arena, the advancement beyond capitalism and toward universal socialism requires some important choices for the Left. Samir Amin has suggested some important directions: charging the World Trade Organization with planning access to the use of major natural resources of the globe and the prices of raw materials, and with planning targets for interregional trade in industrial products; improving the incomes of disadvantaged workers; and reconciling general competitiveness with distributional criteria favoring disadvantaged regions of the globe.[100] In addition, excess finance must be channeled toward productive investment in peripheral countries, accompanied by a rethinking of the international monetary system in the direction of regional monetary systems that guarantee the relative stability of exchange rates, etc. A prerequisite is that the bourgeois Left—largely inconscient of its own reactive theoretical moves—confronts the contradictions inherent in the politics of its own theorizing.

Capitalism's supposed inevitability, and history's presumed failure to defang existing capitalist social relations, have brought about an ethos of panic and despair among the Left. The conventional wisdom—even among many former members of the Marxist intelligentsia—is that there is no realistic alternative to the market. The collapse of Soviet communism and the decline of Marxist parties and movements in many parts of the world has, in the minds of many, once and for all refuted Marx and his heirs and has contributed to the current refusal among many Leftist constituencies to take anticapitalist struggle seriously. Conveniently forgotten by our archivists of historical memory is the fact that Soviet communism was, in effect, an overly bureaucratized and cumbersome (not to mention corrupt) form of state capitalism. As Ian Birchall remarks:

> 'Socialism in one country' failed, not because it abolished the market, but because it failed to escape the world market that Marx so vividly described, a world market mediated through the arms race and international trade, which turned the workers' state into its opposite, bureaucratic and tyrannical state capitalism.[101]

Historical alternatives to capitalism are considered to exist only in the realm of science fiction. A politically motivated forgetfulness surrounds many examples of working-class self-activity, such as the workers' democracy of the Paris Commune of 1871; the first years of the Russian Revolution; Spain in 1936 to 1937; Hungary in 1956; the French action committees of 1968; the Chilean *cordones* of 1973; the Portuguese workers' commissions of 1974 to 1975; the Iranian *Shoras* of 1979; and the initial rise of *Solidarity* in Poland in 1980.

The siren call of the postmodernists—that we should reject a systematic explanation of material reality and the world historical struggle to abolish its exploitative systems of production—follows their conviction that the social division of labor, and the surplus labor that structures it, has been replaced by information, and that the circulation and the consumption of "sign value" has superseded the practices and relations of production. In admonishing us to believe that labor has been replaced by technology as the basis of social wealth, postmodernists tread dangerously close to simply updating the ideology of the dominant regime of capital and wage-labor and facilitating its transnational expansion under the guise of exposing representation's "metaphysics of presence." According to Perry Anderson, the "long downswing" from postwar capitalism to the 1980s, and the "battering down of labour in core regions, outsourcing of plants to cheap wage locations in the periphery, displacement of investment into services and communications, expansion of military expenditure, and vertiginous rise in the relative weight of financial speculation at the expense of innovative production" brought about "all the deteriorated elements of the postmodern," such as "unbridled nouveau riche display, teleprompt statecraft, boll-weevil consensus."[102] Anderson writes that with the advent of postmodernism, oppositional politics aligned against capitalism have all but disappeared:

> The universal triumph of capital signifies more than just a defeat for all those forces once arrayed against it, although it is also that. Its deeper sense lies in the cancellation of political alternatives. Modernity comes to an end, as Jameson observes, when it loses any antonym. The possibility of other social orders was an essential horizon of modernism. Once that vanishes, something like postmodernism is in place.[103]

The inexorably downward spiral toward dystopian resignation, brought about by the postmodernist assault on material reality and any radical attempts to change it, must be confronted by radical hope. It must be confronted by a "contraband pedagogy" that conjugates hope with revolutionary struggle in the search for an alternative to capitalist social relations of exploitation. One primary objective should be the translocation of past socialist struggles into the corridors of our historical imaginations, as a condition of possibility for transformative change and a necessary prelude to our own history-making activity. Such an objective would overcome despair in the face of capital's destructive and imperializing force by outbidding it with an affirmation of collective solidarity.

While mainstream pedagogy has conjured away the idea that education should play a central role in the struggle for social justice, contraband pedagogy rests on the twin notions that the macrostructural frameworks of capitalism do not fully annihilate possibilities for resistance and revolution, and that modernity has not been fully consummated. Contraband pedagogy is not reconciled to the postmodern insight that authentic agency has been eclipsed by the systems of symbolic mediation that create desires that can only be false or always already alienating. We still remain loyal to the conviction that the responsible, self-reflecting subject can exist and that self-knowledge can lead to self-determination and eventually revolutionary praxis. Contraband pedagogy does not seek to help individuals empower themselves. Empowerment is a liberal option that enables people to gain control over the conditions of their daily lives. Contraband pedagogy is not about gaining control of the 'always already' but is about struggling and transforming the conditions that delimit the horizons of daily life and prohibit the acquisition of the material necessities that would enable a decent and just livelihood for all the toilers of the world. Sometimes this struggle calls for armed resistance and opposition. Sometimes it calls for negotiation.

Contraband pedagogy's deployment as a weapon in the fight against globalization can benefit from an engagement with the new wave of Marxist educational scholarship in Britain, particularly the work of educationalists Mike Cole, Andy Green, Dave Hill, and Glenn Rikowski. While lacking the tradition of Marxist scholarship that has benefited education scholars in Great Britain, the educational Left in the United States can nevertheless begin to revitalize educational reform efforts by assessing the limitations of prevailing Leftist paradigms built around postmodernist forms of cultural critique. Given the exacerbating contradictions of capital—seen in the growing numbers of homeless in the streets of major U.S. cities, the increasing vulnerability of the middle class, and in the growth of the militarized, gated communities of the ruling class—a socialist alternative may not seem as farfetched as it does today among the vast majority of United States workers.

Like many other educators and activists, we face a daunting challenge. In Los Angeles, where we live and labor, we face not so much a bourgeois-driven apathy from our colleagues and students as an overwhelmingly active despair, exacerbated by the entrenched belief that the ideological hegemony and social practices of the United States capitalist class is far too powerful to resist (even though at some level most people recognize that all forms of hegemony are leaky). Outraged by the vainglorious attempts of politicians to propagate the myth that the United States represents the best of all possible worlds, and disgusted by the swelling numbers of United States citizens who are following in the ideological footsteps of Christian fundamentalist politicians such as Pat Robertson (whose recent televised address to millions of U.S. citizens included a warning that a gay activist event held in Florida could provoke God to send an asteroid to destroy the earth, and joins similar condemnations of public schooling as an un-American socialist enterprise that is antifamily and that teaches students to reject God and the marketplace in favor of the perils of drugs, sexual promiscuity, homosexuality and union membership), many of us spend time teaching in other countries, including Latin America, where we feel our revolutionary politics has more potential to effect a measure of material change in the lives of the toilers of the world. While to a certain extent and in certain contexts this might be true, we believe that efforts to dismantle the exploitative relations of transnational capitalism have to begin here. As one Central American *campesina* activist, Elvia Alvarado, puts it:

> It's hard to think of change taking place in Central America without there first being changes in the United States. As we say in Honduras, "*Sin el perro, no hay rabia*"—without the dog, there wouldn't be rabies.
> So you Americans who really want to help the poor have to change your own government first. You Americans who want to see an end to hunger and poverty have to take a stand. You have to fight just like we're fighting—even harder. You have to be ready to be jailed, to be abused, to be repressed. And you have to have the character, the courage, the morale, and the spirit to confront whatever comes your way.

If you say, "Oh, the United States is so big and powerful, there's nothing we can do to change it," then why bother talking about solidarity? If you think like that, you start to feel insignificant and your spirit dies. That's very dangerous. For as long as we keep our spirits high, we continue to struggle.

We campesinos are used to planting seeds and waiting to see if the seeds bear fruit. We're used to working on harsh soil. And when our crops don't grow, we're used to planting again and again until they take hold. Like us, you must learn to persist.[104]

We are hardpressed to find a better clarion call for the contraband pedagogy we are advocating.

Notes

1. Karl Marx, *Capital Vol. 1* (New York: Vintage Books, 1977), 159.

2. Julie Graham and Katherine Gibson, "Waiting for the Revolution, or How to Smash Capitalism while Working at Home in Your Spare Time," in *Marxism in the Postmodern Age: Confronting the New World Order*, ed. Antonio Callari, Stephen Cullenberg and Carole Biewener (New York: Guilford Press, 1995), 190.

3. Aijaz Ahmad, "Issues of Class and Culture: An Interview Conducted by Ellen Meiksins Wood," in *Defense of History: Marxism and the Postmodern Agenda*, ed. Ellen Meiksins Wood and John Bellamy Foster (New York: Monthly Review Press, 1997), 102.

4. Albert Einstein, "Why Socialism?" *Monthly Review* 50, no. 1 (1998): 5.

5. See David C. Korten, "The Mystic Victory of Market Capitalism," in *The Case against the Global Economy and for a Turn toward the Local*, ed. Jerry Mander and Edward Goldsmith (San Francisco: Sierra Club Books, 1996), 183–191.

6. Samir Amin, "Imperialism and Culturalism Complement Each Other," *Monthly Review* 48, no. 2 (1996): 3.

7. See Kim Moody, *Workers in a Lean World: Unionism in the International Economy* (London: Verso Books, 1997).

8. Doug Henwood, "The Bull's Sour 16," *The Nation* 267, no. 7 (1998): 5.

9. See Peter McLaren, "The Pedagogy of Che Guevara: Critical Pedagogy and Globalization—Thirty Years after Che," *Cultural Circles*, no. 3 (1998): 28–103 and "Revolutionary Pedagogy in Post-Revolutionary Times: Rethinking the Political Economy of Critical Education," *Educational Theory* 48, no. 4 (fall 1998): 431–462.

10. Earlier versions of this chapter have appeared under the title of "Critical Pedagogy, Postmodernism, and the Retreat from Class: Towards a Contraband Pedagogy" in *Postmodern Excess in Educational Theory: Education and the Politics of Human Resistance* ed. Dave Hill, Peter McLaren, Mike Cole, and Glenn Rikowski (London: Tufnell Press, 1999), 167–202, and in *Theoria: A Journal of Social and Political Theory*, no. 93 (June 1999): 83–115.

11. See Sharon Zukin, *Landscapes of Power: From Detroit to Disneyland* (Berkeley: University of California Press, 1991).

12. Moody, *Workers in a Lean World*, 287.

13. Robert Brenner, "The Economics of Global Turbulence," *New Left Review* 229 (1998): 207.

14. Brenner, "The Economics," 238.

15. Moody, *Workers in a Lean World*, 308.

16. See Marx, *Capital Vol. 1*.

17. Michael Parenti, *America Besieged* (San Francisco: City Lights Books, 1998), 84–145.

18. See Saskia Sassen, *Globalization and Its Discontents* (New York: New Press, 1998).

19. See Sassen, *Globalization and its Discontents.*

20. Moody, *Workers in a Lean World*, 296–297.

21. David Harvey, "The Geography of the Manifesto," in *Socialist Register: The Communist Manifesto Now*, ed. Leo Panitch and Colin Leys (New York: Monthly Review Press, 1998), 68.

22. Our claim is that while globalization is not a new phenomenon, its temporal character has been affected by instant financial transactions.

23. See Andy Green, "Postmodernism and State Education," *Journal of Education Policy* 9, no. 1 (January–February 1994): 67–83.

24. Perry Anderson, *The Origins of Postmodernity* (London: Verso Books, 1998), 115.

25. See Stanley Aronowitz and Henry Giroux, *Postmodern Education* (Minneapolis: University of Minnesota Press, 1991); Patti Lather, *Getting Smart: Feminist Research and Pedagogy with/in the Postmodern* (London: Routledge, 1991); William Doll Jr., *A Post-Modern Perspective on Curriculum* (New York: Teachers College Press, 1993); Joe Kincheloe, *Towards a Critical Politics of Teacher Thinking: Mapping the Postmodern* (Westport, Conn.: Bergin & Garvey, 1993); Robin Usher and Richard Edwards, *Postmodernism and Education* (London: Routledge, 1994); Andy Hargreaves, *Changing Teachers, Changing Times* (New York: Teachers College Press, 1994); Henry Giroux and Peter McLaren, *Between Borders: Pedagogy and the Politics of Cultural Studies* (London: Routledge, 1994); Richard Smith and Philip Wexler, eds., *After Post Modernism* (London: Falmer Press, 1995).

26. See Patti Lather, "Critical Pedagogy and Its Complicities: A Praxis of Stuck Places," *Educational Theory* 48, no. 4 (fall 1998): 487–498.

27. See Peter McLaren, *Critical Pedagogy and Predatory Culture: Oppositional Politics in a Postmodern Era* (London: Routledge, 1995) and *Revolutionary Multiculturalism: Pedagogies of Dissent for the New Millennium* (Boulder, Colo.: Westview Press, 1997); Teresa L. Ebert, *Ludic Feminism and After: Postmodernism, Desire, and Labor in Late Capitalism* (Ann Arbor: University of Michigan Press, 1996); Mike Cole and Dave Hill, "Games of Despair and Rhetorics of Resistance: Postmodernism, Education and Reaction, *British Journal of Sociology of Education* 16, no. 2 (1995): 165–183; Mike Cole, Dave Hill, and Glenn Rikowski, "Between Postmodernism and Nowhere: The Predicament of the Postmodernist, " *British Journal of Educational Studies* 45, no. 2 (1997): 187–200.

28. Aijaz Ahmad, "The Communist Manifesto and the Problem of Universality," *Monthly Review* 50, no. 2 (1998): 22.

29. Samir Amin, *Capitalism in the Age of Globalization* (London: Zed Books, 1997), 151.

30. See, for example, Michael W. Apple, *Cultural Politics and Education* (New York: Teachers College Press, 1996); Michael W. Apple, *Official Knowledge: Democratic Education in a Conservative Age* (New York: Routledge & Kegan Paul, 1993); Henry A. Giroux, *Border Crossings: Cultural Workers and the Politics of Education* (New York: Routledge, 1992); Richard A. Brosio, *A Radical Democratic Critique of Capitalist Education* (New York: Peter Lang, 1994); Henry A. Giroux, *Teachers as Intellectuals: Towards a Critical Pedagogy of Learning* (South Hadley, Mass.: Bergin & Garvey, 1988); Geoff Whitty, *Sociology and School Knowledge: Curriculum Theory, Research and Politics* (London: Methuen Books, 1985).

31. See Mike Cole, ed., *Bowles and Gintis Revisited: Correspondence and Contradictions in Educational Theory* (London: Falmer Press, 1988).

32. Carole A. Stabile, "Pedagogues, Pedagogy, and Political Struggles," in *Class Issues: Pedagogy, Cultural Studies, and the Public Sphere*, ed. Amitava Kumar (New York: New York University Press, 1997), 209.

33. This observation comes from Dave Hill, in a personal communication.

34. Gary Teeple, *Globalization and the Decline of Social Reform* (New Jersey: Humanities Press, 1995).

35. See Moody, *Workers in a Lean World.*

36. James Petras and Chronis Polychroniou, "Capitalist Transformation: The Relevance of and Challenges to Marxism," in *Marxism Today: Essays on Capitalism, Socialism, and Strategies for Social Change*, ed. Chronis Polychroniou and Harry R. Targ (London: Praeger, 1996), 101.

37. See Nathan Gardels, "Globalization with a Human Face," *New Perspectives Quarterly* 14, no. 4 (1997): 48–49.

38. See John Fornäs, *Cultural Theory and Late Modernity* (London: Sage, 1995).

39. Fornäs, *Cultural Theory*, 220.

40. See Andy Green, "Postmodernism and State Education," 67–83.

41. See Ebert, *Ludic Feminism.*

42. See Mike Cole and Dave Hill, "Games of Despair," 165–183.

43. Rick Joines, "The Academic Left Today," *Political Affairs* 76, no. 6 (1997): 30.

44. See Boris Frankel, "Confronting Neoliberal Regimes: The Post-Marxist Embrace of Populism and Realpolitik," *New Left Review*, no. 226 (1997): 57–92.

45. Samir Amin, *Spectres of Capitalism: A Critique of Current Intellectual Fashions* (New York: Monthly Review Press, 1998), 103.

46. Anti-essentialism and antifoundationalism can be characterized as a postmodern philosophical position that criticizes the notion that reality exists as an entity independent of appearances.

47. Cited in Da Cunha, Oliveria Maria Gomez, "Black Movements and the 'Politics of Identity' in Brazil," in *Cultures of Politics, Politics of Culture: Re–visioning Latin American Social Movements*, ed. Sonia L. Alvarez, Evelina Dagnino, and Arturo Escobar (Boulder, Colo.: Westview Press, 1998), 243.

48. See Amin, *Spectres of Capitalism.*

49. Barbara Ehrenreich, "Beyond Monica—the Future of Clinton's Past," *The Nation* 267, no. 7 (1998): 13.

50. Ebert, *Ludic Feminism*, 47.

51. Carl Boggs, "The Great Retreat: Decline of the Public Sphere in the Late Twentieth Century," *Theory and Society* 26 (1997): 767.

52. Hilary Wainwright, *Arguments for a New Left: Answering the Free Market Right* (London: Blackwell, 1994), 100.

53. See Ziauddin Sardar, *Postmodernism and the Other: The New Imperialism of Western Culture* (London: Pluto, 1998).

54. See Terry Eagleton, *The Illusions of Postmodernism* (Malden, Mass.: Blackwell, 1996); McLaren, *Critical Pedagogy and Predatory Culture*; Green, "Postmodernism and State Education," 67–83.

55. See Ahmad, "The Communist Manifesto," 21–22.

56. Amin, *Capitalism, Globalization*, 151.

57. Sardar, *Postmodernism and the Other*, 86.

58. See Dave Hill and Mike Cole, "Marxist State Theory and State Autonomy Theory: The Case of 'Race' Education in Initial Teacher Education," *Journal of Educational Policy* 10, no. 2 (1995): 221–232; Glenn Rikowski, "Left Alone: End Time for

Marxist Educational Theory?" *British Journal of Sociology of Education* 17, no. 4 (December 1996): 415–451.

59. Alex Callinicos, *Against Postmodernism: A Marxist Critique* (New York: St. Martin's Press, 1989), 36.

60. Alex Callinicos, *Theories and Narratives: Reflections on the Philosophy of History* (Durham, N.C.: Duke University Press, 1995), 39.

61. See Eagleton, *The Illusions*.

62. Eagleton, *The Illusions*, 65.

63. See Paul Gilroy, *There Ain't No Black in the Union Jack: The Cultural Politics of Race and Nation* (Chicago: University of Chicago Press, 1991).

64. Amin, *Capitalism, Globalization*, 103.

65. Amin, *Capitalism, Globalization*, 137.

66. Rick Joines, "Derrida's Ante and the Call of Marxist Political Philosophy," *Cultural Logic,* 2001, <http://eserver.org/projects/clogic/3–1%262/joins.html> (July 2001), 7.

67. Joines, "Derrida's Ante," 9.

68. Patti Lather, "Ten Years Later, Yet Again: Critical Pedagogy and Its Complicities," in *Feminist Engagements: Reading, Resisting, and Revisioning Male Theorists in Education and Cultural Studies,* ed. Kathleen Weiler (New York: Routledge, 2001), 183–195.

69. Ralph Rentiera, in a personal communication.

70. Joines, "Derrida's Ante," 12.

71. Amin, *Capitalism, Globalization*, 137.

72. Sherry Ortner, "Identities: The Hidden Life of Class," *Journal of Anthropological Research* 54, no. 1 (1998), 8–9.

73. Ortner, "Identities," 9.

74. Ortner, "Identities," 4.

75. Ortner, "Identities," 14.

76. Ellen Meiksins Wood, "The Communist Manifesto after 150 Years," *Monthly Review* 50, no. 1 (1998): 34.

77. Martha E. Gimenez, "The Production of Divisions: Gender Struggles under Capitalism," in *Marxism in the Postmodern Age: Confronting the New World Order*, ed. Antonio Callari, Stephen Cullenberg and Carole Biewener (New York: Guilford Press, 1995), 262.

78. Carole A. Stabile, "Feminism without Guarantees: The Misalliances and Missed Alliances of Postmodernist Social Theory," in *Marxism in the Postmodern Age*, ed. Antonio Callari, Stephen Cullenberg and Carole Biewener (New York: Guilford Press, 1996), 289.

79. Gimenez, "The Production of Divisions," 258.

80. Samir Amin, "Spectres of Capitalism," 36–39. See Jürgen Habermas, *The Philosophical Discourse of Modernity: Twelve Lectures*, trans. F. Lawrence (Cambridge, Mass.: MIT Press, 1989); Mike Cole and Dave Hill, "Games of Despair," *British Journal of Sociology of Education* 16, no. 2 (June 1995): 165–183.

81. Roselyn W. Bologh and Leonard Mell, "Modernism, Postmodernism, and the New World (dis)Order: A Dialectical Analysis and Alternative," *Critical Sociology* 20, no. 2 (1994): 85.

82. Bologh and Mell, "Modernism, Postmodernism," 86.

83. See Kenan Malik, "Universalism and Difference: Race and the Postmodernists," *Race and Class* 37, no. 3 (January–March 1996): 1–17.

84. Ahmad, "The Communist Manifesto, 103.

85. See Malik, "Universalism and Difference", McLaren, *Revolutionary Multiculturalism*.

86. Parenti, *America Besieged*, 94.

87. Douglas Kellner, "The End of Orthodox Marxism," in *Marxism in the Postmodern Age: Confronting the New World Order*, ed. Antonio Callari, Stephen Cullenberg and Carole Biewener (New York: Guilford Press, 1995), 37.

88. See Ernesto Laclau and Chantal Mouffe, *Hegemony & Socialist Strategy: Towards a Radical Democratic Politics* (London: Verso Books, 1985).

89. Amin, "Imperialism and Culturalism," 8.

90. Amin, "Imperialism and Culturalism," 9–10.

91. Graham and Gibson, "Waiting for the Revolution," 59.

92. See Richard Wolff and Stephen Resnick, "Power, Property, and Class," *Socialist Review* 16, no. 2 (1986): 97–124.

93. Wolff and Resnick, "Power, Property, and Class," 120.

94. Adam Bregman, "All for One: Chumbawamba Sells Out to Help Out," *L.A. Weekly* 20, no. 19 (April 3–9, 1998): 43.

95. István Mészáros, "Globalizing Capital," *Monthly Review* 49, no. 2 (1998): 13.

96. Sam Bowles and Herb Gintis, *Schooling in Capitalist America: Educational Reform and the Contradictions of Economic Life* (New York: Basic Books, 1976).

97. Meiksins Wood, "The Communist Manifesto," 22.

98. Ian McKay, "The Many Deaths of Mr. Marx: Or, What Left Historians Might Contribute to Debates about the "Crises of Marxism," *Left History* 3.2 and 4.1 (1995–1996): 10.

99. McLaren, *Critical Pedagogy and Predatory Culture* and *Revolutionary Multiculturalism*.

100. See Amin, *Capitalism, Globalization*.

101. Ian Birchall, "The Manifesto Remains a Guide", *New Politics* 4, no. 4 (1998): 120.

102. Anderson, *Origins of Postmodernity*, 92.

103. Anderson, *Origins of Postmodernity*, 91–92.

104. Elvia Alvarado, *Don't Be Afraid Gringo: A Honduran Woman Speaks from the Heart*, trans. and ed. Medea Benjamin (New York: Harper and Row, 1987), 144.

Chapter 12

Postmodernism Adieu: Toward a Politics of Human Resistance

Peter McLaren, Dave Hill,
Mike Cole and Glenn Rikowski

Under the guise of a liberal heterogeneity with a front-line value of 'democracy,' the hegemonic market capitalist agenda has set in tandem a brutal abandonment of systems of social protection, longer working hours, reduced welfare benefits, a lessening of resources and freedom of maneuver, and a transformation of governments into security forces for multinational corporations.[1]

Over half the largest economies on the planet are not countries but multinational corporations that relentlessly scour the globe for places where workers can be exploited for cheaper and cheaper labor. However, just as workers are being encrypted by business and government elites into a more severe form of worldwide neocolonial status, they are at the same time being plagued by the consumer capitalist imperative to nourish recycled desires for new commodities (see Peter McLaren and Ramin Farahmandpur, chapter 11). Compelled to degrammaticalize their sensorium and function as irrational consumer-citizens unfettered by the discomfiting propinquity of reason and self-reflexivity, the oppressed are motivated by an unstoppable desire to consume. As a way of mitigating the pernicious malaise that accrues daily in the domains of unemployed misery and of employment in routinized and alienating jobs, in the law, in health, and in education, they dream of one day achieving a hallowed place in commodity utopia. It is in the interests of the corporations to keep this dream alive. Accordingly, many of the international accords (such as the Multinational Agreement on Investments) are negotiated behind closed doors so that the main purpose of the game—to facilitate the movement of money and production facilities across international borders in order to shore up profits and power for the few at the expense of the toil and labor of the many—can be kept out of the public eye. Others, like the Maastricht convergence criteria for the economies of the European Union, so confident of the supremacy of capitalist imperatives, are trumpeted as such—the depletion of social programs and of budget deficits being openly and publicly held to be incontestable.

At this millennial moment, postmodernism, with all its self-propelling capacity, has found a favorable constituency among neoconservatives and neoliberals—who, conjoining together (as Reaganites and Thatcherites and their successors) have enjoyed tremendous success at promoting an antigovernment, unregulated markets agenda, and whose representatives benefit the most from the extraterritoriality of capital. The supply-side politics of conservative politicians and their wealthy benefactors, who regularly turn a blind eye to market inequities or failure, has prompted wage stagnation, rising inequality, real and hidden unemployment, and anti-poor legislation across the capitalist world, both advanced and developing.

The growth in Britain and the United States over the last twenty-five years of right-wing think tanks and their pundits, to whom the media is more than willing to give a friendly hearing, has created a powerful infrastructure able and willing to promote a social and public policy agenda fundamentally based on unregulated markets and limited government, and the excision of government from macro-economic policy.[2] Cutbacks in social spending, which disproportionately affect the poor, will continue to drastically increase social tension in the years ahead (see Peter McLaren and Ramin Farahmandpur, chapter 11). According to Zygmunt Bauman, "One of the most seminal consequences of the new global freedom of movement is that it becomes increasingly difficult, perhaps altogether impossible, to re-forge social issues into effective collective action."[3] We are not so pessimistic. This new global freedom may apply particularly to finance capital,[4] but industrial capital is not nearly as mobile,[5] and while industrial action and protest action by individual social movements (and by coalitions of movements—see Dave Hill, Mike Sanders and Ted Hankin, chapter 8) clearly has its contingently located periods of amazing strength and of quietist retrenchment, the late 1990s and beginning of the twenty-first century have seen, across the United States and Western Europe, for example, highly successful industrial and progressive action, such as the UPS and Teamsters' action in the United States and the Anti-Poll Tax movement and riot in Britain.[6]

The right has subjectively adduced copious reasons why the poor should be held responsible for their own poverty. And their arguments become all the more powerful in an era of economic insecurity in which people are looking for somebody to blame. In September 1995, at San Francisco's Fairmount Hotel, five hundred of the world's leading politicians (including George Bush, George Shultz, and Margaret Thatcher), businessmen, and scientists gathered, at the invitation of Mikhail Gorbachev, to spend three days of discussion on the economic future of the planet. The future was summed up by the numbers '20 to 80.' It was proposed that 20 percent of the population of the planet was all that was needed to keep the world economy going. The 'global brain trust' at the Fairmount calculated that a fifth of all job-seekers will be enough to produce all the commodities and services that the world society will be able to afford. Since business leaders argued that it would be unreasonable to expect corporations to look after the unemployed, the bottom 80 percent will be left without jobs (with the exception of volunteer services) and therefore in need of narcoticization, of having their senses dulled down by the mass media machinery through a form of "tittytainment."[7] Europe and North America are eager to join the privatization movement and become part of that future 20 percent who will be lucky enough to be part of the ranks of the employed.

In the United States, the voucher initiative has become a neoliberal juggernaut, smashing through the infrastructure of public education. In England and Wales, while there is no formal voucher system, the combination of per capita funding for schools and 'open enrolment,' together with an increase in the number of different types of schools—including state schools owned and run by private companies ('choice,' for some)—have, in effect, instituted a quasi-voucher system.[8]

While the rhetoric of choice sounds appealing (working-class families can choose to send their children to a public or private school of their choice), the reality has serious implications that threaten to eviscerate the public sphere of education and, in the United States, turn it into a theme park for Christian Sunday School banality. When an African-American student, Tenasha Taylor, gave a speech in her English class at the private University School of Milwaukee, and proceeded to criticize what she perceived as racist practices at the school, she was suspended until the following fall. She sued the school on the grounds of free speech but lost when Federal Judge Terrance Evans argued that protections afforded by the Bill of Rights do not apply to private actors such as the University School.[9] Private schools in Milwaukee are often used to escape desegregation in a district where 60 percent of the students are African American. In some of the private Catholic schools, the proportion is 3 to 5 percent. In addition, private schools do not have to hire certified teachers, do not have to require college degrees for their teachers, do not have to release information on employee wages and benefits. Further, private schools are not required to release test scores or attendance or suspension or dropout rates. Religious private schools can fire teachers who do not support the religious views of the school, or who support abortion, who are gay, etc. Within private schools, teachers who teach that the Holocaust did not happen, or that evolution is a lie, will have an easier job to make their case unimpeded by objectivity, and will find that fewer bureaucratic obstacles stand between them and promoting the reactionary, racist agendas of new right enthusiasts.

From the perspective of the privateers/privatizers in the United States, the democratically controlled public school system with its structure of public weight and responsibility is little more than a 'socialist' practice and is, therefore, 'demonic.' In Britain, the Blair government's post-2001 general election victory invitation to dramatically extend the role of private business in the running of individual schools, supplementing the role of 'business' in running groups of schools (grouped in Education Action Zones), and 'failing' (democratically accountable) local education authorities, promises—or threatens—to replicate the U.S. experience.[10]

Sally Covington suggests that in the United States, vouchers will help to erode middle-to-upper class support for public education, since parents would save·more in taxes by reducing public expenditure on education than they would lose in decreased education subsidy for their children's education.[11] Vouchers also have strong anti-union implications by offering one way to break the power of public sector unions.[12] Vouchers play into the ideology of the wealthy and the powerful who support a minimalist social welfare state, and effectively disguise the exploitation of the poor and the inequality of the classes. The larger ideology that supports the anti-union, anti-government, and anti-public school constituencies denies that social problems are particular conjunctural problems, related to specific times and places. In other words, it denies that social problems are fundamentally structural and linked to the devastating social consequences of the free market. It denies that these social problems are directly related to institutional structures of power in society, and practices such as capital flight, industrial relocation, the reallocation of state resources toward subsidizing services and suburbs, and providing tax incentives for businesses.[13] The ideology that demonizes the poor for their poverty and calls for 'personal responsibility' among the disenfranchised, who survive in the margins and interstices of the social order, effectively polarizes the class structure and undermines collective mobility among the poor. Postmodernism plays into this logic of local initiatives over collective action (see Peter McLaren and Ramin Farahmandpur, chapter 11).

As the chapters of this volume have clearly shown, ghosted into postmodern theory is a promiscuous fascination with epistemological exoticisms, with difference, with schizophrenia and desire, with the return of the erstwhile eclipsed Other, with a subsumption of criticality within the spectacle, and with the fragmentation of unacknowledged commonalties and potential bases for oppositional force.

It is our wish to reclaim the best that Marxist analysis has to offer—as it has been able so successfully to track humanity's long and arduous journey from the extension of industrialism into what has been termed 'postindustrialism,' from market capitalism to monopoly capitalism, to multinational capitalism—and derail capital's progress before it leads to oblivion. We are not concerned here with a dialectical reading of the conditions of emergence of Marxist theory, only to stress that we continue to learn enduringly from Marx. We are not disinterring Marxism from the catacombs of history—it is, if not in the United States, a vibrant, living body of political and theoretical action and analysis (see Dave Hill, Mike Sanders and Ted Hankin, chapter 8). We are taking its defining principles and theoretical texts and seeing how historical shifts may be registered in them and creatively applied to present circumstances. Marxism is the best response to capitalism that exists. At this current historical juncture we are more subordinated by capital than in Marx's time,[14] and this should not be so much a cause for a paralyzing despair as an important opportunity to articulate the contradictions of capitalism and its unfolding (see Glenn Rikowski, chapter 6).

Somewhere between the recurring cycles of anticipated futures and reconstructed pasts, critical pedagogy needs to needs to bid *adieu* to postmodernism and to accomplish more than a voguish challenge (at the level of the mandatory doctrines of mainstream culture) to those dominant Eurocentric forms of education that have been acculturated in advanced capitalism and that so ardently imprison us. And while we agree that the dominant trope of the white, Western male as the narrativing subject of history must be challenged, and that individualism and agency linked to the autonomous subject be made more hybrid and heterogeneous, we must at the same time safeguard those communal forms through which subjectivity can be transformed into collective political agency. Agency cannot be relinquished for the prize of cynicism. In its attachment to the idea of identity as a transhistorical unconscious plasma unconnected to social relations of production, postmodernism has already conceded too much in the struggle for liberation by denying self-reflexive agency. It also has all but eclipsed the concept of the state (see Michael W. Apple and Geoff Whitty, chapter 4). It has also occluded the totality of patriarchy, virtually ignoring the intimate connections between women's position in society and in the paid workplace (see Jane Kelly, chapter 10). Dismissing objective knowledge in its valorization of the "conflict between discourses" (see Jane Kelly, chapter 10, including her critique of Patti Lather; also Peter McLaren and Ramin Farahmandpur's critique of Lather, in chapter 11), postmodern feminism fails to recognize the contributions of thinkers such as Alexandra Kollontai and Leon Trotsky, who both argued that women need to be liberated from unpaid domestic labor (see Jane Kelly, chapter 10).

And while critical pedagogy must certainly partake of a politics of critical mapping that challenges hegemonic forms of representation such as Eurocentrism and Western models of identity, and while it must also challenge the creation of coherent, transparent identities in which verisimilitude is connected to a master narrative of certainty, it must never fail to situate such a politics in a larger narrative of liberation from the constraints of capital (see Jenny Bourne, chapter 9). While we agree that narratives of liberation cannot be settled in advance, and that the complexities of the 'concrete historical instance' must be teased out in critical detail (see Michael W. Apple and Geoff Whitty, chapter 4), all pedagogies underwritten by a politics of liberation must nevertheless be underwritten by a critical utopianism and political praxis that take the concept of totality seriously. Underlayered by a conviction that inequalities are social and eliminable, critical pedagogy must remain amenable to arbitration and collective decision-making. We remain steadfastly committed to a dialectical approach, which situates reality as a process founded upon contradictions; one can understand the parts only in relation to their totality. And once such an understanding is acquired, agency is possible, if we understand agency to be the ability of people to change social structures over time.

The dialectical reality that we all face is that we are both inside of nature and outside of it. The signifier and the signified are not one and the same. While one cannot understand human needs and desires outside of a symbolic frame of reference, one also cannot escape the mediations of the economy and the reproduction of material life. Ruling ideologies are those that intervene in discourse to secure particular social configurations over others, creating dependent hierarchies that serve to contain hegemonically sliding signifiers of meaning and to halt the progress of historical understanding. Articulating mechanisms are always historically contingent but are secured by the specific activity of social forces. For instance, capital and its institutions are one such force that exists to contain the power of labor (see Michael Neary, chapter 7). Unpaid surplus labor is extracted from direct producers, determining the relationship between capital and labor and labor to itself; labor, in capital, is constitutive of the mediation of social relations (see Michael Neary, chapter 7; also Glenn Rikowski, chapter 6). We need a politics of representation, and a politics of identity, but even as we admit to this we also must at the same time admit to the necessity of recognizing that while the self is constituted through language and representation, all representation is conditioned by the history of social relations and class struggle. Postmodernism understands the first part of this proposition but ignores— sometimes willfully so—the second.

As educators who recognize that we need to build a society where socialism can flourish, we acknowledge that there are some immediate positions on globalization that critical educators and cultural workers can take. Some of these have recently been summarized by William Greider: global expansion must be made more stable and must abide by more realistic rules; the United States must give up its commitment to neocolonial capitalism; the new architecture for a global economy must not be fashioned mainly by bankers and economists but by social activists, poor nations, labor, and environmentalists; capital controls must moderate the behavior of investors; countries must be given sovereign self-protection; and floating exchange rates among national currencies must be abandoned. Since the persistent overcapacity in productive output has always led to the search for cheaper labor, wage incomes must be rebalanced with capital incomes; capital needs to be funneled into domestic industrial development and not just exports; sweatshops and child labor must be abandoned; the G-7 industrial nations must adopt emergency controls on capital; central banks should temporarily relax balance sheet rules for commercial banks; progrowth business executives should run the IMF and stop austerity plans; and the IMF and the World Bank should forgive the poorest nations for their debts.[15]

Ultimately, of course, these perspectives sound no more satisfying than those posed by Roberto Mangabeira Unger and Cornel West. Unger and West are in favor of a productivist program designed to "deepen democracy" while challenging "the stark divisions between vanguard and rearguard—between advanced and backward sectors of the economy."[16] They call this a "politics of tinkering"—"a broad-based and market-friendly effort to lift up the economic rearguard."[17] They envisage a venture capitalist enterprise that can be used to broaden the access of finance and technology through the establishment of independently administered venture-capital funds chartered to invest in the rearguard, a project that would involve diversifying investment portfolios, establishing the coexistence of private and social property, and a strengthening of labor laws. Unger and West refer to this as a form of "democratic experimentalism," a "motivated, sustained and cumulative tinkering with the institutionalist arrangements of the government and the economy" by an engaged and informed citizenry.[18]

Of course, there is something all too reformist in these proposals. Are these not unlike the strategies of the 'resistance postmodernists' (reactionary postmodernists of course eschew such questions), accommodating the imperatives of capital to the existing structures of exploitation while claiming to make minor particularistic adjustments in order to make them less harmful to those most vulnerable in our society? What, in this perspective, is to prevent neoliberals from continuing to threaten unemployment and competition in the labor market as a means of depressing wages and increasing the rate of exploitation and profit? (see Mike Cole and Dave Hill, chapter 5; also Jane Kelly, chapter 10.) Surely this position poses a major dilemma facing the Left today.

Martin Carnoy's recent introduction to *Pedagogy of the Heart* by Brazilian educator Paulo Freire,[19] captures some of the dynamics of this dilemma. On the one hand, Carnoy makes some complimentary remarks about Fernando Enrique Cardoso who, he claims, expanded educational enrollment and democratized educational policies while president, refashioning an involvement in politics of the masses of poor and marginalized, and who solidified democratic political stability. According to Carnoy, Cardoso wanted to bring about equalization of income and wealth by undoing the economic debt of the 1980s, and expanding political participation even if it is tilted toward neoliberal economic stabilization and delays equalization. Yet according to Carnoy, Paulo Freire believes that the process of equalization itself is needed to develop the Brazilian economy outside of global neoliberalism.

We believe that social democratic economic strategies such as those articulated by Unger, West, and Cardoso, by way of a social democratic "tinkering" with the economy (i.e., democratically distribute the social wealth), while well-intentioned, clearly ignore the crisis-ridden nature of global capitalism and end up as little more than a capitulation to the expansion of capital and the proliferation of labor-power surrendered to capital (see Glenn Rikowski, chapter 6).[20] This sounds very much like the challenge of 'Third Way' politicians such as Tony Blair and Bill Clinton—"figuring out how to make accommodating to globalization consistent with progressive social values."[21] We believe that this is the wrong challenge to be pitched by the Left because, as Leo Panitch notes, the "overarching priority will remain that of fostering the penetration of capitalist values into every dimension of state-society relations as well as every corner of the globe and every facet of human life."[22] Panitch articulates the problem as the failure of social democracy. He writes:

> an efficient capitalist state is, increasingly, what social democracy itself stands
> for today. It has adopted global competition as a goal, which the state must
> foster, rather than regarding it as a constraint which must eventually be over-
> come. Social democracy still recognizes the importance of liberal democratic
> institutions, but it has lost that broader democratic vision that originally im-

pelled socialists to try to use those institutions as building blocks for organizing societies on cooperative rather than competitive principles. So extensive is this accommodation to globalization that social democracy (incorporating as it does now most former Communists in Eastern Europe) is largely reduced, even in the face of continuing mass unemployment in Western Europe, to undercutting social benefits in order to advance labor-market flexibility while still promoting the new "cargo cult" of training. ("If you train them the jobs will come.") It is as though, seeing a man on the street, hungry and homeless, you approach his problem only through the optic of his not being motivated enough, entrepreneurial enough, skilled enough to get a job, rather than through the optic of there being something fundamentally wrong with the capitalist system. There is nothing much socialist in a value system that does not begin, morally, from the latter optic.[23]

Here we side with Freire, who writes:

> The criticism of capitalism I put forth, from an ethical point of view, derives as much from the educator as it does from the activist, which I seek to continue to be in my own way. My activism can never become dissociated from my theoretical work; on the contrary, the former has its tactics and strategies formulated on the latter. The moment we recognize that food production around the world could be sufficient to feed twice its population, it is desolating to realize the numbers of those who come into the world but do not stay, or those who do but are forced into early departure by hunger. My struggle against capitalism is founded on that—its intrinsic perversity, its antisolidarity nature.[24]

We are aware that socialism must assume many different forms. Yet the struggle ahead must never waver from the direct overthrow of current practices of global capitalism, and it must be a universal struggle because capital itself, while from its beginning being essentially international and global always has been, but has become to an unprecedented extent, a globalized system. In this sense it must remain fundamentally a politics of emancipation fired by forms of human resistance to the social domination of capital that simultaneously challenge social inequalities generated by capitalist markets.[25] Exploiting the inner contradiction within the capital relation (see Michael Neary, chapter 7), a new class of economic actors—from grassroots activists, workers, small-scale producers, cooperatives, to peasant collectives—must jointly transform the capitalist system. Since abstract labor creates forms of sociality that young people reject, it is imperative that young people—recognized as a specific form of human sociability (see Michael Neary, chapter 7)—be given the theoretical tools to develop a language of social critique and transformation. The struggle will also have to involve diverse social movements and worker-run enterprises that can wrest control of the economy from the multinational corporations. It is imperative that community and labor forces control the means of production. This will include workers councils and trade unions but also communities of self-interest— all of which must be profoundly internationalist in character.

In order to accomplish this, critical pedagogy will have to wrest itself away from bourgeois social theory to the extent that it recognizes some of its major danger points. One of the most confounding overstatements of postmodernism has been the notion that discourse does not correspond in any way with external reality. From this perspective it is difficult to capture the underlying structure of reality, especially in terms of its patterns and relations of exploitation, since it is not even postulated that an independently existing reality occurs at all or that the natural world exists independently of our knowledge of it. In our view, theories must in some fundamental way correspond with external reality or else they become superfluous appendages in the struggle for social justice. There are no timeless, ahistorical or pristine discourses out of which our pedagogies of liberation are to be constructed. Conversely, acknowledging that 'race' and gender and sexuality are 'socially constructed' or 'floating signifiers' does not imperil their everyday lived social reality—a reality that does not care whether 'race' and gender are social constructions or not. Postmodernists too often forget that we have become capitalized life forms (transformed into human capital) who remain centered by capital, even as self-reflexivity itself becomes inflected by capital (see Glenn Rikowski, chapter 6).

Our knowledge must be forged out of the flux and flow of the material world; it must be tested dialectically over time in the arena of praxis. Antiracism and antisexism as part of a pedagogy of liberation must employ dialectical reasoning and not be left to psychoanalytically based models (see Jenny Bourne, chapter 9). A nonreductionist dialectical materialism provides insights into the nature of society that are unavailable from any other perspective, and is indispensable as a weapon in the overthrow of the capitalist system. A theory of pedagogy can only be adequate to the struggle ahead if it takes into consideration the historical development of capitalism. Some of the insights of postmodernism can be conscripted into the struggle against globalized capital, as long as we are aware of their limitations within the broader context of theory-building in general (see Michael W. Apple and Geoff Whitty, chapter 4). Critical educators need an engagement with postmodernism since that can deepen the conceptual reservoirs of Marxist theories by pointing out the limitations of such thought. If this engagement is successful it must eventually banish postmodernist theory to the dustbin of history. Marxist theory has, for example in this volume, pungently and clearly addressed issues pertaining to feminism, transgendered identities, and antiracist struggle. Yet there remains much to accomplish in these areas. Postmodern theories provide a limited explanatory power in exploring such issues. But we want to be clear that unless feminism and identity politics cultivated in the soil of poststructuralism ally themselves more squarely with a politics of class struggle, their contributions will not nourish the revolutionary praxis necessary in the struggle ahead, and will, at best, be second-order contributions.

Notes

1. See Zygmunt Bauman, *Globalization: The Human Consequences* (New York: Columbia University Press, 1998).

2. Sally Covington, "How Conservative Philanthropies and Think Tanks Transform US Policy," *Cover Action Quarterly*, no. 63 (1998): 6–16.

3. Bauman, *Globalization*, 69.

4. See, for example, Roger Burbach, Orlando Nunez, and Boris Kagarlitsky, *Globalization and Its Discontents* (London: Pluto Press, 1997), 67–68. Mike Cole has argued that 'globalization' is used ideologically to justify competitiveness and modernization in the interests of British and global capitalism, in "Globalization, Modernization and Competitiveness: A Critique of the New Labour Project in Education," *International Studies in the Sociology of Education* 8, no. 3 (1998).

5. Ellen Meiksins Wood, "A Reply to A. Sivanandan," *Monthly Review Press* 48 (1997): 21–32.

6. See chapter 8. Also, Sheila Cohen and Kim Moody, "Unions, Strikes and Class Consciousness Today," in *Socialist Register 1998*, ed. Leo Panitch and Colin Leys (Rendlesham, U.K.: Merlin, 1998); Glenn Rikowski, *The Battle in Seattle* (London: Tufnell Press), and the pages of the Left and Marxist press, such as *Socialist* (formerly *Militant*), *Socialist Worker* and *Tribune* in Britain.

7. Hans-Pieter Martin and Harald Schumann, *The Global Trap: Globalization and the Assault on Democracy and Prosperity* (London: Zed Books, 1997).

8. See Dave Hill, "Equality in British Schooling: The Policy Context of the Reforms," in *Promoting Equality in Primary Schools*, ed. Mike Cole, Dave Hill and Saranjeet Shan (Brighton, U.K.: Institute for Education Policy Studies, 1997) also the chapters "Global Capital, Neo-Liberalism, and Privatisation: The Growth of Educational Inequality" and "Equality, Ideology and Education Policy," both in *Schooling and Equality: Fact, Concept and Policy*, ed. Dave Hill and Mike Cole (London: Kogan Page, 2001); also, Geoff Whitty, Sally Power and David Halpin, *Devolution and Choice in Education: The School, the State and the Market* (Buckingham, U.K.: Open University Press, 1998).

9. Barbara Miner, "Target: Public Education," *The Nation* 267, no. 18 (1998): 4–6.

10. Dave Hill, *New Labour and Education: Policy, Ideology and the Third Way* (London: Tufnell Press, 1999), also "Global Capital," "Equality, Ideology" and *Education, Education, Education: Capitalism, Socialism and the Third Way* (Brighton, U.K.: Institute for Education Policy Studies, 2002); Peter McLaren, Mike Cole, Dave Hill and Glenn Rikowski, "An Interview with Three UK Marxist Educational Theorists," *International Journal of Education Reform* 10, no. 2 (2001): 145–162.

11. Covington, "Conservative Philanthropies."

12. Covington, "Conservative Philanthropies"; Alex Molnar, *Giving the Kids the Business: The Commercialization of America's Schools* (Boulder, Colo.: Westview Press, 1996).

13. James Petras and Chronos Polychroniou, "Clinton and Volunteerism: The Poverty of American Social Policy at the End of the Century," *New Political Science* 20, no. 2 (1998): 223–231.

14. See Dave Hill, "State Theory and the Neo-Liberal Reconstruction of Schooling and Teacher Education: A Structuralist Neo-Marxist Critique of Postmodernist, Quasi-Postmodernist and Culturalist Neo-Marxist Theory," *The British Journal of Sociology of Education* 22, no. 1 (March 2001): 137–157.

15. William Greider, "The Global Crisis Deepens: Now What?" *The Nation* 267, no. 12 (1998): 11–16.

16. Roberto Mangabeira Unger and Cornel West, "Progressive Politics and What Lies Ahead," *The Nation* 267, no. 17 (1998): 13.

17. Unger and West, "Progressive Politics," 13.

18. Unger and West, "Progressive Politics," 15.

19. Martin Carnoy, "Foreword," in *Pedagogy of the Heart*, ed. Paulo Freire (New York: Continuum, 1998).

20. See also Rikowski, *Battle in Seattle*.

21. Leo Panitch, "'The State in a Changing World': Social Democratizing Global Capitalism?" *Monthly Review* 50, no. 5 (1998): 20.

22. Panitch, "The State," 20.

23. Panitch, "The State," 20–21.

24. Paulo Freire, ed., *Pedagogy of the Heart* (New York: Continuum, 1998), 88.

25. Moishe Postone, *Time, Labor and Social Domination: A Reinterpretation of Marx's Critical Theory* (Cambridge: Cambridge University Press, 1996).

Bibliography

Adnett, Nick. "Recent Education Reforms: Some Neglected Macroeconomics and Mis-applied Microeconomics." *Review of Policy Issues* 3, no. 3 (summer 1997): 59–77.

Adonis, Andrew, and Stephen Pollard. *A Class Act, the Myth of Britain's Classless Society.* London: Hamish Hamilton, 1997.

Ahmad, Aijaz. *In Theory: Classes, Nations, Literatures.* London: Verso, 1992.

———. "The Politics of Literary Postcoloniality." *Race and Class* 36, no. 3 (January–March 1995): 1–19.

———. "Interview I: Culture, Nationalism and the Role of Intellectuals." In *In Defense of History: Marxism and the Postmodern Age.* Edited by Ellen Meiksins Wood and John Bellamy Foster. New York: Monthly Review Press, 1997.

———. "Interview II: Issues of Class and Culture." In *In Defense of History: Marxism and the Postmodern Age.* Edited by Ellen Meiksins Wood and John Bellamy Foster. New York: Monthly Review Press, 1997.

———. "The Communist Manifesto and the Problem of Universality." *Monthly Review* 50, no. 2 (1998): 12–38.

Ainley, Pat. *Class and Skill: Changing Divisions of Knowledge and Labour.* London: Cassell, 1993.

Albritton, Robert. *Dialectics and Deconstruction in Political Economy.* New York: St. Martin's, 1999.

Allman, Paula. *Revolutionary Social Transformation: Democratic Hopes, Political Possibilities, and Critical Education.* Westport, Conn.: Bergin & Garvey, 1999.

———. "Foreword: Education on Fire!" In *Red Chalk: On Schooling, Capitalism and Politics.* Edited by Mike Cole, Dave Hill, Peter McLaren and Glenn Rikowski. Brighton, U.K.: Institute of Education Policy Studies, 2001.

———. *Critical Education against Global Capital: Karl Marx and Revolutionary Critical Education.* Westport, Conn.: Bergin & Garvey, 2001.

Allman, Paula, and John Wallis. "Gramsci's Challenge to the Politics of the Left in 'Our Times.'" *International Journal of Lifelong Learning Education* 14, no. 2 (March–April 1995): 120–143.

Altbach, Philip G. "Professors and Politics: An International Perspective." In *The Politics of Educators Work and Lives.* Edited by Mark B. Ginsburg. New York: Garland Publishing, 1995.

Althusser, Louis. "Ideology and Ideological State Apparatuses." In Louis Althusser, *Lenin and Philosophy and Other Essays.* London: New Left Books, 1971.

———. *Lenin and Philosophy and Other Essays.* London: New Left Books, 1971.

Alvarado, Elvia. *Don't Be Afraid Gringo: A Honduran Woman Speaks from the Heart.* Translated and edited by Medea Benjamin. New York: Harper and Row, 1987.

Amin, Samir. "Imperialism and Culturalism Compliment Each Other." *Monthly Review* 48, no. 2 (1996): 1–11.

———. *Capitalism in the Age of Globalization.* London: Zed Books, 1997.

———. *Spectres of Capitalism: A Critique of Current Intellectual Fashions.* New York: Monthly Review Press, 1998.

———. "Spectres of Capitalism: A Critique of Current Intellectual Fashions." *Monthly Review* 50, no. 1 (1998): 36–39.

Anderson, Perry. *The Origins of Postmodernity.* London: Verso Books, 1998.

Ansell-Pearson, Keith. *Viroid Life: Perspectives on Nietzsche and the Transhuman Condition.* London: Routledge, 1997.

———. "Viroid Life: On Machines, Technics and Evolution." In *Deleuze and Philosophy: The Difference Engineer.* Edited by Keith Ansell-Pearson. London: Routledge, 1997.

Apple, Michael W. *Ideology and Curriculum.* London: Routledge and Kegan Paul, 1979.

———. *Education and Power.* London: Ark Paperbacks, 1985.

———. *Official Knowledge: Democratic Education in a Conservative Age.* New York: Routledge and Kegan Paul, 1993.

———. *Education and Power.* New York: Routledge, 1995.

———. *Power/Knowledge/Pedagogy.* Boulder, Colo.: Westview Press, 1993.

———. "Remembering Capital: On the Connections Between French Fries and Education." *Journal of Curriculum Theorizing* 11, no. 1 (spring 1995): 113–128.

———. "Power, Meaning, and Identity." *British Journal of Sociology of Education* 17, no. 2 (June 1996): 125–144.

———. *Cultural Politics and Education.* New York: Teachers College Press, 1996.

———. "Can Critical Pedagogies Interrupt Rightist Policies?" *Educational Theory* 50, no. 2 (spring 2000): 229–254.

Aronowitz, Stanley. *The Politics of Identity.* New York: Routledge, 1992.

Aronowitz, Stanley, and Henry Giroux. *Education under Siege: The Conservative, Liberal and Radical Debate over Schooling.* London: Routledge and Kegan Paul, 1986.

———. *Postmodern Education: Politics, Culture, and Social Criticism.* Minneapolis: University of Minnesota Press, 1991.

Ash Ra Tempel. Dutch Radio broadcast, November 1996.

Atkinson, Elizabeth. "What Can Postmodern Thinking Do for Educational Research?" Paper presented at the annual meeting of the American Educational Research Association, New Orleans, April 2000.

———. "In Defence of Ideas, or Why 'What Works' Is Not Enough." *British Journal of Sociology of Education* 21, no. 3 (September 2000): 317–330.

———. "The National Literacy Strategy as Cultural Performance: Some Reflections on the Meaning(s) of Literacy in English Primary Classrooms." Paper presented at the joint meeting of the European Council for Educational Research and the Scottish Educational Research Association, Edinburgh, Scotland, September 2000.

———. "Behind the Enquiring Mind: Exploring the Transition from External to Internal Enquiry." *Reflective Practice* 1, no. 2 (2000): 149–164.

———. "The Promise of Uncertainty: Education, Postmodernism and the Politics of Possibility." *International Studies in Sociology of Education* 10, no. 1 (2000): 81–99.

———. "Critical Dissonance and Critical Schizophrenia: The Struggle between Policy Delivery and Policy Critique." *Research Intelligence*, no. 73 (November 2000): 14–17.

———. "The Responsible Anarchist: Postmodernism and Social Change." Paper presented to the Symposium "If We Aren't Pursuing Improvement, What Are We Doing?" At the annual meeting of the British Educational Research Association Conference, Cardiff University, Wales, September 7–9, 2000.

Atkinson, Elizabeth. "Deconstructing Boundaries: Out on the Inside?" *International Journal of Qualitative Studies in Education* 14, no. 3 (May–June 2001): 1–10.

———. "The Responsible Anarchist: Postmodernism and Social Change." *British Journal of Sociology of Education* 23, no. 1 (2002).

Baker, Kenneth. "A Bright New Term for London's Children." *Evening Standard*, March 30, 1990.

Ball, Stephen J. *Politics and Policy-Making in Education: Explorations in Policy Sociology*. London: Routledge, 1990.

———. *Education Policy*. Lewes, U.K.: Falmer Press, 1994.

———. *Education Reform: A Critical and Post-Structural Approach*. Buckingham, U.K.: Open University Press, 1994.

Banfield, Grant. "Schooling and the Spirit of Enterprise: Producing the Power to Labour." *Education and Social Justice* 2, no. 3 (summer 2000): 23–28.

Banks, Olive. *Parity and Prestige in English Secondary Education*. London: Routledge, 1955.

Barnard, Nick. "Most Research Is 'Waste of Time.'" *Times Educational Supplement* September 12, 1997.

Baudrillard, Jean. *The Illusion of the End*. Palo Alto, Calif.: Stanford University Press, 1995.

Bauman, Zygmunt. *Globalization: The Human Consequences*. New York: Columbia University Press, 1998.

Beechey, Veronica. *Unequal Work*. London: Verso, 1987.

Benn, Tony. *The Benn Diaries*. London: Arrow Books, 1996.

Benton, Ted. *The Rise and Fall of Structural Marxism: Althusser and His Influence*. London: Macmillan, 1984.

Bertsch, Charlie. "Pedagogy of the Depressed." *Bad Subjects*, no. 27 (September 1996), 7 pages at < http://eserver.org/bs/01/Bertsch.html.> (April 2001).

Bertsch, Charlie, and Joe Lockard. "Marx without Monsters." *Bad Subjects*, no. 45 (November 1999) at <http://english-www.hss.cmu.edu/bs/45/editors.html> (November 30, 1999).

Best, Steven, and Douglas Kellner. *Postmodern Theory: Critical Interrogations*. Basingstoke, U.K.: Macmillan, 1991.

Beyer, Landon E., and Daniel P. Liston. "Discourse or Moral Action? A Critique of Postmodernism." *Educational Theory* 42, no. 4 (fall 1992): 371–393.

Bhabha, Homi. "Interview with Homi Bhabha, The Third Space." In *Identity: Community, Culture, Difference*. Edited by Jonathan Rutherford. London: Lawrence & Wishart, 1990.

Biesta, Gert. "Say You Want a Revolution. . . . Suggestions for the Impossible Future of Critical Pedagogy." *Educational Theory* 48, no. 4 (fall 1998): 499–510.

Birchall, Ian. "The Manifesto Remains a Guide." *New Politics* 4, no. 4 (1998): 114–121.

Blackmore, Jill. "Breaking Out of Masculinist Politics in Education." In *Gender and Changing Education Management*. Edited by B. Limerick and Bob Lingard. Rydalmere, NSW: Hodder, 1995.

Blair, Tony. *The Third Way*. London: Fabian Society, 1998.

Blake, Nigel. "Between Postmodernism and Anti-Modernism: The Predicament of Educational Theory." *British Journal of Educational Studies* 44, no. 1 (March 1996): 371–393.

————. "A Postmodernism Worth Bothering About: A Rejoinder to Cole, Hill and Rikowski." *British Journal of Educational Studies* 45, no. 3 (September 1997): 293–305.

Blake, Nigel, Paul Smeyers, Richard Smith and Paul Standish. *Education in an Age of Nihilism*. London: Routledge-Falmer, 2000.

Blake, Nigel, and Richard Smith. "Beware a Totalising Society." *Times Educational Supplement*, October 10, 1997: 22.

Boggs, Carl. "The Great Retreat: Decline of the Public Sphere in the Late Twentieth Century." *Theory and Society* 26 (1997): 741–780.

Bologh, Roselyn W., and Leonard Mell. "Modernism, Postmodernism, and the New World (Dis)order: A Dialectical Analysis and Alternative." *Critical Sociology* 20, no. 2 (1994): 81–120.

Bonefeld, Werner. "Human Practice and Perversion: Between Autonomy and Structure." *Common Sense, Journal of the Edinburgh Conference of Socialist Economists* 15 (April 1994): 43–51.

————. "Capital as Subject and the Existence of Labour." In *Open Marxism, Volume III. Emancipating Marx*. Edited by Werner Bonefeld, Richard Gunn, John Holloway and Kosmas Psychopedis. London: Pluto, 1995.

Bonefeld, Werner, Richard Gunn and Kosmas Psychopedis, eds. *Open Marxism, Volume 1. Dialectics and History*. London: Pluto, 1992.

———— , eds. *Open Marxism, Volume II. Theory and Practice*. London: Pluto, 1992.

Bonefeld, Werner, Richard Gunn, John Holloway and Kosmas Psychopedis, eds. *Open Marxism Volume III. Emancipating Marx*. London: Pluto, 1995.

Boron, Atilio. "Embattled Legacy: Post-Marxism and the Social and Political Theory of Karl Marx." *Latin American Perspectives* 27, no. 4 (2000): 49–79.

Bourne, Jenny. "Cheerleaders and Ombudsmen: The Sociology of Race Relations in Britain." *Race and Class* 21, no. 4 (spring 1980): 331–352.

————. *Homelands of the Mind: Jewish Feminism and Identity Politics*. London: Institute for Race Relations (IRR), 1987.

————. *Towards an Anti-racist Feminism*. London: IRR, 1987.

————. "The War of the Words: The Political Correctness Debate." *Race and Class* 36, no. 3 (January–March 1995): 89–91.

Bowe, Richard, and Stephen J. Ball, with Ann Gold. *Reforming Education and Changing Schools*. London: Routledge, 1992.

————. "The Policy Process and the Processes of Policy." In *Diversity and Change: Education, Policy and Selection*. Edited by John Ahier, Ben Cosin and Margaret Hales. London: Routledge, 1996.

Bowles, Sam, and Herb Gintis. *Schooling in Capitalist America: Educational Reform and the Contradictions of Economic Life*. New York: Basic Books, 1976.

Boyne, Richard, and Ali Rattansi, eds. *Postmodernism and Society*. London: Macmillan, 1990.

Bregman, Adam. "All for One: Chumbawamba Sells Out to Help Out." *L.A. Weekly* 20, no. 19 (April 3–9, 1998): 43.

Brenner, Robert. "The Economics of Global Turbulence." *New Left Review*, no. 229 (1998): 1–264.

Brosio, Richard. "One Marx, and the Centrality of the Historical Actor(s)." *Educational Theory* 35, no. 1 (winter 1985): 73–83.

————. "Capitalism's Emerging World Order: The Continuing Need for Theory and Brave Action by Citizen-Educators." *Educational Theory* 43, no. 4 (fall 1993): 467–482.

Brosio, Richard. *A Radical Democratic Critique of Capitalist Education.* New York: Peter Lang Publishing, 1994.

———. "Late Capitalism and Postmodernism: Educational Problems and Possibilities." *Studies in Philosophy and Education* 15, no. 1 (January–April 1996): 5–12.

———. *Philosophical Scaffolding for the Construction of Critical Democratic Education.* New York: Peter Lang Publishing, 2000.

Brown, Phillip, and Hugh Lauder. "Education, Economy and Social Change." *International Studies in the Sociology of Education* 1, no. 1 (1991): 3–24.

Brown, Sally, Jill Duffield and Shiela Riddell. "School Effectiveness Research: The Policy Makers' Tool for School Improvement?" *EERA Bulletin* (March 1995): 6–15.

Brown, Sally, Shiela Riddell and Jill Duffield. "Classroom Approaches to Learning and Teaching: The Social Class Dimension." Paper presented at the annual conference of the European Educational Research Association, Seville, Spain, September 1997.

Bruegel, Irene. "The Reserve Army of Labour, 1974–1979." In *Waged Work: A Reader.* Edited by Feminist Review. London: Virago, 1986.

Brunt, Rosalind "Bones in the Corset." *Marxism Today* (October 1988): 20–23.

Bryan, Beverly, S. Dadzie and S. Scafe. *The Heart of the Race: Black Women's Lives in Britain.* London: Virago, 1985.

Burbach, Roger, Orlando Nunez and Boris Kagarlitsky. *Globalization and Its Discontents.* London: Pluto Press, 1997.

Burke, Barry. "Karl Marx and Informal Education: What Significance Does Marx Have for Educators Today?" <http://infed.org/thinkers/et-marx.html> (November 6, 2000).

Butler, Judith. *Gender Trouble: Gender and the Subversion of Identity.* London: Routledge, 1990.

———. "Contingent Foundations: Feminism and the Question of 'Postmodernism.'" In *Feminists Theorize the Political.* Edited by Judith Butler and Joan Scott. New York: Routledge, 1992.

———. *Bodies That Matter: On the Discursive Limits of Sex.* London: Routledge, 1993.

———. *Excitable Speech: A Politics of the Performative.* London: Routledge, 1997.

———. "Merely Cultural." *New Left Review* 227 (1998): 33–44.

Callard, Frances. "The Body in Theory." *Environment and Planning D: Society and Space* 16 (1998): 387–400.

Callinicos, Alex. *Against Postmodernism: A Marxist Critique.* Cambridge, U.K.: Polity Press, 1989.

———. *Against Postmodernism: A Marxist Critique.* New York: St. Martin's, 1989.

———. *Race and Class.* London: Bookmarks, 1993.

———. *Theories and Narratives: Reflections on the Philosophy of History.* Durham, N.C.: Duke University Press, 1995.

———. *Social Theory: A Historical Introduction.* New York: New York University Press, 1999.

———. *Equality.* Cambridge, U.K.: Polity, 2000.

———, ed. *Marxist Theory.* Oxford: Oxford University Press, 1989.

Carnoy, Martin. "Foreword." In *Pedagogy of the Heart.* Edited by Paulo Freire. New York: Continuum, 1998.

Carvel, John. "5m Britons Living on the Breadline." *Guardian,* March 8, 2001.

Carvel, John. "Report from Social Trends 2001." *Guardian,* March 8, 2001.

Charter, David. "Schools Must Not Blur Boundary of Culture, Says Curriculum Chief." *Times,* February 8, 1996.

Chitty, Clyde. "The School Effectiveness Movement: Origins, Shortcomings and Future Possibilities." *The Curriculum Journal* 8, no. 1 (spring 1997): 45–62.

Chodorow, Nancy. *The Reproduction of Mothering: Psychoanalysis and the Sociology of Gender.* Berkeley: University of California Press, 1978.

Chomsky, Noam. *The Prosperous Few and the Restless Many.* Tuscon, Ariz.: Odonian Press, 1994.

Chubb, John E., and Terry M. Moe. *Politics, Markets, and America's Schools.* Washington, D.C.: Brookings Institution, 1990.

Clarke, Simon. *Keynesianism, Monetarism and the Crisis of the State.* Aldershot, U.K.: Edward Elgar, 1988.

———. *Marx, Marginalism and Modern Sociology.* London: Macmillan, 1991.

Cliff, Tony, and Donny Gluckstein. *The Labour Party: A Marxist History.* London: Bookmarks, 1996.

Cohen, Gerry A. "Review of A. W. Wood (Karl Marx)." *Mind* 92 (1983): 444.

Cohen, Phil. *Anti-racist Cultural Studies: A Curriculum Development Project in School and Community Education.* London: London University Institute of Education, 1986.

———. "The Perversions of Inheritance: Studies in the Making of Multi-racist Britain." In *Multi-racist Britain.* Edited by Phil Cohen and Harwant Bains. London: Macmillan, 1988.

———. *Monstrous Images, Perverse Reasons.* London: Centre for Multicultural Education, University of London Institute of Education, 1991.

———. "'It's Racism What Dunnit': Hidden Narratives in Theories of Racism." In *'Race', Culture and Difference.* Edited by James Donald and Ali Rattansi. London: Sage, 1992.

———. *Rethinking The Youth Question, Education, Labour and Cultural Studies.* Basingstoke, U.K.: Macmillan, 1997.

Cohen, Shiela, and Kim Moody. "Unions, Strikes and Class Consciousness Today." In *Socialist Register 1998.* Edited by Leo Panitch and Colin Leys. Rendlesham, U.K.: Merlin, 1998.

Cole, Mike. "From Reductionist Marxism and Revolutionary Socialism to Post-Liberal Democracy and Ambiguity: Some Comments on the Changing Political Philosophy of Bowles and Gintis." *British Journal of Sociology* 34, no. 3 (September 1988): 452–462.

———. "Racism, History and Educational Policy: From the Origins of the Welfare State to the Rise of the Radical Right." Unpublished Ph.D. thesis: Department of Sociology, University of Essex, 1992.

———. "Globalisation, Modernisation and Competitiveness: A Critique of the Labour Project in Education." *International Studies in Sociology of Education* 8, no. 3 (1998): 315–332.

———. "Globalisation, Modernisation and New Labour." In *Business, Business, Business: New Labour's Education Policy.* Edited by Martin Allen, Caroline Benn, Clyde Chitty, Mike Cole, Richard Hatcher, Nico Hirtt and Glenn Rikowski. London: Tufnell Press, 1999.

———. *Education, Equality and Human Rights: Issues of Gender, 'Race,' Sexuality, Special Needs and Social Class.* London: Routledge-Falmer, 2000.

———. "Time to Liberate the Mind: Primary Schools in the New Century." *Primary Teaching Studies* 11, no. 2 (autumn 2000): 4–9.

———. "Educational Postmodernism, Social Justice and Social Change: An Incompatible Ménage à Trois." *The School Field: International Journal of Theory and Research in Education* 12, nos. 1–2 (2001).

———. "Conclusion." In *Schooling and Equality: Fact, Concept and Policy.* Edited by Dave Hill and Mike Cole. London: Kogan Page, 2001.

Cole, Mike, ed. *Bowles and Gintis Revisited: Correspondence and Contradiction in Educational Theory.* Lewes, U.K.: Falmer Press, 1988.

Cole, Mike, and Dave Hill. "Postmodernism, Education and Contemporary Capitalism: A Materialist Critique." In *Teacher Education and Values Education.* Edited by Odete Valente, Amália Bárrios, Alberto Gaspas and V. D. Teodoro. Lisbon: Faculty of Science, Department of Education, University of Lisbon, 1995.

————. "Games of Despair and Rhetorics of Resistance: Postmodernism, Education and Reaction." *British Journal of Sociology of Education* 16, no. 2 (June 1995): 165–218.

————. "'Resistance Postmodernism': Emancipatory Politics for a New Era or Academic Chic for a Defeatist Intelligentsia?" In *Information Society: New Media, Ethics and Postmodernism.* Edited by Karamjit S. Gill. London: Springer-Verlag, 1996.

————. "'New Labour,' Old Policies: Tony Blair's 'Vision' for Education in Britain." *Education Australia,* no. 37 (1997): 17–19.

————. "Into the Hands of Capital: The Deluge of Postmodernism and the Delusions of Resistance Postmodernism." In *Postmodernism in Educational Theory: Education and the Politics of Human Resistance.* Edited by Dave Hill, Peter McLaren, Mike Cole and Glenn Rikowski. London: Tufnell Press, 1999.

————. "Ex-Left Academics and the Curse of the Postmodern." *Education and Social Justice* 1, no. 3 (1999): 28–30.

Cole, Mike, Dave Hill, Peter McLaren and Glenn Rikowski. *Red Chalk: On Schooling, Capitalism and Politics.* Brighton, U.K.: Institute for Education Policy Studies, 2001.

Cole, Mike, Dave Hill and Glenn Rikowski. "Between Postmodernism and Nowhere: The Predicament of the Postmodernist." *British Journal of Educational Studies* 45, no. 2 (1997): 187–200.

Cole, Mike, Dave Hill and Sharanjeet Shan, eds. *Promoting Equality in Primary Schools.* London: Cassell, 1997.

Cole, Mike, and Bob Skelton, eds. *Blind Alley: Youth in a Crisis of Capital.* Ormskirk, U.K.: G. W. and A. Hesketh, 1980.

Colley, Helen. "Exploring Myths of Mentor: A Rough Guide to the History of Mentoring from a Marxist Feminist Perspective." Paper presented at the annual meeting of the British Educational Research Association Annual Conference, Cardiff University, Wales, September 7–10, 2000.

Comer, Lee Sanders. "Functions of the Family under Capitalism." In *Conditions of Illusion.* Edited by Sandra Allen, Lee Sanders and Jan Wallis. Leeds, U.K.: Feminist Books, 1974.

Connell, Robert. "Transformative Labour: Theorizing the Politics of Teachers Work." In *The Politics of Educators Work and Lives.* Edited by Mark B. Ginsburg. New York: Garland Publishing, 1995.

Cousin, Glynis. "Failure through Resistance: Critique of Learning to Labour." *Youth and Policy,* no. 10 (autumn 1984): 37–40.

Covington, Sally. "How Conservative Philanthropies and Think Tanks Transform U.S. Policy." *Cover Action Quarterly,* no. 63 (1998): 6–16.

Crichton, Michael. *Jurassic Park.* London: Arrow, 1991.

Crichton, Michael. *The Lost World.* London: Century, 1995.

Crook, Stephen. "The End of Radical Social Theory? Notes on Radicalism, Modernism and Postmodernism." In *Postmodernism and Society.* Edited by Roy Boyne and Ali Rattansi. London: Macmillan, 1990.

Croteau, David. *Politics and the Class Divide: Working People and the Middle-Class Left.* Philadelphia: Temple University Press, 1995.

Curtis, Bruce. *True Government by Choice Men?* Toronto: University of Toronto Press, 1992.

Da Cunha, Oliveria Maria Gomez. "Black Movements and the 'Politics of Identity' in Brazil." In *Cultures of Politics, Politics of Culture: Re-visioning Latin American Social Movements.* Edited by Sonia L. Alvarez, Evelina Dagnino and Arturo Escobar. Boulder, Colo.: Westview Press, 1998.

Dale, Roger. "The Thatcherite Project in Education." *Critical Social Policy* 9, no. 3 (1989): 4–19.

Davies, Andrew. "The Cheapening of Education." *Fight Racism, Fight Imperialism!* 143 (June–July 1998): 11.

Debord, Guy. *The Society of the Spectacle.* Detroit: Black and Red, 1977.

Deer, Brian. "Still Struggling after All These Years." *New Statesman,* August 23, 1996: 12–13.

Derrida, Jacques. *Of Grammatology.* Translated by Spivak Gayatri. London: Johns Hopkins University Press, 1976.

———. *Specters of Marx: The State of the Debt, the Work of Mourning.* New York: Routledge, 1994.

Dinerstein, Ana. "Marxism and Subjectivity: Searching for the Marvellous (Prelude to a Notion of Action)." *Common Sense, Journal of the Edinburgh Conference of Socialist Economists,* no. 22 (December 1997): 83–96.

Dinerstein, Ana, and Michael Neary. "Modernity or Capitalism: Abstract Theory or Theory of Abstraction?" Paper presented at the second meeting of the ESRC Seminar on "Social Theory and Major Social Transformations," University of Sussex, Brighton, U.K., October 10–11, 1997.

Docherty, Thomas, ed. *Postmodernism: A Reader.* London: Harvester Wheatsheaf, 1993.

Doll, William Jr. *A Post-Modern Perspective on Curriculum.* New York: Teachers College Press, 1993.

Donald, James. "Interesting Times." *Critical Social Policy* 9, no. 3 (1989).

Donald, James, and Ali Rattansi, eds. *'Race,' Culture and Difference.* London: Sage, 1992.

Donnelly, Clara, Matthew Nimmo and Paul Convery. *The New Deal Handbook.* London: Unemployment Unit and Youthaid, 1998.

Duffield, Jill. "School Support for Lower Achieving Pupils." *British Journal of Special Education* 25, no. 3 (February 1998): 126–134.

———. *Unequal Opportunities or Don't Mention the (Class) War.* Paper presented at the annual meeting of the Scottish Educational Research Association (SERA), Dundee, 1998.

———. "Learning Experiences, Effective Schools and Social Context." *Support for Learning* 13, no. 1 (February 1998): 3–8.

Dunning, Ray. "Plus Ca Change. " *Education,* July 8, 1988: 38.

Eagleton, Terry. *The Illusions of Postmodernism.* Malden, Mass.: Blackwell Publishers, 1996.

———. "Where Do Postmodernists Come From? " In *In Defense of History: Marxism and the Postmodern Agenda.* Edited by Ellen Meiksins Wood and James Bellamy Foster. New York: Monthly Review, 1997.

———. "Utopia and its Oppositions." In *Socialist Register 2000.* Edited by Leo Panitch and Colin Leys. Suffolk, U.K.: Merlin Press, 1999.

———. *The Idea of Culture.* Oxford, U.K.: Blackwell Publishers, 1999.

Ebert, Teresa L. *Ludic Feminism and After: Postmodernism, Desire, and Labor in Late Capitalism.* Ann Arbor: University of Michigan Press, 1996.

Ehrenberg, John. "Civil Society and Marxist Politics." *Socialism and Democracy* 12, no. 1–2 (1998): 15–46.

Ehrenreich, Barbara. "Beyond Monica—the Future of Clinton's Past." *The Nation* 267, no. 7 (1998): 13–14.

Einstein, Albert. "Why Socialism?" *Monthly Review* 50, no. 1 (1998): 1–10.

Eisner, Elliot W., and Alan Peshkin, eds. *Qualitative Inquiry in Education.* New York: Teachers College Press, 1991.

Engels, Freidrich. *The Origin of the Family, Private Property and the State* [1844]. Peking: Foreign Language Press, 1978.

Engler, Allen. *Apostles of Greed: Capitalism and the Myth of the Individual in the Market.* Boulder, Colo.: Pluto Press, 1995.

Equal Pay Task Force, *Just Pay.* London: Equal Opportunities Commission, 2001. <http://www.eoc.org.uk> (June 20, 2001).

Evans, John, and Dawn Penney. "The Politics of Pedagogy: Making a National Curriculum Physical Education." *Journal of Education Policy* 10, no. 1 (January–February 1994): 27–44.

Fekete, Liz. "Let Them Eat Cake." *Race and Class* 39, no. 3 (1998): 77–82.

Ferguson, Margaret, and Jennifer Wicke, eds. *Feminism and Postmodernism.* London: Duke University Press, 1994.

Fermont, Clare. "Four Years Hard Labour." *Socialist Review* 251 (2001): 9–11.

Fielding, Shaun, and Glenn Rikowski. "Resistance to Restructuring? Post-Fordism in British Primary Schools." Paper presented at the School of Education, University of Birmingham, U.K., November 1996.

Finn, Dan. *Training without Jobs, New Deals and Broken Promises.* London: Macmillan, 1987.

Firestone, Shulamith. *The Dialectic of Sex.* New York: Bantam, 1970.

Fiske, James. *Understanding Popular Culture.* London: Routledge, 1991.

Flax, Jane. "Postmodernism and Gender Relations in Feminist Theory." *Signs* 12 (1987): 621–643.

Fornäs, John. *Cultural Theory and Late Modernity.* London: Sage Publications, 1995.

Foster, Hal. *Recordings: Art, Spectacle, Cultural Politics.* Port Townsend, Wash.: Bay Press, 1985.

———, ed. *The Anti-aesthetic: Essays on Postmodern Culture.* Port Townsend, Wash.: Bay Press, 1983.

Frankel, Boris. "Confronting Neoliberal Regimes: The Post-Marxist Embrace of Populism and Realpolitik." *New Left Review*, no. 226 (1997): 57–92.

Fraser, Nancy. *Justice Interruptus: Critical Reflections on the 'Postsocialist' Condition.* New York: Routledge, 1997.

Fraser, Nancy, and Linda Gordon. "A Genealogy of Dependency." *Signs* 19 (winter 1994): 309–336.

Fraser, Nancy, and Linda J. Nicholson. "Social Criticism without Philosophy: An Encounter between Feminism and Postmodernism." In *Feminism/Postmodernism.* Edited by Linda J. Nicholson. London: Routledge, 1990.

Freeman-Moir, John. "Reflections on the Methods of Marxism." *Educational Philosophy and Theory* 24, no. 2 (1992): 98–128.

Freeman-Moir, John, and Alan Scott. "Looking Back at Education: the Abandonment of Hope." *New Zealand Journal of Educational Studies* 26, no. 2 (1991): 109–124.

Freeman-Moir, John, Alan Scott and Hugh Lauder. "Reformism or Revolution: Liberalism and the Metaphysics of Democracy." In *Bowles and Gintis Revisited: Corre-*

spondence and Contradiction in Educational Theory. Edited by Mike Cole. London: Falmer Press, 1988.

Freire, Paulo, ed. *Pedagogy of the Heart.* New York: Continuum, 1998.

Frith, Simon. *Sound Effects: Youth, Leisure and the Politics of Rock.* London: Constable, 1983.

Fryer, Peter. *Staying Power.* London: Pluto, 1984.

Gadotti, Moacir. *Pedagogy of Praxis: A Dialectical Philosophy of Education.* Translated by John Milton. Albany: State University of New York Press, 1996.

Gamman, Linda, and Merrja Makinen. *Female Fetishism.* New York: New York University Press, 1994.

Gane, Mike, ed. *Baudrillard Live: Selected Interviews.* London: Routledge, 1993.

Gardels, Nathan. "Globalization with a Human Face." *New Perspectives Quarterly* 14, no. 4 (1997): 48–49

Gee, Paul. "On Mobots and Classrooms: The Converging Languages of the New Capitalism and Schooling." *Organization* 3, no. 3 (1996): 385–407.

Geras, Norman. "The Controversy about Marx and Justice." In *Marxist Theory.* Edited by Alex Callinicos. Oxford: Oxford University Press, 1989.

Gewirtz, Sharon, Stephen J. Ball and Richard Bowe. *Markets, Choice and Equity in Education.* Buckingham, U.K.: Open University Press, 1995.

Giddens, Anthony. *The Third Way.* Cambridge, U.K.: Polity Press, 1998.

———. *The Third Way and Its Critics.* Cambridge: Polity Press, 2000.

———. *The Global Third Way Debate.* Cambridge: Polity Press, 2001.

Gillborn, David. "Articulating the Relationship between EAL, African Caribbean Pupil Achievement and Race Equality." *NALDIC News* 23 (March 2001): 4–6.

Gillborn, David, and Deborah Youdell. *Rationing Education: Policy, Practice, Reform and Equity.* Buckingham, U.K.: Open University Press, 2000.

Gilligan, Carol. *In a Different Voice: Psychological Theory and Women's Development.* Cambridge, Mass.: Harvard University Press, 1983.

Gilroy, Paul. *There Ain't No Black in the Union Jack: The Cultural Politics of Race and Nation.* Chicago: University of Chicago Press, 1991.

———. *Black Atlantic: Modernity and Double Consciousness.* London: Verso, 1993.

Gimenez, Martha E. "The Production of Divisions: Gender Struggles under Capitalism." In *Marxism in the Postmodern Age: Confronting the New World Order.* Edited by Antonio Callari, Stephen Cullenberg and Carole Biewener. New York: Guilford Press, 1995.

Giroux, Henry A. "Theories of Reproduction and Resistance in the New Sociology of Education: A Critical Analysis." *Harvard Education Review* 53, no. 3 (1983): 257–293.

———. *Teachers as Intellectuals: Towards a Critical Pedagogy of Learning.* South Hadley, Mass.: Bergin and Garvey, 1988.

———. *Border Crossings: Cultural Workers and the Politics of Education.* London: Routledge, 1992.

———. "Living Dangerously: Identity, Politics and the New Cultural Racism." In *Between Borders: Pedagogy and Politics of Cultural Studies.* Edited by Henry Giroux and Peter McLaren. London: Routledge, 1994.

———. "Radical Pedagogy and Prophetic Thought: Remembering Paulo Freire." *Rethinking Marxism* 9, no. 4 (winter 1996–1997): 76–87.

Giroux, Henry A., ed. *Postmodernism, Feminism, and Cultural Politics.* New York: State University of New York Press, 1990.

Giroux, Henry, and Peter McLaren. *Critical Pedagogy, the State and Cultural Struggle.* New York: State University of New York Press, 1988.

Gitlin, Andrew, ed. *Power and Method.* New York: Routledge, 1994.

Glenn, Charles Leslie. *The Myth of the Common School.* Amherst: University of Massachusetts Press, 1987.

Gordon, David, and Peter Townsend, eds. *Breadline Europe: The Measurement of Poverty.* Bristol, U.K.: Policy Press, 2001.

Gordon, F. "Workers and Masses." *Open Polemic* (March 11, 1995). PO Box 1169, London, W3 9PF.

Grace, Gerald. "Welfare Labourism and the New Right: The Struggle in New Zealand's Education Policy." *International Studies in Sociology of Education* 1, no. 1 (1991): 25–42.

Graham, Julie, and Katherine Gibson. "Waiting for the Revolution, or How to Smash Capitalism while Working at Home in Your Spare Time." In *Marxism in the Postmodern Age: Confronting the New World Order.* Edited by Antonio Callari, Stephen Cullenberg and Carole Biewener. New York: Guilford Press, 1995.

———. *The End of Capitalism (As We Knew It): A Feminist Critique of Political Economy.* Malden, Mass.: Blackwell Publishers, 1996.

Green, Andy. "Postmodernism and State Education." *Journal of Education Policy* 9, no. 1 (January–February 1994): 67–83.

———. *Education, Globalization and the Nation State.* Basingstoke, U.K.: Macmillan, 1997.

Green, Tony, and Geoff Whitty. "The Legacy of the New Sociology of Education." Paper presented at the annual meeting of the American Educational Research Association (AERA), New Orleans, April 1994.

Greider, William. "The Global Crisis Deepens: Now What?" *The Nation* 267, no. 12 (1998): 11–16.

The Guardian. "Brain Implants Allow Patients to Work Computer by Thought-Power." *Guardian,* October 15, 1998: 7.

Gunn, Richard. "Against Historical Materialism: Marxism as a First-Order Discourse." In *Open Marxism, Volumes 1 and 2.* Edited by Werner Bonefeld, Richard Gunn and Kosmas Psychopedis. London: Pluto, 1992.

Habermas, Jurgen. "Modernity vs. Postmodernity." *New German Critique* 2 (1981): 3–14.

———. "Modernity—an Incomplete Project." In *The Anti-Aesthetic: Essays on Postmodern Culture.* Edited by Hal Foster. Port Townsend, Wash.: Bay Press, 1983.

———. *The Philosophical Discourse of Modernity.* Cambridge, Mass.: MIT Press, 1987.

———. *The Philosophical Discourse of Modernity: Twelve Lectures.* Cambridge, Mass.: MIT Press, 1990.

Hall, Stuart. "Brave New World." *Marxism Today,* Special Issue (October 1988): 24–29.

———. "Cultural Studies: Two Paradigms." In *Cultural Studies.* Edited by Lawrence Grossberg, Cary Nelson and Paula Treichler. New York: Routledge, 1992.

———. "New Ethnicities." In *'Race,' Culture and Difference.* Edited by Ali Rattansi and James Donald. London: Sage, 1992.

———. "The Great Moving Nowhere Show: Blair Has Failed to Break with Neoliberalism and thereby Squandered a Golden Opportunity." *Marxism Today* (November–December 1998): 9–14.

Hall, Stuart, Charles Critcher, Tony Jefferson, John Clarke and Brian Roberts. *Policing the Crisis: Mugging, the State and Law and Order.* London: Macmillan, 1978.

Hall, Stuart, and Martin Jacques, eds. *New Times: The Changing Face of Politics in the 1990s*. London: Lawrence & Wishart, 1989.

Hall, Stuart, and Tony Jefferson, eds. *Resistance through Rituals: Youth Subculture in Post-War* Britain. London: Hutchinson, 1975.

Halpin, David. "Getting By through Failing to Deliver Simple Truths." *British Journal of Educational Studies* 46, no. 1 (March 1998): 1–7.

Halsey, A. H., Hugh Lauder, Philip Brown and Amy Stuart Wells, eds. *Education, Culture and Economy*. Oxford: Oxford University Press.

Halstead, J. M. *The Case for Muslim Voluntary-Aided Schools*. Cambridge: Islamic Academy, 1986.

Haraway, Donna. "Situated Knowledges: The Science Question in Feminism and the Privilege of Partial Perspectives." *Feminist Studies* 14, no. 3 (fall 1988): 575–599.

———. *Simians, Cyborgs, and Women: The Reinvention of Nature*. New York: Routledge, 1991.

Hardt, Michael, and Antonio Negri. *Labor of Dionysus*. Minneapolis: University of Minnesota Press, 1994.

Hargreaves, Andy. *Changing Teachers, Changing Times*. New York: Teachers College Press, 1994.

———. "Restructuring Restructuring: Postmodernism and the Prospects for Educational Change." *Journal of Education Policy* 9, no. 1 (January–February 1994): 47–66.

Harman, Chris, and Socialist Workers Party. *In the Heat of the Struggle: 25 Years of Socialist Worker*. London: Socialist Worker and Bookmarks, 1993.

Harris, Kevin. *Education and Knowledge*. London: RKP, 1979.

———. "Two Contrasting Theories." *Education with Production* 3, no. 1 (July 1984): 13–33.

———. "Teachers, Curriculum and Social Reconstruction." *Forum of Education* 47, no. 2 (1988): 3–21.

———. "Schooling, Democracy and Teachers as Intellectual Vanguard." *New Zealand Journal of Educational Studies* 27, no. 1 (1992): 21–33.

———. *Teachers: Constructing the Future*. London: Falmer Press, 1994.

Hartley, David. "Confusion in Teacher Education: A Postmodern Condition?" In *International Analyses of Teacher Education*. Edited by Peter Gilroy and Michael Smith. London: Carfax Publishing Company, 1993.

Harvey, David. *The Condition of Postmodernity*. Oxford, U.K.: Basil Blackwell, 1989.

———. "Class Relations, Social Justice and the Politics of Difference." In *Principled Positions*. Edited by Judith Squires. London: Lawrence & Wishart, 1993.

———. "The Body as an Accumulation Strategy." *Environment and Planning D: Society and Space* 16 (1998): 401–421.

———. "The Geography of the Manifesto." In *Socialist Register: The Communist Manifesto Now*. Edited by Leo Panitch and Colin Leys. New York: Monthly Review Press, 1998.

Harvie, David. "Alienation, Class and Enclosure in U.K. Universities." *Capital and Class*, no. 71 (summer 2000): 103–132.

Hatcher, Richard. "Labour, Official School Improvement and Equality." *Journal of Education Policy* 13, no. 4 (July–August 1998): 485–499.

———. "Social Justice and the Politics of School Effectiveness and Improvement." *Race, Ethnicity and Education* 1, no. 2 (October 1998): 267–289.

Hatcher, Richard. "Getting Down to Business: Schooling in the Globalised Economy." *Education and Social Justice* 3, no. 2 (spring 2001): 45–59.

Hatcher, Richard, and Barry Troyna. "The Policy Cycle: A Ball by Ball Account." *Journal of Education Policy* 9, no. 2 (March–April 1994): 155–170.

Hatton, Derek. *Inside Left, the Story So Far.* London: Bloomsbury Publishing, 1988.

Hawkes, David. *Ideology.* London: Routledge, 1996.

Hayes, Dennis. "Confidence and the Academy." Paper presented at the annual meeting of the British Educational Research Association, Cardiff University, Wales, September 7–9, 2000.

Haymer, Rupert. "How 11-Plus Divided Twin Brothers with the Same IQ." *Sunday Mirror,* February 18, 2001.

Hebdige, Dick. *Subculture: The Meaning of Style.* London: Methuen, 1979.

———. *Hiding in the Light.* London: Routledge, 1988.

Hennessy, Rosemary. *Materialist Feminism and the Politics of Discourse.* New York: Routledge, 1993.

Henwood, Doug. "The Bull's Sour 16." *The Nation* 267, no. 7 (1998): 5.

Her Majesty's Stationery Office (HMSO). *General Household Survey.* London: Stationery Office, 1971.

———. *General Household Survey.* London: Stationery Office, 1971.

———. *General Household Survey.* London: Stationery Office, 1994.

———. *Population Trends.* London: Stationery Office, 1971.

———. *Population Trends.* London: Stationery Office, 1987.

———. *Population Trends.* London: Stationery Office, 1997.

———. *Population Trends.* London: Stationery Office, 1999.

———. *Social Trends 31.* London: Stationery Office, 2001.

Herrnstein, Richard J., and Charles Murray. *The Bell Curve.* New York: Free Press, 1994.

Hewitt, Marsha. "Illusions of Freedom: The Regressive Implications of 'Postmodernism.'" In *Real Problems, False Solutions. Socialist Register.* Edited by Ralph Miliband and Leo Panitch. London: Merlin Press, 1993.

Hickey, Tom. "Class and Class Analysis for the Twenty-first Century." In *Education, Equality and Human Rights.* Edited by Mike Cole. London: Routledge-Falmer, 2000.

Hill, Dave. *Charge of the Right Brigade: The Radical Right's Attack on Teacher Education.* Brighton, U.K.: Institute for Education Policy Studies, 1989 (<http://www.ieps.org.uk.html>).

———. *Something Old, Something New, Something Borrowed, Something Blue: Schooling, Teacher Education and the Radical Right in Britain and the USA.* London: Tufnell Press, 1990.

———. "Seven Ideological Perspectives on Teacher Education Today and the Development of a Radical Left Discourse." *Australian Journal of Teacher Education* 16, no. 2 (1991): 5–29.

———. "Cultural Diversity and Initial Teacher Education." In *Cultural Diversity and the Curriculum, Vol. 4. Cross-Curricular Contexts, Themes and Dimensions in Primary Schools.* Edited by Gajendra Verma and Peter Pumfrey. London: Falmer Press, 1994.

———. "Reflection in Teacher Education." In *Educational Dilemmas: Debate and Diversity, Volume 1: Teacher Education and Training.* Edited by Keith Watson, Sohan Modgil and Celia Modgil. London: Cassell, 1997.

———. "Equality in Primary Schooling: The Policy Context, Intentions and Effects of the Conservative 'Reforms.'" In *Promoting Equality in Primary Schools.* Edited by Mike Cole, Dave Hill and Sharanjeet Shan. London: Cassell, 1997.

Hill, Dave. "Social Class and Education." In *An Introduction to the Study of Education.* Edited by David Matheson and Ian Grosvenor. London: David Fulton, 1999.

————. *New Labour and Education: Policy, Ideology and the Third Way.* London: Tufnell Press, 1999.

————. "Interview." Rupert Haymer, "How 11-Plus Divided Twin Brothers with the Same IQ." *Sunday Mirror,* February 18, 2000: 6–7.

————. "Reclaiming Our Education from the Neo-Liberals: Markets in Education, James Tooley, and the Struggle for Economic and Social Justice." Paper presented at the Campaign for Free Education Conference on "Reclaiming Our Education," University of East London, U.K., August 2000.

————. "The Third Way Ideology of New Labour's Educational Policy in England and Wales." In *Combating Social Exclusion through Education: Laissez faire, Authoritarianism or Third Way?* Edited by Guido Walraven, Chris Day, Carl Parsons and Dolf Van Deen. Leuven-Apeldoon, Belgium: Garant, 2000.

————. "The Third Way in Britain: Capitalism, Neo-Liberalism and Education Policy." Paper presented at the annual meeting of the European Educational Research Association Annual, University of Edinburgh, Scotland, September 2000.

————. "New Labour's Neo-Liberal Education Policy." *Forum for Promoting Comprehensive Education* 42, no. 1 (spring 2000): 8–11.

————. "Radical Left Principles for Social and Economic Justice in Education Policy." Paper presented to the Day Seminar on *Approaching Social Justice in Education: Theoretical Frameworks for Practical Purposes,* Faculty of Education, Nottingham Trent University, U.K., April 2000.

————. "State Theory and the Neo-Liberal Reconstruction of Schooling and Teacher Education: A Structuralist Neo-Marxist Critique of Postmodernist, Quasi-Postmodernist and Culturalist Neo-Marxist Theory." *British Journal of Sociology of Education* 22, no. 1 (March 2001): 137–156.

————. "Equality, Ideology and Education Policy." In *Schooling and Equality: Fact, Concept and Policy.* Edited by Dave Hill and Mike Cole. London: Kogan Page, 2001.

————. "Global Capital, Neo-Liberalism, and Privatisation: The Growth of Educational and Economic Inequality." In *Schooling and Equality: Fact, Concept and Policy.* Edited by Dave Hill and Mike Cole. London: Kogan Page, 2001.

————. "The National Curriculum, the Hidden Curriculum and Inequality in Schooling." In *Schooling and Equality: Fact, Concept and Policy.* Edited by Dave Hill and Mike Cole. London: Kogan Page, 2001.

————. *Education, Education, Education: Capitalism, Socialism and the Third Way.* Brighton, U.K.: Institute for Education Policy Studies, 2002.

Hill, Dave, and Mike Cole. "Marxist State Theory and State Autonomy Theory: The Case of 'Race' Education in Initial Teacher Education." *Journal of Educational Policy* 10, no. 2 (1995): 221–232.

————. "Materialism and the Postmodern Fallacy: The Case of Education." In *Proceedings of the Second International Conference of Sociology of Education in Portugal.* Edited by Joao Viegas Fernandes. Faro, Portugal: Escola Superior de Educacao da Universidade do Algarve, 1996.

————. "Social Class." In *Schooling and Equality: Fact, Concept and Policy.* Edited by Dave Hill and Mike Cole. London: Kogan Page, 2001.

Hill, Dave, and Mike Cole, eds. *Promoting Equality in Secondary Schools.* London: Cassell, 1999.

Hill, Dave, and Mike Cole, eds. *Schooling and Equality: Fact, Concept and Policy.* London: Kogan Page, 2001.

Hill, Dave, Peter McLaren, Mike Cole and Glenn Rikowski, eds. *Postmodernism in Educational Theory: Education and the Politics of Human Resistance.* London: Tufnell Press, 1999.

Hillcole Group. *Changing the Future: Redprint for Education.* Edited by Clyde Chitty. London: Tufnell Press, 1991.

Hillcole Group. *Rethinking Education and Democracy: A Socialist Alternative for the Twenty-first Century.* London: Tufnell Press, 1997.

Hillgate Group. *The Reform of British Education.* London: Claridge Press, 1987.

Hird, Myra J. "Theorising Student Identity as Fragmented: Some Implications for Feminist Critical Pedagogy." *British Journal of Sociology of Education* 19, no. 4 (December 1998): 517–527.

Hirom, Kate. "Gender." In *Schooling and Equality: Fact, Concept and Policy.* Edited by Dave Hill and Mike Cole. London: Kogan Page, 2001.

Hirtt, Nico. "The 'Millennium Round' and the Liberalisation of the Education Market." *Education and Social Justice* 2, no. 2 (2000): 12–18.

Hobsbawm, Eric. "The Death of Neo-Liberalism: The Present Global Crisis Marks the End of Market Fundamentalism." *Marxism Today*, November–December 1998: 4–8.

Hollands, Robert. *The Long Transition.* London: Macmillan, 1990.

Holloway, John. "In the Beginning Was the Scream." *Common Sense, Journal of the Edinburgh Conference of Socialist Economists,* no. 11 (1991): 69–78.

———. "Open Marxism, History and Class Struggle." *Common Sense, Journal of the Edinburgh Conference of Socialist Economists,* no. 13 (January 1993): 76–86.

———. "The Freeing of Marx." *Common Sense, Journal of the Edinburgh Conference of Socialist Economists,* no. 14 (October 1993): 17–21.

———. "From Scream of Refusal to Scream of Power: The Centrality of Work." In *Open Marxism: Volume III. Emancipating Marx.* Edited by Werner Bonefeld, Richard Gunn, John Holloway and Kosmas Psychopedis. London: Pluto Press, 1995.

Holst, John. *Social Movements, Civil Society, and Radical Adult Education.* Westport, Conn.: Bergin & Garvey, 2001. <http://www.acm.usl.edu/ ~dca6381/ c2_mirror/xi/ entropy.html> (April 2001).

Hudis, Peter. "Can Capital be Controlled?" News and Letters (April 2000). <http://www.newsandletters.org/4.00essay.html> (March 1, 2001).

———. "Marx in the Mirror of Globalization." <http:www.britannica.com/bcom/ original/article/print/0.5749.11673.00.html>(January 1, 2001).

Hunter, I. *Rethinking the School.* Boston: Allen & Unwin, 1994.

Hutton, Will. "The Rich Aren't Cleverer, Just Richer." *Observer,* April 1, 2001.

International Communist Union. "Public Education under Attack." *Class Struggle,* no. 30 (January–February 2000): 14–19.

Jacques, Martin. "As We Move into a New Era, New Labour Remains Firmly Stuck in the Old One." *Marxism Today.* Special Issue (October 1998): 2–3.

Jameson, Frederic. "Postmodernism and the Cultural Logic of Capitalism." *New Left Review,* no. 146 (1984): 59–92.

———. *Postmodernism or the Cultural Logic of Late Capitalism.* Durham, N.C.: Duke University Press, 1991.

———. *Postmodernism.* London: Verso, 1992.

Jarvis, Darryl S. L. "Postmodernism: A Critical Typology." *Politics and Society* 26, no. 1 (March 1998): 95–142.

Jay, Martin. *Cultural Semantics: Keywords of Our Time.* Amherst: University of Massachusetts Press, 1998.

Jenkins, Robin. *The Production of Knowledge at the Institute of Race Relations*. London: Independent Labour Party, 1971.

Jessop, Bob. *State Theory: Putting Capitalist States in Their Place*. Cambridge: Polity Press, 1990.

Johnson, Richard. "Three Problematics: Elements of a Theory of Working-Class Culture." In *Working Class Culture*. Edited by John Clarke, Charles Critcher and Richard Johnson. London: Hutchinson, 1979.

Joines, Rick. "The Academic Left Today." *Political Affairs* 76, no. 6 (1997): 29–33.

Joines, Rick. "Derrida's Ante and the Call of Marxist Political Philosophy." In *Cultural Logic*, 2001. <http://eserver.org/projects/clogic/3-1%262/joins.html> (July 2001), 7.

Kay, Geoffrey, and James Mott. *Political Order and the Law of Labour*. London: Macmillan, 1982.

Kelley, Robin D. G. "A Poetics of Anticolonialism." *Monthly Review* 51, no. 6 (1999): 1–21.

Kellner, Douglas. "The End of Orthodox Marxism." In *Marxism in the Postmodern Age: Confronting the New World Order*. Edited by Antonio Callari, Stephen Cullenberg and Carole Biewener. New York: Guilford Press, 1995.

Kelly, Duncan. "Multicultural Citizenship: The Limitations of Liberal Democracy." *The Political Quarterly* 71, no. 1 (2000): 31–41.

Kelly, Jane. "Postmodernism and Feminism." *International Marxist Review*, no. 14 (winter, 1992): 39–55.

———. "Postmodernism and Feminism: The Road to Nowhere." In *Postmodernism In Educational Theory: Education and the Politics of Human Resistance*. Edited by Dave Hill, Peter McLaren, Mike Cole and Glenn Rikowski. London: Tufnell Press, 1999.

———. "Gender and Equality: One Hand Tied behind Us." In *Education, Equality and Human Rights: Issues of Gender, 'Race,' Sexuality, Special Needs and Social Class*. Edited by Mike Cole. London: Routledge-Falmer, 2000.

Kelly, Jane, Mike Cole and Dave Hill. "Resistance Postmodernism and the Ordeal of the Undecidable." Paper presented at the meeting of the *British Educational Research Association*, September 1999.

Kelsh, Deb. "Desire and Class: The Knowledge Industry in the Wake of Poststructuralism (Parts 1 and 2)." *Cultural Logic* 1, no. 2 (spring 1998). <http://eserver.org/clogic/1-2/kelsh.html> (May 2001).

Kenway, Jane. "Having a Postmodern Turn or Postmodernist Angst: A Disorder Experienced by an Author Who Is Not Yet Dead or Even Close to It." In *Education: Culture, Economy, Society*. Edited by A. H. Halsey, Hugh Lauder, Philip Brown, and Amy Stuart Wells. Oxford: Oxford University Press, 1997.

Kincheloe, Joe. *Toward a Critical Politics of Teacher Thinking: Mapping the Postmodern*. Westport, Conn.: Bergin & Garvey, 1993.

Kleinberg Neumark, Mark. "If It's So Important, Why Won't They Pay for It? Public Higher Education at the Turn of the Century." *Monthly Review* 51, no. 1 (1999): 20–31.

Korten, David C. "The Mystic Victory of Market Capitalism." In *The Case against the Global Economy and for a Turn toward the Local*. Edited by Jerry Mander and Edward Goldsmith. San Francisco: Sierra Club Books, 1996.

Krehm, William. "The Co-Failure of Communism and Capitalism in Russia." *Comer* 12, no. 7 (2000): 9–19.

Kroker, Arthur, and David Cook. *The Postmodern Scene: Excremental Culture and Hyper-Aesthetics*. New York: St. Martin's, 1986.

Kuhn, Annette, and AnnMarie Volpe, eds. *Feminism and Materialism: Women and Modes of Production*. London: Routledge and Kegan Paul, 1978.

Laclau, Ernesto. *Politics and Ideology in Marxist Theory*. London: Verso, 1979.

———. *Reflections on the New Revolutions of Our Times*. London: Verso, 1991.

Laclau, Ernesto, and Chantal Mouffe. *Hegemony and Socialist Strategy: Towards a Radical Democratic Politics*. London: Verso, 1985.

Larrain, Jorge. "Identity, the Other, and Postmodernism." In *Post-ality: Marxism and Postmodernism*. Edited by Mas'ud Zavarzadeh, Teresa Ebert and Donald Morton. Washington, D.C.: Maisonneuve Press, 1995.

Lash, Scott. *Sociology of Postmodernism*. London: Routledge, 1990.

Lather, Patti. "Critical Theory, Curricular Transformation, and Feminist Mainstreaming." *Journal of Education* 166, no. 1 (March 1984): 49–62.

———. *Getting Smart: Feminist Research and Pedagogy with/in the Postmodern*. London: Routledge, 1991.

———. "Critical Pedagogy and Its Complicities: A Praxis of Stuck Places." *Educational Theory* 48, no. 4 (fall 1998): 487–497.

———. "Ten Years Later, Yet Again: Critical Pedagogy and its Complicities." In *Feminist Engagements: Reading, Resisting and Revisioning Male Theorists in Education and Cultural Studies*. Edited by Kathleen Weiler. London: Routledge, 2001.

Lauder, Hugh, John Freeman Moir and Alan Scott. "What Is to Be Done with Radical Academic Practice?" *Capital and Class*, no. 29 (1986): 83–110.

Lauder, Hugh, David Hughes, Sue Watson, Sietske Waslander, Martin Thrupp, Rob Strathdee, Ibrahim Simiya, Ann Dupuis, Jim McGlinn and Jennie Hamlin. *Trading in Futures: The Nature of Choice in Educational Markets in New Zealand*. Wellington: Victoria University of Wellington, 1995.

Lawton, Dennis. *Class, Culture and the Curriculum*. London: Routledge, 1975.

Lebowitz, Michael. *Beyond Capital: Marx's Political Economy of the Working Class*. Basingstoke, U.K: Macmillan, 1992.

Lenin, Vladimir Ilyich. "A Great Beginning." In *Collected Works: Volume 29*. Moscow: Progress Publishers, 1965.

Levidow, Les. "Marketizing Higher Education: Neoliberal Strategies and Counter-Strategies." *Education and Social Justice* (summer 2001).

Leys, Colin, and Leo Panitch. "The Political Legacy of the Manifesto." In *Socialist Register 1998*. Edited by Leo Panitch and Colin Leys. Rendlesham, U.K.: Merlin, 1998.

Liston, Daniel. *Capitalist Schools: Explanation and Ethics in Radical Studies of Schooling*. London: Routledge, 1988.

———. "Faith and Evidence: Examining Marxist Explanations of Schools." *American Journal of Education* 96, no. 3 (1988): 323–350.

Livingstone, David. "Searching for the Missing Links: Neo-Marxist Theories of Education." *British Journal of Sociology of Education* 16, no. 1 (March 1995): 53–73.

Livingstone, Ken. *If Voting Changed Anything, They'd Abolish It*. London: Collins, 1987.

Longhurst, Ross. "Education as a Commodity: The Political Economy of the New Further Education." *Journal of Further and Higher Education* 20, no. 2 (summer 1996): 49–66.

Low Pay Unit. "Problems in Search of a Solution." *The New Review* 48 (November–December 1997): 6–9.

Low Pay Unit. "One Small Step for Woman (and Man) Kind." *The New Review* 66 (November–December 2000): 6–8.

Luke, Tim. "'Moving at the Speed of Life?' A Cultural Kinematics of Telematic Times and Corporate Values." In *Time and Value*. Edited by Scott Lash, Andrew Quick and Richard Roberts. Oxford, U.K.: Blackwell, 1998.

Mahony, Pat, and Christine Zmroczek. *Class Matters: 'Working-Class' Women's Perspectives on Social Class*. London: Taylor and Francis, 1997.

Malik, Kenan. "Universalism and Difference: Race and the Postmodernists." *Race and Class* 37, no. 3 (January–March 1996): 1–17.

———. "The Mirror of Race: Postmodernism and the Celebration of Difference." In *In Defense of History: Marxism and the Postmodern Agenda*. Edited by Elizabeth Meiksins Wood and John Bellamy Foster. New York: Monthly Review Press, 1997.

Marginson, Simon. *Markets in Education*. St. Leonards, New South Wales: Allen and Unwin, 1997.

Margonis, Frank. "Theories of Conviction: The Return of Marxist Theorizing." *Educational Theory* 48, no. 1 (winter 1998): 87–101.

Martin, Hans-Peter, and Harald Schumann. *The Global Trap: Globalization and the Assault on Democracy and Prosperity*. London: Zed Books, 1997.

Martin, Jane. "Barbarians at the Gate: Gender, Education and the New Millennium." In *Education, Equality and Human Rights: Issues of Gender, 'Race,' Sexuality, Special Needs and Social Class*. Edited by Mike Cole. London: Routledge-Falmer, 2000.

Martinot, Steve. "The Racialized Construction of Class in the United States." *Social Justice* 27, no. 1 (2000): 43–60.

Marx, Karl. "Excerpts from James Mill's 'Elements of Political Economy'" [1844]. In *Karl Marx: Early Writings*. Edited and translated by Rodney Livingstone and Gregor Benton. London: Penguin Classics-New Left Review, 1992.

———. *Economic and Philosophical Manuscripts of 1844* [1844]. Moscow: Progress Publishers, 1977.

———. "Economic and Philosophical Manuscripts of 1844" [1844]. In *Karl Marx: Early Writings*. Edited and translated by Rodney Livingstone and Gregor Benton. London: Penguin Classics-New Left Review, 1992.

———. "Theses on Feuerbach" [1845]. In *The Marx-Engels Reader*. Edited by Robert C. Tucker. New York: W. W. Norton, 1978.

———. "The Poverty of Philosophy" [1847]. In *The Marx-Engels Reader*. Edited by Robert C. Tucker. New York: W. W. Norton, 1978.

———. "Wage-Labour and Capital" [1847]. In *Selected Works—Volume 1*. Edited by Scott Lash, Andrew Quick and Richard Roberts. Moscow: Progress Publishers, 1977.

———. "The Eighteenth Brumaire of Louis Bonaparte" [1852]. In *Surveys from Exile*. Edited by David Fernbach. New York: Vintage Books, 1974.

———. "General Introduction" [1857]. In *Grundrisse: Foundations of the Critique of Political Economy (Rough Draft)*. Translated by Martin Nicolaus. Harmondsworth, U.K.: Penguin, 1973.

———. *Grundrisse: Foundations of the Critique of Political Economy (Rough Draft)* [1858]. Translated by Martin Nicolaus. Harmondsworth, U.K.: Penguin, 1973.

———. *A Contribution to the Critique of Political Economy* [1859]. Moscow: Progress Publishers, 1977.

———. *Theories of Surplus Value—Part 1* [1863]. London: Lawrence & Wishart, 1969.

———. *Theories of Surplus Value—Part 1* [1863]. Moscow: Progress Publishers, 1975.

———. *Theories of Surplus Value—Part 2* [1863]. London: Lawrence & Wishart, 1969.

———. *Theories of Surplus Value—Part 3* [1863]. London: Lawrence & Wishart, 1975.

Marx, Karl. *Capital: A Critique of Political Economy—Volume 3* [1865]. London: Lawrence & Wishart, 1977.

———. *Capital: A Critique of Political Economy—Volume 3* [1865]. Harmondsworth, U.K.: Penguin, 1981.

———. "Capital: A Critique of Political Economy—Volume 3" [1865]. In *The Marx-Engels Reader*. Edited by Robert C. Tucker. New York: W. W. Norton, 1978.

———. "Wages, Price and Profit" [1865]. In *Selected Works—Volume 2*. Moscow: Progress Publishers, 1976.

———. "Results of the Immediate Process of Production" [1866]. In *Capital: A Critique of Political Economy—Volume 1*. Harmondsworth, U.K.: Penguin, 1979.

———. *Capital: A Critique of Political Economy—Volume 1* [1867]. Moscow: Foreign Languages Publishing House, 1959.

———. *Capital: A Critique of Political Economy—Volume 1* [1867]. London: Lawrence & Wishart, 1977.

———. *Capital: A Critique of Political Economy—Volume 1* [1867]. New York: Vintage Books, 1977.

———. *Capital: A Critique of Political Economy—Volume 1* [1867]. Harmondsworth, U.K.: Penguin, 1986.

———. *Preface to the First German Edition of 'Capital' (Volume 1)* [1867]. London: Lawrence & Wishart, 1977.

———. *Capital: A Critique of Political Economy—Volume 2* [1878]. Harmondsworth, U.K.: Penguin, 1978.

———. *Karl Marx: Early Writings*. Edited and translated by Rodney Livingstone and Gregor Benton. London: Penguin Classics-New Left Review, 1992.

Marx, Karl, and Freidrich Engels. *The German Ideology* [1846]. Moscow: Progress Publishers, 1976.

———. *The Communist Manifesto* [1848]. Harmondsworth, U.K.: Penguin Classics, 1985.

———. "The Communist Manifesto" [1848]. In *The Marx-Engels Reader*. Edited by Robert C. Tucker. New York: W. W. Norton, 1978.

Marxist Collective at Syracuse University (MCSU). "Capitalism and Your University Education." *The Alternative Orange* 3, no. 2 (1993) <http://www.geocities.co/Capitol Hill/Lobby/2072/AOVol2-2CapUniv.html> (April 2001).

Maynard, Mary. "Feminism and the Possibilities of a Postmodern Research Practice." *British Journal of Sociology of Education* 14, no. 3 (September 1993): 327–331.

Mayo, Peter. *Gramsci, Freire and Adult Education: Possibilities for Transformative Action*. London: Zed Books, 1999.

McCarthy, Cameron, and Warren Crichlow, eds. *Race, Identity, and Representation in Education*. New York: Routledge, 1993.

McChesney, Robert W. "Introduction." In Noam Chomsky, *Profit Over People: Neoliberalism and Global Order*. New York: Seven Stories Press, 1999.

McGreal, John, and Phil Corrigan. *Ideology in 'Colour and Citizenship'*. London: LSE, 1970.

McKay, George. *Senseless Acts of Beauty: Cultures of Resistance since the Sixties*. London: Verso, 1996.

McKay, Ian. "The Many Deaths of Mr. Marx: Or, What Left Historians Might Contribute to Debates about the 'Crises of Marxism.'" *Left History*, nos. 3.2 and 4.1 (1995–1996): 9–84.

McLaren, Peter. "Postmodernity and the Death of Politics: A Brazilian Reprieve." *Educational Theory* 36, no. 4 (fall 1986): 389–401.

McLaren, Peter. "Multiculturalism and the Postmodernist Critique: Towards a Pedagogy of Resistance and Transformation." In *Between Borders: Pedagogy and the Politics of Cultural Studies*. Edited by Henry Giroux and Peter McLaren. London: Routledge, 1994.

————. *Critical Pedagogy and Predatory Culture: Oppositional Politics in a Postmodern Age*. London: Routledge, 1995.

————. *Revolutionary Multiculturalism: Pedagogies of Dissent for the New Millennium*. Boulder, Colo.: Westview Press, 1997.

————. "Critical Pedagogy and Globalization: Thirty Years after Che." Keynote Address at the Annual Convention for the National Association for Multicultural Education, Albuquerque, New Mexico, October 31, 1997.

————. "The Pedagogy of Che Guevara: Critical Pedagogy and Globalization—Thirty Years after Che." *Cultural Circles*, no. 3 (1998): 28–103.

————. "Revolutionary Pedagogy in Post-Revolutionary Times: Rethinking the Political Economy of Critical Education." *Educational Theory* 48, no. 4 (fall 1998): 431–462.

————. *Life in Schools: An Introduction to Critical Pedagogy in the Foundations of Education*. Harlow, U.K.: Longman, 1998.

————. "The Educational Researcher as Critical Social Agent: Some Personal Reflections on Marxist Criticism in Post-Modern Times of Fashionable Apostasy." In *Multicultural Research: A Reflective Engagement with Race, Class, Gender and Sexual Orientation*. Edited by Carl Grant. London: Falmer Press, 1999.

————. "Traumatizing Capital: Oppositional Pedagogies in the Age of Consent." In *Critical Education in the New Information Age*. Edited by Manuel Castells, Ramon Flecha, Paulo Freire, Henry Giroux, Donald Macedo and Paul Willis. Lanham, Md.: Rowman & Littlefield, 1999.

————. *Che Guevara, Paulo Freire, and the Pedagogy of Revolution*. Lanham, Md.: Rowman & Littlefield, 2000.

————. "Gang of Five." In *Red Chalk: On Schooling, Capitalism and Politics*. Edited by Mike Cole, Dave Hill, Peter McLaren and Glenn Rikowski. Brighton, U.K.: Institute of Education Policy Studies, 2001.

McLaren, Peter, and Ramin Farahmandpur. "Critical Pedagogy, Postmodernism, and the Retreat from Class: Towards a Contraband Pedagogy." In *Postmodernism in Educational Theory: Education and the Politics of Human Resistance*. Edited by Dave Hill, Peter McLaren, Mike Cole and Glenn Rikowski. London: Tufnell Press, 1999.

————. "Critical Pedagogy, Postmodernism, and the Retreat from Class: Towards a Contraband Pedagogy." *Theoria*, no. 93 (June 1999): 83–115.

————. "Critical Multiculturalism and the Globalization of Capital: Some Implications for a Politics of Resistance." *Journal of Curriculum Theorizing* 15, no. 4 (winter 1999): 27–46.

————. "Reconsidering Marx in Post-Marxist Times: A Requiem for Postmodernism?" *Educational Researcher* 29, no. 3 (April 2000): 25–33.

————. "Educational Policy and the Socialist Imagination: Revolutionary Citizenship as a Pedagogy of Resistance." *Educational Policy* 15, no. 3 (July 2001): 343–378.

McLaren, Peter, Mike Cole, Dave Hill and Glenn Rikowski. "Education, Struggle, and the Left Today." Interview of Mike Cole, Dave Hill and Glenn Rikowski by Peter McLaren. *International Journal of Education Reform* 10, no. 2 (spring 2000): 145–162.

McLaren, Peter, Gustavo Fischman, Silvia Serra and Estanislao Antelo. "The Specters of Gramsci: Revolutionary Praxis and the Committed Intellectual." *Journal of Thought* 33, no. 3 (fall 1998): 9–41.

McLaren, Peter, and Colin Lankshear. "Critical Literacy and the Postmodern Turn." In *Critical Literacy: Politics, Praxis, and the Postmodern*. Edited by Colin Lankshear and Peter McLaren. New York: State University of New York Press, 1993.

McMurtry, John. "A Failed Global Experiment: The Truth about the U.S. Economic Model." *Comer* 12, no. 7 (2000): 10–11.

McNally, David. *Against the Market: Political Economy, Market Socialism and the Marxist Critique*. London: Verso, 1993.

———. "The Present as History: Thoughts on Capitalism at the Millennium." *Monthly Review* 51, no. 3 (1999): 134–145.

McRobbie, Angela. *Postmodern and Popular Culture*. London: Routledge, 1994.

McVicar, John. *By Himself*. London: Arrow, 1979.

Meagher, Nigel. "What Do Employers Require from Their Young Recruits?" Paper from the Department of Education, University of Newcastle, U.K., 1998.

Meiksins Wood, Ellen. *The Retreat from Class*. London: Verso, 1986.

———. *Democracy against Capitalism: Renewing Historical Materialism*. Cambridge: Cambridge University Press, 1996.

———. "A Reply to A. Sivanandan." *Monthly Review* 48 (1997): 21–32.

Meiksins Wood, Ellen, and John Bellamy Foster, eds. *In Defense of History: Marxism and the Postmodern Agenda*. New York: Monthly Review Press, 1997.

———. "The Communist Manifesto after 150 Years." *Monthly Review* 50, no. 1 (1998): 14–35.

Mercer, Kobena. "Welcome to the Jungle: Identity and Diversity in Postmodern Politics." In *Identity: Community, Culture, Difference*. Edited by Jonathan Rutherford. London: Lawrence & Wishart, 1990.

Mészáros, István. "Marxism, the Capital System, and Social Revolution: An Interview with István Mészáros." *Science and Society* 63, no. 3 (1999): 338–361.

———. "Globalizing Capital." *Monthly Review* 49, no. 2 (1998): 27–37.

———. *The Power of Ideology*. New York: New York University Press, 1991.

Miliband, Ralph. *Divided Societies*. Oxford: Oxford University Press, 1991.

Miller, Richard. "Rawls and Marxism." In *Reading Rawls: Critical Studies on Rawls' "A Theory of Justice."* Edited by Norman Daniels. Palo Alto, Calif.: Stanford University Press, 1989.

Miner, Barbara. "Target: Public Education." *The Nation* 267, no. 18 (1998): 4–6.

Mizen, Phil. *The State, Young People and Youth Training: In and against the Training State*. London: Mansell, 1995.

Molnar, Alex. *Giving the Kids the Business: The Commercialization of America's Schools*. Boulder, Colo.: Westview Press, 1996.

Moody, Kim. *Workers in a Lean World: Unions in the International Economy*. London: Verso, 1997.

More, Max. "The Post Human Sub-page." Extracts in Robert Pepperell, *The Post-Human Condition*. Exeter: Intellect Books, 1997.

Morris, Brian. *Western Conceptions of the Individual*. Oxford, U.K.: Berg, 1991.

Mosley, Walter. *Workin' on the Chain Gang: Shaking off the Dead Hand of History*. New York: Ballantine Publishing Group, 2000.

Muchhala, Bhumika. *Student Voices: One Year after Seattle*. Washington, D.C.: Institute of Policy Studies, 2000. <http://www.ips-dc.org.html> (April 9, 2001).

Murray, Nancy. "Anti-racists and Other Demons: The Press and Ideology in Thatcher's Britain." In Nancy Murray and Chris Searle, *Racism and the Press in Thatcher's Britain*. London: Institute of Race Relations (IRR).

Nash, Kate. "The Feminist Production of Knowledge: Is Deconstruction a Practice for Women?" *Feminist Review* 47 (summer 1994): 65–77.

Neary, Michael. *Youth, Training and the Training State: The Real History of Youth Training in the Twentieth Century.* Basingstoke, U.K.: Macmillan, 1997.

———. "Situating the Situationists: The Most Modern Discourse." *Radical Chains* 5 (1998): 26–31.

———. "Youth, Training and the Politics of 'Cool.'" In *Postmodernism in Educational Theory: Education and the Politics of Human Resistance.* Edited by Dave Hill, Peter McLaren, Mike Cole and Glenn Rikowski. London: Tufnell Press, 1999.

———. "Labour: The Poetry of the Future." In *Global Humanisation: Studies in the Manufacture of Labour.* Edited by Michael Neary. London: Mansell, 1999.

Neary, Michael, and Glenn Rikowski. "Deep Possession: Marx, Labour and the Trans-human." (Forthcoming 2003).

Neary, Michael, and Graham Taylor. *Money and the Human Condition.* London: Macmillan, 1998.

Nederveen Pieterse, Jan. *Emancipations, Modern and Postmodern.* London: Sage, 1992.

Negri, Antonio. *Revolution Retrieved, Selected Writings on Marx, Keynes, Capitalist Crisis and New Social Subjects 1967–1983.* London: Red Notes, 1988.

———. *Marx beyond Marx. Lessons on the Grundrisse.* Brooklyn, N.Y.: Automedia and Pluto Press, 1991.

Neuman, Yair, and Zvi Bekerman. "Organic versus Symbolic Pedagogy: Against the Commercialization of Knowledge." *Education and Society* 17, no. 1 (1999): 53–61.

Nichol, Claire. "Patterns of Pay: Results from the 1997 New Earnings Survey." *Labour Market Trends* (November 1997): 469–478.

Nicholson, Linda J. "Feminism and the Politics of Postmodernism." In *Feminism and Postmodernism.* Edited by Margaret Ferguson and Jennifer Wicke. Durham, N.C.: Duke University Press, 1994.

———, ed. *Feminism/Postmodernism.* London: Routledge, 1990.

Nikolinakos, Marios. "Notes towards a General Theory of Migration in Late Capitalism." *Race and Class* 17, no. 1 (summer 1975): 5–17.

Norris, Christopher. *Uncritical Theory.* London: Lawrence & Wishart, 1992.

Noumoff, Sam J. *Globalization and Culture.* Pullman: Washington State University Press, 1999.

O'Connor, James. *Natural Causes: Essays in Ecological Marxism.* New York: Guilford Press, 1998.

Ormer, Mimi, Janet Miller and Elizabeth Ellsworth. "Excessive Moments and Educational Discourses That Try to Contain Them." *Educational Theory* 46, no. 1 (spring 1996): 71–91.

Ortner, Sherry. "Identities: The Hidden Life of Class." *Journal of Anthropological Research* 54, no. 1 (1998): 1–17.

Ozga, Jennifer. "Policy Research and Policy Theory." *Journal of Education Policy* 5, no. 4 (October–December 1989): 359–362.

Pakulski, Jan. "Social Movements and Class: The Decline of the Marxist Paradigm." In *Social Movements and Social Classes.* Edited by Louis Maheu. London: Sage, 1995.

Pan. *Dictionary of Philosophy.* London: Pan Books, 1979.

Panitch, Leo. "The State in a Changing World: Social Democratizing Global Capitalism?" *Monthly Review* 50, no. 5 (1998): 11–22.

Parenti, Michael. *America Besieged.* San Francisco: City Lights Books, 1998.

Parker, Stuart. *Reflective Teaching in the Postmodern World: A Manifesto for Education in Postmodernity.* Buckingham, U.K.: Open University Press, 1997.

Parmar, Prathiba. "Young Asian Women: A Critique of the Pathological Approach." In *Multiracial Education* 9, no. 5 (1981).

Parmar, Prathiba. "Black Feminism: The Politics of Articulation." In *Identity: Community, Culture, Difference.* Edited by Jonathan Rutherford. London: Lawrence & Wishart, 1990.

Pepperell, Robert. *The Post-Human Condition.* Exeter: Intellect Books, 1997.

Perrucci, Robert, and Earl Wysong. *The New Class Society.* Lanham, Md.: Rowman & Littlefield, 1999.

Petras, James, and Chronis Polychroniou. "Capitalist Transformation: the Relevance of and Challenges to Marxism." In *Marxism Today: Essays on Capitalism, Socialism, and Strategies for Social Change.* Edited by Chronis Polychroniou and Harry R. Targ. London: Praeger, 1996.

———. "Clinton and Volunteerism: The Poverty of American Social Policy at the End of the Century." *New Political Science* 20, no. 2 (1998): 223–231.

Phillips, Melanie. "Why Black People Are Backing Baker." *Guardian*, September 9, 1988.

Population Trends. London: HMSO, 1971.

Postone, Moishe. *Time, Labour and Social Domination: A Reinterpretation of Marx's Critical Theory.* Cambridge: Cambridge University Press, 1993.

———. *Time, Labour and Social Domination: A Reinterpretation of Marx's Critical Theory.* Cambridge: Cambridge University Press, 1996.

Raduntz, Helen. "Researching a Hegelian-Marxian Dialectic for a Theory of Australian Catholic Schooling." Paper presented at the Conference of the Australian Association for Education Research (RAD 98259) in 1998. Revised version, January 7, 1999.

———. "A Marxian Critique of Teachers' Work in an Era of Capitalist Globalization." Paper presented at the AARE-NZARE Conference (RAD 99520), Melbourne, Victoria, November–December 1999.

Rahman, Mohibur, Guy Palmer, Peter Kenway and Catherine Howarth. *Monitoring Poverty and Social Exclusion 2000.* York, U.K.: Joseph Rowntree Foundation, 2001. (<http://www.jrf.org.uk.html>).

Rattansi, Ali. "Modern Racisms, Racialized Identities." In *Racism, Modernity and Identity: On the Western Front.* Edited by Ali Rattansi and Sally Westwood. Cambridge: Polity, 1994.

Rattansi, Ali, and James Donald. "Introduction." In *'Race,' Culture and Difference.* Edited by Ali Rattansi and James Donald. London: Sage, 1992.

Redhead, Steven. *Rave Off.* Aldershot, U.K.: Avebury, 1993.

Rifkin, Jeremy. *The Age of Access: The New Culture of Hypercapitalism Where All of Life Is a Paid-For Experience.* New York: Tarcher-Putman Books, 2000.

Rikowski, Glenn. "The Recruitment Process and Labour Power." Paper presented at Division of Humanities and Modern Languages, Epping Forest College, U.K., 1990.

———. "Labour-Power Once More." Paper presented at Division of Humanities and Modern Languages, Epping Forest College, U.K., 1990.

———. "Work Experience Schemes and Part-Time Jobs in a Recruitment Context," *British Journal of Education and Work* 5, no. 1 (1992): 19–46.

———. "Education Markets and Missing Products." Paper presented at the Conference of Socialist Economists, University of Northumbria at Newcastle, July 7–9, 1995.

———. "Left Alone: End Time for Marxist Educational Theory?" *British Journal of Sociology of Education* 17, no. 4 (December 1996): 415–451.

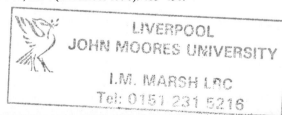

Rikowski, Glenn. "Apprenticeship and the Use-Value Aspect of Labour Power." Paper prepared for the ESRC Seminar Series on Apprenticeship, Nene College, Northampton, May 31, 1996.

———. "Revealed Recruitment Criteria through the Use-Value Aspect of Labour Power." Paper prepared for the ESRC Seminar Series on Apprenticeship, Nene College, Northampton, May 31, 1996.

———. "Scorched Earth: Prelude to Rebuilding Marxist Educational Theory." *British Journal of Sociology of Education* 18, no. 4 (December 1997): 551–574.

———. "Nietzsche's School? The Roots of Educational Postmodernism." Paper presented at the Education Research Seminar, A Marxist Critique of Postmodernism, convened by Mike Cole, School of Education, University of Brighton, November 19, 1997.

———. "Only Charybdis: The Learning Society Through Idealism." In *Inside the Learning Society*. Edited by Stewart Ranson. London: Cassell, 1998.

———. "Three Types of Apprenticeship, Three Forms of Mastery: Nietzsche, Marx, Self and Capital." Departmental Paper, University of Birmingham (U.K.), School of Education, June 5, 1998.

———. "Nietzsche, Marx and Mastery: The Learning Unto Death." In *Apprenticeship: Towards a New Paradigm of Learning*. Edited by Patrick Ainley and Helen Rainbird. London: Kogan Page, 1999.

———. "Lifelong Learning and the Political Economy of Containment." Paper for Faculty of Education, University of Central England, November 1999.

———. "Third Fantasy from the Right." *Education and Social Justice* 1, no. 3 (summer 1999): 25–27.

———. "Why Employers Can't Ever Get What They Want. In Fact, They Can't Even Get What They Need." Paper presented to the School of Post-compulsory Education and Training Staff-Student Seminar, University of Greenwich, London, March 27, 2000.

———. "Education and Social Justice within the Social Universe of Capital." Paper presented to the British Educational Research Association Day Seminar on Approaching Social Justice in Education: Theoretical Frameworks for Practical Purposes, Faculty of Education, Nottingham Trent University (U.K.), April 10, 2000.

———. "New Labour's Knowledge Economy versus Critical Pedagogy: The Battle in Seattle and Its Significance for Education." Paper presented at the Conference of Socialist Economists 2000, Global Capital and Global Struggles: Strategies, Alliances, Alternatives, University of London Union, July 1–2, 2000.

———. "Marxist Educational Theory Transformed." *Education and Social Justice* 2, no. 3 (summer 2000): 60–64.

———. "Messing with the Explosive Commodity: School Improvement, Educational Research, and Labour-Power in the Era of Global Capitalism." Paper presented to the Symposium on If We Aren't Pursuing Improvement, What Are We Doing? at the British Educational Research Association Conference, Cardiff University, Wales, September 7–9, 2000.

———. "That Other Great Class of Commodities: Repositioning Marxist Educational Theory." Paper presented at the British Educational Research Association Conference, Cardiff University, Wales, September 7–9, 2000.

———. "The Rise of the Student-Worker." In *A Compact for Higher Education*. Edited by Moti Gokulsing and Cornel DaCosta. Aldershot, U.K.: Ashgate, 2000.

———. *The Battle in Seattle: Its Significance for Education*. London: Tufnell Press, 2001.

Rikowski, Glenn. "Education for Industry: A Complex Technicism." *Journal of Education and Work* 13, no. 1 (February 2001): 29–49.

———. Comments on "Global Capital, Neo-Liberalism, and Privatisation: the Growth of Educational Inequality" by Dave Hill. In *Schooling and Equality: Fact, Concept and Policy.* Edited by Dave Hill and Mike Cole. London: Kogan Page, 2001.

———. "Marxist Educational Theory Unplugged." *Historical Materialism: Research in Critical Marxist Theory,* 2002.

———. "The Repressed Anarchist: Postmodernism as Theoretic Anxiety Attack, and the Consequences for Educational Theory, Practice and Politics." <http://www.leeds.ac.uk/educol/2002> 2002.

Rikowski, Glenn, and Michael Neary. "Working Schoolchildren in Britain Today." *Capital and Class* 63 (autumn 1997): 25–35.

Roman, L., and Michael W. Apple. "Is Naturalism a Move Beyond Positivism?" In *Qualitative Inquiry in Education.* Edited by E. Eisner and A. Peshkin. New York: Teachers College Press, 1990.

Rorty, Richard. *Philosophy and the Mirror of Nature.* Princeton, N.J.: Princeton University Press, 1980.

Rosaldo, Michelle. *Woman, Culture, and Society.* Palo Alto, Calif.: Stanford University Press, 1974.

Rose, Eliot Joseph Benn et al. *Colour and Citizenship: A Report on British Race Relations.* London: Oxford University Press–Institute of Race Relations, 1972.

Rosenau, Pauline Marie. *Postmodernism and the Social Sciences: Insights, Inroads, and Intrusions.* Princeton, N.J.: Princeton University Press, 1992.

Rosenberg, Chanie, and Kevin Ovenden. *Education: Why Our Children Deserve Better than New Labour.* London: Socialist Workers Party, 1999.

Rowbotham, Sheila, Lynne Segal and Hilary Wainwright. *Beyond the Fragments.* London: Merlin, 1979.

Rutherford, Jonathan. "A Place Called Home: Identity and the Cultural Politics of Difference." In *Identity: Community, Culture, Difference.* Edited by Jonathan Rutherford. London: Lawrence & Wishart, 1990.

———. "Scholars Squeezed By Market Muscle." *Times Higher Education Supplement,* January 6, 2001: 20.

Said, Edward. *Orientalism.* London: Routledge, 1978.

———. *Culture and Imperialism.* New York: Vintage, 1993.

Sanders, Claire, Tony Tysome and Olga Wojtas. "Is a Return to Grants Really the Answer?" *Times Higher Education Supplement,* March 9, 2001.

Sardar, Ziauddin. *Postmodernism and the Other: The New Imperialism of Western Culture.* London: Pluto Press, 1998.

Sargent, Lydia, ed. *The Unhappy Marriage of Marxism and Feminism: A Debate on Class and Patriarchy.* London: Pluto Press, 1986.

Sarup, Madan. *Marxism and Education.* London: Routledge and Kegan Paul, 1978.

———. *Education, State and Crisis.* London: Routledge and Kegan Paul, 1982.

———. *Marxism / Structuralism / Education: Theoretical Developments in the Sociology of Education.* Lewes, U.K.: Falmer Press, 1983.

Sassen, Saskia. *Globalization and Its Discontents.* New York: New Press, 1998.

Saunders, Murray, and Helen Sambili. "Can Vocational Programmes Change Use and Exchange Value Attributions of School Leavers?" *Educational Review* 47, no. 3 (November 1995): 319–331.

Saville, John. *The Consolidation of the Capitalist State 1800–1850.* London: Pluto Press, 1994.

Schuchardt, Reader Mercer. "Swoosh! The Perfect Icon for an Imperfect Postliterate World." *UTNE Reader*, no. 89 (1998): 76–77.

Searle, Chris. OFSTEDed, Blunketted and Permanently Excluded: An Experience of English Education. *Race and Class* 38, no. 1 (July–September 1996): 21–38.

———. *Living Community, Living School.* London: Tufnell Press, 1997.

Segal, Lynne. "Whose Left? Socialism, Feminism and the Future." *New Left Review* 185 (1991): 81–91.

———. *New Sexual Agendas.* London: Macmillan, 1997.

Seve, Lucien. *Marxism and the Theory of Human Personality.* London: Lawrence & Wishart, 1975.

Sharp, Rachel. "Introduction." In *Capitalist Crisis and Schooling: Comparative Studies in the Politics of Education.* Edited by Rachel Sharp. South Melbourne: Macmillan Company of Australia, 1986.

Shor, Ira. *Culture Wars: School and Society in the Conservative Restoration 1969–1984.* London: Routledge and Kegan Paul, 1986.

Sivanandan, Ambalavaner. *Race and Resistance: The IRR Story.* London: IRR, 1974.

———. *Race, Class and the State.* London: IRR, 1976.

———. *From Resistance to Rebellion: Asian and Afro-Caribbean Struggles in Britain.* London: IRR, 1982.

———. "Introduction." *Patterns of Racism.* London: IRR, 1982.

———. "Introduction." *Roots of Racism.* London: IRR, 1982.

———. "Challenging Racism: Strategies for the 1980s." *Race and Class* 25, no. 2 (autumn 1983): 1–11.

———. "RAT and the Degradation of Black Struggle." *Race and Class* 26, no. 4 (April 1985): 1–33.

———. "Race, Class and Brent." *Race and Class* 29, no. 1 (summer 1987): 73–77.

———. "All That Melts into Air Is Solid: The Hokum of New Times." *Race and Class* 31, no. 3 (January–March 1990): 1–30.

———. "La Trahison des Clercs." *New Statesman* (July 14, 1995): 20–21.

Skeggs, Beverley. "Postmodernism: What Is All the Fuss About?" *British Journal of Sociology of Education* 12, no. 2 (June 1991): 255–267.

———. *Formations of Class and Gender.* London: Sage, 1997.

Sloterdijk, Peter. *Critique of Cynical Reason.* London: Verso, 1988.

Sly, Frances, Alistair Price and Andrew Risdon. "Women in the Labour Market: Results from the Spring 1996 Labour Force Survey." *Labour Market Trends* (March 1997): 99–120.

Smart, Carol, and Barry Neale. *Family Fragments?* Cambridge, U.K.: Polity Press, 1999.

———. *Social Identities: Journal for the Study of Race, Nation and Culture,* <http://www.tandf.co.uk/Journals/carfax/13504630.html> (20 July 2001).

Smith, Richard, and Philip Wexler, eds. *After Post Modernism.* London: Falmer Press, 1995.

Sohn-Rethel, Alfred. *Intellectual and Manual Labour: A Critique of Epistemology.* London: Macmillan, 1978.

Sparks, Colin. "The Tories, Labour and the Education Crisis." *International Socialism* 74 (spring 1997): 3–40.

Stabile, Carole A. *Feminism and the Technological Fix.* Manchester, U.K.: Manchester University Press, 1994.

———. "Feminism without Guarantees: The Misalliances and Missed Alliances of Postmodernist Social Theory." In *Marxism in the Postmodern Age: Confronting the*

New World Order. Edited by Antonio Callari, Stephen Cullenberg and Carole Biewener. New York: Guilford Press, 1996.

Stabile, Carole A. "Pedagogues, Pedagogy, and Political Struggles." In *Class Issues: Pedagogy, Cultural Studies, and the Public Sphere.* Edited by Amitava Kumar. New York: New York University Press, 1997.

Stephens, Michael. *Japan and Education.* London: Macmillan, 1991.

Stronach, Ian, and Maggie MacLure. *Educational Research Undone: The Postmodern Embrace.* Buckingham, U.K.: Open University Press, 1997.

Stuart, James G. "A Place for Faith." *Comer* 12, no. 7 (2000): 7.

Taaffe, Peter, and Tony Mulhearn. *Liverpool: A City That Dared to Fight.* London: Fortress Books, 1988.

Taylor, Gary. "Socialism and Education: Marx and Engels." *General Educator* 32 (January–February 1995): 22–23.

———. "Socialism and Education: 'The German Ideology.'" *General Educator* 33 (March–April 1995): 21–23.

———. "Marx on Education, Industry and the Fall of Capitalism. *General Educator* 35 (July–August 1995): 19–22.

Teeple, Gary. *Globalization and the Decline of Social Reform.* New Jersey: Humanities Press, 1995.

Thompson, Willie. *The Left in History: Revolution and Reform in Twentieth-century Politics.* London: Pluto Press, 1997.

Thornett, Alan. *Inside Cowley.* London: Porcupine Press, 1998.

Thorpe, Geraldine, and Patrick Brady. "The Labour Process in Higher Education." Paper presented at the Conference of Socialist Economists, University of Northumbria at Newcastle, July 12–14, 1996.

Thrupp, Martin. *Schools Making a Difference: Let's Be Realistic!* Buckingham, U.K.: Open University Press, 1999.

———. "Compensating for Class: Are School Improvement Researchers Being Realistic?" *Education and Social Justice* 2, no. 2 (summer 2000): 2–11.

Trigg, Roger. *Ideas of Human Nature: An Historical Introduction.* Oxford, U.K.: Blackwell, 1988.

Trotsky, Leon. *Women and the Family.* New York: Pathfinder Press, 1973.

Tucker, Robert C., ed. *The Marx-Engels Reader.* New York: W. W. Norton, 1978.

Unger, Roberto Mangabeira and Cornel West. "Progressive Politics and What Lies Ahead." *The Nation* 267, no. 17 (1998): 11–15.

Urry, John. "Rethinking Class." In *Social Movements and Social Class.* Edited by Louis Maheu. London: Sage, 1995.

Usher, Robin, and Richard Edwards. *Postmodernism and Education: Different Voices, Different Worlds.* London: Routledge, 1994.

Virilio, Paul. *The Art of the Motor.* Translated by Julie Rose. Minneapolis: University of Minnesota Press, 1995.

Vogel, Lise. *Marxism and the Oppression of Women: Towards a Unitary Theory.* London: Pluto Press, 1983.

———. *Woman Questions: Essays for a Materialist Feminism.* London: Pluto Press, 1995.

Wainwright, Hilary. *Arguments for a New Left: Answering the Free Market Right.* London: Blackwell, 1994.

Waite, Geoff. *Nietzsche's Corpse: Aesthetics, Politics, Prophecy, or the Spectacular Technoculture of Everyday Life.* Durham, N.C.: Duke University Press, 1996.

Walford, Geoffrey, and Henry Miller. *City Technology College*. Milton Keynes, U.K.: Open University Press, 1991.

Walker, Pat, ed. *Between Labour and Capital*. Brighton, U.K.: Harvester Press, 1979.

Walkerdine, Valerie. *Schoolgirl Fictions*. London: Verso, 1990.

Walkling, Phillip, and Chris Brannigan. "Anti-sexist/Anti-racist Education: A Possible Dilemma." *Journal of Moral Education* 15, no. 1 (January 1986): 16–25.

Wandor, Micheline. "The Family under Capitalism: The Conditions of Illusion." In *Conditions of Illusion*. Edited by Sandra Allen, Lee Sanders and Jan Wallis. Leeds, U.K.: Feminist Books, 1974.

Waugh, Colin. *Marx and Engels' Concept of Education*. Unpublished paper, July 27, 1996.

———. "Marx and Engels' Concept of Education." *General Educator* 43 (December 1996): 21–23.

Weedon, Chris. *Feminist Practice and Poststructuralist Theory*. Oxford, U.K.: Blackwell, 1987.

Wegner, Morton G. "Idealism Redux: The Class-Historical Truth of Postmodernism." *Critical Sociology* 20, no. 1 (1993–1994): 53–78.

Wexler, Philip. *Becoming Somebody*. Lewes, U.K.: Falmer, 1992.

White, Judith. "The Family in Capitalist Society." *Socialist Woman* (July–August 1971): 3–4.

White, Michael. "Blair Hails Middle Class Revolution." *Guardian*, January 15, 1999.

Whitty, Geoff. *Sociology and School Knowledge: Curriculum Theory, Research and Politics*. London: Methuen, 1985.

———. "Education Policy and the Inner Cities." In *The Contemporary British City*. Edited by P. Lawless and C. Raban. London: Harper and Row, 1986.

———. "The New Right and the National Curriculum—State Control or Market Forces?" *Journal of Education Policy* 4, no. 4 (October–December 1989): 329–341.

———. "Recent Educational Reform: Is It a Postmodern Phenomenon?" Paper presented at the Conference on Reproduction, Social Inequality and Resistance, Germany: University of Bielefeld, 1991.

———. "Education Reform and Teacher Education in England in the 1990s." In *International Analyses of Teacher Education*. Edited by Peter Gilroy and Michael Smith. London: Carfax, 1993.

———. "Creating Quasi-Markets in Education." In *Review of Research in Education* 22. Edited by Michael W. Apple. Washington, D.C.: American Educational Research Association, 1997.

———. "Marketization, the State, and the Re-formation of the Teaching Profession." In *Education, Culture and Economy*. Edited by A. H. Halsey, Hugh Lauder, Phillip Brown and Amy Stuart Wells. Oxford: Oxford University Press, 1997.

———. "Citizens or Consumers? Continuity and Change in Contemporary Education Policy." In *Power/Knowledge/Pedagogy*. Edited by Dennis Carlson and Michael Apple. Boulder, Colo.: Westview Press, 1998.

———. "New Labour, Education and Social Justice." *Socialist Teacher*, no. 65 (spring 1998): 2–8.

Whitty, Geoff, Tony Edwards and Sharon Gewirtz. *Specialisation and Choice in Urban Education*. London: Routledge, 1993.

Whitty, Geoff, and Ian Menter. "Lessons of Thatcherism: Education Policy in England and Wales, 1979–88." *Journal of Law and Society* 16, no. 1 (1989): 42–64.

Whitty, Geoff, Sally Power and David Halpin. *Devolution and Choice in Education: The School, the State and the Market*. Buckingham, U.K.: Open University Press, 1998.

Wichterich, Christa. *The Globalized Woman: Reports from a Future of Inequality.* Translated by Patrick Camiller. London: Zed Books, 2000.

Willis, Paul. *Learning to Labour: How Working Class Kids Get Working Class Jobs.* Farnborough, U.K.: Saxon House, 1977.

Willis, Paul. *Consuming Passions.* Milton Keynes, U.K.: Open University Press, 1990.

———. *Moving Culture.* London: Calouste Gulbenkian Foundation, 1990.

———. "Labor Power, Culture, and the Cultural Commodity." In *Critical Education in the New Information Age.* Edited by Manuel Castells, Ramon Flecha, Paulo Freire, Henry Giroux, Donaldo Macedo and Paul Willis. Lanham, Md.: Rowman & Littlefield, 1999.

Wolff, Richard, and Stephen Resnick, "Power, Property, and Class." *Socialist Review* 16, no. 2 (1986): 97–124.

Wolpe, Anne Marie. "'Experience' as Analytical Framework: Does It Account for Girls' Education?" In *Bowles and Gintis Revisited: Correspondence and Contradiction in Educational Theory.* Edited by Mike Cole. Lewes, U.K.: Falmer Press, 1988.

Wright, Tony, and Matt Carter. *The People's Party: The History of the Labour Party.* London: Thames and Hudson, 1997.

Wyn, Johanna, and Robert White. *Rethinking Youth.* London: Sage, 1997.

Yamamoto, Oswaldo, and Antonio Neto. "Sociology of Education and Marxism in Brazil." *Sociological Research Online* 4, no. 1 (1999). <http://www.socresonline.org.uk. html> (April 2001).

Yandell, John. "A Victory in the Eduworkplace." *Education and Social Justice* 3, no. 1 (autumn 2000): 56–58.

Yates, Michael. "An Essay on Radical Labor Education." *Cultural Logic* 2, no. 1 (fall 1998). <http://eserver.org/clogic/2-1/yates.html> (May 19, 2001).

Yeatman, Anna. "A Feminist Theory of Social Differentiation." In *Feminism/Postmodernism.* Edited by Linda Nicholson. New York: Routledge, 1990.

Zavarzadeh, Mas'ud. "Post-ality: The (Dis)Simulations of Cybercapitalism." In *Postality: Marxism and Postmodernism.* Edited by Mas'ud Zavarzadeh. Washington, D.C.: Maisonneuve, 1995.

Zeichner, Kenneth, and Daniel Liston. "Teaching Student Teachers to Reflect." *Harvard Educational Review* 57, no. 1 (February 1987): 23–48.

Zipin, L. "Emphasising 'Discourse' and Bracketing People." In *Governmentality Through Education.* Edited by Thomas Popkewitz and M. Brennan. New York: Teachers College Press, 1998.

Zukin, Sharon. *Landscapes of Power: From Detroit to Disneyland.* Berkeley: University of California Press, 1991.

Zweig, Michael. *The Working Class Majority: America's Best Kept Secret.* London: ILR Press, 2000.

Index

Of Names

Of Subjects

Index

Totality, 23, 35, 41, 115–117, 140, 296;
social universe of capital as, 23.
See also social universe of
capital

Trade unions, 61, 280, 299; gays and,
280; lesbians and, 280; women
and, 245, 280

Trades Union Congress (TUC),
166n39, 166n45

Training, 3, 7, 10, 19, 162, 194,
205n80; culture, 10;
recomposition of youth and, 162;
regimes, 162; role in the
capitalization of humanity, 137–
139. *See also* capitalist training,
and vocational education and
training

Tragedy, of fragmentation, 9

Transhuman, 56, 118, 120–123, 136,
142; as capitalization of
humanity, 142; capital and the,
118; condition, 120; definition
of, 120, 135; theory, 9, 122, 137.
See also posthuman
transhumanism, 6, 133
tranhumanization, 141–142

Truth, 5, 226, 229, 260; claims of, 267;
postmodernist rejection of
universal, 264

Tuition fees, 204n76

Two-nation project, 109n34

Underclass, 108n34, 169

Underdetermination, 266

Unions. *See* trade unions

United Auto Workers, 198n27

United Parcel Services, 198n27

United States, 83–84, 198n27, 200n44,
201n52, 246n1, 293–296; right-
wing think tanks in, 292

Universalism, 42, 49, 83, 215, 264

University School of Milwaukee, 293

Use-value, 23, 123, 131, 155–157,
263–264. *See also* value,
exchange-value, and surplus-
value

Utopia, capitalist form of, 291;
postmodern, 269

Value, 4, 10, 17, 22–23, 41, 56, 116,
122–124, 131, 136, 157;
education and, 23; form of labor,
3, 6, 146n48; form of production,
131; law of, 51, 58, 154, 158,
266, 270; magnitude of, 156;
substance of, 156. *See also*
surplus-value, exchange-value,
and use-value

Vocational education and training,
history of in UK, 159–160. *See
also* training

Vouchers, school, 293–294

Wage-labor, 156, 184, 282. *See also*
labor

Wages, 126, 130

Washington, vii

Welfare, standards, 21

Welfare State, attacks on, 242

White economy, 55

Whiteness, 54

Women, 67, 96, 181, 226, 228, 230–
231, 237, 247n37, 280; caring
role of, 244; devalued by
capitalist society, 16; exchange-
value and, 56; labor and, 244;
labor market participation of,
243; part of the industrial reserve
army, 243; pay of, 11, 241,
249n76; poverty, and, 181; rights
of at risk, 258; role in home of,
239; struggles by, 238;
workforce activity of, 240–243,
245, 249n75, 258; working
conditions of, 11

Women against Pit Closures, 238

Women of the Waterfront, 238

Women's Liberation Movement
(WLM), 225–226, 236–237

Women's Studies, 225, 227, 246

Workers, attacks on, 11; white, 55

Workers councils, 299